POVERTY IN THE PANDEMIC

T0378008

POVERTY IN THE PANDEMIC
POLICY LESSONS FROM COVID-19

Zachary Parolin

Russell Sage Foundation • New York

The Russell Sage Foundation

The Russell Sage Foundation, one of the oldest of America's general purpose foundations, was established in 1907 by Mrs. Margaret Olivia Sage for "the improvement of social and living conditions in the United States." The foundation seeks to fulfill this mandate by fostering the development and dissemination of knowledge about the country's political, social, and economic problems. While the foundation endeavors to assure the accuracy and objectivity of each book it publishes, the conclusions and interpretations in Russell Sage Foundation publications are those of the authors and not of the foundation, its trustees, or its staff. Publication by Russell Sage, therefore, does not imply foundation endorsement.

Library of Congress Cataloging-in-Publication Data

Names: Parolin, Zachary, author.
Title: Poverty in the pandemic : policy lessons from COVID-19 / Zachary Parolin.
Description: New York : Russell Sage, [2023] | Includes bibliographical references and index. | Summary: "Poverty in the Pandemic is interested in poverty during the COVID-19 pandemic in the U.S., as well as what the pandemic teaches us about how to think about poverty, and policies designed to reduce it, well after the pandemic subsides. Four main questions guide the book's focus. First, how did poverty influence the consequences of the COVID-19 pandemic? Second, what was the role of government income support in reducing poverty during the pandemic? Third, what lessons does the COVID-19 pandemic offer for the way we measure and conceptualize poverty in the U.S.? And fourth, what policy lessons should we take from the pandemic for efforts to improve the economic well-being of households in the future? In answering these four questions, this book not only provides a comprehensive, descriptive portrait of policy and poverty outcomes during the pandemic but also identifies policy takeaways for improving economic opportunity beyond the pandemic" — Provided by publisher.
Identifiers: LCCN 2023009003 (print) | LCCN 2023009004 (ebook) | ISBN 9780871546722 (paperback) | ISBN 9781610449236 (ebook)
Subjects: LCSH: Poor — United States — History — 21st century. | Poverty — United States — History — 21st century. | COVID-19 Pandemic, 2020 — Influence. | COVID-19 Pandemic, 2020 — Economic aspects. | COVID-19 Pandemic, 2020 — Social aspects.
Classification: LCC HC110.P63 P37 2023 (print) | LCC HC110.P63 (ebook) | DDC 305.5/690973 — dc23/eng/20230314
LC record available at https://lccn.loc.gov/2023009003
LC ebook record available at https://lccn.loc.gov/2023009004

Text design by Suzanne Nichols.

RUSSELL SAGE FOUNDATION
112 East 64th Street, New York, New York 10065
10 9 8 7 6 5 4 3 2 1

Contents

Illustrations

Tables

Figures

About the Author

Zachary Parolin is an assistant professor of social policy at Bocconi University and a senior research fellow at Columbia University's Center on Poverty and Social Policy.

Acknowledgments

THIS BOOK IS dedicated to those who in recent years completed the income and well-being surveys on which this book is based. In sharing your life experiences—often voluntarily and almost always with large, impersonal institutions—you provided the research and policy communities with vital information on trends in the country's economic, social, psychological, and physical well-being. Your participation provides the data infrastructure necessary to investigate which public policies work (and which do not) in making life better for the nation's residents. This book, and a great deal of policy research in general, would not be possible without your willingness to share your experience.

This book is also dedicated to the Rainbow House's Homeless Youth Program in Columbia, Missouri, and to its staff and residents. Our work together from 2009 to 2012 motivates my research interests to this day.

Few readers would pick up a book entitled *Poverty in the Pandemic* in search of a lighthearted, feel-good read, but I do hope that readers will find this book worthwhile and instructive. I have used data from dozens of different sources to provide a comprehensive account of the challenges that U.S. households faced during the COVID-19 pandemic relating to physical health, employment, poverty, food and housing hardship, mental health, school closures, and childcare closures. I have also carefully documented, and extracted lessons from, the extraordinary policy response that led to a record-low poverty rate in the United States in 2020 and then again in 2021. This book offers not merely a record of past events, but also a blueprint for smarter policy action moving forward. Specifically, the book takes seriously the challenge of confronting the conventional ways we think about poverty, identifying which policies worked in reducing poverty and hardship during the pandemic and deriving lessons from the COVID-19 era to promote greater economic well-being after the pandemic subsides.

I owe a tremendous amount of gratitude to many who have influenced this book, either directly or indirectly, throughout its development and my own development as an early-career researcher. Jane Waldfogel and Christopher Wimer of Columbia University's Center on Poverty and Social Policy deserve particular credit. As a third-year PhD student living outside the United States, I was not the likeliest choice to join Jane and Chris as a postdoctoral researcher, yet they provided me with that opportunity and a unique environment in which to develop my research. When the COVID-19 pandemic arrived in New York, one year after I moved to the city, Chris, Jane, and I reflected on how our team could be useful in the moment; one eventual answer was to develop the monthly, near-real-time poverty measure that this book will discuss and that informed the federal government's policy response throughout 2020 and 2021. At Columbia, I was also fortunate to directly collaborate with and learn from Elizabeth Ananat, Sophie Collyer, Megan Curran, Qin Gao, Irwin Garfinkel, Christal Hamilton, Robert Hartley, Sonia Huq, Benjamin Glasner, Neeraj Kaushal, Jordan Matsudaira, Ronald Mincy, and others affiliated with the Center on Poverty and Social Policy.

I wrote the vast majority of this book from my current home at Bocconi University in Milan. The book benefited tremendously from early feedback from Gøsta Esping-Andersen, Francesco Billari, Giulia Giupponi, Marlene Jugl, and other colleagues who participated in an early reading group on the book's introductory chapter.

I am grateful to Emma Lee and Marcela Rubio, who provided terrific research assistance throughout phases of this book's development, and to Kosar Jahani and the Bill & Melinda Gates Foundation for their early support of our work on measuring poverty during the pandemic. The European Research Council's Starting Grant (number 101039655, *ExpPov*) provided support that overlapped with the final six months of book preparation.

I appreciate the early and ongoing support for this project from Suzanne Nichols, Sheldon Danziger, and others on the Russell Sage Foundation team, and I am also grateful to the anonymous peer reviewers they organized for thorough and constructive comments on the initial draft of this book.

To Mom and Dad, to my siblings, and to our growing family: You know, with no need for me to elaborate here, how much you mean to me. To Minna especially: Thank you for your love and support. It is my greatest joy to spend every day by your side.

Many researchers and colleagues have influenced my work, either directly by reviewing the book's contents or indirectly by discussing the book's themes in conversations, at conferences, and through emails. In addition to those cited earlier, I am appreciative of discussions with Jacob Bastian, Lauren Bauer, David Brady, Andrea Brandolini, Bea Cantillon, Christina Cross, Matthew Desmond, Stefano Filauro, Liana Fox, Robert

Greenstein, Jacob Goldin, Bradley Hardy, David Harris, Hilary Hoynes, David Johnson, Jennifer Laird, Wim Van Lancker, Elaine Maag, Laurie Maldonado, Ive Marx, Robert Moffitt, Brian Nolan, Rourke O'Brien, José Pacas, Natasha Pilkauskas, Diane Schanzenbach, Daniel Schneider, Luke H. Shaefer, Arloc Sherman, Timothy Smeeding, Danilo Trisi, Scott Winship, Jim Ziliak, and many others.

I do not anticipate that all of these scholars will agree with the conclusions that I draw in this book. I hope all readers, however, will find the book to be an honest, accurate, and comprehensive account of poverty during the COVID-19 pandemic. For researchers of poverty, I hope the lessons I elaborate on here will encourage critical thinking of the conventional tools and frameworks we use to evaluate living conditions among the nation's most vulnerable individuals. For policymakers, I hope that the specific policy lessons proposed here will inform efforts to expand economic opportunity moving forward. For the casual reader who can relate to the themes of this book, I thank you for your trust and for your time.

Chapter 1

Three Perspectives on Poverty in the Context of COVID-19

HOUSEHOLDS IN the United States faced their fair share of struggles well before January 18, 2020, the date on which the Centers for Disease Control and Prevention (CDC) confirmed the country's first recorded case of COVID-19. Throughout the prior year, before masks and school closures became standard sources of the day's concerns, more than 1.4 million children in the nation's public schools had experienced homelessness or severe housing instability.[1] In New York City alone, more than 100,000 children had faced some form of homelessness in 2019, a number large enough to fill every seat at the New York Yankees' and Mets' baseball stadiums combined.

In addition to family homelessness, other forms of material hardship, such as food insecurity, were relatively high. In 2019—well before "contact tracing" or "flatten the curve" were enshrined in our vocabulary—one in ten households across the United States experienced food insecurity.[2] One in four families who paid for formal childcare arrangements spent more than 10 percent of their annual income on the cost of that care, while even more families faced challenges in navigating work and care responsibilities.[3] An estimated 29 million individuals lacked access to health insurance, while millions more reported concern about being unable to afford their medical treatment.[4] At the close of 2019, 11.7 percent of U.S. residents lived in poverty—a record low at the time, but still amounting to 40 million Americans whose income was insufficient to meet their basic needs.[5]

And then the COVID-19 pandemic arrived.

This book investigates what happened next. Specifically, this book analyzes poverty in the United States during the COVID-19 pandemic, as well as what the pandemic teaches us about how to think about poverty, and about policies designed to reduce it, well after the pandemic subsides. Four questions guide the book's focus. How did poverty influence the

1

consequences of the COVID-19 pandemic? What was the role of government income support in reducing poverty during the pandemic? What lessons does the COVID-19 pandemic offer for how we measure and conceptualize poverty in the United States? And finally, what policy lessons from the pandemic should we bring to our efforts to improve the economic well-being of households in the future? In answering these four questions, this book not only provides a comprehensive, descriptive portrait of policy and poverty outcomes during the pandemic but also identifies policy takeaways for improving economic opportunity after the pandemic.

A first challenge in documenting poverty during COVID-19 is confronting the fact that poverty is a contested concept, with no single agreed-upon way to measure it. Even the most advanced methodological approaches to quantifying it overlook the fact that poverty is not merely a point-in-time state. Instead, poverty is an economic condition that, once experienced, often lingers throughout an individual's life, inflicting costs that range from poorer health conditions to reduced long-run economic opportunity. Estimating point-in-time poverty during the pandemic, for example, may overlook the impact of individuals' persistent exposure to poverty *prior to* the pandemic on their physical, mental, and economic well-being during COVID-19. As such, this introductory chapter presents a three-part framework that offers a tool for more comprehensively studying households' experiences with poverty. This framework's three perspectives on poverty help to reconcile the many contradictions in the economic, social, and health outcomes of U.S. households during the pandemic.

Consider, for example, that the onset of the COVID-19 pandemic sent the U.S. unemployment rate soaring toward 19 percent in April 2020—the highest rate since the Great Depression—but the national poverty rate in 2020 did not increase. In fact, the 2020 poverty rate declined from its 2019 level, reaching its lowest level in modern U.S. history (that is, since at least 1967, when reliable income data were first made available). In the midst of immense economic and social turmoil, poverty rates declined to record lows in 2020 for Black, White, Asian, and Hispanic individuals alike, and for children as well as for adults.

Consider that initial reports of food insecurity during the COVID-19 pandemic pointed to a doubling or tripling of hardship relative to pre-crisis levels, but that official government statistics later pointed to no meaningful change in food insecurity from 2019 to 2020.

Consider that despite the federal government's massive investment in direct income support for families—spending on new income transfers in 2020 alone surpassed spending on all new income transfers provided during the Great Recession—mental health challenges, including frequent anxiety and worrying, remained at concerningly high levels throughout the pandemic, particularly for low-income families with children.

Consider that despite the record declines in poverty in 2020 (and then again in 2021), a disproportionate number of those who died from the COVID-19 virus were those individuals who had greater preexisting health challenges, were relatively less able to work from home, lived in more crowded conditions, and were more financially vulnerable—all conditions that were more common among individuals who experienced poverty prior to the onset of the pandemic.

Consider that school closures and distance learning affected nearly all U.S. families with children in April 2020, yet inflicted the greatest declines in educational performance on students from lower-income families, potentially exacerbating long-run disparities in educational outcomes.

Consider that existing accounts of the pandemic's distributional consequences range from claims that COVID increased inequality in America[6] to arguments that inequality declined throughout the pandemic.[7]

This book aims to make sense of these conflicting perspectives on disparities during the pandemic. To do so, I rely on several original data sources and empirical advancements, including a new framework for tracking poverty rates in the United States on a monthly basis, the first national databases of school closures and childcare closures during the pandemic, comprehensive and causal evidence on the effects of government policy interventions during COVID-19, and more.

In addition to informing our thinking of poverty, the pandemic offers many lessons for the design of public policies that serve low-income households. As the COVID-19 virus spread throughout the country in March 2020, the federal government prioritized a rapid distribution of income support—to households and businesses alike—amounting to more than $1 trillion in spending. Beyond the magnitude of the spending, the characteristics of many of the policies implemented differed from the traditional features of the American welfare state. The pandemic policy response thus unleashed a set of experiments in a relatively condensed time period. These experiments—making unemployment benefits widely available to jobless adults, delivering cash payments each month to most families with children, distributing resources to small businesses to prevent job loss, and more—were conducted in a peculiar economic, social, and health context. Nonetheless, these policy experiments provided a base of empirical evidence that can be cautiously analyzed to help answer questions such as: To what extent did expansions in unemployment benefits sever the relationship between joblessness and poverty? Were expansions to the access or generosity of unemployment benefits more consequential for reducing poverty? In times of economic recession, should the federal government prioritize the incomes of unemployed adults or the preservation of jobs? What are the trade-offs of these two approaches? What are the benefits and costs of providing an unconditional, near-universal cash benefit to families with children? How does the timing of cash payments to families with children differentially affect their consumption behaviors and general well-being? More broadly, how can the federal government and state governments better serve households when they face a life disruption?

The pandemic policy response offers evidence on each of these questions, with implications for how the country supports low-income households in the future.

The Eve of the Pandemic: A Fragile Victory

Understanding the peculiarities of the U.S. welfare state and labor market institutions on the eve of the pandemic is a necessary first step toward understanding poverty and the federal government's subsequent policy response during the pandemic.

In light of the low U.S. poverty rate in 2019, one might have predicted that the country would be well equipped to navigate the economic crisis that 2020 was about to bring on. Consider that from 2011, the peak of the Great Recession, to 2019, the national poverty rate (when using the Supplemental Poverty Measure) fell from 16.1 to 11.7 percent, the lowest on record since at least 1967.[8] That rate was buoyed by the lowest national unemployment rate in recent history: 3.5 percent at the end of 2019.[9]

On top of that, the United States had been steadily shifting to a work-based welfare state for more than two decades.[10] A bevy of income transfers, such as the Earned Income Tax Credit (EITC) and the Child Tax Credit (CTC), were targeted exclusively at working adults, and at working parents especially. Given that households receiving these benefits had market earnings already, their income was likely to be just under the poverty line, if they were in poverty at all, and thus the targeted EITC and CTC transfers could easily lift them above the poverty line. The low unemployment rate combined with these large income transfers for working parents created socioeconomic conditions that can best be described as a fragile victory: though poverty rates were low in 2019, they were one employment shock away from unraveling.

The work-based welfare state that the United States had developed in recent decades was predicated not only on enhancing benefits for working families but also on steadily eroding the available income support for nonworking adults.[11] Since "welfare reform" and the introduction of the Temporary Assistance for Needy Families (TANF) program in the mid-1990s, cash assistance for jobless adults in the United States has been increasingly difficult to acquire; moreover, benefit levels for those who are able to acquire it have been shrinking. Consider, for example, that a jobless single parent with two children in Missouri could receive a maximum of $292 per month ($3,504 per year) in cash support in 2019 (although, in reality, only one in seven children in poverty in Missouri actually received this benefit in recent years).[12] If that single parent were to instead work and earn $15,000 per year (say, by working full-time at the federal minimum wage of $7.25 per hour), the federal government would instead hand her $5,828 in EITC benefits and $1,875 in refundable CTC benefits over the year. Combined, the benefits provided to the working single parent from these two programs alone would amount to around $7,700—more than double the level of direct cash support provided to the jobless single parent, who would presumably be more in need of the support, given her lack of earnings.

This work-first approach was extremely effective at reducing poverty in 2019. The EITC, which alone lifted 7.5. million individuals out of poverty, was the most effective income transfer program in the arsenal of the American welfare state (aside from Social Security benefits, most of which are targeted at retirement-age adults).[13] But this fragile victory was about to meet its greatest threat: an unemployment rate that climbed to 19 percent in April 2020, forcing millions of U.S. residents to confront a welfare state that was deeply unprepared to help those who were suddenly out of work.

Beyond the lack of income support for jobless families, several other institutional features of the United States made it particularly vulnerable to the consequences of a global pandemic. Unequal access to decent health care may have been the most important factor in shaping overall well-being during the COVID-19 pandemic. As noted, 29 million U.S. residents entered the pandemic without health insurance, while millions more relied on employer-provided insurance to meet their family's health care needs.[14] Moreover, U.S. residents were not as healthy as the populations of other high-income countries prior to the arrival of COVID-19, and poor health was closely associated with greater exposure to poverty.[15]

Meanwhile, the country's labor market institutions, and especially workers' lack of power, had led to workers having little say in their working conditions. In 2019, workers' power relative to their employers was near a historic low, at least as represented in rates of union membership, which had declined from 24 percent of the labor force in 1970 to 10 percent.[16] The share of workers covered under any type of collective bargaining agreement in the United States is far lower than in peer nations, and especially compared to European Union (EU) countries.[17] Not surprisingly, then, many workers who kept their jobs after the first wave of layoffs in early April 2020 had little choice but to report to work in-person despite the spread of a contagious and lethal virus.[18]

Beyond the challenges related to out-of-work support, health care access, and low worker power, U.S. households were also challenged by expensive childcare services, large inequalities in housing and neighborhood conditions, and a divided political system that was not particularly known for its ability to work cohesively for the common good. In short, the United States was an economically strong country that, despite its wealth, featured welfare state and labor market institutions that were particularly unfit to protect against the onset of widespread health concerns, mass job loss, and exacerbation of families' care responsibilities. In the span of several months in early 2020, however, each of those concerns became reality.

On March 1, 2020, New York City—the city hit hardest in the initial phase of the pandemic—recorded its first case of COVID-19.[19] By the end of the month, its count had skyrocketed to thirty thousand cases. Mayor Bill DeBlasio ordered all schools to close and all non-essential businesses to suspend operations.[20] As New York City hospitals filled up and thousands of the city's residents lost their jobs, uncertainty, as well as COVID-19, spread throughout the rest of the country.

By the start of April 2020, New York's experience was replaying in cities across the United States. That month the unemployment rate spiked and millions of jobless adults filed for unemployment benefits, only to encounter lengthy delays in benefit receipt as states' antiquated application systems were overwhelmed.[21] Childcare centers across the nation shut down or reduced their intake capacity.[22] All but two states mandated a shift to distance learning, exacerbating many parents' struggles with balancing their work and care responsibilities.[23] Meanwhile, the virus continued to sweep throughout the world, eventually claiming more than a million lives in the United States alone—more than the combined number of American deaths in World War II and subsequent wars in Vietnam, Korea, Iraq, and Afghanistan.[24]

For the next two years and perhaps beyond, the United States was faced with what was first and foremost a health crisis. But even those who were fortunate enough to avoid the worst health effects of the virus still faced a number of overlapping and related crises that threatened their well-being in the short term as well as their physical, social, or economic well-being in the long run. This book addresses seven of the crises that households faced throughout the pandemic: challenges related to physical health, employment, income, material hardship, mental health, children's educational outcomes, and childcare. Some of these crises had different impacts on different populations: school and childcare closures hit families with children harder than childless families, the health consequences of the pandemic were felt most acutely by older adults, and childless adults of all ages faced job loss and difficulties in making ends meet. This book gives attention to each of these age groups and family types, though the chapter on school and childcare closures focuses more intensively on the unique challenges faced by families with children.

To view these crises through the lens of poverty, however, requires critical reflection on how we should think about poverty in the context of a global economic and health crisis. The primary goal of this chapter is to put forth a framework for building a more complete understanding of poverty that can help us make sense of the many complexities in households' experiences during the COVID-19 pandemic.

How Should We Understand Poverty in the COVID-19 Pandemic?

Poverty, most simply defined, is the state of having a shortage of resources relative to need.[25] What constitutes "resources" or "need" is a source of constant debate, but most scholars and government institutions tend to compare a household's income (resources) to a poverty threshold (need) when identifying whether it is in poverty.[26] For the average two-parent, two-child family renting a home in the United States in 2020, the first year of the pandemic, the annual poverty threshold was $30,150 when using the Supplemental Poverty Measure (SPM), the measure of poverty that most U.S. researchers and government institutions prefer.[27] Poverty is measured once per year as a binary indicator (you are either in poverty or not in poverty) for each resource-sharing unit (most often equivalent to the household; see note 26). If a household has an annual income less than the poverty threshold, it is in poverty.

A tremendous amount of scientific work has been invested in producing meaningful measures of poverty. The SPM, for example, is the product of years of deliberation and research by government agencies and academic researchers.[28] Like other scientifically grounded measures of poverty, the SPM is a useful tool for tracking economic well-being across people, places, and time and for evaluating how different policy interventions can improve the conditions of the nation's most vulnerable residents. However, an understanding of poverty that is filtered solely through this binary, once-per-year indicator of a household's economic status is insufficient for understanding the challenges that low-income households faced in the context of a global pandemic.

I argue that we must broaden our perspective if we are to deepen our understanding of the interrelation of poverty with the health, employment, income, education, and care challenges that the pandemic presented. Specifically, I argue that we must move beyond the typical academic conceptualization of poverty and simultaneously view it through three distinct perspectives.

The first perspective sees poverty as a preexisting *risk factor* that increases the likelihood of experiencing a life disruption and its consequences. A life disruption can refer to any number of events that threaten a household's ability to maintain its current standard of living: the loss of a job, the loss of a family member, the birth of a child, the closure of a childcare center, a personal health setback, and more. Life disruptions do not, of course, occur only during pandemics: before 2020, households already faced the threat of job loss, family changes, and health challenges. A unique and terrifying feature of the pandemic, however, was how quickly it expanded the reach and accelerated the pace of life disruptions: for example, it was not uncommon for a U.S. resident to lose a job, lose a family member, and face a personal health challenge in just a few months in the spring of 2020. This perspective on poverty argues that persistent and lifelong exposure to poverty makes individuals more likely to experience some of these life disruptions and their associated consequences. Individuals who had experienced high levels of exposure to poverty prior to the COVID-19 pandemic found themselves on a more direct path to the many life disruptions that it spawned, such as greater exposure to the virus's health risks and a higher likelihood of job loss.

The second perspective on poverty focuses on a household's *current resources*, seeing poverty as the immediate state of lacking adequate resources. This view of poverty is most directly captured in the official government statistics used to report the national poverty rate each year. These indicators are important for representing economic well-being in the here and now. That said, any point-in-time estimate of poverty or hardship, on its own, incompletely captures the broader consequences of sustained economic vulnerability.[29] Income transfers can reduce the poverty rate at any given point in time—as they did for millions during the pandemic—but the long-run consequences of sustained exposure to poverty will persist for those who have faced it throughout their lives.[30]

The third perspective understands poverty as a *stratifying feature* that moderates the short- and long-run consequences of a life disruption. In contrast to the first perspective, which examines differential *exposure* to life disruptions, this perspective captures the differential *consequences* of a life disruption for lower- and higher-income families. Several kinds of life disruptions, such as the birth of a child, are not necessarily more likely among lower-income individuals or households, but when they do occur, lower-income individuals often face greater challenges in adapting to the new reality. Experiencing poverty prior to the COVID-19 pandemic did not make an individual more likely to be exposed to school closures or

Table 1.1   Three Perspectives for Understanding Poverty during the COVID-19 Pandemic

Perspective	Focus	Example
Risk factor: Exposure to poverty increases the likelihood that an individual will experience a life disruption and its consequences.	Persistent exposure to poverty can make an individual more vulnerable to a life disruption and its economic, social, psychological, and health consequences.	Adults who entered the COVID-19 pandemic in poorer health and who lived in a multigenerational home—two correlates of poverty—were more likely to contract and die from COVID-19.
Current resources: Poverty is the immediate state of lacking adequate resources to meet basic needs.	This perspective provides a descriptive measure of the share of individuals who experience poverty or hardship at a specific point in time.	The share of U.S. individuals experiencing poverty declined from 15.5 percent in January 2020 to 13.9 percent in April 2020.
Stratifying feature: As a stratifying feature, poverty moderates the short- and long-run consequences of a life disruption.	Even when poverty does not directly increase the likelihood of a life disruption, persistent exposure to poverty nonetheless amplifies the challenges of adapting to a life disruption when one does occur.	Lower-income families were not more likely to face school closures, but they did struggle more than higher-income families to adapt to distance learning, with potential long-run consequences for learning outcomes.

Source: Author's compilation.

distance learning, but preexisting poverty did make it far more difficult for families with children to adapt to distance learning, with consequences for income-based gaps in educational performance (see chapter 7). For a summary of the three perspectives on poverty, see table 1.1.

Scholars have investigated each of these themes; we have strong evidence, for example, that, in a pattern consistent with our first perspective on poverty, lower-income Black workers are often the first to lose their jobs during economic downturns.[31] A large body of research has sought to understand the determinants of point-in-time poverty rates, consistent with the second perspective.[32] And we can see poverty acting as a stratifying feature, for example, in the greater struggle of low-income adults to cope with adverse health events compared with higher-income adults.[33] These themes are not new to this book but have emerged, often in isolation, throughout the long history of poverty research.

I argue in this book that the three perspectives can be united and explicitly put forth as an organizing framework for a more systematic analysis of poverty—in this case, an analysis focused on the COVID-19 pandemic. My purpose in doing so is functional: I argue that this framework is an appropriate tool for answering the four primary questions that this book aims to answer. Beyond its application to my own analysis, the formalization of these three perspectives on poverty can stimulate future policy and poverty research, a theme I return to in the final chapter. Here I elaborate on these three perspectives, focusing on their application to the pandemic.

Perspective 1: Poverty as a Preexisting Risk Factor That Increases the Likelihood of Experiencing a Life Disruption and Its Consequences

The dominant focus in contemporary poverty research is on understanding point-in-time estimates of poverty. For example, we might ask: How have poverty rates changed over time? Why do some groups of people have higher poverty rates than others? How does a policy of interest impact poverty rates? These economic snapshots are useful, but they tell us only one part of the story about households' experience of poverty, particularly in the context of COVID-19.

For a fuller understanding, we must recognize that a household's experience during COVID-19 depended not merely on its point-in-time poverty status in 2020 and 2021 but also on its economic circumstances at the onset of the pandemic. Specifically, we must understand how sustained exposure to poverty before the pandemic contributed to how likely individuals were to enter the pandemic in poorer health, to have access to health care, to live in a multigenerational household, or to work in a high-risk occupation. Looking at poverty as a preexisting risk factor that increases the likelihood of experiencing a life disruption—the first perspective on poverty—acknowledges accumulated disadvantages that form as early as childhood.

The term "preexisting" in this context specifically refers to an individual's experience with poverty prior to the onset of COVID-19. Imagine, for example, a person who grew up in the United States and is now around thirty years old. According to data from the Panel Study of Income Dynamics (PSID)—a source of panel data that tracks economic conditions over the life course of many thousands of respondents—

Table 1.2   Exposure to Childhood Poverty and Characteristics in Young Adulthood, by Race or Ethnicity, 2013–2019

Race or Ethnicity	Percent of Childhood in Poverty	Percent of Young Adulthood in Poverty	Lacked Health Insurance in Young Adulthood	Lacked a College Degree	Worked in a High-Risk Occupation
All	16.2	10.3	17.2	52.8	36.4
White	8.8	7.1	13.6	44.7	31.5
Black	40.8	20.9	28.5	78.1	55.6
Hispanic	20.8	13.3	20.4	50.5	39.9

Source: Author's calculations from the Panel Study of Income Dynamics.
Note: Sample is limited to adults between the ages of twenty-five and thirty-five from 2013 to 2019 who were observed for at least five years during their childhood (birth through age ten). Poverty is measured using a post-tax/transfer income definition (inclusive of SNAP and EITC) relative to an OPM poverty threshold given the lack of SPM poverty thresholds in the PSID. High-risk occupations (measured as a share of employed adults) are service, care, or clerical support jobs, all of which were vulnerable to job loss at the onset of COVID-19. $N = 9,395$.

the average young adult (between the ages of twenty-five and thirty-five) spent 16.2 percent of their childhood in poverty.[34] For young Black adults, that percentage is much higher: the average young Black adult in the 2010s spent 40.8 percent of their childhood in poverty, compared to 8.8 percent for young White adults. Table 1.2 documents these facts and shows their association with other disadvantages in young adulthood, such as lacking health insurance, lacking a college degree, or working in a particularly high-risk occupation in the context of COVID-19—such as a high-contact service job—that was more vulnerable to job loss during the pandemic.

Past research has shown that those who have been more exposed to poverty, particularly during the formative period of childhood, generally have lower educational performance, are less likely to graduate from high school or to attend college, have more health challenges as well as reduced cognitive development, and are more likely to live in poverty during adulthood.[35] It is no surprise, then, that young Black adults—who were exposed to child poverty at nearly five times the rate of young White adults—also experience higher rates of poverty (20.9 percent) in young adulthood compared to young White adults (7.1 percent) and are less likely to have health insurance (28.5 percent versus 13.6 percent), less likely to have a college degree (78.1 percent versus 44.7 percent), and more likely to work in a job that became high-risk during the COVID-19 pandemic (55.6 percent of employed young Black adults versus 31.5 percent of employed young White adults). Similarly, young Hispanic adults face greater exposure to child poverty relative to young White adults and are more likely to live in poverty in adulthood, less likely to have health insurance or a college degree, and more likely to work in a higher-risk job.[36]

The consequences of sustained exposure to poverty are concerning enough in non-pandemic times, but during a global health crisis they are particularly dangerous. Poverty's association with poorer health, less access to health care, less family stability, lower-paying jobs in less flexible workplaces, and other challenges in adulthood created a set of "risk factors" that made those living in poverty vulnerable to the pandemic's overlapping crises. And given the large racial/ethnic differences in exposure to poverty prior to the pandemic, it was largely Black, Hispanic, and Native American families who were most vulnerable at the start of the pandemic.[37]

As chapter 2 documents, higher pre-pandemic poverty rates were directly linked to higher COVID case rates and fatality rates and to reduced access to vaccine distribution. That Black and Hispanic adults were far more exposed to poverty helps to explain the large racial and ethnic disparities in the health consequences of COVID-19. For these groups, temporary improvements in income as a result of government transfers during COVID-19 could not offset the damage already inflicted by persistent exposure to poverty prior to the pandemic.

Perspective 2: Poverty as the Immediate State of Lacking Adequate Resources to Meet Basic Needs

The second perspective on poverty is the one most in line with the measurement of poverty in current academic and policy research. From this perspective, an individual's or family's poverty status is most often assessed through their current level of income relative to a "needs" standard, which is generally represented by a poverty threshold.[38]

The measurement of poverty in this form carries immense influence and power. Behind President Lyndon B. Johnson's "War on Poverty," behind the United Kingdom's 1999 pledge to "end child poverty," and behind the European Union's pledge to "cut poverty by at least 20 million people" were critical decisions on how to actually measure poverty. In a notable indication of the contentious and never-ending search for the most appropriate measure of poverty, each of these initiatives applied a different measure to quantify the extent of poverty.[39]

In measuring a household's annual resources, the SPM, which U.S. scholars generally agree is a useful measure of poverty, takes into account all taxes and transfers, including once-per-year refundable tax credits, such as those provided by the EITC, as well as SNAP benefits.[40] In setting the poverty threshold, the SPM takes into account recent consumption standards for food, housing, clothing, utilities, and a little more, and it adjusts poverty thresholds by local costs of living. As a result, the poverty threshold is higher in high-cost areas, such as San Francisco and New York City, and lower in lower-cost areas, such as rural Missouri.

Point-in-time conceptualizations of poverty, such as the SPM poverty rate, are the backbone of empirical research in poverty and social policy research.[41] When comparing poverty rates across countries, regions, or demographic groups, scholars tend to focus on this annual binary snapshot of a given group to determine what share lives in poverty. For example, in 2019, just before the pandemic hit the United States, the national poverty rate was 11.7 percent, but the rate was higher for Black (18.3 percent) and Hispanic (18.9 percent) individuals relative to White individuals (8.2 percent).[42] As noted, the national poverty rate was lower in 2019 than in any other year since 1967, the first year for which we have reliable income data.

In some circumstances, however, such as the COVID-19 pandemic, the conventional approach to measuring poverty in the United States does not adequately represent households' experiences of poverty. Specifically, the standard approach to measuring poverty faces three major shortcomings that, I argue, warrant the introduction of a new measure of poverty to supplement the traditional annual measure.

First, measures of poverty are generally based on a household's *annual* income. A household's poverty status in 2019, for example, was based on the combined sum of the income that the household members received from January through December 2019. The incomes and living conditions of U.S. households, however, have become increasingly volatile from month to month, and this was particularly true during the COVID-19 pandemic.[43] A household's income in February 2020, just before the pandemic hit, may have borne little resemblance to its economic situation in April 2020, when millions were filing for unemployment benefits. Similarly, a jobless adult's income in July 2020, when the federal government was supplementing unemployment benefits with an additional $600 per week, may have looked nothing like that person's income in August 2020, when those benefits had expired. Though many families can use assets, savings, and debt to smooth their consumption and live "normally" during months with lower-than-expected incomes, many low-income families cannot, as this book later demonstrates empirically.

Second, measures of poverty are generally produced *only once a year*. Consistent with the collection of annual income data, government agencies produce an annual poverty rate that summarizes economic conditions for a given year. One time each year we learn about the poverty status of the country for the prior year; during the rest of the year we gain no new direct information about the national poverty rate or about changes in families' experiences with poverty during the year.

Third, official estimates of poverty are released after a *long delay*. Consider, for example, that the U.S. Census Bureau did not release its poverty rate for 2020 until September 2021—eighteen months after the start of the pandemic.[44] If estimates of poverty are to inform policy action, or at least offer knowledge of current economic conditions, then such long delays in reporting the poverty estimates reduce their usefulness.

To address these shortcomings, this book introduces a monthly measure of poverty that accounts for a household's monthly resources and can be released as soon as two weeks after the end of a given month. The monthly poverty rate incorporates the features of the SPM—it accounts for all taxes and transfers and uses the same measurement principles when defining the poverty threshold—but it more appropriately accounts for the intrayear volatility in poverty that many households experience.

As I document in later chapters, levels and trends in the monthly SPM poverty rate closely correspond with levels and trends in measures of material hardship, such as food insufficiency, and they outperform monthly unemployment rates and other measures of poverty in predicting households' economic well-being. Tracking monthly poverty rates allows us to produce near-real-time estimates of the economic status of households across the country as well as the effectiveness of government transfers in enhancing economic well-being throughout the pandemic.

Importantly, the monthly measure of poverty should be understood as a supplement to, rather than a substitute for, the typical annual measure of poverty. In nonpandemic years, the monthly poverty measure is likely to add less value to the annual poverty measure. Moreover, since the monthly measure currently cannot be created without a number of technical procedures (which chapter 5 documents), its estimation is more subject to potential measurement errors. For these reasons and more, the monthly and annual measures should generally be evaluated in tandem; chapter 5 evaluates trends in both measures, tracking their changes from prior to the pandemic through the end of 2021.

One of chapter 5's central findings is that even as the massive job loss after the onset of the pandemic threatened to send the monthly poverty rate soaring in April 2020, the federal government's unprecedented distribution of cash assistance to households across the country managed to *reduce* levels of poverty. From the pre-pandemic month of January 2020 to April 2020, after the onset of the pandemic, the monthly poverty rate declined from 15.5 percent to 13.9 percent, entirely owing to government income support. The annual poverty rate fell from 11.8 percent to 9.1 percent from 2019 to 2020. That record-high unemployment can lead to record-low poverty is no surprise in light of the federal government's efforts to temporarily double the size of income support by passing the Coronavirus Aid, Relief, and Economic Security Act (CARES Act) in March 2020 and subsequently authorizing other policy interventions (discussed in detail in chapter 4). The federal policy interventions throughout the pandemic generated the largest reductions in poverty since at least 1967 and the lowest child poverty rate in recorded U.S. history.

Perspective 3: Poverty as a Stratifying Feature That Moderates the Short- and Long-Run Consequences of a Life Disruption

The consequences of poverty extend beyond increased exposure to life disruptions or point-in-time consumption challenges. Even when poverty did *not* lead to greater exposure to job loss, school closures, health risks, or the pandemic's other threats, the conditions of poverty may nonetheless have made it more challenging for households to adapt to these challenges. From this third perspective, poverty acts as a stratifying feature that moderates the consequences of life disruptions.

The example of school closures illustrates the difference between the first and third perspectives on poverty. Given that nearly all states mandated the closure of schools in April 2020, wealthy families and poor families alike were comparably exposed to distance learning. However, pre-pandemic poverty status still affected how well a family could cope with school closures. Put differently, preexisting poverty had no bearing on who was directly exposed to school closures in April 2020 (the focus of the first perspective), but it did potentially moderate the consequences of school closures for students' learning outcomes.

Many wealthy families were able to adapt to the new reality by forming learning pods with other students in the neighborhood, using reliable internet access and dedicated laptops for learning, and addressing any potential learning loss with after-hours tutoring. Poorer families, in contrast, were less likely to have a reliable internet connection or a dedicated working space so that their children could tune in to virtual instruction. Exacerbating the challenges of balancing work and family responsibilities during COVID-19 was the frequent inability of working parents in lower-income families to take time off from work or to work remotely.

Chapter 7 focuses specifically on school closures and distance learning. Using cell-phone data to create the first nationwide database on school closures in the United States, I show that lower-income families were not necessarily more exposed to school closures, but that lower-income students nonetheless suffered the greatest learning losses in the initial year of the pandemic. To be sure, school closures were probably necessary to protect children's health and slow the spread of COVID-19. But an important side effect was exacerbation of the educational performance gaps between lower- and higher-income students.

Contributions to Poverty Knowledge

These three perspectives on poverty are not limited to the context of the pandemic: poverty long predated COVID-19, and many households experience life disruptions in the absence of a global health or economic crisis. Studying the three perspectives simultaneously is necessary, however, to appropriately document and understand the challenges facing low-income households during the pandemic years of 2020 and 2021; to revisit standard conceptualizations of poverty in the social sciences; and to extract policy lessons that can be applied to nonpandemic years to improve the lives of low-income U.S. residents.

More generally, the evidence presented here on the complexities of poverty during the COVID-19 pandemic allows us to draw several broader conclusions regarding the *consequences, measurement,* and *sources* of poverty. These conclusions contribute to what Alice O'Connor refers to as "poverty knowledge"—or, more broadly, social scientific thinking on the phenomenon of poverty.[45] I preview these contributions here and elaborate on each in the book's final chapter.

The findings presented here deepen our understanding of the *consequences* of poverty by reinforcing the fact that reducing point-in-time poverty, while an important policy achievement, is far different from eliminating the disadvantages associated with cumulative poverty exposure. Despite poverty reductions during the pandemic, systemic inequalities in exposure to poverty as far back as childhood led directly to increased risk of COVID-19's consequences. Summarizing this evidence, table 1.3 documents the link between exposure to poverty as a child and COVID-related outcomes across several dimensions that subsequent chapters cover in detail.

Specifically, table 1.3 provides estimated outcomes for two types of adults: adults who spent none of their childhood in poverty and adults who spent all of their childhood in poverty (row 1). According to the PSID, these different starting points were associated with different incomes relative to the poverty line for adults in 2019 (row 2): the average

Table 1.3   Differential Risks during the COVID-19 Pandemic by Exposure to Childhood Poverty

Outcome	No Childhood Poverty	High Childhood Poverty
Share of childhood spent in poverty	0%	100%
Income relative to poverty line in 2019 (predicted)	3.6	0.9
Likely in poverty as adult in 2019?	No	Yes
Likelihood of COVID-related fatality (ages twenty-five to sixty-five)	0.07%	0.18%
Likelihood of being unemployed in April 2020	18.1%	35.9%
Likelihood of being unemployed in January 2021	6.6%	20.5%
Likelihood of being able to work remotely (if employed) in April 2020	33.6%	21.0%
Reported receipt of monthly Child Tax Credit payments	70.0%	62.4%
Likelihood of SPM poverty in 2020	5.1%	33.8%
Likelihood of food insufficiency during pandemic	7.6%	29.0%
Likelihood of attending a school engaged in remote learning in January 2021	46.3%	50.3%
Mean reduction in math progress if school was mostly in remote learning mode (standard deviation)	0.30	0.46

Source: Author's calculations from the Panel Study of Income Dynamics, Current Population Survey, and SafeGraph data.
Note: SPM = Supplemental Poverty Measure. See methods for calculation in the chapter 1 appendix. The estimates of mean reduction in math progress assume that the average child with high (low) exposure to poverty experienced learning loss comparable to the average student at a high-poverty (low-poverty) school that prioritized remote learning in 2020–2021.

adult with no childhood poverty exposure had an income around 3.6 times the poverty line in 2019, while the more disadvantaged adult had an income just under the poverty line in 2019.

The subsequent rows document how these disadvantages dating back to childhood are associated with average outcomes during the COVID-19 pandemic. Compared to the adult with no childhood poverty exposure, the adult with high childhood poverty exposure was about twice as likely to die from COVID, twice as likely to be unemployed in April 2020, about three times as likely to be unemployed in January 2021, and, if employed, about one-third less likely to be able to work from home in the first month of the pandemic. Worse, the more disadvantaged adult was less likely, on average, to access the monthly CTC payments, more likely to be living in poverty in 2020, and around four times more likely to face food insufficiency during the pandemic. Children in poverty in 2019 were not much more likely to face school closures or distance learning, but in schools that prioritized remote learning they did experience larger average reductions in math progress compared to children not in poverty. The appendix to this chapter provides more details on these estimates, and the subsequent chapters discuss each outcome in more detail.

As demonstrated in table 1.3, the lifelong accumulation of disadvantage sets the foundation for the point-in-time disparities in economic, social, and health outcomes that poverty scholars tend to analyze. As I elaborate in chapter 8, these findings point to the need for policies that reduce disadvantages as early as childhood, as well as for further research on the long-term benefits of policy interventions that reduce exposure to poverty.[46]

On the *measurement* of poverty, this book demonstrates that the way scholars measure and conceptualize poverty can, in certain contexts, misrepresent the burdens of poverty for low-income households. Moreover, an income-specific measure of poverty conceals layers of hardship that extend further up the income distribution: consider that most U.S. families experiencing food insufficiency in the first year of the pandemic were not in SPM-level poverty (see chapter 5). How can researchers better ensure that the concept they call "poverty" appropriately aligns with low-income families' day-to-day reality? The evidence within this book will help us make progress toward that aim.

On the *sources* (or *determinants*) of poverty, this book informs us on the relative role of individual and behavioral characteristics in shaping poverty rates. A long-running debate in the academic literature on poverty is the extent to which we should understand differences in poverty across place, time, or groups as a product of individual behavior, structural economic features, or political and institutional features.[47] Individualist perspectives on poverty have largely focused on family structure and employment as two dominant drivers of poverty rates.[48] The COVID-19 pandemic, however, demonstrated that increases in joblessness need not translate into increases in poverty.

Consider that in March 2020, Congress passed the CARES Act, which authorized the distribution of stimulus checks and $600 per week top-ups to unemployment benefits, plus a large expansion in access to unemployment benefits. The CARES Act alone put nearly $930 billion directly into the pockets of U.S. households in 2020.[49] A year later, in March 2021, Congress passed the Biden administration's American Rescue Plan Act, which authorized another round of stimulus checks, a revival of the weekly unemployment benefit top-ups (this time set at $300 per week), and, perhaps most notably, a temporary expansion of the Child Tax Credit that, for six months in 2021, provided most U.S. families with a monthly check of up to $300 per child.[50] This book uses a variety of data sources to identify the distributional implications of these policy responses throughout the pandemic. One particular finding stands out: a record-high unemployment rate coincided with a record-low poverty rate.

That the federal government's interventions severed the relationship between joblessness and poverty raises several questions. To what extent should the federal government replicate its generous unemployment benefits supplements in nonpandemic years? Would state governments be better off expanding access to, or the generosity of, their unemployment support? What impacts would these policy changes have on employment rates?

I return to these questions in chapter 8, where I argue that the life-altering events experienced by a large share of Americans during the COVID-19 pandemic—job loss, health challenges, unfair demands from employers, food hardship, inability to pay rent, and more—are regular events in the lives of a smaller subset of U.S. residents even in the absence of an economic recession or global pandemic. Although caution is needed in translating policy lessons from an atypical context (a pandemic) to more normal contexts, the policy experiments from 2020 and 2021 nonetheless offer many lessons for the everyday challenges that low-income households face in the United States.

Some of these policy lessons relate to the challenge of preparing the policy infrastructure to more efficiently respond to future economic downturns. Particularly during moments of crisis, policymakers must grapple with balancing the *timeliness*, *targeting*, and *duration* of economic support.[51] Quick distribution of benefits can help mitigate the pain of an economic downturn, but often at the cost of imperfect targeting: during COVID-19, for example, the Internal Revenue Service (IRS) was tasked with rapidly distributing stimulus checks, but at the cost of missing many of the lowest-income tax units. Meanwhile, the Small Business Administration (SBA) was tasked with quickly implementing the Paycheck Protection Program (PPP), which was intended to offer a lifeline to COVID-impacted businesses with fewer than five hundred employees; the program was implemented with little targeting and few accountability mechanisms to ensure a moderately progressive use of the $800 billion worth of resources (see chapter 4 for a detailed discussion of these programs). Policymakers' decisions on the duration of a given income support policy, such as unemployment benefit supplements, required providing sufficiently steady income support while not impeding the subsequent employment recovery. In reality, the federal government's response during COVID-19 was to implement four months of generous unemployment benefit supplements (April to July 2020), followed by five months without the benefit supplements, followed by a period when most jobless adults could again receive unemployment supplements (January to summer 2021), followed by a period in which twenty-six state governments decided to no longer allow residents of their state to receive the supplements.[52]

An examination of these stops and starts, as well as the successes and shortcomings of the COVID-era policy response more generally, offers a blueprint for proactively preparing for economic crises in the future. But there are also several lessons to be gleaned that could be applied to noncrisis contexts. Among the policy experiments that the pandemic unleashed were an unconditional child allowance, an expansion of food and nutrition supports, the largest onetime increase in education spending in U.S. history, and a loosening of eligibility criteria for the receipt of unemployment benefits. The distinct designs of some of these policies offer lessons in themselves. This book provides data from the expanded CTC, for example, on how a monthly provision of cash support differentially affects families' consumption responses relative to a once-per-year, lump-sum provision of income support. Taken together, this evidence (elaborated in chapter 8) points to ten policy lessons that can be applied to improving economic opportunity in a post-COVID economy.

The Plan of the Book

The next seven chapters apply the three perspectives on poverty to understand how households across the United States coped with the pandemic's overlapping crises, discuss what the results teach us about the study of poverty, and draw out lessons for improved policymaking in the future.

Chapters 2 and 3 document poverty as a preexisting risk factor for suffering the consequences of COVID-19. Chapter 2 presents evidence on the connection between pre-pandemic exposure to poverty and COVID cases, fatalities, and vaccinations. More than other observable characteristics of counties, poverty is central to explaining disparities in COVID-related health outcomes. In explaining why poverty led to worse health outcomes, the chapter documents how the consequences of persistent poverty exposure—poorer health conditions, reduced health care access, poorer neighborhood and housing conditions, and unequal reliance on high-risk jobs—generated more perilous health conditions for Black and Hispanic adults in particular during the pandemic. Chapter 3 focuses on the employment crisis, demonstrating that preexisting poverty—more than gender, parenthood, age, or race/ethnicity—was central to understanding disparities in job loss throughout 2020.

Chapters 4, 5, and 6 focus on poverty as the immediate state of lacking adequate resources to meet basic needs (the second perspective). The dramatic increase in joblessness threatened to send poverty rates soaring, particularly given the weak welfare state described earlier. But in March 2020, the federal government stepped in and passed one of the most ambitious income support packages in modern U.S. history. Chapter 4 discusses these policy interventions, tracking the spending from the CARES Act and, later, the American Rescue Plan Act to document the enormity of the response. Chapter 5 shifts attention to income and poverty by documenting the impact of the policy response on poverty rates throughout the pandemic. This chapter will introduce the framework for producing monthly estimates of poverty, document trends in poverty for different groups throughout the pandemic, and place the poverty reduction of 2020 and 2021 into historical and international context.

Poverty is only one indicator, however, of economic well-being. I bring in new evidence in chapter 6 on trends in material hardship and mental health throughout COVID-19, as well as the role of the policy response in keeping levels of hardship in check. I walk through the competing accounts of the extent to which food hardship increased (or did not) during the pandemic and document how the expanded Child Tax Credit dramatically lowered levels of food hardship for low-income families. However, the chapter's findings are not entirely happy: I show that though income transfers meaningfully reduced food hardship, they were less successful at promoting mental health and subjective well-being during the pandemic. The complexity of the crisis left many adults with high levels of anxiety that temporary income transfers could not ease.

To capture the role of poverty as a stratifying feature that moderates the consequences of life disruptions, chapter 7 focuses on school and childcare closures. The chapter relies on original data collection to track school and care facility closures across nearly all counties in the United States during each month of the pandemic. The findings point to unequal exposures to school and care-facility closures across place and race/ethnicity. Importantly, the chapter documents that even equal exposure to closures by poverty status portends widening long-run gaps in educational and economic performance between lower- and higher-income families.

Finally, chapter 8 presents takeaways from the pandemic for future public policy decisions related to improving life in low-income America. Building on evidence presented throughout the book, I argue that the experiences of low-income households throughout the pandemic should prompt several changes to the public policies and services that federal and state governments provide, and I point to several specific changes to achieve those aims. The lessons from the pandemic need not be applied only during times of crisis; the United States can learn much from its experience during COVID-19 to reduce poverty and promote well-being long after the pandemic subsides.

Chapter 1 Appendix

In table 1.3, I provide generalized associations of the link between childhood poverty and COVID-era disadvantages, using data sources, assumptions, and estimation strategies that vary by indicator.

To estimate adults' income-to-poverty ratio in 2019, conditional on their exposure to childhood poverty, I use the PSID data for the sample of adults in 2019 who were observed for at least five years during their childhood. I measure their post-tax, post-transfer income (using the income variables modified by the Cross-National Equivalent File, or CNEF) relative to the OPM poverty threshold, given that SPM thresholds are not generally replicable in the PSID. This leads to the predicted income-to-poverty ratios of 3.6 for an adult with no exposure to childhood poverty and 0.9 for an adult with full exposure to childhood poverty. I simplify from these estimates that the more advantaged adult was not in poverty in 2019, while the less advantaged adult was in poverty, particularly given the latter's income-to-needs ratio of below 1.

To calculate the likelihood of a COVID-related fatality between the ages of twenty-five and sixty-five, I use data from the research of Amy Finkelstein and her colleagues, specifically from their 2022 paper's figure 6, which plots excess deaths per ten thousand (ages twenty-five to sixty-four) across the family income-to-poverty ratio.[53] I apply the estimated income-to-poverty ratios derived earlier from the PSID to proxy for the average COVID-related fatality rates for the more and less disadvantaged adults characterized in table 1.3.

For the three employment indicators in table 1.3 (rows 5 to 7), I link the 2020 CPS ASEC (covering income year 2019) to the 2020 monthly files to estimate unemployment trends conditional on SPM poverty status in 2019. I discuss this linking process in more detail in the chapter 3 appendix.

To measure monthly CTC receipt conditional on the income-to-needs ratio, I use the 2022 CPS ASEC (covering the income year 2021) and produce a revised income-to-needs ratio based on the SPM income definitions; however, I exclude CTC benefits from this specific ratio. I then estimate the likelihood of reported receipt of the advance (monthly) CTC payments among SPM family units with children as a product of the income-to-needs ratio and its square (given that I expect benefit receipt to initially increase with income, then decline among households as their income disqualified them for the benefit). I then predict benefit receipt based on the two estimated income-to-needs ratios for the more and less disadvantaged adults characterized in table 1.3.

To measure the likelihood of SPM poverty in 2020 conditional on 2019 poverty status, I link the 2021 and 2020 CPS ASEC files (covering the 2020 and 2019 income years) and compute the mean poverty rate in 2021 by poverty status in 2020.

I measure food insufficiency during the pandemic using the 2021 wave of the PSID, which includes a direct question on whether the household's food often or sometimes did not last owing to insufficient resources. I link this directly to the 2019 income-to-needs ratios observed in the PSID.

The likelihood of attending a school engaged in remote learning in January 2021 is based on the SafeGraph data on school closures that I present in chapter 7. Here I estimate the share of students who were (or were not) eligible for free or reduced-price lunch (an imperfect proxy for poverty status but the best available) and who were exposed to schools with at least a 50 percent decline in in-person visits from the same month in 2019. Chapter 7 elaborates on this data set.

To estimate the mean reduction in math progress if the school was mostly using remote learning, I apply a simplified assumption that the average child in poverty attended a "high-poverty" school (a school with other children who were more likely to be in poverty) and that the average child not in poverty attended a "low-poverty" school (a school with other children who were less likely to be in poverty). I take estimates of learning loss from the work of Dan Goldhaber and his colleagues, who find that, "within school districts that were remote for most of 2020–21, high-poverty schools experienced 50 percent more achievement loss than low-poverty schools (e.g., .46 vs. .30 standard deviations in math)."[54] These authors produced these estimates using testing data from 2.1 million students in ten thousand schools in forty-nine states. They define "low-poverty" schools as those with fewer than 25 percent of their students receiving free or reduced-price lunch and "high-poverty" schools as those where more than 75 percent of students receive benefits from the federal lunch programs. Thus, the estimates in table 1.3 assume that the average child with high exposure to poverty experienced learning loss comparable to that of the average student at a high-poverty school.

Chapter 2

Poverty as a Risk Factor, Part 1: The Unequal Health Consequences of COVID-19

EW EXPERIENCES capture the unequal landscape of American poverty so succinctly as the eleven-stop subway ride from the Wall Street station, situated in the center of American finance, to the 167th Street stop in the Bronx, situated next to schools where more than 20 percent of kindergarten students experienced homelessness in 2019.[1] The ten-mile, forty-five-minute journey transports one across the "two Americas" that Martin Luther King Jr. spoke about in 1967: one America where "young people grow up in the sunlight of opportunity," and another where "they find themselves perishing on a lonely island of poverty in the midst of a vast ocean of material prosperity."[2]

These two Americas have long experienced vastly different prospects for economic opportunity, and during 2020 and 2021 they also experienced two different pandemics. In the Bronx, where 29 percent of the county's residents live in poverty, the COVID-related death rate by the end of 2021 was 408 of every 100,000 residents—the highest rate in the state and among the highest in the nation.[3] In wealthier Manhattan (New York County), by contrast, the death rate was 242 of every 100,000 residents; though still higher than the national mean, this death rate was less than two-thirds of the rate of the neighboring Bronx. The disparities in poverty rates and COVID-related fatalities mirror the racial and ethnic disparities across New York City: more than half of Bronx residents are Hispanic (the largest share among the state's counties), and just under one-third are Black (second only to Brooklyn in the state), while only 11 percent are White (by far the lowest percentage in the state).

New York City's disparities are not unique; rather, they are a microcosm of the inequalities in exposure to poverty—and in turn, inequalities in COVID-related fatalities—that were made evident across the United States during the pandemic. As this chapter demonstrates, long-run exposure to poverty prior to the onset of the pandemic—which Black and Hispanic individuals experienced more than White individuals—was a direct risk factor for the health consequences of COVID-19. This finding is in line with what we would expect to see through the lens of the first of the three perspectives on poverty introduced in chapter 1: poverty as a *preexisting risk factor* that increases the likelihood of experiencing a life disruption and its consequences.

Specifically, this chapter sets out to answer three questions: How was pre-pandemic exposure to poverty associated with health outcomes and behaviors during the pandemic, such as rates of COVID-19 cases, COVID-19 fatalities, and vaccinations? How did poverty and racial discrimination work hand in hand to generate the racial/ethnic disparities in COVID-19 health outcomes? And through which set of mechanisms did entering the pandemic in poverty affect an individual's likelihood of facing the harshest health consequences of COVID-19? The findings show that the Bronx's comparatively high rate of COVID-related fatalities was no aberration: across the United States, sustained exposure to poverty prior to the pandemic was a dominant driver of COVID case rates, death rates, and vaccination access in 2020 and 2021.

The Strong Relation of Poverty to COVID-19 Health Outcomes

To understand how poverty related to health outcomes during the COVID-19 pandemic, we can look beyond the example of New York City's boroughs and examine differences in COVID cases, deaths, completed vaccination cycles, and first vaccination boosters across all counties in the United States. Figure 2.1 documents the association of counties' poverty rates prior to the pandemic with COVID-related health outcomes. Each of the four COVID-related health outcomes presented is a cumulative rate from the start of the pandemic through December 2021.

Panel A of figure 2.1 shows a strong, nearly linear relationship between counties' poverty rates and cumulative COVID-19 cases per 100,000 residents. The lowest-poverty counties, for example, had a case rate of around 14,000 cases per 100,000 residents as of December 2021; the highest-poverty counties, in contrast, had rates closer to 18,000 cases per 100,000 residents. The upward-sloping line shows that, relative to the lowest-poverty counties, the counties with higher poverty rates had increasingly high COVID-19 case rates.

Panel B shows an even stronger relationship when we look at COVID-19 death rates. The lowest-poverty counties had death rates below 200 per

Figure 2.1   COVID-19 Cases, Deaths, Vaccinations, and Vaccination Boosters by Counties' Pre-Pandemic Poverty Rates through December 2021

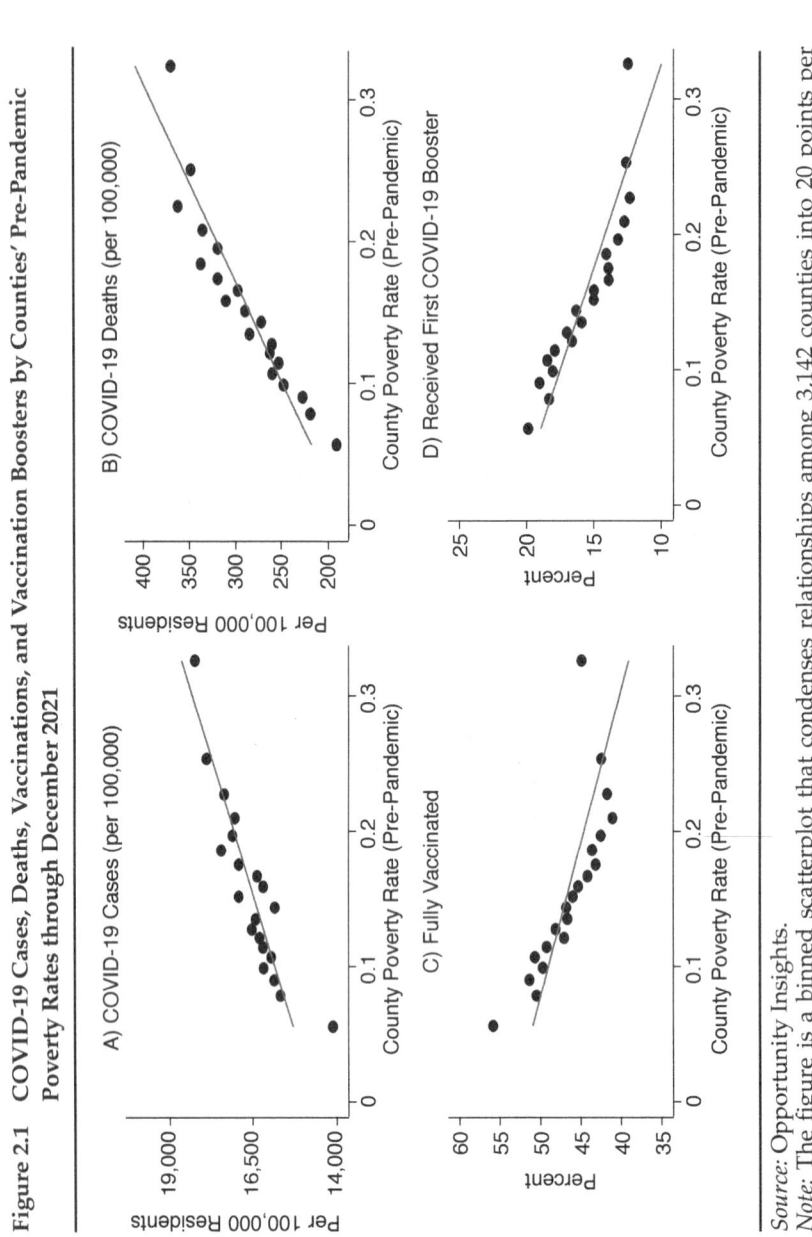

Source: Opportunity Insights.
Note: The figure is a binned scatterplot that condenses relationships among 3,142 counties into 20 points per figure. The COVID-19 cases and deaths are cumulative counts per 100,000 residents in the county up to December 2021. Vaccination and booster rates are percentages of the county population as of December 2021. Counties are not weighted for population size; results that do weight for population size show similar associations, but with higher average values of vaccination rates and booster rates across all bins.

100,000 residents; for the highest-poverty counties, the death rates were closer to 400 per 100,000 residents, or twice the rate of the lowest-poverty counties. Again, the nearly linear, upward-sloping lines show that knowing a county's poverty rate gives us a strong indication of its COVID-inflicted death rate, with higher poverty being associated with higher mortality rates.

To get a better sense of how wide these disparities are, we can compare the death rates in the low- and high-poverty counties to death rates observed across the world. The highest-poverty counties in the United States had COVID-related death rates above 350 per 100,000 residents, as panel B documents, a rate comparable to COVID-related death rates in Romania (351), the poorest country in the European Union.[4] In contrast, the lowest-poverty counties in the United States had death rates around 200 per 100,000 residents, comparable to Germany (199) and Luxembourg (192), two of Europe's wealthiest countries. The differences across the United States were not simply due to the greater poverty levels of some states, on average, compared to others: even within the same state (or city), we can find large disparities in death rates. In Missouri, for example, low-poverty Platte County had a death rate of 68 residents per 100,000, while neighboring Jackson County, with twice the poverty rate (15.5 percent compared to 7 percent in Platte), had nearly twice the COVID-related death rate (120 per 100,000 residents).

Panel C shifts the focus to vaccination rates as of December 2021 (defined as completing the full initial vaccine cycle, such as two shots of the Pfizer vaccine).[5] Among the lowest-poverty counties, more than 55 percent of residents were fully vaccinated by the end of 2021; however, there were near-linear decreases in this rate among counties with higher pre-pandemic poverty rates. The highest-poverty counties, for example, had vaccination rates between 40 and 45 percent as of December 2021. Panel D shows similar disparities among those who received the first COVID-19 booster vaccine: the lowest-poverty counties had the highest rate of booster receipt. Later in this chapter I discuss why high poverty went hand in hand with low vaccination and booster rates.

This descriptive evidence shows a clear relationship between a county's poverty rate and COVID health outcomes. But pre-pandemic poverty rates are not the only factor associated with COVID-19 cases, deaths, and vaccinations. Other factors, such as age, also go a long way toward determining COVID health risks. The CDC reports that, unlike the effect of poverty status, there are no notable differences across age groups in the likelihood of testing positive for COVID-19.[6] But among those who do get hit with the virus, the risks of hospitalization and death vary dramatically: sixty-five- to seventy-four-year-olds are five times more likely than eighteen- to twenty-nine-year-olds to be hospitalized, and sixty times more likely to die as a result of COVID-19 complications. Among adults ages eighty-five and older, the rate of hospitalization is fifteen times greater than for eighteen- to twenty-nine-year-olds, while the death rate is 340 times higher. Older adults with low pre-pandemic incomes were particularly vulnerable.[7]

Does accounting for the age composition of counties thus offer a stronger predictor of place-based variation in COVID health outcomes? Not really. Figure 2.2 evaluates the strength of a broader set of county-level characteristics in explaining variation in counties' COVID-related health outcomes, including their age structure. The figure shows how a higher level of a given county-level characteristic (such as its pre-pandemic poverty rate, or its share of residents of a given race/ethnicity) relative to other counties is associated with variation in COVID-19 health outcomes.[8] The other county-level characteristics included are the share of the county's population that lacked health insurance; the share age sixty or older; the share between ages twenty and twenty-nine; the share that were White, Black, Hispanic, or Asian (with separate indicators for each); the share who were single parents or born outside of the United States; and the population density of the county. This list of possible correlates of COVID-related health challenges is not, of course, exhaustive, but it may allow us to understand which county characteristics were most strongly correlated with pandemic health outcomes.

Panel A of figure 2.2 shows again that a higher poverty rate is associated with higher COVID-19 case rates. (A one standard deviation higher poverty rate is associated with a tenth of a standard deviation higher rate of COVID cases per 100,000 residents.) The association with poverty is stronger in absolute terms than it is with any of the other indicators observed, with the exception of the share of the population age sixty or older (which is negatively associated with COVID cases). Also noteworthy, counties with higher shares of Black or Hispanic residents tend to have higher COVID-19 case rates, while counties with higher shares of White residents generally have lower case rates.

Panel B shows similar findings for COVID-19 death rates. The strongest predictor of more COVID-19 deaths per capita remains a county's poverty status, closely followed by the share of the population without health insurance. A higher share of adults age sixty or older in a county's population, meanwhile, is associated with a higher share of COVID-19 deaths per capita, though this county characteristic is less strongly associated with COVID deaths than poverty. Counties with either higher shares of Black or Hispanic residents or lower shares of White residents experienced more COVID-19 deaths per capita relative to other counties.

Figure 2.2   County-Level Characteristics as Predictors of COVID-19 Cases, Deaths, Vaccinations, and Vaccination Boosters, January 2020 to December 2021

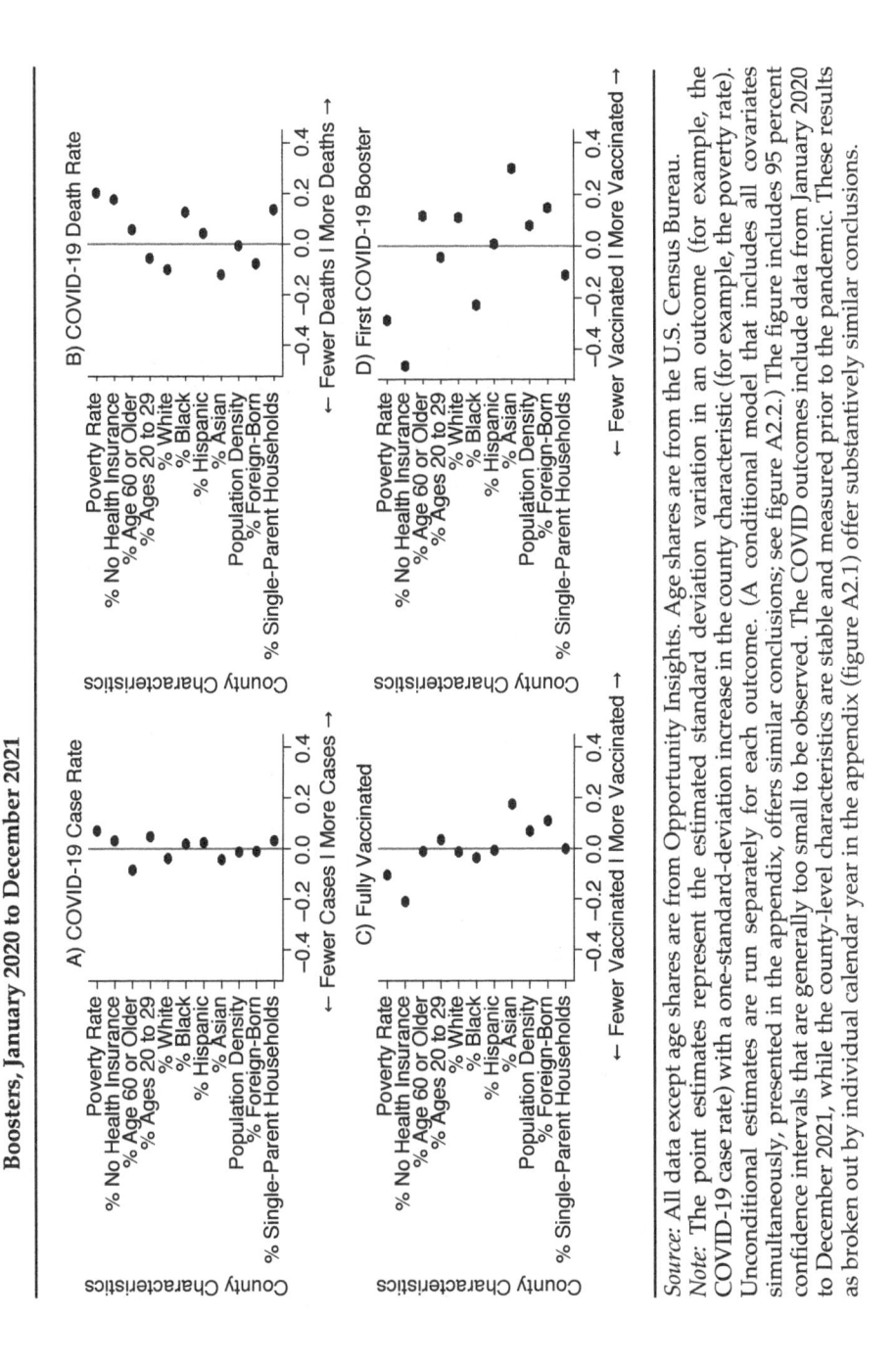

Source: All data except age shares are from Opportunity Insights. Age shares are from the U.S. Census Bureau.
Note: The point estimates represent the estimated standard deviation variation in an outcome (for example, the COVID-19 case rate) with a one-standard-deviation increase in the county characteristic (for example, the poverty rate). Unconditional estimates are run separately for each outcome. (A conditional model that includes all covariates simultaneously, presented in the appendix, offers similar conclusions; see figure A2.2.) The figure includes 95 percent confidence intervals that are generally too small to be observed. The COVID outcomes include data from January 2020 to December 2021, while the county-level characteristics are stable and measured prior to the pandemic. These results as broken out by individual calendar year in the appendix (figure A2.1) offer substantively similar conclusions.

Turning to vaccination and booster rates in panels C and D, we see that a county's poverty rate still stands out—the higher a county's poverty rate, the fewer of its residents had been vaccinated—but this indicator is overtaken in magnitude by another: the share of a county's population lacking health insurance. Where fewer residents had health insurance, vaccine participation was far lower. As I discuss later, lack of health insurance is a key driver of the link between poverty and COVID health risks and in fact was one way in which the U.S. welfare state directly generated inequalities in health outcomes during the pandemic.

Three takeaways emerge from figures 2.1 and 2.2. First, pre-pandemic exposure to poverty is directly connected to the likelihood of experiencing COVID-19, dying from COVID-related complications, and not being sufficiently vaccinated against the virus. Second, at least at the county level, poverty status is generally more strongly associated with variation in COVID cases and deaths than other characteristics of a county's population, including the county's age structure. With respect to vaccinations, however, lack of health insurance, which is closely connected to poverty, stands out as the strongest predictor of fewer completed vaccination cycles or booster shots. Third, the results of figure 2.2 point to strong disparities by race/ethnicity; Black and Hispanic residents in particular experienced greater exposure to COVID cases and deaths.

These descriptive findings illustrate that beginning the pandemic in poverty was directly associated with poorer health outcomes during the pandemic.[9] These findings are focused on counties rather than people, but other studies confirm that lower-income individuals faced a disproportionate share of health challenges during the pandemic.[10] The average adult with an income below half the poverty line was around three times more likely to die of COVID-related causes relative to the average adult with an income more than three times the poverty line.[11] The disparities by race/ethnicity are also consistent with other evidence: a study of one thousand children who were tested for COVID-19 at the same testing center showed that racial/ethnic minority and low-income children had higher COVID-19 positivity rates than non-Hispanic White and higher-income children.[12] Other studies have also shown higher case and mortality rates for COVID-19 among Black and Hispanic individuals, as well as more severe clinical outcomes, when compared to their White counterparts.[13]

As a consequence of these racial/ethnic inequalities in COVID-related mortality rates, the reported life expectancies of racial/ethnic minority populations have greatly decreased relative to the life expectancy of White populations in the United States. One study estimates that Black and Hispanic populations experienced stronger declines in life expectancy (3.5 years and 3.7 years, respectively) owing to the COVID-19 pandemic than White populations (2.0 years).[14] Though data on the Native American population are scarcer, one study estimates that declines in life expectancy among this population were between 4.5 and 6.4 years relative to pre-pandemic life expectancy.[15]

The Relationship between Racial/Ethnic Disparities in Poverty and Disparities in COVID-19 Health Outcomes

The large racial and ethnic disparities in COVID-19 cases and deaths point to a broader fact about American society that deserves elaboration: racial/ethnic discrimination and poverty go hand in hand. Together, they contributed to many of the unequal health outcomes observed during the pandemic.

A large body of academic and survey-based research has documented that the average American has strongly racialized perceptions about who is more likely to receive social assistance benefits in the United States. Specifically, evidence suggests that White individuals are more likely to perceive Black Americans as lazy or undeserving.[16] Martin Gilens, for example, finds evidence that White Americans tend to believe that Black Americans' relative disadvantage is due to a lack of effort.[17] Such perceptions subsequently shape individual attitudes toward the welfare state. Katherine Krimmel and Kelly Rader find that symbolic racism — defined as "the belief that Blacks get more assistance than they deserve from government" — is four times stronger than an individual's income in predicting negative attitudes toward redistribution.[18] I have demonstrated in my own research that the Temporary Assistance for Needy Families (TANF) program, which distributes cash assistance to low-income families, contributes to larger Black-White gaps in child poverty because state governments with higher shares of Black residents provide less generous support.[19] Even when programs are not explicitly racialized, disparities across the United States in welfare state provisions may still generate racial inequalities. Consider that the average Black individual is more likely than the average White individual to live in a state without expanded access to Medicaid, without state supplements to the Earned Income Tax Credit, with less generous Unemployment Insurance benefits, or without a minimum wage beyond the federal minimum.[20]

This unequal policy environment has directly contributed to unequal exposure to poverty for non-White (and especially Black) children compared to White children. Higher exposure to poverty during childhood then creates the conditions for a lifetime of disadvantage, as individuals who grew up with fewer resources and/or in more stressful environments

Figure 2.3   Poverty Rate in Adulthood and Poverty Rate in Childhood by Adult Poverty Status, 2019

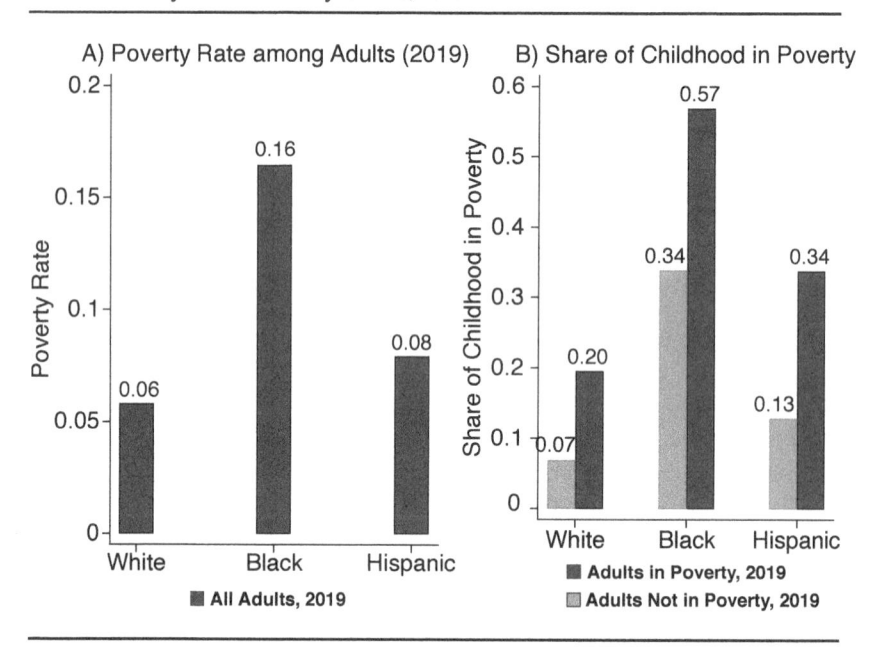

Source: Author's calculations from the Panel Study of Income Dynamics.
Note: Sample is limited to adults who were at least age thirty in 2019. Poverty is measured using a post-tax/transfer income definition (inclusive of SNAP and EITC) relative to an OPM poverty threshold given the lack of SPM poverty thresholds in the PSID.

face poorer health, education, and employment outcomes in later life, as well as a higher likelihood of being poor in adulthood.

Figure 2.3 contextualizes the extent of racial/ethnic disparities in exposure to poverty prior to the pandemic. Panel A provides a simple, point-in-time snapshot of poverty rates among adults by race/ethnicity in 2019, just prior to the onset of the pandemic. Six percent of White adults in our PSID sample lived in poverty in 2019, compared to 16 percent of Black adults and 8 percent of Hispanic adults. These point-in-time estimates point to well-known disparities in racial/ethnic economic conditions, but they also conceal different histories of accumulated disadvantage.

Elaborating on this point, panel B documents the share of childhood that each group spent in poverty, broken up by race/ethnicity (as in panel A) but also by whether the adults were in poverty in 2019. Three main takeaways emerge. First, the average Black adult in poverty in 2019 had a different economic past than the average White or Hispanic adult in poverty in 2019. Specifically, the average Black adult in poverty in 2019 had spent 57 percent of his or her childhood in poverty; in contrast, the average White adult in poverty in 2019 had spent 20 percent of her or his childhood in poverty. Many point-in-time evaluations of poverty would treat the Black and White adults in poverty in a given year as if they were in a comparable social and economic state, but this is not the case. Black (and to a lesser extent, Hispanic) adults in poverty experienced longer stretches of their most critical developmental years (childhood) in a state of economic destitution than White adults in poverty did. As such, accounting for current poverty status is insufficient to understand racial/ethnic differences in health risks during the COVID-19 pandemic. This finding reinforces the need to understand the consequences of poverty through a lens other than a point-in-time economic state.

The second takeaway is similar, but reversed: there were meaningful racial/ethnic differences in the economic histories of even those adults who were *not* in poverty in 2019. The Black adults who were not identified as living in poverty in 2019 nonetheless had spent an average of one-third of their childhoods in poverty, compared to 7 percent for White adults. This fact implies that point-in-time disadvantage may be explained more usefully by accounting for exposure to childhood poverty rather than current poverty status. In fact, the evidence presented later in this chapter demonstrates direct links between exposure to poverty as early as childhood and health outcomes during the pandemic.

Third, figure 2.3 shows that for all racial/ethnic groups, greater exposure to childhood poverty is associated with a greater likelihood of being in poverty in adulthood (and with entering the pandemic with fewer economic resources). The mechanisms through which childhood poverty affects poverty in adulthood are varied, but differential educational attainment has long been central to understandings of the lack of upward mobility among adults living in poverty.[21] Children growing up in poverty are less likely to finish high school, less likely to complete a college degree, and less likely to secure stable employment in adulthood. Each of these outcomes, in turn, contributes to a higher likelihood of poverty in adulthood. The consequences of this higher risk of poverty are severe enough in nonpandemic times; during the pandemic, they were directly connected to the gravest health risks of COVID-19.

Connecting Poverty to COVID-19 Health Outcomes

The evidence presented thus far demonstrates that pre-pandemic poverty status, which is notably higher among Black and Hispanic individuals, was closely connected to COVID-19 health outcomes. But through which

Figure 2.4   Pathways through Which Poverty and Racial/Ethnic Discrimination Affected COVID-19 Health Disparities

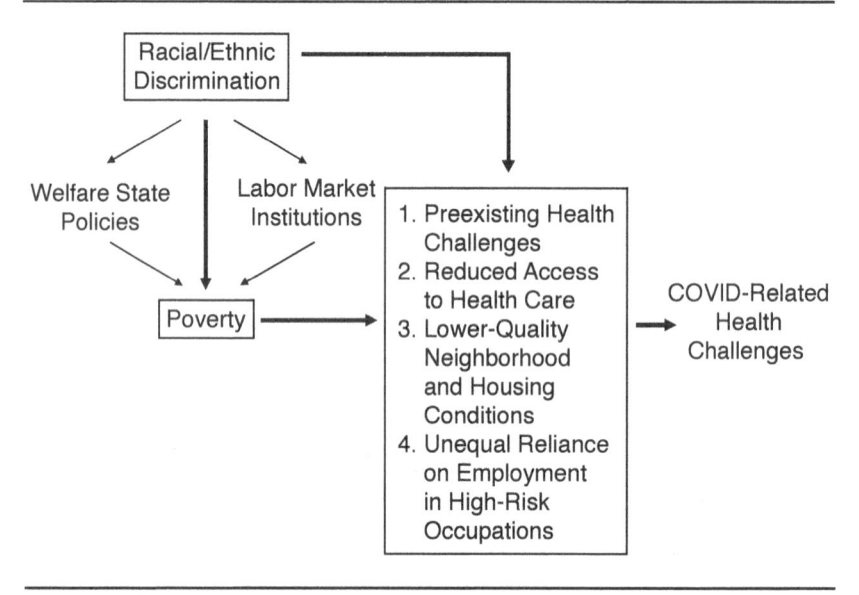

Source: Author's compilation.

specific pathways did greater exposure to poverty affect health outcomes during the pandemic? What was it about the higher poverty rates in the Bronx relative to Manhattan—to return to our earlier example—that contributed to its higher COVID-related deaths? I identify four important pathways through which poverty affected the health disparities observed in the pandemic: greater preexisting health challenges, reduced access to health care, lower-quality neighborhood and housing conditions, and unequal reliance on employment in high-risk occupations. These pathways are summarized in figure 2.4.

Pathway 1: Greater Preexisting Health Challenges

The first pathway connecting poverty to COVID-related health outcomes, *greater preexisting health challenges*, refers to the underlying health conditions that made individuals more vulnerable to COVID-19-related hospitalization, intensive-care treatment, and mortality. Age, of course, is a critically important factor in this pathway: older age is already associated with more health challenges, and older adults faced the greatest mortality rates after catching COVID-19 (see figure 2.2). Across age groups, however, income-based and racial/ethnic disparities persisted. Lower-income individuals and racial/ethnic minorities were more likely to have underlying medical conditions such as cancer, chronic lung disease, diabetes, heart conditions, and HIV, all of which the CDC has identified as capable of exacerbating the medical impact of COVID-19.[22] One study suggests that 35 percent of non-elderly adults with a household income of less than $15,000 had a higher risk for serious illness related to COVID-19 compared to only 16 percent of non-elderly adults with a household income greater than $50,000.[23] Racial/ethnic minorities are also more likely to have an underlying health condition than White individuals, in part owing to their greater exposure to poverty.[24]

Figure 2.5 returns to our PSID data to corroborate the link between exposure to poverty and adult health outcomes. The figure plots the share of each group with low self-reported health status, defined as answering "fair" or "poor" (as opposed to "excellent," "very good," or "good") when asked to summarize their health condition. Of course, as a broad measure, self-reported health status can capture perceptions of a wide range of health ailments; nonetheless, it also provides us with a glimpse into patterns of eve-of-pandemic health disparities.

The left panel of figure 2.5 documents that 11 percent of White adults had low self-reported health status compared to 14 percent of Hispanic adults and 20 percent of Black adults. The right panel shows the link between these health perceptions and childhood poverty exposure. Among adults who spent more than one-fifth of their childhood in poverty, the rate of lower self-reported health status was 22 percent, compared to 12 percent among the group that never experienced childhood poverty (though the group that had spent 1 to 20 percent of their childhood in poverty did not vary much from the no-poverty group).

Again, this broad, self-reported health indicator only points to potential risk factors that made an individual more vulnerable to COVID-19. But the patterns align with broader evidence that high levels of exposure to childhood poverty, which Black and Hispanic adults experienced at higher levels than White adults, were connected to poorer health outcomes on the eve of the pandemic.[25] The pattern also aligns with the reality on the ground in the pandemic: the Bronx had the highest rates of asthma, diabetes, and high blood pressure among New York City's boroughs, as well as the lowest-ranked health outcomes across all of the state's counties.[26] Sustained poverty, racial discrimination, and health challenges worked in tandem to influence the borough's comparatively high rate of COVID-19 fatalities.

Pathway 2: Reduced Access to Health Care

Preexisting health disparities are closely linked to the second pathway: *reduced access to health care*. Lower-income individuals are less likely to have health insurance than higher-income individuals.[27] Among individuals with underlying health conditions who were at risk for

Figure 2.5   Self-Reported Health Status in Adulthood by Amount of Time Spent in Poverty as a Child, 2019

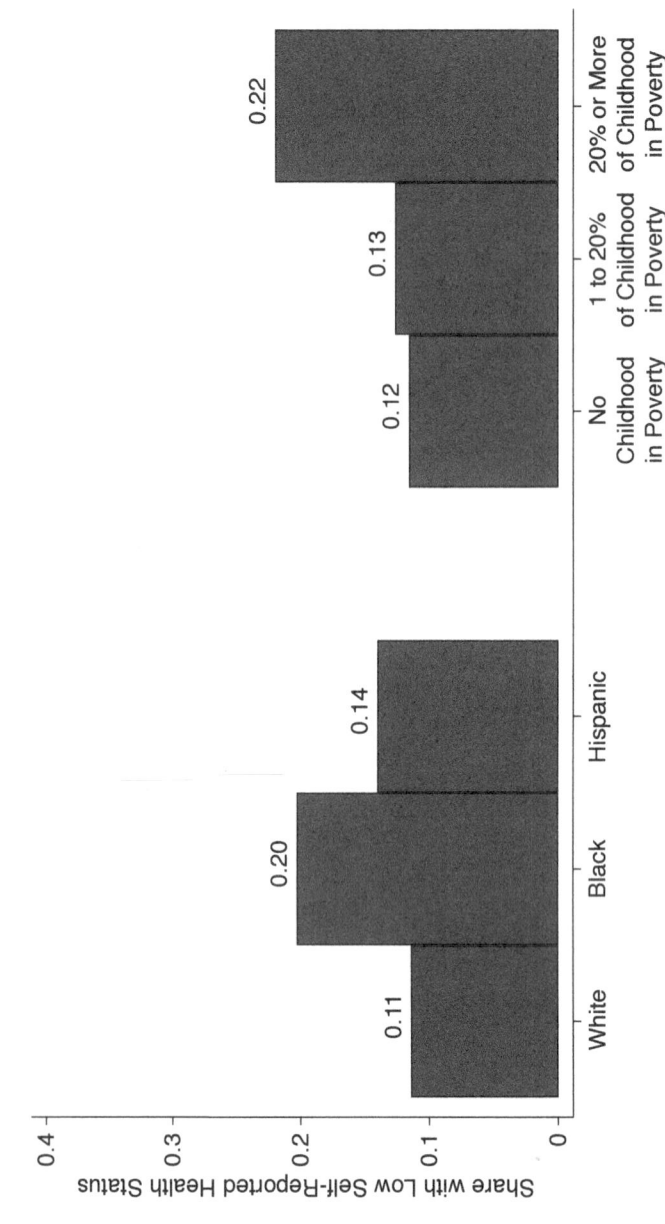

Source: Author's calculations from the Panel Study of Income Dynamics.
Note: "Low self-reported health status" is defined as a report of being in "fair" or "poor" health rather than "excellent," "very good," or "good" health. The sample is limited to adults who were at least age thirty in 2019. Poverty is measured using a post-tax / transfer income definition (inclusive of SNAP and EITC) relative to an OPM poverty threshold given the lack of SPM poverty thresholds in the PSID.

severe COVID-19 health outcomes, 18.2 million were uninsured or underinsured (defined as skipping a visit to the doctor in the past year owing to the expense) at the start of the pandemic.[28]

These patterns are also evident in our PSID data, as figure 2.6 documents. An estimated 21 percent of Black adults did not have access to health insurance leading up to the pandemic, in contrast to 9 percent of White adults and 19 percent of Hispanic adults. The right panel shows variations in health insurance access depending on individuals' exposure to childhood poverty. Among adults with no exposure to childhood poverty, only 8 percent lacked health insurance. That rate climbed to 12 percent for the adults with lower exposure (1 percent to 20 percent of childhood spent in poverty). Among the high-poverty group (those who spent one-fifth or more of their childhood in poverty), the share without health insurance was 20 percent—more than double the rate for the no-poverty group.

Childhood poverty and a lack of health care coverage are particularly linked in the United States, where access to health care is not guaranteed by the state, varies regionally, and is generally costly. For example, the low-income residents of the thirteen U.S. states that had yet to expand Medicaid coverage by the start of the pandemic had more difficulty accessing affordable health care.[29] During the pandemic, lower rates of health insurance contributed to worse health outcomes, and states that had not yet expanded Medicaid experienced higher shares of COVID-related deaths in 2020.[30] In non-expansion states, individuals with health risks that made them vulnerable to COVID complications were 52 percent more likely to be uninsured or underinsured than comparable individuals in states that had implemented the Medicaid expansion.[31]

Unequal access to vaccine distribution, particularly in the early months of the vaccine rollout, is likely to have also exacerbated COVID-related health disparities for lower-income populations and racial/ethnic minorities. Recall from figure 2.2 that the strongest county-level predictor of having completed the vaccination cycle was whether or not an individual had health insurance. This is unsurprising: many individuals without health insurance do not have access to a primary care provider and consequently may lack a trusted source of vaccination information.[32]

Pathway 3: Lower-Quality Neighborhood and Housing Conditions

The third pathway connecting poverty to COVID-related health outcomes is *lower-quality neighborhood and housing conditions*, which includes both neighborhood characteristics and living conditions such as the

Figure 2.6   Lack of Health Insurance in Adulthood by Amount of Time Spent in Poverty as a Child, 2019

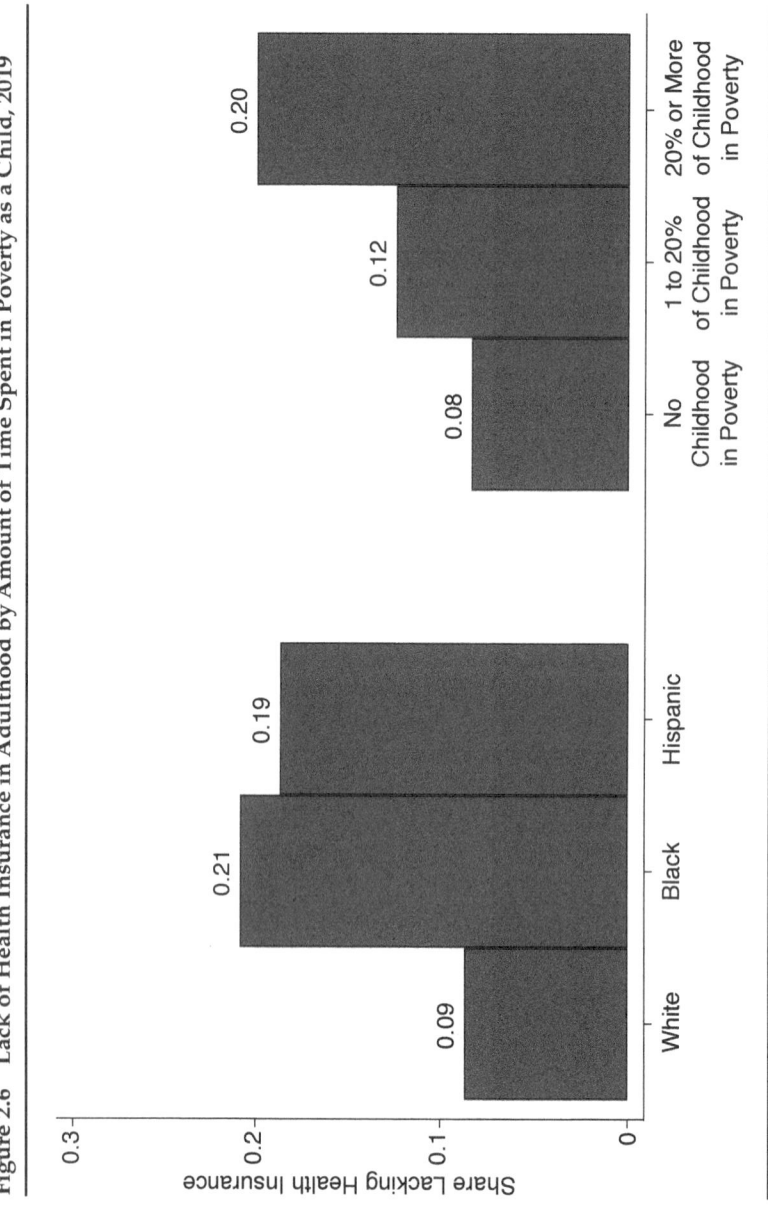

Source: Author's calculations from the Panel Study of Income Dynamics.
Note: The sample is limited to adults who were at least age thirty in 2019. Poverty is measured using a post-tax/transfer income definition (inclusive of SNAP and EITC) relative to an OPM poverty threshold given the lack of SPM poverty thresholds in the PSID.

number of household members or the characteristics of living environments in the community.

At the neighborhood level, economic and racial residential segregation has been associated with a more severe COVID-19 impact on lower-income Black and Hispanic populations. This is also true at the county level, as figure 2.2 demonstrates: higher poverty as well as higher shares of Black or Hispanic residents are associated with higher COVID case and mortality rates. The disparities are not limited to high-density cities: Black-majority suburban and rural counties, as well as Hispanic-majority rural counties, had higher COVID-19 mortality rates than White-majority counties.[33]

Returning to the Bronx, we see sufficient evidence of the influence of neighborhood and housing conditions on these health disparities. Nearly one-quarter of households across much of the Bronx are "overcrowded," defined as having more than one resident per living space (excluding kitchens and bathrooms) in a home.[34] In the context of the pandemic, overcrowding accelerated the spread of COVID-19 among individuals who entered the pandemic with lower incomes and poorer health status. Across the country, overcrowded and multi-generational households are more likely to be headed by racial/ethnic minorities.[35] Specifically, 26 percent of Hispanic families, 17.2 percent of Asian families, and 14.4 percent of Black families, compared to only 10.1 percent of White families, live in households with five or more individuals.[36] My own estimates from the Current Population Survey (CPS) suggest that the poverty rate (using the SPM) among households with more than one family living together is 26 percent, or more than double the poverty rate for single-family households (12 percent).

Overcrowding is also a major concern where people live communally, such as in homeless shelters, immigration detention centers, and prisons.[37] Similarly, the lower quality of broader housing conditions in lower-income areas, such as sanitation and proper ventilation of common areas, further contributed to the spread of the virus.[38]

Neighborhood and housing conditions also affect the accessibility of COVID-19 vaccinations. As one example, Black individuals were more likely than White individuals to have to travel more than ten miles to a vaccination center.[39] Moreover, individuals lacking adequate internet access or technological resources—who are primarily racial/ethnic minorities or from lower-income households—were more likely to experience barriers to acquiring the COVID-19 vaccination.[40]

In short, poverty contributes to lower-quality neighborhood and housing conditions, which in turn contributed to large disparities in COVID cases, testing and vaccination rates, and mortality rates, with households in the lowest-income neighborhoods generally facing the most severe consequences.

Pathway 4: Unequal Reliance on Employment in High-Risk Occupations

The fourth pathway connecting poverty to COVID-related health outcomes is *unequal reliance on employment in high-risk occupations*. Prior to the onset of the pandemic, the federal minimum wage was $7.25 per hour (unchanged since 2009), union membership was low, and the safety net for the unemployed had been gradually weakened.[41] As a result, a large share of working-age individuals worked in low-paying and low-quality jobs. During the pandemic many of these jobs became hazardous because they offered no option to workers to perform their duties remotely.

"Essential workers" in particular were at increased risk for COVID-19 infection and death. As defined by the CDC, essential workers are employed in occupations that are necessary "to ensure the continuity of critical functions of the U.S."[42] These workers include health care workers and non-health-related workers employed in sectors such as education, critical retail, public transportation, and food production. These workers were more likely than "less essential" workers to have low incomes and to be Black or Hispanic.[43]

Essential workers were at increased risk of contracting COVID-19 owing in part to their inability to work remotely, but also because of inadequate working conditions and health regulations. Essential workers reported working conditions that did not follow standard COVID-19 protocols, such as a lack of social distancing, insufficient provision of personal protective equipment, and inadequate facilities to maintain personal hygiene and sanitation.[44] In a survey of service-sector workers during the spring of 2020, Daniel Schneider and Kristen Harknett found that only one-fifth of workers reported that their employers had made masks available, and only 7 percent reported that mask-wearing was mandatory in their workplace.[45] The lack of safety standards was particularly prevalent in non-unionized workplaces.[46] Several studies have pointed to excess mortality rates among workers in these high-contact occupations.[47]

Figure 2.7 shows that working in service-sector jobs—which are generally higher-contact occupations and thus posed greater risk to workers during the pandemic—is itself associated with long-standing economic disadvantages. In the PSID, roughly half of employed Black adults worked in the service sector, compared to 35 percent of Hispanic adults and 29 percent of White adults. As with other findings reported in this

Figure 2.7   Employment in a Service Occupation by Exposure to Childhood Poverty, 2019

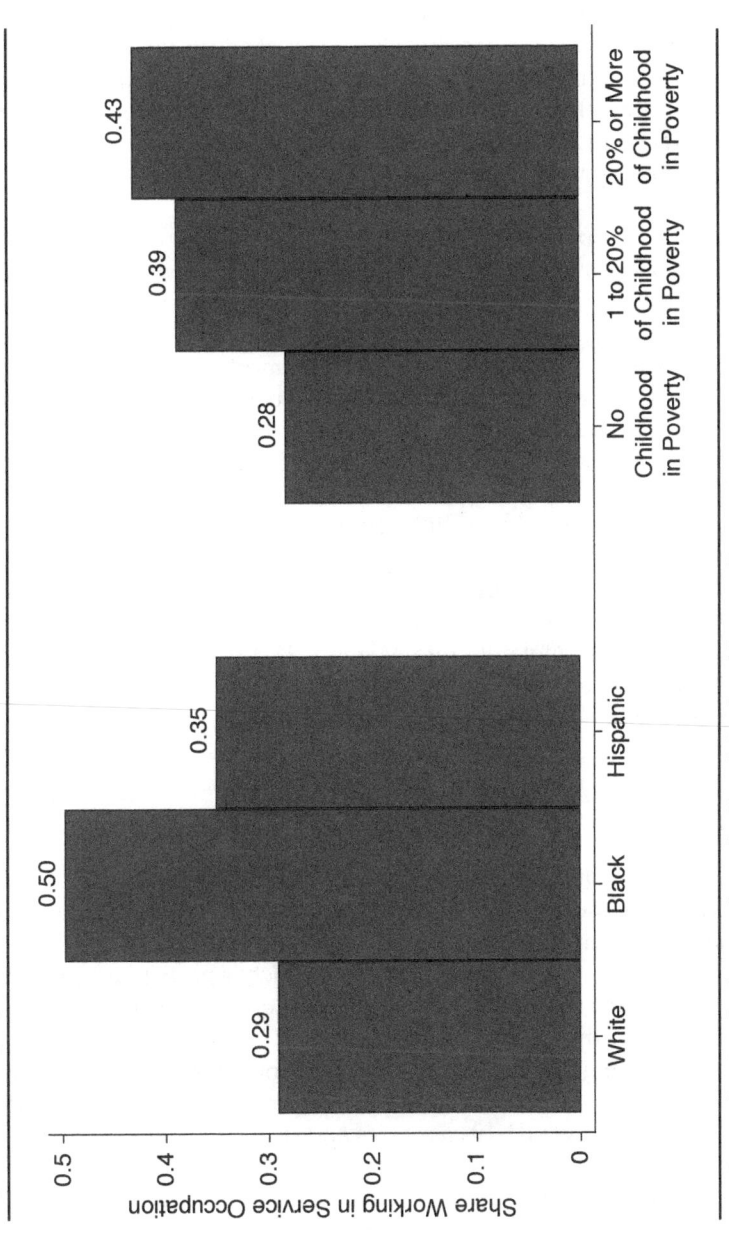

Source: Author's calculations from the Panel Study of Income Dynamics.
Note: The sample is limited to adults who were at least age thirty in 2019. Poverty is measured using a post-tax/transfer income definition (inclusive of SNAP and EITC) relative to an OPM poverty threshold given the lack of SPM poverty thresholds in the PSID.

chapter, there is a direct link to disadvantage as far back as childhood: 28 percent of adults who spent no time in childhood poverty worked in service occupations, compared to 39 percent of adults with lower childhood poverty exposure, and 43 percent of adults with higher childhood poverty exposure. This evidence is consistent with work from Jonathan Rothwell and Ember Smith, who find that low income levels were associated with two to three times greater physical harm during the pandemic, primarily because of occupation-related exposures to COVID-19.[48]

The racial disparities in who worked in these high-exposure jobs, combined with the racial disparities in health challenges, health care access, and living conditions, contributed to racial disparities in health outcomes during COVID-19. Among essential workers in California and Massachusetts, for example, COVID-19 mortality rates were higher among Hispanic and Black workers.[49] Age-adjusted mortality rates among workers in Massachusetts were four times higher for Hispanic and Black workers in high-risk occupations than for their White counterparts.[50]

These disparities in employment conditions also affected vaccine access and contributed to the link between poverty and low vaccination rates documented in figure 2.1. Despite being among the first individuals to have access to the vaccination, essential and frontline workers experienced inflexible work schedules and difficulty in taking time off work to receive the vaccine. Not until mid-March 2021 did some states, including New York and California, begin to mandate paid leave for workers to receive the COVID-19 vaccination.[51]

Preexisting Poverty as a Risk Factor for the Health Consequences of COVID-19

If we were to predict a given adult's health vulnerability during the pandemic, a telling indicator, beyond the individual's age, would have been the share of her childhood spent in poverty. The cumulative disadvantages of exposure to childhood poverty—which is particularly common among Black and Hispanic individuals in the United States—translate directly by adulthood into disadvantages in health status, health care coverage, housing and neighborhood conditions, and occupation. These risk factors associated with higher poverty rates were directly associated with higher COVID-19 case rates and death rates and lower access to vaccine distribution.

To further contextualize the extent of income-based disparities in health outcomes, consider the following: in 2019, the average income-to-needs ratio (household income relative to the poverty line) of an adult who spent her entire childhood in poverty was 0.9, which corresponded with a 0.18 percent likelihood of dying from COVID in 2020. In contrast, an adult with no exposure to childhood poverty had an income-to-needs ratio of 3.6, which corresponds with less than half the likelihood (0.07 percent) of dying from COVID.[52] In other words, these estimates suggest that someone who spent her entire childhood in poverty, compared to someone who experienced no childhood poverty, had twice the likelihood of falling victim to COVID-19.

More broadly, the gaps in death rates between high-poverty counties and low-poverty counties in the United States were equivalent to the gaps in death rates between Romania and Luxembourg in the European Union. The pandemic did not strike all individuals equally; instead, it hit the America living on that "lonely island of poverty," in the words of Dr. King, with substantially more force than the America in "the sunlight of opportunity."

These findings underscore that poverty cannot simply be viewed as a temporary economic state. The dramatic reductions in poverty during the pandemic years of 2020 and 2021 that this book will document represent a remarkable policy achievement; even so, historic exposure to poverty is a fixed risk factor that hovers over an individual's life even when current resources exceed a poverty line. During the COVID-19 pandemic, past exposure to poverty generated a set of preexisting risk factors for experiencing the gravest consequences of the virus.

Even those in poverty who managed to avoid the worst of the pandemic's health consequences, however, still faced many other challenges in adapting to the economic and social turmoil of COVID-19. Especially in the months after the onset of the pandemic, working adults who entered the pandemic with low incomes experienced particularly high rates of job loss—the focus of the next chapter.

Chapter 2 Appendix

Figure A2.1 Standardized Association of County-Level Characteristics with COVID-19 Cases, Deaths, and Full Vaccinations, 2020, 2021, and 2022

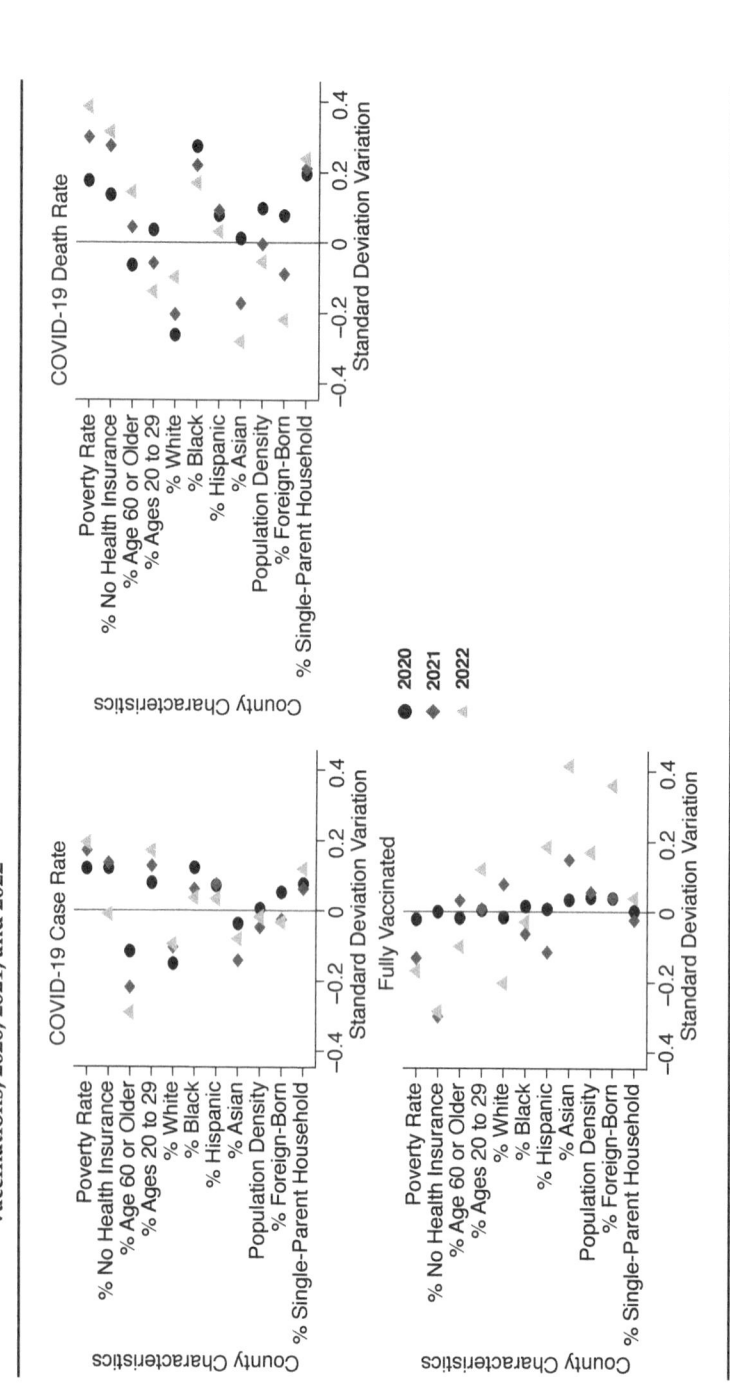

Source: All data, except for the age shares, are from Opportunity Insights. The age shares are from the U.S. Census Bureau. *Note:* The point estimates represent the estimated standard deviation variation in the labeled outcome (for example, the COVID-19 case rate) with a one-standard-deviation increase in the county characteristic (such as the poverty rate). Unconditional estimates are run separately for each outcome. The COVID outcomes include data from the specified calendar year, while the county-level characteristics are stable and were measured prior to the pandemic.

Figure A2.2 Conditional Models: Standardized Association of County-Level Characteristics with COVID-19 Cases, Deaths, Full Vaccinations, and First Vaccination Booster, 2020, 2021, and 2022

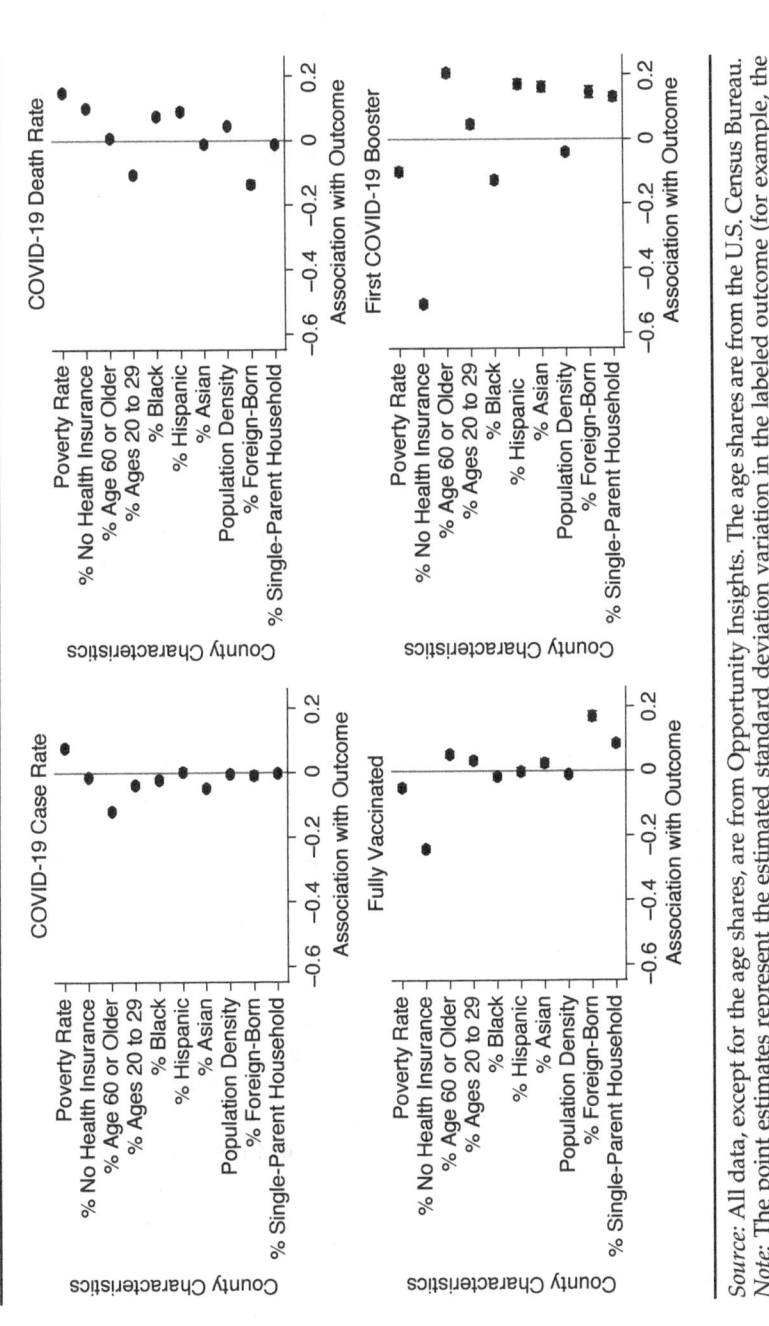

Source: All data, except for the age shares, are from Opportunity Insights. The age shares are from the U.S. Census Bureau. *Note:* The point estimates represent the estimated standard deviation variation in the labeled outcome (for example, the COVID-19 case rate) with a one-standard-deviation increase in the county characteristic (such as the poverty rate). The coefficients are from a single model per outcome that includes all covariates at once. The COVID outcomes include data from 2020 to 2022, while the county-level characteristics are stable and were measured prior to the pandemic.

Chapter 3

Poverty as a Risk Factor, Part 2: Disparities in Job Loss and Job Quality

As COVID-19 began to spread across the United States, leaders at every level of government were forced to respond quickly and with incomplete information to try to limit the rise in cases and hospitalizations. Aside from the closure of schools (the focus of chapter 7), one of the widest-reaching actions that many policymakers took was to temporarily issue stay-at-home orders and/or mandate the closure of non-essential businesses. During the week of March 19, 2020, for example, nineteen states imposed stay-at-home orders, including California and New York.[1] By the start of April, most states had imposed temporary closures of establishments deemed not immediately essential to the functioning of the broader economy. Restaurants, shopping centers, cinemas, hair salons, and similar service-oriented institutions were among those most directly affected by the closures. Even where such establishments remained open, declining demand for in-person services pressured many businesses to cut hours and lay off (or furlough) employees.

The dramatic reduction in the foot traffic so important to these establishments is likely to have reduced the spread of COVID-19 and thus saved many lives.[2] Few can doubt the necessity of temporarily mandating closures in the early months of the pandemic given the low access to COVID-19 testing, the scarcity of masks, and the uncertainties around transmission of the virus. The closures did, however, contribute to a notable side effect: job loss on an unprecedented scale. By the end of April 2020, more than 20 million U.S. workers had lost their jobs.[3] The widespread job loss threatened to drastically increase economic insecurity for a large proportion of the U.S. population, with particularly harsh consequences for adults who entered the pandemic in poverty.

Many analyses of the disparate employment consequences have focused on gender, race/ethnicity, or age. For example, studies have determined that women were more likely to work in the industries that were hit hardest by the pandemic, while many mothers faced an added challenge of fulfilling care responsibilities, leading to claims that the country was experiencing a "she-cession."[4] Studies have also documented the disproportionate job losses among Black and Hispanic adults in the early months of the pandemic.[5] Others described the double-edged sword for older adults as they navigated the health risks while trying to meet their income needs.[6] These analyses are insightful and warranted. They tend to overlook, however, the strongest dividing line between the employed and the unemployed during the COVID-19 pandemic for any given demographic group: the economic situation that individuals had inherited as they faced the onset of the pandemic.

More than an employment crisis that hit one demographic harder than others, this was a crisis that disproportionately took jobs from those who entered the pandemic in or near poverty, whether they were men or women, mothers or fathers, White or Black, young or old, or otherwise. This chapter demonstrates that, more than most other demographic characteristics of interest, pre-pandemic poverty status (and its correlates) was the strongest driver of unemployment disparities throughout the pandemic.

The argument made here is not intended to undermine the very real disparities that some demographic groups faced compared to others. Intersectional disadvantages were large and persistent: Black adults with low pre-pandemic incomes, for example, faced some of the highest unemployment rates during the early months of the pandemic, and they were certainly higher than rates for White adults with low pre-pandemic incomes. Meanwhile, low-income mothers with children faced an incomparable set of challenges in balancing work and family life, even if they did not exit the labor market in comparatively large numbers (as this chapter shows). Older adults in the labor force with lower incomes, moreover, were more vulnerable than younger workers with lower incomes to the acute health risk associated with COVID-19.

But just as lower-income Americans faced a double dose of COVID-related health challenges, they also faced double the rate of job loss. More broadly, one in three adults who started the pandemic in poverty were unemployed in April 2020. Among Black adults who were already in poverty, the rate of unemployment climbed above 40 percent.[7] This chapter examines how these disparities played out in practice by documenting the wage distribution of occupations that faced higher rates of job loss, as well as differences in job quality for those workers who, for better or worse, were able to hang on to their jobs.[8]

Poverty and Job Loss

Before we dive into the unemployment trends, it is worth a brief return to the three perspectives on poverty outlined in chapter 1 to help us think through the connections between poverty and employment. From the perspective of poverty as *the immediate state of lacking adequate resources to meet basic needs*, the potential consequences of job loss during the pandemic were straightforward. For most working-age adults, earnings from employment are the central source of income. If earnings disappear without adequate income support from other sources, the likelihood of poverty increases, as poverty statistics from before the onset of the pandemic make evident. In 2019, the poverty rate for employed working-age adults (ages eighteen to sixty-five) was 6.6 percent, and the poverty rate for unemployed working-age adults was 18.3 percent.[9] The surge in unemployment in April 2020 was all the more dramatic given that the pre-pandemic rate of unemployment had been at its lowest level (3.5 percent) in years.[10] Combined with the work-based welfare state, which funneled income support to low-wage workers, the low rate of unemployment led to a low rate of poverty, but the spike in joblessness after March 2020 threatened to quickly reverse that progress.

We can also view the employment trends throughout the COVID-19 pandemic from the perspective of an individual's pre-pandemic poverty status. In understanding poverty as *a stratifying feature that moderates the short- and long-run consequences of a life disruption*, we can evaluate whether poverty intensified the challenges in adjusting to job loss. Most adults entering the pandemic in poverty had reduced access to savings and liquid assets, as well as a reduced ability to debt-finance their consumption, intensifying the difficulty of coping with the earnings loss. Though many of these adults were temporarily held afloat through generous income transfers, the lowest-income individuals who experienced job loss were less likely to be able to access those transfers.

These two perspectives on poverty are helpful in thinking about how people dealt with earnings losses, but this chapter's primary focus is on a different perspective: *poverty as a preexisting risk factor that increases the likelihood of experiencing a life disruption and its consequences*. Using the panel component of the Current Population Survey, which allows us to track some individuals across several consecutive months and two consecutive years, I demonstrate that workers' poverty status in 2019 was directly linked to their likelihood of job loss after the onset of COVID-19. And yes, employment and poverty often go hand in hand: in 2019, 63 percent of all households in poverty had at least one working adult.[11] In this chapter's appendix, I elaborate on the technical details of how

I link pre-pandemic poverty status to current employment status and offer validations of the estimation procedures used to identify each individual's pre-pandemic poverty status.

Trends in Unemployment by Pre-Pandemic Poverty Status

The national trends in unemployment through the pandemic are well documented: the unemployment rate climbed from 3.5 percent in February 2020 to 14.7 percent in April 2020, a record high in the postwar era.[12] Adjusted for misclassification errors, the unemployment rate was closer to 19 percent.[13] The change in the rate of non-employment (the share of all jobless adults whether seeking employment or not) was just as stark: it climbed from 22.7 percent in February 2020 to 34.5 percent in April 2020 among working-age adults.[14] But how did unemployment trends vary for adults who entered the pandemic with lower versus higher incomes?

Figure 3.1 documents disparities in unemployment in April 2020, since that was when monthly unemployment reached its peak; subsequent figures examine trends throughout 2020 and 2021 more broadly. Specifically, figure 3.1 visualizes the levels of unemployment in April 2020, as well as percentage-point changes in unemployment from February to April 2020, across the 2019 distribution of incomes relative to the poverty line. A value below 1 on the x-axis indicates that individuals had incomes below the poverty line in 2019, while values above 1 indicate that individuals were not in poverty in 2019.

The dashed gray line, which indicates the level of unemployment in April 2020, shows that more than one-third of individuals who entered the pandemic in poverty were unemployed in April 2020. This is higher than the unemployment rate of adults who had 2019 incomes above the poverty line (right half of the figure). Adults who had 2019 incomes between 25 and 50 percent of the poverty line had an unemployment rate of 38 percent in April 2020, the highest point estimates of any income group. In general, the higher the 2019 income relative to the poverty line, the lower the rate of April 2020 unemployment: among adults with an income at least four times the poverty line, for example, the unemployment rate was around 10 percent, a rate that is one-third the value of the in-poverty group, yet still high relative to pre-pandemic standards.

Given that adults in poverty prior to the pandemic were more likely to be unemployed in the first place, these April 2020 levels could simply reflect preexisting disparities in employment rather than changes from before the pandemic to April 2020. The black line in figure 3.1

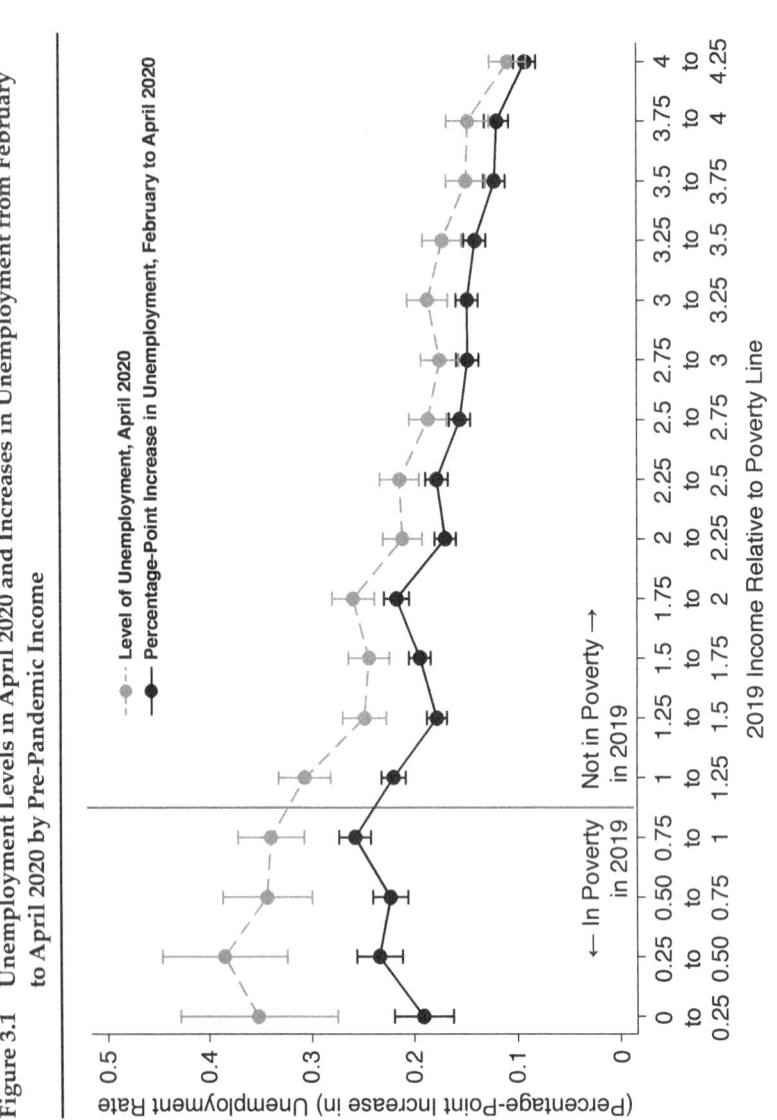

Figure 3.1   Unemployment Levels in April 2020 and Increases in Unemployment from February to April 2020 by Pre-Pandemic Income

Source: Author's calculations from the 2020 Current Population Survey Annual Social and Economic Supplement (with income for the 2019 calendar year) merged with 2020 basic monthly files.
Note: Estimates are for adults between ages eighteen and sixty-four. The error bars represent 95 percent confidence intervals.

thus visualizes the percentage-point change in unemployment from February to April 2020 for each income group. The results again point to widespread increases in unemployment across the income distribution, but with particularly large job losses among those who were working and poor in 2019. Adults who were just below the poverty line (75 to 100 percent) in 2019 experienced the highest percentage-point increases in unemployment: a twenty-four-percentage-point increase in unemployment, twice the magnitude as for those with a 2019 income at four times the poverty line. At the same time, the high rates of job loss throughout the income distribution threatened to increase the share of adults falling into poverty. Adults with pre-pandemic incomes between three and four times the poverty line, for example, still faced more than a ten-percentage-point increase in unemployment from February to April 2020.

Pre-pandemic poverty status, however, is only one relevant predictor of job loss in the initial months of the pandemic. To provide a broader portrait of unemployment risk factors, figure 3.2 displays the relative likelihood of job loss between April and June 2020 by pre-pandemic poverty, gender, parenthood status, race/ethnicity, age, and education. The figure confirms that the strongest predictor of job loss during the initial months of the pandemic was whether workers entered the pandemic in poverty. Specifically, pre-pandemic poverty status was associated with an 8-percentage-point increase in the likelihood of having lost a job. The next strongest predictors were being between the ages of eighteen and twenty-nine (6.6-percentage-point increase in likelihood of job loss) and having a college degree (a 6.2-percentage-point decline in the likelihood of job loss).

Across gender and parenthood, two findings stand out. First, mothers and childless women faced near-identical levels of job loss from April to June 2020 (1.1-percentage-point increases in the likelihood of job loss). Second, these two groups both faced higher likelihoods of job loss relative to fathers and childless men. Subsequent figures will track these trends throughout the pandemic and elaborate further on the gender- and parenthood-based differences. Across race/ethnicity, figure 3.2 shows that Hispanic workers faced higher likelihoods of job loss in the initial months of the pandemic, followed by Black workers. White workers, meanwhile, were less likely to face job loss.

What this figure does not show, however, is whether these disparities in job loss across gender, parenthood, race/ethnicity, age, and education persisted throughout 2020 and 2021. Moreover, the figure does not inform us how differences in unemployment between women and men, mothers and fathers, White adults and Black adults, and younger adults and older adults compare to differences by pre-pandemic poverty status

Figure 3.2   Likelihood of Job Loss from April to June 2020 by Characteristic

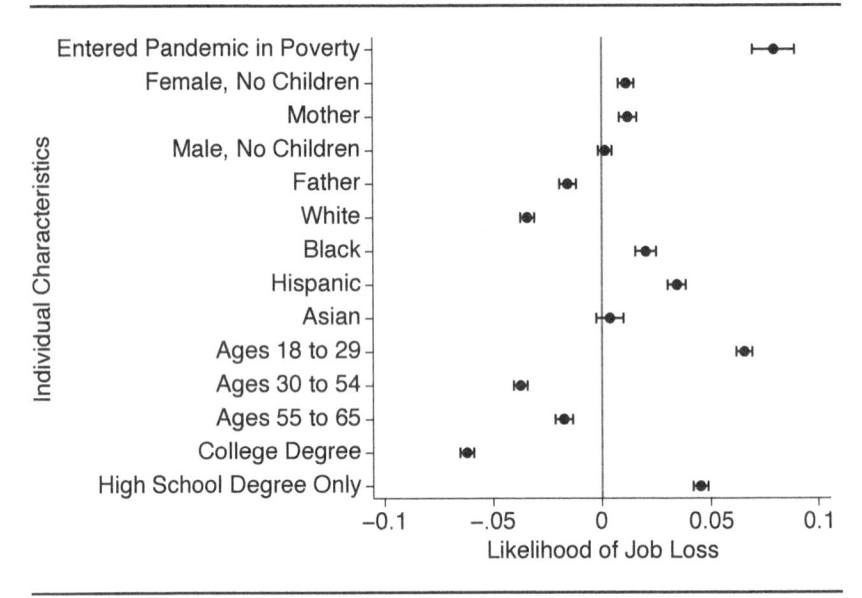

Source: Author's calculations from the Current Population Survey.
Note: Each coefficient represents the unconditional association of the labeled characteristic with job loss from April to June 2020. The sample is limited to adults between ages eighteen and sixty-five. Poverty status in 2019 is based on the SPM and is observed in matched data as described in the appendix. Error bars represent 95 percent confidence intervals.

within each of these demographic groups. In other words, we can ask: Were differences in job loss by pre-pandemic poverty status generally larger than average differences in job loss across age, gender, or race/ethnicity? The answer is a resounding and consistent *yes*.

Unemployment across Age Groups

Let's start with age disparities in poverty and divide the population into three groups: younger workers (ages eighteen to twenty-nine), prime-age workers (ages thirty to fifty-four), and older workers (ages fifty-five and older). Importantly, there are large differences in the share of each of these age groups who are active in the labor force and therefore potentially countable as unemployed. Among the eighteen- to twenty-nine-year-olds, 73 percent were actively seeking employment in January 2020 (many are still pursuing an education during this life stage), compared to 83 percent of the thirty- to fifty-four-year-olds and 40 percent of the population over fifty-five (many are retired at this point). Recall that the

Figure 3.3   Unemployment Trends by Poverty Status and Age, January 2020 to December 2021

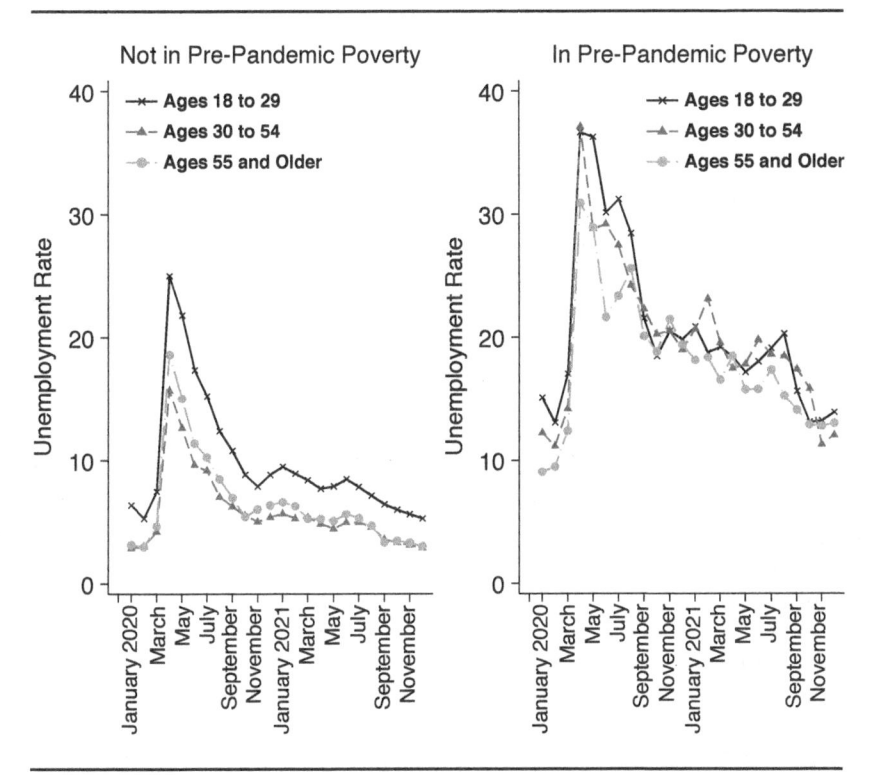

Source: Author's calculations from the Current Population Survey.
Note: Pre-pandemic poverty refers to poverty status in 2019, which is based on the SPM and is observed in matched data and/or estimated based on the procedure described in the appendix. Group differences in the "not in pre-pandemic poverty" and "in pre-pandemic poverty" estimates are statistically significant.

status of being "unemployed" is calculated only for workers who are active in the labor market.

Figure 3.3 documents the differences in unemployment trends by poverty status and age. The left panel displays the unemployment rate for those adults not in poverty in 2019; the right panel displays the unemployment rate for those adults who were in poverty before the pandemic.

The differences in unemployment rates between pre-pandemic poverty status far exceed differences by age group. Among adults who were in poverty in 2019, the percentage-point increases in unemployment from January 2020 to April 2020 ranged from 21.6 percentage points (for eighteen- to twenty-nine-year-olds) to 24.9 percentage points (for thirty- to fifty-four-year-olds). For each age group, these increases were larger than for adults who were not in poverty in 2019, and they were larger than any between-group disparities (for example, ages thirty to fifty-four versus ages fifty-five and older) in unemployment trends during this time period. More than age, pre-pandemic poverty status was central to disparities in job loss.

That said, there are some notable differences across age groups that deserve elaboration. Among younger workers, even those not in poverty in 2019 saw particularly large unemployment increases: the rate jumped from 6.4 percent in January 2020 to 25 percent in April 2020, an increase of 18.6 percentage points. Their high unemployment rate in April 2020 was larger than that of prime-age or older adults who did not enter the pandemic in poverty. The particularly large spike in unemployment for young adults was primarily due to the types of jobs in which they tend to be employed: nearly one-quarter of employed young adults worked in leisure and hospitality, one of the sectors that experienced the largest shocks after the onset of the pandemic.[15] Though their unemployment rates had largely recovered to pre-crisis levels by December 2021, the young adults making life transitions during 2020 and 2021—whether graduating from college, leaving home, or entering the labor market—may have paid an economic penalty from their early period of unemployment that will persist for years to come. Research from the Great Recession has shown that young adults who graduated from college and entered the workforce during the economic downturn of 2010 faced the longer-run "scarring" effect of lower employment rates years after graduating.[16] The negative consequences were particularly large for young adults with a high school degree or less, a group that was more likely to be concentrated in the 37 percent of young adults who entered the pandemic in poverty and who were unemployed in April 2020.[17]

For prime-age workers (ages thirty to fifty-four), the April 2020 gap in unemployment between those who did, versus did not, enter the pandemic in poverty was a particularly steep 18.6 percentage points (37.1 percent versus 15.7 percent). Whereas younger workers across the income distribution were hard hit, pre-pandemic poverty status was more strongly linked with unemployment risk among these prime-age workers. This finding is unsurprising: at this life stage, more fortunate workers tend to have more consistent work experience, stronger job-specific skills, and greater power within their respective firms. They are less dispensable, and even when they are not indispensable, they are harder to dispense with nonetheless. In contrast, the workers in this age group who entered the pandemic in poverty were largely concentrated in service occupations, as this chapter later discusses in more detail.

More than the other age groups, older adults faced a double-edged sword as they navigated employment during the pandemic.[18] Most older adults, especially those over sixty-five, were already inactive in the labor market (because they were retired) before the onset of the pandemic. Those who remained employed during the pandemic often did so at their own peril, given the unique health risks of COVID-19 for older adults.[19] Moreover, older adults, and especially those with low incomes to begin with, are far less likely than other age groups to work remotely, owing in part to differences in occupations but also to their lower likelihood of having a computer and reliable internet at home.[20] The unemployment rate of these older workers reached a peak of 18.6 percent for those who did not enter the pandemic in poverty and 30.9 percent for those who did, before falling back toward baseline by the end of 2021. Older adults in particular, however, were also more likely to exit the labor force during the pandemic: nearly 2 million older workers dropped out of the labor market in 2020–2021, and they have been less likely to return to work than younger adults who left the labor market.[21]

Unemployment across Gender and Parenthood

As noted at the start of this chapter, gender gaps in employment trends rightfully attracted much media and public attention throughout the pandemic. The closure of schools and childcare centers placed a heavy burden on the parents of young children, and on mothers especially given that they tend to do a disproportionate share of domestic care work. But to what extent did women, and mothers especially, face job loss relative to men and/or fathers? And how do these divisions compare to the gaps *among* mothers—for example, by pre-pandemic poverty status? Figure 3.4 provides evidence on these questions. Trends are broken out for four demographic groups: fathers with at least one child present in the household, childless men, and the same two categories for women. Within each group, I again depict divisions based on pre-pandemic poverty status.

The left panels present trends for adults who were not in poverty at the onset of the pandemic. Fathers experienced an increase in unemployment of 10.9 percentage points (2.7 percent to 13.6 percent) from January to April 2020, compared to an increase in unemployment of 14.8 percentage points for mothers. Both groups had recovered to January 2020 levels by December 2021. Notably, however, childless women who were not in poverty at the onset of the pandemic experienced an even stronger 17.2-percentage-point increase in unemployment.

Note: The sample is limited to adults between ages eighteen and sixty-five. Poverty status in 2019 is based on the SPM and is observed in matched data and/or estimated based on the procedure described in the appendix. Group differences in the "not in pre-pandemic poverty" and "in pre-pandemic poverty" estimates are statistically significant.

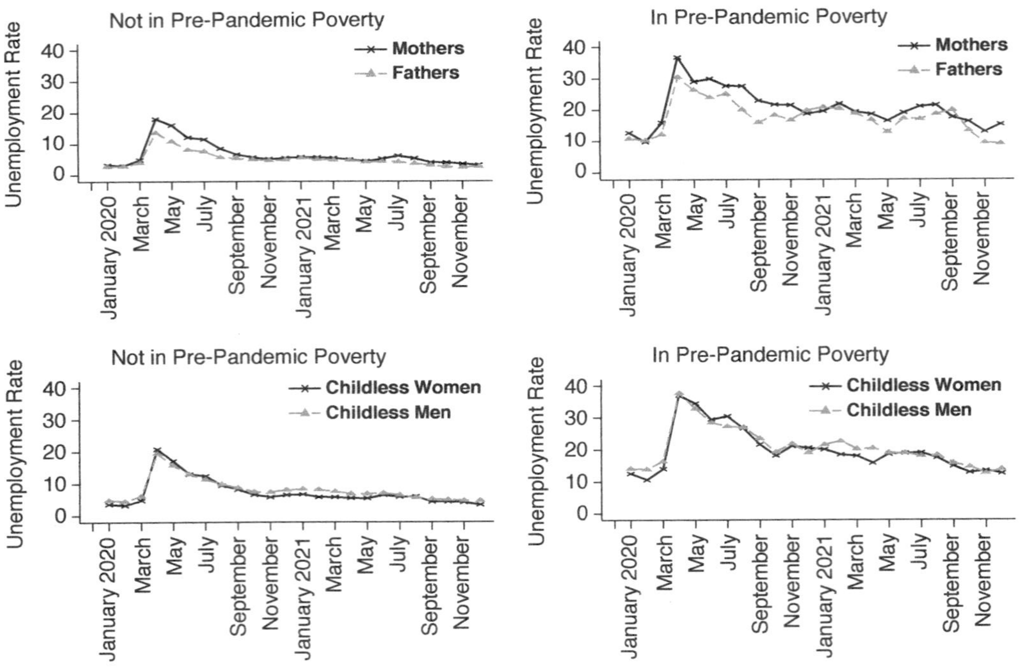

Source: Author's calculations from the Current Population Survey.

Figure 3.4   Unemployment Rates during the Pandemic by Gender, Parenthood Status, and Poverty Status, January 2020 to December 2021

Employment losses were far greater among those who entered the pandemic in poverty, as the right two panels display. Fathers in poverty in 2019 saw a 19.6-percentage-point increase (10.8 percent to 30.4 percent) in unemployment, while childless adults saw a 23.6-percentage-point increase (14.1 percent to 37.7 percent). Among women, the patterns are largely comparable. Unemployment among mothers who were in pre-pandemic poverty increased by 23.9 percentage points, compared to a 14.8-percentage-point increase for mothers who were not in poverty in 2019. Thus, the differences in job loss between lower- and higher-income mothers were around three times the size of the differences between low-income mothers and low-income fathers.

That mothers and childless women experienced similar increases in unemployment suggests that factors other than childcare responsibilities—such as the occupations and industries in which women are more likely to work—were the primary drivers behind the gender disparities in unemployment, especially given that the rates at which they exited the labor force were also similar for mothers and childless women. From January 2020 to April 2020, the share of working-age mothers in the labor force declined by 3.6 percentage points (from 72.4 percent to 68.8 percent), while the decline for working-age childless women was a nearly identical 3.7 percentage points (from 70.5 percent to 66.8 percent). Both groups had fully recovered to pre-pandemic activity levels by December 2021.

The economist Claudia Goldin and the team of Jason Furman, Melissa Kearney, and Willie Powell conclude in their respective studies that while care burdens undoubtedly made life more challenging for parents, and for mothers especially, those responsibilities cannot explain much of the gap between men's and women's employment rates.[22] Furman, Kearney, and Powell find that mothers with young children experienced slightly larger declines in employment compared to other adults (consistent with the evidence in figure 3.4), but owing to gender-based differences in occupation and industry rather than to added childcare responsibilities.[23] Working women were more likely than working men to be in occupations that the pandemic directly affected, such as service-, education-, and care-related work.

Goldin, a leading expert on gender disparities in labor markets, goes further in confronting claims of a "she-cession," writing that "the pandemic produced both a he- and a she-cession. Relative to previous recessions, women have been harder hit. But the largest differences in pandemic effects on employment are found between education groups rather than between genders within educational groups."[24] In response to a *New York Times* headline suggesting that the "Pandemic Will 'Take Our Women 10 Years Back' in the Workplace," Goldin writes that "individual experiences reported in the news are those containing the most adversity," contributing to popular media coverage during the pandemic that exaggerated demographic (and specifically gender-based) differences in employment consequences.[25]

While true that gender and parenthood are not dominant dividing lines in explaining COVID employment disparities, Goldin's critique may go too far. Even when employment declines were relatively consistent for parents and nonparents, and for women and men, the heightened stress and anxiety induced by the pandemic nonetheless created immense uncertainty for parents, and for mothers especially, even if the worst-case employment scenarios envisioned during that uncertain period did not always pan out.

As chapter 6 documents, mental health and well-being remained concerningly poor for many people throughout the pandemic, particularly for parents, and these factors were more detached from actual incomes and employment than in nonpandemic years, for understandable reasons. Moreover, as chapter 7 documents, widespread school and childcare closures increased the amount of time that parents, and mothers especially, needed to spend on care work, even when that did not translate into widespread withdrawal from the labor market. Indeed, as Goldin's study also shows, childcare time in families with young children approximately doubled for mothers and fathers alike, but absolute gains in hours of care were larger for mothers.[26]

Women faced larger employment declines relative to men, and women who entered the pandemic in poverty, in particular, faced the largest employment penalties throughout the crisis. But changes in formal employment capture only one dimension of the many challenges that women, and mothers especially, experienced relative to men and fathers throughout 2020 and 2021.

Unemployment across Race and Ethnicity

Even if parents in general did not face notably different employment trends relative to childless adults, some groups of adults—Black and Hispanic workers in particular—experienced more employment instability, especially if they entered the pandemic with low incomes. Figure 3.5 presents the same trends in unemployment for four racial/ ethnic groups: White (non-Hispanic), Black, Hispanic, and Asian working-age adults. This figure provides further insight into the intersecting disadvantages of race/ethnicity and poverty status.

The differences in trends across the two panels again demonstrate that pre-pandemic poverty status is a strong driver of unemployment trends throughout 2020 and 2021. The right panel of figure 3.5 shows that 40.3 percent of Black adults who entered the pandemic in poverty were

Figure 3.5   Unemployment Rates by Racial/Ethnic Group and Pre-Pandemic Poverty Status, January 2020 to December 2021

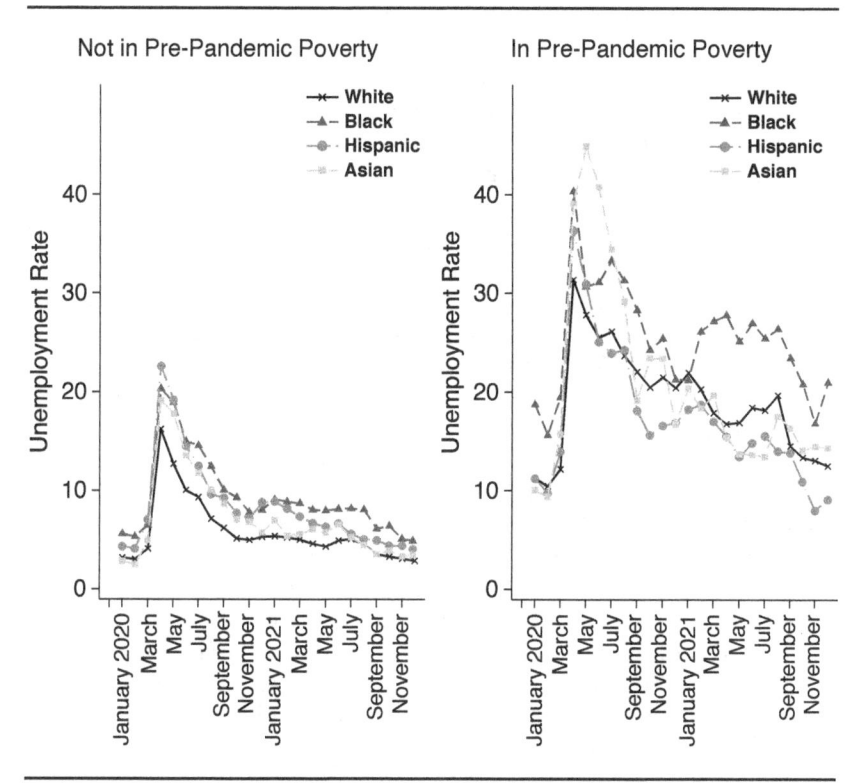

Source: Author's calculations from the Current Population Survey.
Note: The sample is limited to adults between ages eighteen and sixty-five. Poverty status in 2019 is based on the SPM and is observed in matched data and/or estimated based on the procedure described in the appendix. Group differences in the "not in pre-pandemic poverty" and "in pre-pandemic poverty" estimates are statistically significant.

unemployed in April 2020, and one-fifth remained unemployed even at the end of 2021 (comparable to the level in January 2020). These unemployment rates are around ten percentage points higher than for White workers who entered the pandemic in poverty, and higher than for similar Asian and Hispanic workers. These findings are consistent with patterns observed in prior recessions: Black workers are often the first to lose their jobs during a crisis.[27] Moreover, these patterns reflect the persistent barriers, including structural racism, that Black workers face in accessing and maintaining good jobs.[28] Among Black men, specifically, who entered the pandemic in poverty (not displayed), the unemployment rate reached a peak of 42 percent in April 2020 (and 39 percent among Black women); among Black fathers with school-age children, unemployment reached 47 percent (and 37 percent for Black mothers). The intersecting disadvantages of low income, racial/ethnic discrimination, and parenthood contributed to the unemployment of nearly half of Black fathers who entered the pandemic in poverty.

Hispanic workers were also hit hard. Among those not in poverty, Hispanic workers experienced the largest increase in unemployment in April 2020: nearly one in four Hispanic workers who were above the poverty line in 2019 were unemployed in April 2020, an increase of 18.3 percentage points. As this chapter shows later, Hispanic workers, more than other racial/ethnic groups, were concentrated in the lowest-paying jobs at the onset of the pandemic—the jobs that were the first to disappear when COVID-19 arrived.

Patterns for Asian workers also stand out. Though Asian workers are less likely to be in poverty in the first place, those who did enter the pandemic in poverty faced a set of unemployment disadvantages similar to those experienced by Black and Hispanic workers in 2020. This group's unemployment rate climbed from 10 percent to 39.1 percent from January to April 2020, the largest percentage-point increase among the racial/ethnic groups observed during these months, though this estimated change is necessarily less precise given the relatively small sample of working Asian adults who were in poverty in 2019.

There are other group differences, such as between-state heterogeneities in unemployment, that this chapter could explore, but these investigations offer little beyond the conclusions already reached through the figures for age, gender, parenthood status, and race/ethnicity. For example, the fifty states (and the District of Columbia) were hit differently by the pandemic, and political and economic responses to the pandemic were also different from state to state. The story across states is similar, however, to conclusions reached in the analyses of the demographic characteristics considered here: within-state differences by pre-pandemic poverty status generally exceeded between-state differences in overall unemployment changes.[29]

The Relationship between Pre-Pandemic Poverty Status and Job Loss during the COVID-19 Pandemic

The observed disparities in unemployment by poverty status, especially for women and non-White adults, are striking. How can we make sense of these disparities? Why, in other words, was pre-pandemic poverty status so strongly connected to job loss during the COVID-19 pandemic?

There are two questions we can ask that go a long way toward explaining the patterns we have observed in this chapter. First, which types of occupations were most likely to face job loss after the onset of the pandemic? And second, what are the characteristics of the workers in these more vulnerable jobs?

Given the shutdowns of non-essential businesses and the declining demand for in-person services more broadly, the jobs most likely to disappear in the early months of the pandemic, not surprisingly, were primarily in service industries. Eight million jobs in leisure and hospitality were lost in April 2020.[30] Education and health services saw 2 million jobs disappear that month, while jobs declined in April in a broad range of other services by 1.4 million. Other sectors were also hit hard: local governments shed 1.2 million jobs in April 2020, while manufacturing lost 1.4 million jobs.

In relative terms, the average worker in these industries was not earning all that much prior to the pandemic. To understand the overlap of income and job loss, it is useful to shift our focus from the types of jobs that were lost to the pre-pandemic *wages* or *incomes* of workers in those jobs.[31] Doing so allows us to evaluate the extent to which earning a low wage prior to the pandemic was associated with job loss during the pandemic.

Figure 3.6 shows this relationship, grouping occupations into five quintiles based on their 2019 hourly wage rate. The lowest-paying occupations are grouped into one category, the next one-fifth of low-paying jobs are grouped into another category, and so on, up to the highest-paying set of jobs in a fifth category. The trend lines represent, for each group, the percentage change in employment for the group relative to January 2020.

In April 2020, employment rates for the lowest-paying occupations had declined by 30 percent relative to their January levels. For the second quintile employment declined by 15 percent, and for the third and fourth quintiles employment dropped by 10 percent and 7 percent, respectively. Meanwhile, the highest-paying jobs saw only a 3 percent decline in employment in April 2020. Thus, those in the lowest-paying jobs saw a rate of job loss around ten times greater than the rate for the highest-paying jobs. This finding is consistent with the evidence presented throughout the first half of this chapter: entering the pandemic with a lower income was strongly associated with job loss during the pandemic.[32]

The employment rates of the lowest-paying jobs also recovered more slowly than was the case with higher-paying jobs. In December 2021, for example, the two highest-paying quintiles of jobs had fully recovered from their COVID-related employment losses (that is, the point estimate

Figure 3.6   Changes in Employment Rates by Pay Level, January 2020 to December 2021

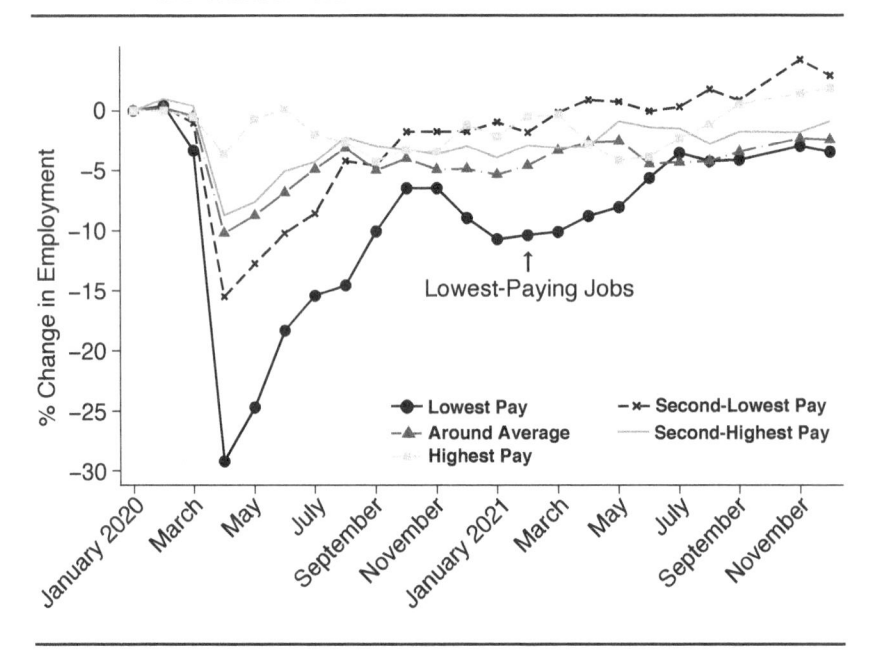

Source: Author's calculations of median hourly wages by occupation from the 2019 Current Population Survey Annual Social and Economic Supplement. Employment changes for occupations in 2020 and 2021 are estimated using the monthly CPS files.

Note: Occupations are sorted into five categories based on their 2019 median hourly wage. The y-axis displays the percentage change in the employment-to-population ratio from January 2020.

climbs above zero, suggesting no relative decline from January 2020). In the same month, the lowest-paying quintile of jobs was still around 4 percent below its January 2020 levels.

With these facts established, we can turn to our second question: Who was more likely to work in those lower-paying jobs? Table 3.1 provides descriptive characteristics of the race/ethnicity, gender, education, and pre-pandemic poverty status of workers in each earnings group.

Nearly all the characteristics listed in table 3.1 linearly increase or decrease when we move from the lowest-paying quintile to the highest-paying quintile. To simplify the descriptive portrait, then, we can focus on differences in the characteristics of workers in the lowest- versus highest-paying jobs. Relative to the highest-paying jobs, workers in the lowest-paying jobs prior to the pandemic had a 2019 poverty rate

Table 3.1   **Characteristics of Workers in Lowest- to Highest-Paying Occupations, January and February 2020**

	First Quintile (Lowest Pay)	Second Quintile	Third Quintile	Fourth Quintile	Fifth Quintile (Highest Pay)
SPM poverty rate (2019)	11.5%	9.9%	5.0%	3.3%	1.9%
White	50.2	57.0	66.2	71.1	69.3
Black	14.9	15.0	12.2	9.6	9.0
Hispanic	27.7	21.2	15.4	12.3	8.4
Asian	6.0	5.5	5.0	5.7	12.6
Male	50.2	51.8	49.2	57.0	54.6
High school degree only	56.5	43.6	31.0	19.7	5.4
College degree	13.9	23.2	36.2	54.9	79.0
Median hourly wage (2019)	$11.58	$16.00	$19.70	$25.29	$38.72

Source: Author's calculations from the Current Population Survey.

(11.5 percent) that was six times greater than the 2019 poverty rate among workers in the highest-paying jobs (1.9 percent). Those in the lowest-paying jobs were less likely to be White or Asian and more likely to be Black or Hispanic. The share of Hispanic workers in the lowest-paying jobs (27.7 percent) was three times the rate of Hispanic workers in the highest-paying jobs (8.4 percent), for example.

Those in the lowest-paying jobs were also more likely to be women compared to workers in the highest-paying jobs (consistent with the prior argument for gender disparities in COVID-era unemployment) and more likely to have only a high school degree. By definition, the 2019 median hourly wage of the jobs in the lowest-paying quintile ($11.58) was far lower than that of the highest quintile ($38.72). These patterns corroborate the claim that pre-pandemic disadvantage translated directly into disparities in job loss during the initial months of the pandemic.

Disparities in Working Conditions among the Employed

The large and unequal increases in joblessness posed a threat to widening inequalities and poverty during the pandemic. It must be noted, however, that working conditions for those who kept their pre-pandemic jobs were also vastly unequal. In other words, though losing a job risked income loss, maintaining employment during a pandemic carried its own set of risks and difficulties.

To start, those who went to work in the midst of the COVID-19 pandemic probably had more face-to-face encounters with other people, either on their commute to work or in the workplace, and thus a higher risk of contracting the virus. The health risks were particularly acute for workers who could not work remotely from home. Access to remote work opportunities varied widely by pre-pandemic poverty status. As with unemployment, disparities by poverty status were generally larger than the differences between demographic groups. Figure 3.7 documents evidence of these disparities by presenting trends in workers' ability to work from home by race/ethnicity and poverty status throughout 2020 and 2021.

Workers who entered the pandemic in poverty had a low likelihood of being able to work from home: at peak levels in May 2020, 22.8 percent of White workers in poverty, 15.9 percent of Black workers in poverty, 11.5 percent of Hispanic workers in poverty, and 26 percent of Asian workers in poverty were able to work remotely. Contrast these rates with the workers who were not in poverty at the onset of the pandemic: relative to workers in poverty in the same racial/ethnic group in the same month, the remote work rates were 17 percentage points higher (39.8 percent) for nonpoor White workers, 15.1 percentage points higher (31 percent) for nonpoor Black workers, 13.5 percentage points higher (24.9 percent) for nonpoor Hispanic workers, and 27.3 percentage points higher (53.3 percent) for nonpoor Asian workers. Underlying these findings is the close (and positive) correlation of the ability to work from home with the average wage earned.[33] The higher-income workers could more comfortably work from home in a safer setting; the lower-income workers still went into work and faced more exposure to the virus.

As discussed in chapter 2, one group of workers had little choice but to show up in person at their workplaces: those in the so-called essential or frontline jobs. These workers generally had lower pre-pandemic incomes than workers not deemed essential, were often directly exposed to the health risks of COVID-19 in the workplace, and experienced higher mortality rates than workers in other jobs.[34]

High Joblessness, High Poverty?

In chapter 2, we also observed that low- and high-income America faced vastly different health consequences during the pandemic. Specifically, an adult who spent most of her childhood in poverty was twice as likely to die from COVID as an adult who had not been exposed to childhood poverty. This chapter has documented that low- and high-income

Figure 3.7 Working-Age Adults Working Remotely by Pre-Pandemic Poverty Status, January 2020 to December 2021

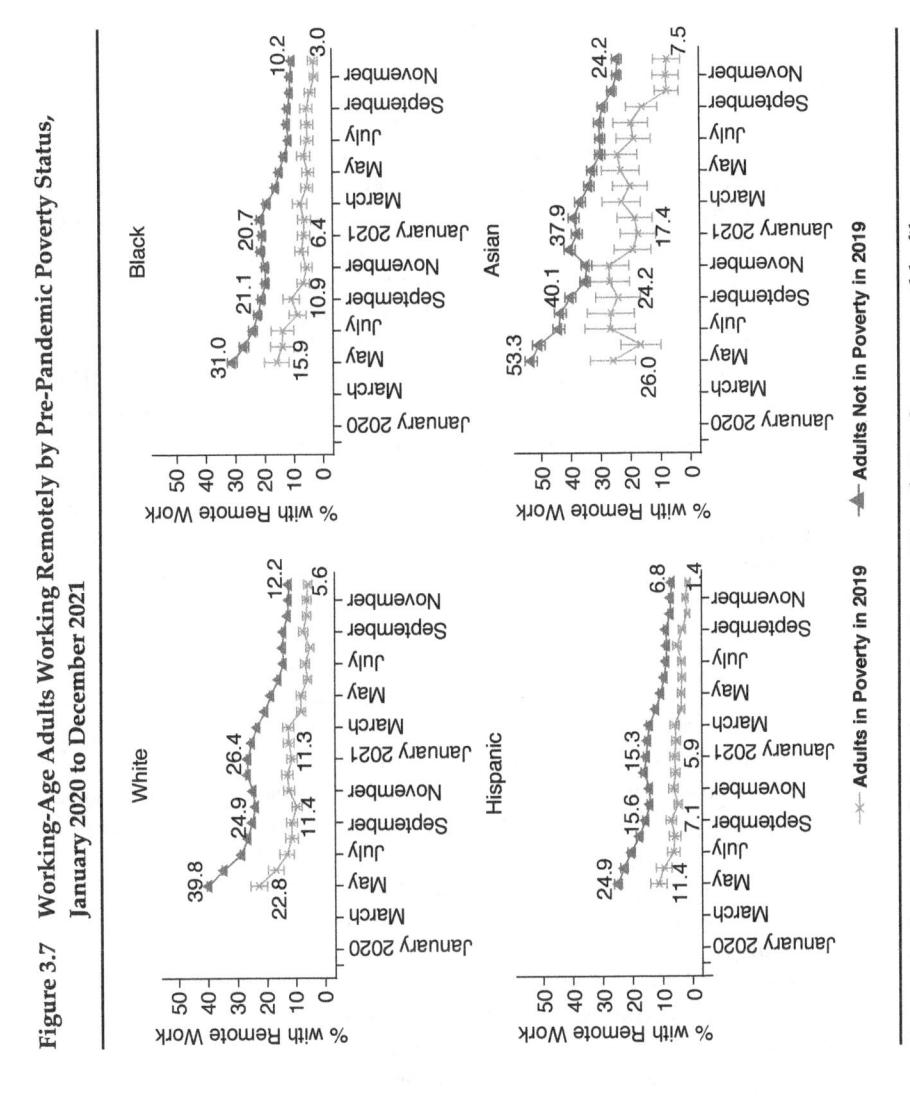

Source: Author's calculations from the Current Population Survey monthly files.

America also faced vastly different employment consequences: those who entered the pandemic in poverty had twice the rate of job loss in April 2020 as working adults who were comfortably above the poverty line. Meanwhile, the better-off workers who managed to keep their jobs were twice as likely to be able to work from home in the spring of 2020 compared to workers who entered the pandemic in poverty. Put differently, poverty served as a preexisting risk factor for the pandemic's employment consequences.

Popular media accounts and much COVID-related research have understandably emphasized demographic differences in unemployment trends.[35] And indeed, evaluating differential employment patterns for parents and nonparents, mothers and fathers, Black workers and White workers, and so on, we can better understand disparities and identify the groups most in need of economic support. This chapter has instead demonstrated, however, that the most appropriate lens through which to understand employment disparities during the pandemic is not demographic differences but pre-pandemic exposure to poverty. The 2020 employment crisis disproportionately took jobs from those who entered the pandemic already in poverty, whether they were men or women, mothers or fathers, White workers or Black workers, young or old, or otherwise. Through an intersectional perspective, economically vulnerable workers who were also young and Black or Hispanic faced particularly large rates of job loss: for example, more than 40 percent of Black adults who entered the pandemic in poverty were unemployed in April 2020.

These unequal (un)employment trends threatened three potential outcomes, with implications for how we should think about poverty in the context of crisis. First, given that adults who already struggled to meet their basic needs suffered a disproportionate share of the job losses, the employment declines threatened to increase the severity and depth of poverty, especially given that the pre-pandemic safety net did relatively little to support jobless adults, as discussed in chapter 1.

Second, the employment declines had important consequences beyond income and beyond affected individuals. We know from prior work that job loss can impose much uncertainty, create more stress, affect family relations, and lead to poorer developmental outcomes for children.[36] Evidence suggests that parental job loss during the pandemic took a toll on children: parents experiencing job loss reported higher levels of anxiety, stress, uncooperativeness, and depressive symptoms in their children and greater intrafamily conflict between parents and children.[37] Beyond individual financial concerns, then, job loss—and disparities in job loss—added another layer of hardship and uncertainty to the lives of an already vulnerable segment of society.

Third, the steep increase in unemployment overall in the initial months of the pandemic threatened to put more people in the ranks of poverty. Though job loss disproportionately hit adults who entered the pandemic in poverty, unemployment was by no means limited to low-wage workers. As even many of those who entered the pandemic comfortably above the poverty line—for example, those with a family income more than three times the poverty threshold—lost jobs, the pool of households at risk of falling into poverty increased. As such, many more people than before the pandemic were at risk of falling into poverty and becoming unable to meet their basic expenses, such as paying for food or rent.

In 2019, high employment and a work-centered welfare state had combined to produce the lowest poverty rate in recent U.S. history. The primary event that could shatter that combination, as I argued in chapter 1, would have been a strong, sudden spike in unemployment. The COVID-19 pandemic delivered just such a spike, the likes of which had not been seen in the postwar era. The American welfare state, poorly equipped to offset income declines from job loss prior to the pandemic, was now tasked with sustaining the incomes of more than 20 million workers and their family members in the early months of 2020. In the Great Recession, the American welfare state had largely failed in this task: the poverty rate climbed from 13.8 percent in 2006 to 16.1 percent in 2011.[38] And it was not just poverty that climbed: in that earlier crisis, food insufficiency increased from 11.1 percent to 14.9 percent.[39]

Early projections suggested that, absent a major policy response, the COVID-19 pandemic would lead to similar outcomes.[40] Those hit hardest by the pandemic in the early months, Black and Hispanic families, were poised to see particularly large increases in poverty without the introduction of new income supports—no surprise given the trends that this chapter has documented. But in late March 2020, the federal government passed the Coronavirus Aid, Relief, and Economic Security Act (CARES Act), a $2 trillion piece of legislation that would have greater consequences for poverty and hardship than any other legislation in the postwar era.

Chapter 3 Appendix

The 2019 Supplemental Poverty Measure poverty rates are observed for a subset of the sample from January to June 2020 and imputed for the remainder of respondents. In both cases, the analyses merge the 2020 CPS ASEC (with poverty rates from the 2019 calendar year) with the 2020 CPS Basic Monthly files. Given the 4-8-4 sampling procedure of the CPS (respondents are interviewed for four consecutive months, then not interviewed for eight months, then interviewed for four months again), a subset of 2020 CPS ASEC respondents are also observed between January and June 2020. We can directly identify the 2019 poverty status of these respondents.

For all other respondents in the Basic Monthly files, I impute 2019 poverty status by estimating a model that predicts the likelihood of 2019 SPM poverty (in the CPS ASEC) based on the share of SPM unit members who are male; who are in five-year age bins spanning from birth to age ninety; who are married; who have a disability; who are White (non-Hispanic), Black, Asian, or Hispanic; who are noncitizens; who are foreign-born; who have only a high school degree; who have a college degree; and who live in a single-adult, no-child household, a single-parent household, a multi-adult, no-child household, or a multi-adult household with children, as well as the metropolitan status and state of their household. After I estimate this model in the ASEC file, I export the conditional probabilities to each monthly file, matching on the same set of observables applied in the ASEC model.

I do not include employment indicators in the model, as doing so would predict notably higher pre-pandemic poverty rates in months in which the observed unemployment rate is higher, thus invalidating the purpose of the model. Using ascriptive or mostly fixed characteristics allows the analysis to consistently identify a disadvantaged group — those likely to have been in poverty in 2019 — regardless of changing employment patterns throughout 2020 and 2021.

Figure A3.1 tests the accuracy of the imputed poverty rates, comparing the unemployment rates of the imputed-poverty group to those of the observed-poverty group. The results show consistent point estimates. In May and June 2020, point estimates for the observed-poverty group were slightly lower than they were for the imputed-poverty group, probably owing to the selective attrition among CPS ASEC panel members observed after March 2020. Nonetheless, the differences in the point estimates are not statistically significant. Results are consistent across the subgroups analyzed in chapter 3.

Figure A3.1   Trends in Unemployment by Poverty Rate for Individuals in Observed SPM Poverty (January to June 2020) versus Imputed SPM Poverty (January to December 2021)

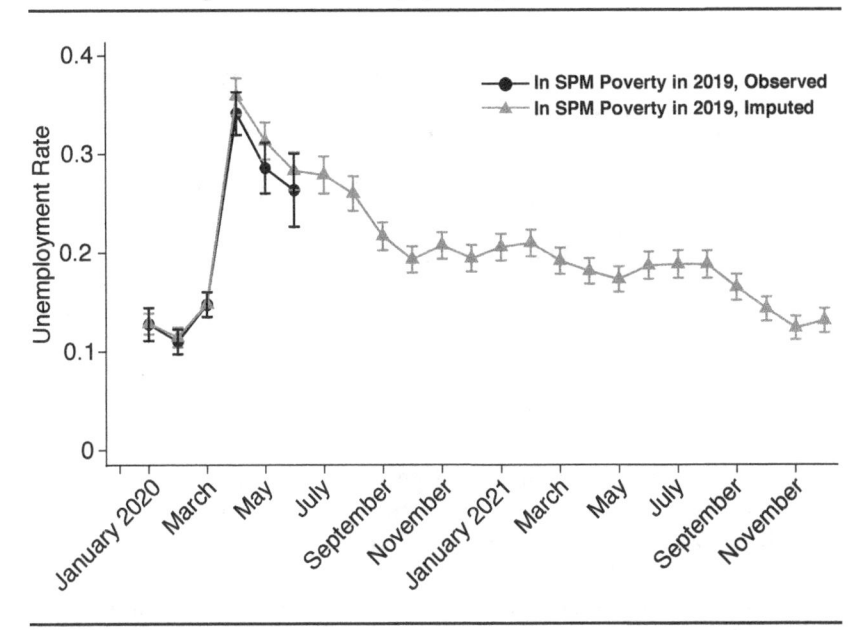

Source: Author's calculations from the Current Population Survey Annual Social and Economic Supplement.
Note: To document how unemployment trends varied by pre-pandemic poverty status, I link the same households that participated in the annual household income survey that produced poverty statistics for 2019 (the 2020 version of the CPS ASEC) with several monthly surveys of labor market activity and household composition in early 2020 (through the CPS Basic Monthly files). For households directly observed in both surveys, I directly assess how 2019 poverty status was associated with the likelihood of unemployment in April, May, and June 2020. For households observed in the monthly surveys but not the annual CPS ASEC, I estimate their 2019 poverty status using fine-grained information on household structure, place of residence, and demographic characteristics.

Chapter 4

The Policy Response: The CARES Act, the American Rescue Plan Act, and the Child Tax Credit

As EMPHASIZED in chapter 1, a large and rapid decline in employment was the precise scenario for which the pre-pandemic American welfare state was least prepared, yet this is what the onset of COVID-19 provided in March and April 2020.

Left to the pre-pandemic welfare state, most of the 20 million adults who lost their jobs after the onset of the COVID-19 would have received relatively little income support to compensate for their losses. A fortunate few would have qualified for Unemployment Insurance (UI) for up to twenty-six weeks, but many would have been left out of UI altogether owing to an inadequate work history. These displaced workers might have received benefits from the Supplemental Nutrition Assistance Program (SNAP, often referred to as "food stamps") and not much else. The uncertainty created by the pandemic, as well as an out-of-work welfare state unequipped to meet the needs of the millions of newly jobless adults, practically demanded that the federal government take action. There was no guarantee of how long the pandemic would last (far longer than most initially suspected, as it turned out), how long it would take the economy to recover (into 2022), and how long the average family could get by on SNAP benefits or time-limited unemployment benefits (not very long).

To the credit of the federal government, the policy response at the onset of the pandemic was swift and massive. In March 2020, Congress passed both the Families First Coronavirus Response Act (FFCRA) and the Coronavirus Aid, Relief, and Economic Security (CARES) Act. The FFCRA expanded access to paid sick leave and increased support for food and nutrition programs, among other changes. It paled in comparison, however, to the CARES Act, a multi-trillion-dollar piece of legislation designed to mitigate the economic consequences of the pandemic, among other things. As this chapter demonstrates, the CARES Act alone put nearly $930 billion directly into the pockets of U.S. households in 2020—more than all of the added income support provided to families over the four-year period from 2009 to 2012 during the Great Recession.

Less than a year later, after the presidential election of Joseph R. Biden, Congress passed another piece of legislation amounting to more than $2 trillion in spending, the American Rescue Plan Act (ARP). The center-piece of the ARP was the expanded Child Tax Credit (CTC), a policy that marked a massive, albeit temporary, break from the country's three-decade shift toward a work-centered welfare state. Rather than limiting the CTC's cash payments to working parents, the program's expansion provided "fully refundable" tax credits to nearly all parents with children, regardless of their level of earnings. And unlike the CTC of the past, which was distributed as a once-per-year payment during tax season, the expanded CTC was paid monthly to families for a six-month period beginning in July 2021. The consequences for poverty and hardship, as I document in this and subsequent chapters, were vast.

Inherent to many of the policy decisions in 2020 and 2021, however, were trade-offs among three goals: (1) ensuring the *timeliness* of income support, (2) *targeting* benefits to the desired populations, and (3) achieving the right *duration* of benefit provision. Since the federal government had no administrative infrastructure to immediately provide income support to all households across the country, for example, it decided to distribute stimulus checks through the Internal Revenue Service. This approach succeeded in being timely, but its targeting was imperfect: some of the lowest-income households across the country were unable to receive their stimulus check payments because they had not needed to file taxes in prior years and thus were not in the IRS system.

This chapter addresses many other examples of these types of trade-offs in COVID-era policy decisions. Their net result was that, despite the massive increase in spending, the many shortcomings of the CARES Act, the ARP, and the expanded CTC limited their potential to reduce poverty. To understand trends in poverty, hardship, and other outcomes throughout 2020 and 2021, we first need to dive into the size and structure of these historic yet imperfect policy interventions and the trade-offs embedded within them.

The Coronavirus Aid, Relief, and Economic Security Act

The CARES Act, passed at the end of March 2020, was designed to simultaneously stabilize a ruptured economy, increase investment in public health measures, support state and local governments, and provide much-needed income support to millions of U.S. families. As a whole, the package amounted to nearly $2 trillion in projected spending. Of that sum, around $500 billion was initially projected to be distributed directly into the pockets of residents across the country, though the real value would climb to around $930 billion.[1]

Another set of funds would eventually be distributed through the Paycheck Protection Program (PPP) to small businesses with the intention of preserving jobs, although most of the money, as discussed later, would not be used for job-protection purposes. The PPP aside, the CARES Act generated two major expansions to income transfer programs: stimulus checks—more formally known as Economic Impact Payments (EIPs)—and expansions to unemployment benefits.

The CARES Act's stimulus checks, distributed in the spring of 2020, provided a one-off payment of $1,200 per eligible adult and $500 per eligible child age sixteen or younger. For example, a family with one adult and two children could receive up to $2,200 if they qualified for the full benefit amount ($1,200 + $500 + $500). Lower-income households typically received the maximum benefit value, though benefits phased out for single tax filers who earned above $75,000 and for spouses filing together who earned above $150,000. Importantly, the payment did not cover dependents who were older than seventeen, and it was not available for immigrants who filed taxes with an Individual Taxpayer Identification Number (ITIN) or for any members of their household, regardless of U.S. citizenship or green-card status.

Total spending on the CARES Act's unemployment benefit expansions was even larger than for the stimulus checks. Building off of existing UI programs, the expansions established three temporary subcomponents of UI that increased benefit levels, expanded benefit eligibility, and increased the maximum duration of benefit receipt.

The first of those subcomponents was Pandemic Unemployment Compensation (PUC), or Federal Pandemic Unemployment Compensation (FPUC), which delivered a $600 per week top-up to all recipients of unemployment benefits. A jobless adult claiming UI benefits, for example, received not only his or her standard UI payments (say, $300 per week) but also the extra federally funded $600 per week bonus. Importantly, the PUC was temporary: it lasted roughly four months, from April to the end of July 2020. (It was renewed again in 2021 with a $300 benefit level.) Those receiving the benefit for all four months brought in around $9,600 in income support from the PUC alone. Given that the receipt of many unemployment benefits was delayed in 2020, the PUC benefits were also paid out retroactively to ensure that those facing delays in benefit receipt could still acquire the full value.

Just as important as the increase in benefit levels was the increase in benefit access. Typically, workers need to earn a certain amount in their job and/or hold the job for a long enough duration to qualify for UI benefits; as a result of this restriction, a minority of unemployed adults receive UI benefits. At the peak of the Great Recession, for example, only 40 percent of unemployed adults were able to access UI benefits.[2] By contrast, the CARES Act's Pandemic Unemployment Assistance (PUA) provided unemployment benefits to jobless adults who had been excluded from regular UI eligibility owing to their type of employment (for example, the self-employed, part-time workers, independent contractors, and gig workers), their work history, or their level of earnings. Unlike before the pandemic, nearly any person who lost a job because of the pandemic could now claim unemployment benefits. Individuals receiving PUA assistance received benefits worth at least half the state's regular minimum payment (around $183 per week) for up to thirty-nine weeks, in addition to the $600 per week PUC benefits. As a result, a person receiving minimum PUA benefits for the full thirty-nine-week duration of the benefits could bring in close to $17,000 in unemployment benefits alone. PUA beneficiaries represented 40 percent of overall UI claims during 2020, and its benefits disproportionately went to lower-income adults.[3]

The third subcomponent built off of existing UI programs addressed the duration of benefit receipt. Pandemic Emergency Unemployment Compensation (PEUC) added thirteen weeks of additional unemployment benefits once regular UI allotments expired (generally after a maximum of twenty-six weeks). In early 2021, the Biden administration again extended the maximum duration of benefit receipt, this time to the start of September 2021.

CARES Act Income Transfers: Unprecedented Social Spending

The CARES Act's stimulus checks and expanded unemployment benefits increased social spending to a level not seen in modern U.S. history. To contextualize the sheer size of the programs, we can compare CARES Act spending to levels of spending on other income transfer programs (excluding Social Security and health care spending) in 2020. Figure 4.1 compares spending on the CARES income transfers to spending on the Earned Income Tax Credit (EITC), SNAP, Supplemental Security Income (SSI), housing assistance, and other forms of (nonretirement) income support available through the American welfare state prior to the pandemic.

Combined, the two components of the CARES Act amounted to around $930 billion in transfers in 2020. To place these sums in context, consider

Figure 4.1   Spending on CARES Act Transfers Compared to Spending on Existing Transfer Programs, 2020

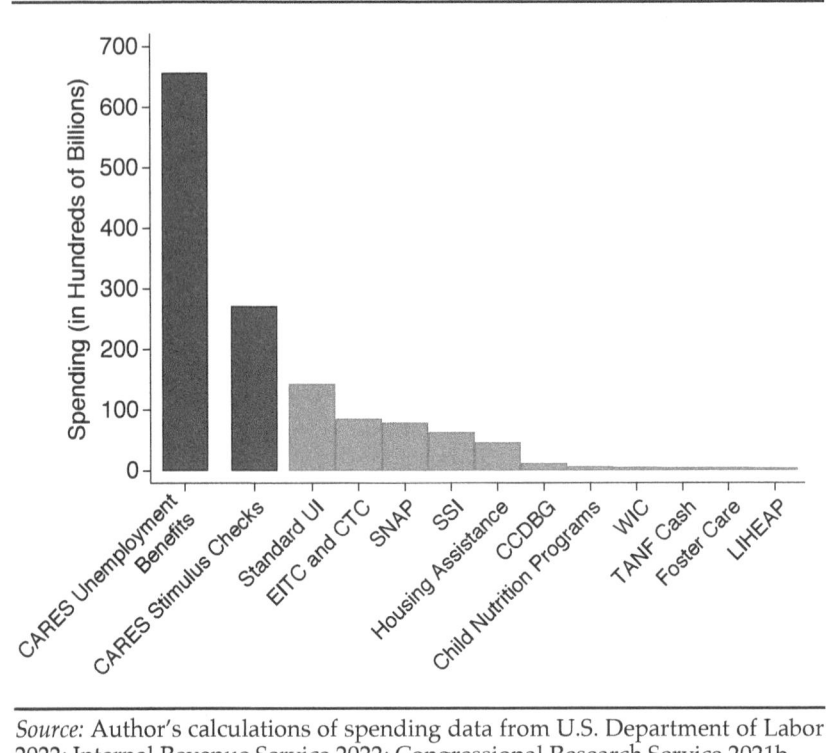

Source: Author's calculations of spending data from U.S. Department of Labor 2022; Internal Revenue Service 2022; Congressional Research Service 2021b.
Note: UI = Unemployment Insurance; SSI = Supplemental Security Income; CCDBG = Child Care and Development Block Grant; WIC = Women, Infants, and Children; LIHEAP = Low Income Home Energy Assistance Program. Spending totals are limited to nonretirement and non-health-care spending.

that all nonretirement and non-health-care spending on other income transfers in 2020 amounted to around $475 billion. Put differently, the CARES Act nearly doubled the size of all nonretirement, non-health-care income transfers to the U.S. population in 2020, an appropriate response given the historic increase in unemployment.[4] Spending in the first round of stimulus checks alone amounted to $270 billion, larger than the combined sum of the EITC, CTC, and SNAP payments distributed in 2020. On their own, the CARES Act's expansions to unemployment benefits added $650 billion in income transfers—more than one hundred times the value of cash transfers provided through the TANF program in the same year.

Keep in mind that these sums do not yet include the second and third stimulus checks that were distributed in late 2020 and early 2021 and also do not account for some other benefits, like the Pandemic EBT support for families with school-age children (discussed later in the chapter). Even without counting those benefits, the CARES-related transfers doubled the amount of cash support distributed to U.S. households.

The CARES Act Compared to the Federal Response to the Great Recession

Another useful comparison is to plot the federal response during COVID-19 to what happened during the Great Recession. Both events precipitated an economic recession, though of course the speed and sources of the economic collapses varied. The Great Recession saw a slow, steady rise of unemployment from 5 percent in December 2007 to 10 percent in October 2009.[5] The doubling of the national unemployment rate during the Great Recession, in other words, took nearly two years. As we observed in chapter 3, the initial months of the COVID-19 pandemic were far different: unemployment more than doubled from March to April 2020. The contexts of the economic crises also influenced the policy responses: a global pandemic—which required, at least temporarily, stay-at-home orders to prevent face-to-face contact—necessitated a different policy response than a more conventional economic collapse. What the two recessions shared in common, however, was the threat to the economic security of American households as millions of adults either lost their jobs or had their hours cut.

From 2008 through 2012, the federal government was reluctant to provide large direct income transfers to U.S. families. One exception came at the start of the crisis: the George W. Bush administration passed the Economic Stimulus Act, which offered tax rebates of up to $1,200 for a married couple ($600 for a single person) for tax units with at least $3,000 in qualifying income in the prior year. These payments amounted to around $175 billion (in 2020 U.S. dollars). From 2009 onward, the primary changes to income support programs were a 15 percent upgrade to SNAP benefits and an extension of the duration of unemployment benefits. Rather than vastly increasing the provision of cash support, the federal government opted for a subtler strategy of reducing taxes (the $112 billion "Making Work Pay" tax credit, for example, reduced the tax liability for wage-earners) and encouraging business investment to stimulate the economy. The underlying weaknesses of the economy during that time (which, again, were vastly different than the sources of the employment shock during COVID-19) led to a strategy that was less concerned with reducing immediate poverty and hardship than with stimulating business activity in hopes of sparking a quicker economic recovery. This priority is all the more evident when we compare social spending on income transfers in 2020 relative to the period of 2008 to 2012.

Spending on new income transfers during the Great Recession amounted to around $955 billion (in 2020 U.S. dollars) over a five-year period.[6] The CARES Act put as much income ($928 billion) into the pockets of families in a single year, 2020. To put it another way, average spending on income transfers per year during the Great Recession amounted to $191 billion, roughly 20 percent of what the CARES Act provided in 2020 alone.

Even these spending totals overestimate the actual policy response in the Great Recession, as they overlook the distribution and form of that spending. For example, because the 2008 stimulus checks and the Making Work Pay tax credit were conditional on prior earnings, working-age adults who had no work at the onset of the crisis were less likely to receive the payments. In contrast, the CARES Act's stimulus checks provided direct support regardless of current or former employment status. Additionally, the Great Recession's spending totals use a generous definition of "income transfers" that includes a small Wounded Warrior Tax Credit, which was available only to firms that hired unemployed veterans; temporary health insurance subsidies (COBRA) for workers who lost their jobs; and a $200 billion payroll tax cut that probably spurred hiring but did little to directly alleviate the hardships of jobless families. In short, besides the astronomical quantitative differences, there were large qualitative differences in the types of federal spending during the Great Recession relative to pandemic spending.

Perhaps a more useful apples-to-apples comparison is to focus on policy changes made to the distribution of unemployment benefits in the Great Recession and during the COVID-19 pandemic. In the American Recovery and Reinvestment Act (ARRA) of 2009, Congress included a $25 per week increase in the value of UI benefits. In the CARES Act, Congress included a $600 per week increase in the value of UI benefits through the PUC. Even accounting for a bit of inflation over the previous decade, the CARES Act expansion was at least ten times more generous than the ARRA intervention. And importantly, the CARES Act's expansion of coverage through the PUA ensured that unemployment benefits were far more accessible. For instance, at the peak of the Great Recession, only 40 percent of unemployed adults were able to access UI benefits.[7] During 2020, in contrast, the share of unemployed adults accessing the benefits was probably close to 80 percent.[8] In fact, the number of UI beneficiaries often exceeded the number of unemployed adults during the pandemic.[9] The federal government did try during the Great Recession to incentivize state governments to expand eligibility for UI benefits through Modernization Act payments, but the realized expansions to benefit access hardly compare to what the PUA accomplished in 2020.

The Potential Poverty Reduction Effect of the CARES Act

For families during COVID-19, these unemployment benefits, combined with other support from the CARES Act, offered a potentially meaningful buffer against income losses from job loss. In fact, the $600 per week in UI benefits actually exceeded the pre-pandemic wages of many low-income workers. The median replacement rate (the share of prior wages compensated for by income transfers after job loss) was 145 percent when the $600 per week PUC was in place.[10] Three-fourths of workers eligible for the PUC had replacement rates above 100 percent, and that was before accounting for the stimulus check payment.

The next chapter will examine how these CARES Act benefits affected real-world poverty trends. As a preview of their potential impact, figure 4.2 shows how receipt of these different income transfers could push a given family type out of poverty. Specifically, the figure shows the level of these benefits relative to the poverty threshold of the Supplemental Poverty Measure for two different household types: a single adult and a single-parent, two-child family. The figure shows the benefit values as a percentage of the overall poverty line, so an income transfer that is equivalent in value to half the household type's poverty threshold is labeled as 50 percent. A combination of benefits that crosses 100 percent of the poverty line is equivalent to saying that receipt of the benefits alone could push that household type out of poverty. For simplicity, I assume here that these two households received their first stimulus check payments and also received minimum unemployment benefits (including the $600 per week top-up) from April through July 2020. The single-parent family also received SNAP benefits in this stylized example. I also assume that they were renting their homes in an average-cost city—say, Phoenix, Arizona—for the purpose of selecting their SPM poverty threshold.

The y-axis in figure 4.2 shows each income transfer pushing each household closer to the poverty line. For the single adult in this example, receiving the standard UI benefits alone for sixteen weeks covered around one-fourth of the poverty threshold (which was $13,825 of annual income for a standard single adult in 2020). The stimulus check (EIP) bumped the total up to nearly 40 percent of the poverty line, while the $600 per week supplement to unemployment benefits (FPUC) pushed this single adult's annual income above the poverty line (assuming receipt for all

Figure 4.2   Stylized Example of Household Resources Relative to Poverty Threshold with Receipt of Standard UI Benefits, FPUC, EIP, and SNAP Benefits, 2020

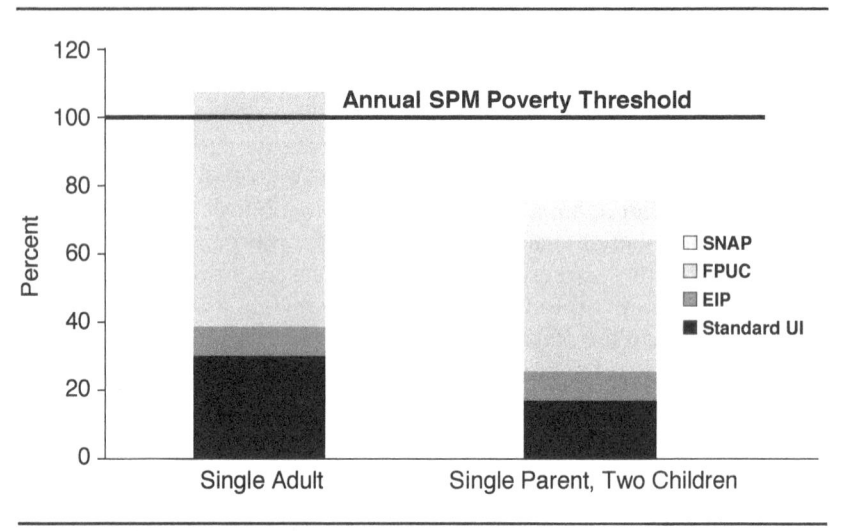

Source: Author's calculations.
Note: The 2020 SPM threshold for a single adult renting in an average-cost city was $13,825. The poverty threshold for a similar single-parent, two-child family was $24,766. Thresholds vary according to living costs; thus, the poverty thresholds for families in New York City are higher than in an average-cost city, while the thresholds for families in rural Missouri are lower.

sixteen weeks). Without even accounting for the earned income from employment that this adult presumably accrued prior to the onset of the pandemic, his or her annual income was above the poverty line thanks to the CARES Act's generous income provisions.

The poverty threshold for the single-parent, two-child family is higher ($24,766 in annual income) than for the single adult, given that such a family needs more resources to get by. As a result, each income transfer did slightly less to push this family out of poverty. Nonetheless, the combination of unemployment benefits, the $600 per week supplement, the stimulus check, and SNAP benefits was sufficient to push the family to around 75 percent of the poverty threshold. If the parent had income from other sources during the year—say, earnings from employment or access to cash support from TANF—then the likelihood of having an annual income above the poverty line only increased.

This stylized example provides a glimpse of the CARES Act's potential for poverty reduction in 2020. However, for all the benefits of its programs, several important caveats are likely to have limited the CARES Act's ability to cut into poverty rates.

Trade-offs: Timeliness, Targeting, and Duration

Policymakers face a series of trade-offs in designing crisis-era policies: How quickly can they get the benefits out? How can they ensure that the money gets into the hands of those who need it most, while keeping it out of the hands of those who should not have access? And how can they ensure that generous benefit provisions last long enough to support households in need but not so long as to slow the economic recovery? Rarely are these three dimensions of crisis-era policies in perfect harmony, and the COVID-era income support policies were no exception. As a result, the poverty reduction impact of CARES Act spending, while vast, still did not live up to its fullest potential, as we see in the following four examples.

The Paycheck Protection Program: The PPP was a textbook illustration of the policy trade-offs between timeliness and targeting. At the onset of the pandemic, the federal government lacked the infrastructure to quickly distribute targeted funds to small businesses. Given the rapid spread of COVID-19 and the sudden decline in employment, the government was faced with a choice: spend months to develop a decently targeted system of loan distribution with appropriate accountability mechanisms or act quickly, at the cost of distributing resources with few conditions and little accountability.[11] With the PPP, the latter choice was made.

The purpose of the PPP was to provide small businesses (defined as those with fewer than five hundred employees) with financial support to reduce their need to shutter or lay off employees. Altogether, the program distributed more than $800 billion in loans to business owners—roughly the amount distributed in the form of stimulus check payments and expanded unemployment benefits. More than 90 percent of these loans were forgivable, that is, no repayment was required. Virtually any small business could access the loans, and most did: David Autor and his coauthors estimate that "94 percent of employees with fewer than 500 employees took up a PPP loan."[12] For perspective, this is higher than the estimated take-up rate of the stimulus checks or the expanded CTC benefits.

Were the payments successful in preserving jobs? Yes, but at an extraordinary cost. Autor and his colleagues estimate that the PPP preserved around 3 million jobs per week between April and June 2020, at a cost of $170,000 to $257,000 per job preserved (which was notably higher than the mean wages of workers in the jobs preserved, estimated at around $58,200).[13] Additionally, Michael Dalton estimates that businesses receiving the loans were 6 percent less likely to close a month after receiving the funds—but again, this somewhat reduced risk of closure came at a high cost.[14]

The elevated costs were due to the fact that most of the PPP funds did not funnel down to workers. Instead, about two-thirds of the funds went to business owners and shareholders—two groups concentrated in the upper rungs of the income distribution. As a result, three-quarters of the PPP benefits went to households in the top fifth of the overall income distribution.[15] To put it more concretely, only $13.2 billion of the $510 billion in PPP loans provided in 2020 made it to households in the bottom fifth of the income distribution (the workers most likely to be in poverty).

The federal government acted at impressive speed to prevent many firms (and workers) from going under during the pandemic. Moreover, the PPP was an admirable attempt to adopt a European-style approach of preserving jobs rather than providing benefits to adults only after they have lost their job. In this, the program succeeded, to an extent: the PPP saved many jobs, prevented some firms from closing, and probably reduced poverty. The flip side of the rapid pace of its rollout, however, was its poor targeting of the resources and its lack of provision for accountability; as a result, most of the $800 billion in payments remained in the hands of the richest households in the country. This outcome stands in stark contrast to the effectiveness of the distribution of payments from the similarly priced unemployment benefit expansions, stimulus checks, and expanded CTC benefits.

Exclusions from stimulus check provisions: Another limitation of the CARES Act's support was the exclusion, by law, of certain low-income families from receiving the income support. Megan Curran and Sophie Collyer of Columbia's Center on Poverty and Social Policy have documented that 30 million income-eligible individuals were excluded from receiving the first stimulus checks.[16] Adult dependents were also excluded from the payments. This large group included high school and college students who were still claimed as dependents on their parents' tax records as well as older adults with disabilities and elderly parents receiving care. Curran and Collyer estimate that the CARES Act excluded around 10 million adults under age twenty-four, most of them students, who were more likely to live in poverty prior to the pandemic and less likely to be able to access other forms of immediate income support. Moreover, according to estimates from the Center on Budget and Policy Priorities, around 5 million of those excluded were elderly individuals with health issues or disabilities, a group that also tends to be economically disadvantaged.[17]

In addition to adult dependents, many undocumented immigrants were explicitly excluded from receiving support. Around 10 million undocumented individuals, including nearly 4 million children who were in fact U.S. citizens, were excluded from receiving the stimulus checks.[18] Undocumented immigrants faced the most explicit exclusions from the CARES Act's unemployment expansions. The PUA was meant to provide unemployment benefits to the self-employed and others with part-time work or an informal work history who lost their jobs during the crisis. However, work authorization was required to access PUA benefits, leaving many undocumented workers without access. According to the Migration Policy Institute, roughly 7 million undocumented individuals were employed in the years prior to the pandemic, and none of these individuals were able to access unemployment benefits, in any form, during 2020.[19]

The exclusion of undocumented immigrants from income support programs in the past has contributed to rising levels of deep and extreme poverty among families with children. In prior work, I have found that between 60 and 70 percent of children in extreme poverty live in households headed by noncitizens, a direct result of most noncitizens' lack of access to basic income support programs in the event of joblessness or loss of income from other sources.[20] The CARES Act only continued this trend, it seems, at a time when finding a job was more difficult and less safe than ever.

Challenges in accessing CARES Act benefits: Beyond the explicit exclusion of certain groups of individuals, the CARES Act's stimulus checks and unemployment benefit expansions both struggled to balance the timeliness of payments with accurate targeting of benefits. At the onset of the pandemic, the federal government lacked the administrative infrastructure to quickly distribute funds to all low-income tax units across the country. The closest it could get to such an infrastructure was the IRS, which has income, address, and often bank account information from submitted tax returns for most tax units across the country. The targeting challenge lay in finding those for whom the IRS lacked information: the tax units with incomes so low that they had not had to file taxes in recent years. Because the IRS was not prepared to distribute stimulus checks to the lowest-income families in the United States, an estimated 12 million Americans were left at risk of not receiving their stimulus checks.[21]

This trade-off—getting the benefits out in a timely manner, but not necessarily reaching the full population that the benefit should have reached—was surely justified: few would argue that the federal government should have withheld income support until it found every last low-income family. But this fact does not diminish the economic consequences for those who missed out on their payments. In the Urban Institute's

Coronavirus Tracking Survey, conducted in May 2020, researchers found that three in ten respondents claimed not to have received a stimulus check. Among families with incomes below the federal poverty line, the reported rate of receipt was only 60 percent, compared to 77.5 percent for families with incomes above the poverty line.[22] The nonrecipients were more likely, as Chuck Marr and his colleagues had projected, to be Black or Hispanic.[23]

It is likely that the final rates of benefit receipt were higher than these survey data suggest.[24] Nonetheless, the imperfect coverage and its clear skew toward the most economically vulnerable families represent a blemish on an otherwise effective policy intervention. The government's inability to distribute payments to nonfilers imposed an "administrative burden"—an extra bureaucratic step—on the lowest-income families to receive their benefits that is likely to have contributed to higher rates of hardship than would have been observed otherwise.[25]

The balance of timeliness and targeting was also evident in the distribution of the expanded unemployment benefits. Unlike the stimulus checks, which the IRS distributed to tax units across all states, the unemployment benefits were distributed through state governments. And unlike the automatic payments from which most stimulus check recipients benefited, the receipt of unemployment benefits required an application process so as to screen applicants and reduce fraud. Screening millions of new UI applicants, however, contributed to a general lack of timeliness: the UI application process was slow and tedious in many states. In Florida, for example, the state's online UI application system became so overwhelmed that the state had to limit the hours that people could visit the website. Thousands of Floridians turned to paper applications instead and waited in long lines outside of state offices to apply for their income support. Moreover, applying for benefits did not guarantee effective receipt, or at least not in a timely manner. In Florida, an estimated one-quarter of UI applicants were denied the income support they presumably needed to get by.[26]

Florida was not, however, the worst-performing state. Data from the Census Household Pulse Survey ("Pulse") suggest that one-third of Alabama residents who applied for UI benefits did not receive them, a rate similar to what was observed in Arkansas.[27] In contrast, roughly 90 percent of Rhode Island residents who applied for UI benefits reported that they received them in 2020. These estimates of success rates among unemployed adults who applied for UI benefits do not, of course, include the many unemployed adults who did not apply for the benefits in the first place.[28]

Survey-based reports of unemployment benefit receipt are likely to understate the true distribution of payments to some extent. Even in nonpandemic years, benefit underreporting in surveys has made it more challenging to estimate the actual effect of income support programs on poverty rates.[29] For example, some surveys suggest that very few unemployed adults received support.[30] Levels of receipt could have been as high as 80 percent, however, according to other surveys, including the 2021 Current Population Survey, and administrative data suggest even higher levels of receipt. Administrative data compiled at the California Policy Center, for example, suggest that the number of UI beneficiaries actually exceeded the number of unemployed adults in many counties within California, and that coverage was about 90 percent in the state as a whole.[31]

Despite variation in reports on the receipt of benefits, there is consistent evidence that, across all states, beneficiaries often experienced delays in receiving their payments. In Kentucky, for example, only one in four recipients of unemployment benefits received the payments within three weeks after applying.[32] California and New York were not much better: only around 40 percent of applicants in these states were receiving payments within three weeks, according to Department of Labor data.[33]

Although state governments often prioritized accurate targeting over timeliness, those efforts were not entirely successful. Individuals attempting to defraud the UI system were applying in large numbers to receive the benefits at the same time as individuals who actually needed (and were eligible for) the support. The Department of Labor estimates that around $45 billion worth of UI benefits were fraudulently claimed. Thousands of investigations are currently ongoing to prosecute the highest-dollar cases.[34]

The CARES Act's inconsistently paid and short-lived benefits: There is another question that arises when implementing crisis-era policy: How long should the benefit supplements last? Benefit provision that ends too quickly (say, before the economy recovers) threatens to leave many households struggling to get by as labor markets heal; benefit provision that lasts too long, by contrast, may inhibit that economic recovery. Few could guess ahead of time how long the COVID-19 pandemic might last, or its immediate economic damage; as such, designing the duration of the initial income supports was no simple task.

As it turned out, some of the more generous income supports introduced early in the pandemic probably ended too soon. As generous as the CARES Act benefits were for those who could receive them, the initial set of benefits left many families with little to no income support from August through December 2020. The stimulus checks were (initially) a onetime payment, and the largest part of the unemployment expansions—the $600 per week PUC bonus—expired in late July 2020, leaving many families with smaller incomes in subsequent months. The initial payments were appropriately timed to direct emergency cash

Figure 4.3   Stylized Example of Income Volatility throughout 2020 for a Single-Parent, Two-Child Family Receiving a Stimulus Payment and Unemployment Benefits

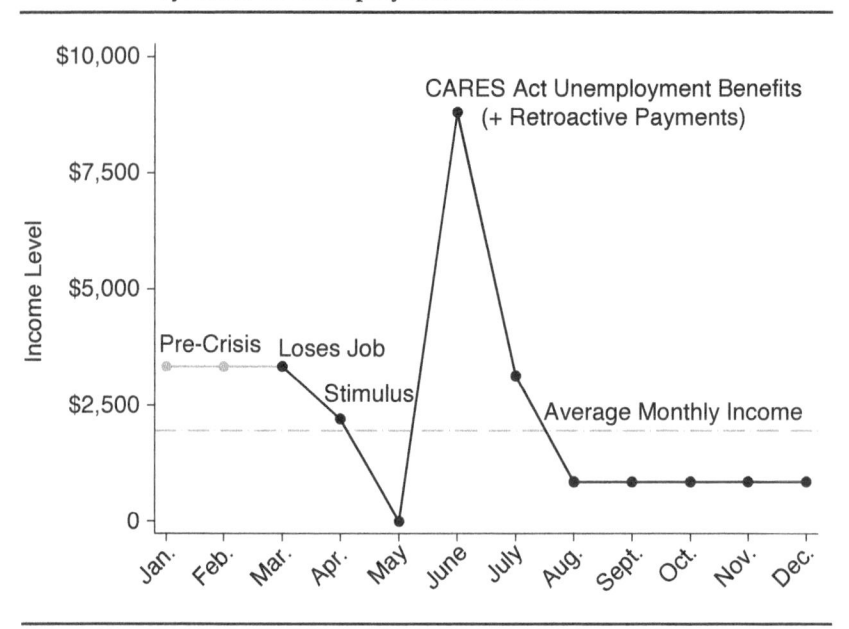

Source: Author's calculations.
Note: The stylized example represents a single-parent, two-child family with an annual income above the poverty threshold and living in a state with average living costs. The parent is assumed to have lost employment in March but was unable to access unemployment benefits until June. This scenario assumes that the parent received the $600 per week PUC bonus through its expiration in July and continued to receive minimum unemployment benefits through December. The family had an annual income above the poverty line despite experiencing several months with low or no income support.

relief to families who had recently lost jobs and other family income at the start of the pandemic. However, these payments did not (and initially, could not) account for the fact that the economic downturn would continue through 2020 and into 2021.

The short-lived benefits, combined with the delays in payments, kept the government's income support volatile for some families throughout 2020. Figure 4.3 provides a stylized example of how this income volatility might look for a single parent with two children who received the stimulus check and expanded unemployment benefits.

Each month is plotted on the x-axis, while the monthly income is plotted on the y-axis. In this example, the parent lost her job in March 2020 but was unable to collect unemployment benefits until June owing to delays in state application and processing procedures. The $2,400 stimulus check in April buffered the loss of market earnings due to job loss in March. However, the family was left with no income support in May. (In reality, this family might have received SNAP benefits, but they would have had no cash support.) In June, the parent received that month's unemployment benefits, as well as retroactive unemployment benefits for April and May. In July, the $600 per week PUC top-up payment expired. From August through December, the parent received the minimum unemployment payments only. This combination of income transfers was just enough for the family's annual total income to stay above the poverty line, despite their experience for much of the year of only modest income support (including one month with no income from earnings or assistance at all). The family's total annual income was also well below what the parent most likely would have been able to earn prior to losing his job at the start of the pandemic.

A well-prepared family might have been able to finance consumption through debt or savings in May, then smooth the large unemployment benefit payments from June over the remaining months of the year, when income support was much smaller. I return to this "consumption smoothing" argument in more detail in the next chapter. For now, I would emphasize two points.

First, many low-income families do not have the option to debt-finance their consumption, nor do many of them have savings or assets to rely on when times get tough. This was particularly true during the COVID-19 pandemic, when families had no way of knowing how many months they would be required to smooth consumption. For families who had little access to credit and were living paycheck to paycheck, delayed receipt of those unemployment benefits (in April or May, in this example) probably increased their risk of hardship while they waited for them to arrive. Second, even if all families could smooth consumption across the year, they should not be required to do so simply to compensate for the state's inability to administer timely payments. Put simply, the welfare state should be designed to make life easier for families rather than create new layers of uncertainties regarding the timeliness and duration of benefit payments.

The CARES Act, in short, was an imperfect yet largely successful intervention by the federal government. By the end of 2020, however, the PUC's $600 per week benefit supplement had been expired for roughly half a year, a new wave of COVID cases was spreading throughout the country, and employment rates had not yet returned to pre-pandemic levels. Thus, in early 2021, a new presidential administration decided to take its own set of actions.

The American Rescue Plan Act

President Joe Biden took office in January 2021, roughly one month after the outgoing Trump administration provided a second round of stimulus checks to much of the U.S. population. By this time, however, most of the CARES Act provisions had expired. To spur the economy and further support the incomes of families, the Democrat-led Congress passed the American Rescue Plan Act (ARP) in March 2021—roughly one year after passage of the CARES Act.

The American Rescue Plan shared many features with the CARES Act: it allocated $400 billion to another stimulus check payment, this time up to $1,400 for each eligible adult and child.[35] Additionally, the ARP extended the PUA for twenty-eight more weeks and added a $300 per week top-up to unemployment benefits; the latter was half as generous as the CARES Act version, but it still approximately doubled the mean value of the standard weekly unemployment benefit. Beyond these features it shared with the CARES Act, the ARP also extended a 15 percent monthly benefit increase in SNAP benefits (initially included in legislation passed under the Trump administration in December 2020), increased the benefit levels of the Earned Income Tax Credit for childless workers, and, perhaps most importantly, temporarily created a fully refundable Child Tax Credit (CTC) to be paid in monthly installments starting in July 2021.

Each of these ARP components provided an important boost to the incomes of families and prevented increases in poverty, as I document in more detail in the next chapter. As in 2020, the levels of 2021 spending as a result of the ARP were guaranteed to exceed the generosity of the income support provided in the Great Recession. Consider that the ARP stimulus checks, SNAP expansions, and CTC expansions alone amounted to more than $500 billion, which was more than twice the average annual spending on income support in the Great Recession.[36]

Beyond the size of the 2021 intervention, there were important changes to the type of income support provided. The most important addition, the expanded CTC, had the potential to mark a historic turning point in the development of the American welfare state.

The Expanded Child Tax Credit
under the American Rescue Plan

Prior to the ARP's expansion of the Child Tax Credit, tax filers could receive a maximum CTC of $2,000 per child per year, but it was not fully refundable. Put differently, parents who were not working were excluded from the benefit altogether, and parents working at the lowest-wage jobs (or in part-time or inconsistent jobs) often did not receive the full benefit value of the CTC. As Sophie Collyer and her colleagues documented in 2019, one in three children in the United States lived in a family who did not receive the full benefit value of the CTC.[37] Children with a single parent, those living in a rural area, Black and Hispanic children, and those in a larger family were disproportionately ineligible for the full credit.[38]

The ARP transformed the CTC into a nearly universal child allowance in 2021. Specifically, the ARP included three fundamental changes to the CTC. First, it made the CTC available to almost all children—including those in the lowest-income families who had previously been excluded—by removing the earnings requirement and making the credit fully refundable. Second, it raised the maximum annual credit amounts to $3,000 for children ages six to seventeen and $3,600 for children under age six. Third, beginning in mid-July 2021, it delivered the credit in monthly installments of up to $250 per older child or up to $300 per younger child, for a period of six months.

The benefit increase was important, but the two most important changes were full refundability and the monthly benefit payments. Full refundability—the payment of benefits even to parents with little or no earnings in the prior year—marked a dramatic shift from the three-decade trend toward a more work-based welfare state.[39] The United States has been one of only a few high-income countries without a universal cash benefit for families with children, regardless of the employment status of the parents. As a result, the country has had high child poverty rates compared to other high-income countries, while the share of American children in families with very little cash income (excluding SNAP) has arguably increased.[40] The expansion of the CTC thus represented a historic deviation from the direction of the U.S. welfare state: for the first time, the United States had a child benefit that compared to that of its peer nations.

The monthly provision of benefits also marked a notable shift in policy. Prior to the ARP, refundable tax credits (the EITC and CTC) were paid out once a year in single, lump-sum payments to families after they filed their taxes. Though these benefits were counted as annual income equivalent to monthly cash payments, consumption data suggest that recipients spent the benefits differently than they would have if the benefits had been distributed evenly throughout the year: many chose to pay down debt and purchase durable items with this money rather than use it to pay for day-to-day expenses.[41]

With the rising benefit levels of these tax-based transfers, a larger share of income transfers to families with children were delivered only in a single month each year (usually in March or April), generating

Figure 4.4   Mean Share of Annual Income Transfers Distributed to Families in Once-per-Year Lump-Sum Payments, 1980–2019

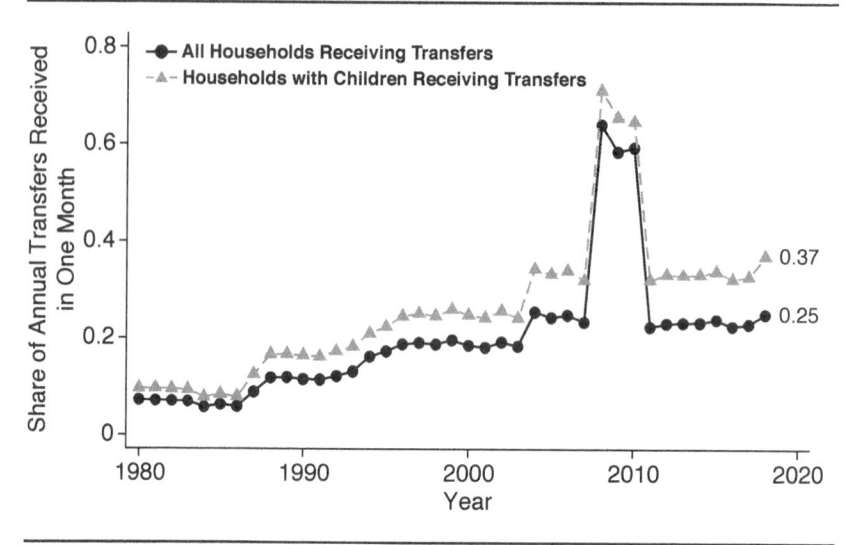

Source: Parolin, Curran, et al. 2022. Reprinted with permission.

Note: Indicator measures the share of lump sum transfers (EITC, CTC, and 2008 stimulus check) relative to all income transfers (including Social Security, TANF cash assistance, SNAP benefits, the value of subsidized school lunches, housing subsidies, UI benefits, SSI benefits, WIC benefits, and energy subsidies). The nonrefundable portion of CTC transfers is excluded. The increase during the period 2008 to 2011 is due to the distribution of onetime stimulus checks and temporary refundable tax credits as part of the ARRA of 2009. These payments covered individuals who did not receive other benefits throughout the year, providing them with a value of 100 percent and increasing the overall mean in these years.

high levels of income volatility and placing the burden on low-income families to try to use these benefits to smooth their consumption over the subsequent eleven months. Figure 4.4 documents the mean share of annual income transfers (primarily the EITC and CTC, though these transfers also included stimulus checks and temporary refundable tax credits during the Great Recession) distributed over time in the form of once-per-year lump-sum payments to households.

Prior to the introduction of the EITC in 1975, no transfers were delivered, by design, as once-per-year lump-sum payments. After 1975, however, the mean share of transfers received as a single payment steadily increased, owing to expansions to the EITC and the pre-ARP version of the CTC. By 2018, when federal legislation again increased the value of the CTC, lump-sum transfers accounted for 37 percent of total annual transfers to average recipients of any income support who lived in a household with children. Among all households, regardless of whether children were present, the mean was 25 percent. Put differently, the average household receiving income transfers received one-quarter of those transfers in a single month (generally February, March, or April) after filing taxes. The volatility of annual income transfers is likely to have increased during 2020, given the onetime stimulus check payments and the short-lived increases to the level of unemployment benefits.

For six months in 2021, by contrast, the vast majority of families in the United States received consistent, predictable payments of up to $300 per child each month. These payments, as I demonstrate in subsequent chapters, had a large effect on the ability of low-income families to make ends meet throughout the latter half of 2021.

The Accessibility of the ARP's Expanded Child Tax Credit Payments

As with the CARES Act's income supports, however, the expanded CTC came with an important caveat: not all eligible children would automatically receive the payments. Most families who did not file taxes in the prior year, presumably because their income was below the tax-filing threshold, had to register with the IRS in order to receive benefits. Several estimates suggest that the total number of children in eligible tax units was 64 to 67 million.[42] In July 2021, the IRS distributed the first CTC payments to tax units covering 59.3 million children.[43] This number increased slightly, to around 61 million, in subsequent months, but still fell well below the total of the full eligible population.

Of particular concern is that, once again, it was the lowest-income families who were most likely to miss out on the benefits. Figure 4.5 documents evidence on the share of families receiving the CTC payments between July and December 2021 by race/ethnicity and income level. The figure demonstrates that 66 percent of children were in households that reported receiving the initial CTC payment, according to data from the Pulse. This is equivalent to approximately 48 million children, or 12 million fewer than the IRS reports. The discrepancy could be due to a number of factors, such as sampling bias in the Pulse, benefit underreporting in the Pulse, the Treasury Department's overestimation of children served, or general measurement error. Nonetheless, the data share the same underlying point as the department's administrative reports: not all families with children actually received the benefit.

The distribution of those who did not receive the benefit is particularly concerning. The results by income bin (left panel of figure 4.5) suggest that

Figure 4.5 Share of Children in Families Receiving Monthly Child Tax Credit Payments, 2021

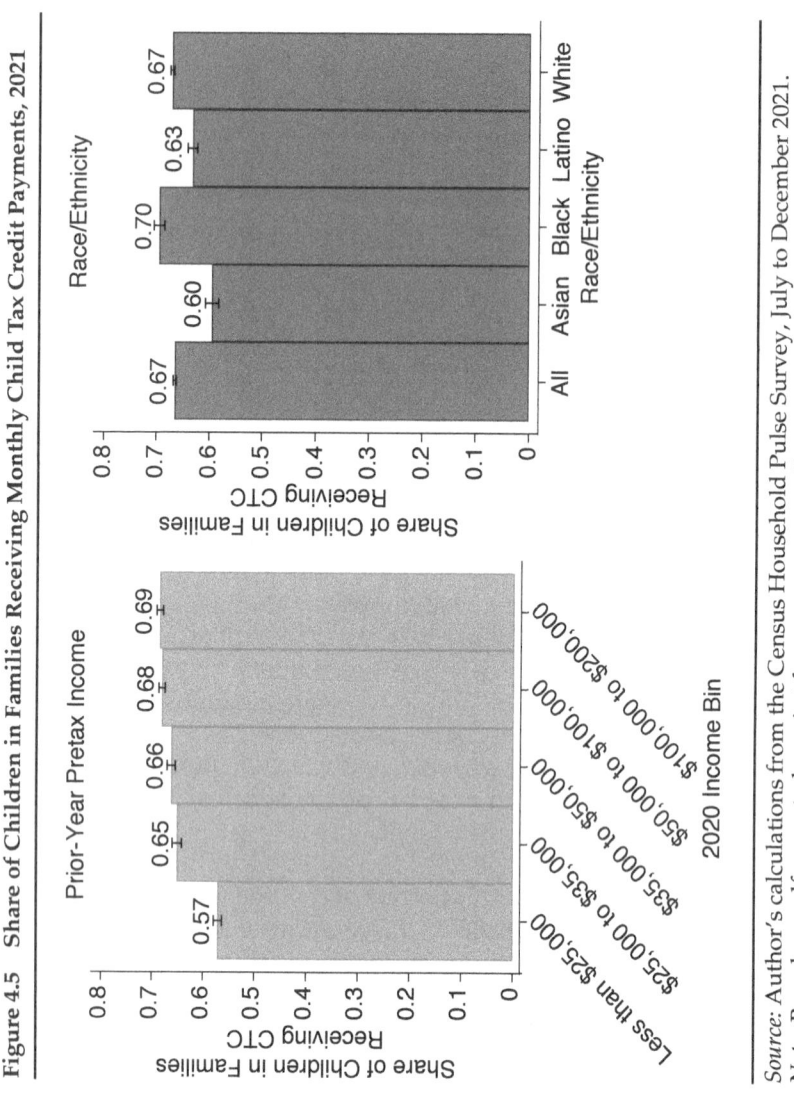

Source: Author's calculations from the Census Household Pulse Survey, July to December 2021.
Note: Based on self-reported receipt from responses to Census Household Pulse Survey. "Race/ethnicity" refers to that of the household head in which the child lives. Coverage rates are across the entire sample of households with children and are not limited to eligible households, as eligibility cannot be inferred with precision in the Pulse.

families with children and with pretax incomes below $25,000 were less likely than higher-income families to have received the benefit. According to the Pulse data, just over half (57 percent) of children in families with incomes under $25,000 received the first or second payment. Rates of (self-reported) receipt rose as incomes rose. Among families with earnings between $25,000 and $35,000, around two-thirds (65 percent) of children received the benefit. Among families with higher incomes, around 70 percent of children received the payment.

The right panel of the figure shows breakdowns by race/ethnicity. An estimated 60 percent of Asian children, 70 percent of Black children, 63 percent of Hispanic children, and 67 percent of White children received the monthly CTC payments in the second half of 2021. The low rates among Asian and Hispanic children stand out: four in ten children were in families who reported not having received the CTC payments. Although some of these families may have been ineligible to receive the CTC given their high income, the reality is that around 90 percent of families in the United States were eligible to receive the benefits, and the racial/ethnic disparities remain even when zooming in on low-income families in the data.

Increases to Food and Nutrition Support

The income support programs that this chapter has concentrated on so far are those that primarily distribute cash directly to adult recipients who can use it to consume any type of good or service they desire, whether that be diapers, food, bus tickets, or a haircut. An evaluation of COVID-era economic assistance, however, is incomplete without discussing enhancements of food and nutrition support.

Providing assistance in the form of nutrition support is a unique feature of the U.S. welfare state compared to other high-income countries. In nonpandemic years, for example, Supplemental Nutrition Assistance Program benefits are among the largest transfers to low-income families, and certainly larger than the sum of cash support from the TANF program. In 2019, SNAP benefits kept 2.5 million people out of SPM poverty, more than eight times the number of those kept out of poverty by cash support from TANF. (Despite being limited to food and nutrition items, SNAP benefits are generally treated as comparable to cash income in measures of family or household income.).[44]

SNAP plays a particularly important role in reducing poverty during economic downturns and is often made more generous during recessionary periods.[45] In the Great Recession, as noted before, the maximum value of SNAP benefits was increased by 15 percent, and caseloads steadily increased. Similarly, during the COVID-19 pandemic, maximum benefit values were upped by 15 percent in December 2020 as part of the Consolidated Appropriations Act. Additionally, states were given the authority to distribute the maximum benefit amount to all SNAP recipients, and most states chose to do so through the end of 2021. The rising benefit values, combined with increased demand for SNAP support and fewer caseload exits among SNAP recipients (thanks in part to temporary extensions to eligibility), contributed to strong increases in spending on SNAP benefits.[46]

The SNAP increases were coupled with the introduction of what became known as the Pandemic Electronic Benefits Transfer (P-EBT) payments, a program that supported families with children exposed to school closures and distance learning. Given that many school-age children relied on schools for their daily lunch and breakfast, the closure of schools threatened to increase food hardship among low-income families with children in particular. P-EBT benefits were delivered in the form of a preloaded debit card (or a top-up to the debit cards families already had) that could be spent on food and nutrition items. P-EBT benefit values ranged from $250 to $400 in the spring of 2020, depending on the state, and may have reached up to two-thirds of school-age children.[47]

The Implications for Poverty during the Pandemic

The large spike in unemployment in 2020 was met with a historic increase in income transfers. Through the CARES Act alone, the federal government exceeded the level of income transfers it provided during the Great Recession over the period from 2008 to 2012, as well as the amount of resources invested in all other direct (nonretirement) income transfers in 2020. The Biden administration then repeated this feat in 2021, ushering in a historic, though temporary, overhaul to the CTC, in addition to another stimulus check and more generous unemployment benefits.

The spending numbers alone point to the immense poverty reduction potential of these policy interventions. It would be hard for $900 billion in spending on direct income transfers in a single year to not affect poverty and hardship in some meaningful way, so long as the benefits were not all skewed toward the highest-income families. That said, the federal and state governments were not sufficiently prepared to distribute these income transfers: the IRS struggled to put stimulus checks in the pockets of the country's lowest-income families, while most state unemployment offices were deeply unprepared for the sudden spike in benefit applicants. Beyond the administrative burdens and bureaucratic complexities associated with the CARES Act, it cruelly excluded some of the country's most vulnerable residents from receiving benefits at all. Simultaneously, those who did receive benefits were often uncertain about when they would arrive, how long they would last, and how they would get by after the most generous support—the $600 per week top-up to unemployment benefits—ended in July 2020.

These two faces of the pandemic policy interventions—their enormity as well as their transience—had different implications for understanding poverty in the United States during the COVID-19 pandemic. As I detail in the next chapter, the sheer size of the ARP and the CARES Act had large impacts on poverty rates, but the two initiatives also challenged several principles underlying how we measure and track poverty trends in the first place.

Chapter 5

Tracking Poverty
in the Here and Now

WITH THE Coronavirus Aid, Relief, and Economic Security Act (CARES Act), the American Rescue Plan Act (ARP), and the expanded Child Tax Credit (CTC), the federal government confronted a historic increase in joblessness with a set of equally historic policy interventions. The new income transfers not only surpassed, by a large magnitude, those provided during the Great Recession but also were larger than spending on all other nonretirement transfers combined in 2020. The programs had their flaws, as discussed in chapter 4, but their potential to reduce poverty was nonetheless extraordinary.

This chapter documents the impact of these income transfers on poverty throughout 2020 and 2021. Revisiting the three perspectives on poverty outlined in chapter 1, the focus of this chapter (and the one that follows) is squarely on the second perspective: *understanding poverty as the immediate state of lacking adequate resources to meet basic needs*. Specifically, the goal of the next two chapters is to understand trends in households' economic well-being and to document the influence of the COVID-era income transfers on those trends. This chapter focuses on income-based poverty rates, while the next chapter looks at material hardship and mental health.

As discussed in chapter 1, the conventional approach to measuring poverty in the United States proved inadequate to measuring conditions during the COVID-19 pandemic. Official poverty estimates produce one measure of poverty per year, focus on annual incomes, and are released only after a considerable lag. Take, for example, the U.S. Census Bureau's official estimate of poverty. In 2020, the Census Bureau produced one estimate of the national Supplemental Poverty Measure (SPM) that captured households' incomes between January and December 2020 and did not release this poverty estimate until September 2021.

While there is no replacement for the quality of the Census Bureau's annual poverty estimates, there are some contexts in which the once-per-year measure of poverty is unfit for the moment. The COVID-19 pandemic was one of those contexts. To start, a household's income situation in January 2020 might have shared no resemblance to its income situation in April 2020, when the pandemic sent unemployment to a record high. Moreover, a household's income in May 2020 might have looked remarkably different from its situation in September 2020, when all of the CARES Act's income support had expired. The month-to-month volatility throughout 2020 limits the usefulness of a single poverty measure that captures income over the entire year. Additionally, the Census Bureau's long delay in reporting 2020 estimates of poverty, which were not released until September 2021, prevented policymakers and the general public from understanding the economic well-being of households across the country in real time.

With these limitations of conventional measures of poverty in mind, this chapter has three aims. First, I discuss the advantages and disadvantages of a shorter income accounting period and a timelier release of poverty estimates. The primary advantages are that, particularly in contexts of rapid economic change, a *monthly* measure of poverty can better track the intrayear volatility of poverty experienced by many households, as well as provide real-time data on the economic conditions of households across the country. But there are also some shortcomings to a one-month income accounting period, as well as moments when a monthly measure of poverty may be less useful.

Second, I present a framework for producing a monthly measure of poverty based on work I have led in collaboration with Jordan Matsudaira, Megan Curran, Christopher Wimer, and Jane Waldfogel from Columbia University.[1] As a third aim, this chapter documents monthly poverty rates throughout 2020 and 2021, as well as annual poverty rates across these years, for the full U.S. population and various subgroups. Particular focus is given to the influence of government-provided transfers—especially those introduced during the pandemic—on levels and trends in poverty.

I should emphasize up front that the monthly poverty measure featured in this chapter is best understood as a supplement to, rather than a substitute for, annual measures of poverty. The monthly poverty measure is more likely to add value in contexts of rapid economic, labor market, or policy change, but to add less value over the annual measure in more stable years. Moreover, there are some purposes that only the annual measure of poverty can meet. How does the U.S. poverty rate compare to the rates of other countries? How does the 2020 or 2021 U.S. poverty rate compare to that of 1967? What was a household's general consumption capability over the course of a year? For these types of questions and more, the standard measure of annual poverty is uniquely

Table 5.1   **Differences between the Standard Measure of Poverty and the Monthly Measure of Poverty**

	Standard Measure of Poverty of U.S. Census Bureau	Monthly Poverty Measure of Parolin, Curran, et al. 2022
How often is poverty measured?	Once per year	Once per month
Over which months do we measure a family unit's income?	Income received over the twelve-month calendar year	Income received in the given month
How quickly is the estimate of poverty released to the public?	Nine months after the end of the calendar year (for example, the 2020 poverty estimate was released in September 2021)	Two weeks after the end of the month (for example, the January 2021 poverty estimate was released in mid-February 2021)
What counts as income?	Pretax/transfer income plus all taxes and transfers from the prior year	Pretax/transfer income plus all taxes and transfers, including those from new or altered income support programs
Which data sources are used?	Current Population Survey Annual Social and Economic Supplement (CPS ASEC)	CPS ASEC and CPS Basic Monthly files

Source: Author's compilation.
Note: "Pretax/transfer income" includes all resources other than government transfers and taxes, especially earnings from employment. The income definitions follow the Supplemental Poverty Measure.

valuable. This chapter thus presents evidence for both the monthly and annual measures of poverty.

Table 5.1 recaps the primary differences between the Census Bureau's annual estimate of poverty and the monthly measure of poverty. The monthly estimates of poverty presented in this chapter differ from the standard approach in that they (1) measure poverty once per month rather than once per year; (2) measure income received in a single month rather than over a twelve-month period; (3) can be released relatively quickly; and (4) can incorporate the introduction of, or changes to, income support programs such as the CARES Act, the ARP, and the CTC.

The Advantages and Disadvantages of a Monthly Poverty Measure

A primary advantage of a monthly poverty measure is that it may more accurately represent the level of economic insecurity that a household faces throughout the year. This advantage is especially important in contexts such as the COVID-19 pandemic and also for lower-income households, which may not have the resources (or access to debt or liquid assets) to smooth consumption over longer periods of unemployment or income loss.[2]

The late Tony Atkinson made a similar argument in his final book, where he wrote that the choice between a monthly estimate of poverty and an annual one depends on "the assumptions made about the effect of short-term fluctuations on the economic well-being of individuals and households."[3] If transitory declines in income tend to contribute to higher rates of hardship or lower levels of well-being, then an accounting period of less than a year may be warranted. A 1976 report on "The Measure of Poverty" from the U.S. Department of Health, Education, and Welfare's Poverty Studies Task Force agreed: whether poverty is measured over "a week, month, year or lifetime, depends on the particular purpose the definition of poverty is meant to serve . . . for designing programs which deal with emergencies or temporary low income, like temporary unemployment, a shorter accounting period is more appropriate."[4]

Sufficiently high rates of intrayear variability of incomes do warrant a shorter accounting period for poverty measurement as a supplement to the standard annual measure.[5] As documented in chapter 4, the U.S. welfare state has been a strong source of income variability, not only during the COVID-19 pandemic but also for decades prior given the once-per-year payments from the Earned Income Tax Credit (EITC) and Child Tax Credit (CTC).

Aside from the welfare state, the labor market is another source of intrayear volatility. Recent scholarship focusing on month-to-month volatility has found that lower-income individuals face particularly high rates of volatility—the earnings or income they receive in one month might be very different from their earnings or income the next month. Lower-income households tend to experience several months throughout the year when their monthly income is at least 25 percent lower than their annual average monthly income.[6] Similarly, Neil Bania and Laura Leete as well as Pamela Morris and her colleagues find that intrayear income volatility is high and rising among lower-income families with children.[7] Focusing on working hours rather than incomes, Joe LaBriola and Daniel Schneider find that low-educated workers experience high and rising rates of volatility in work hours relative to higher-educated workers.[8] In short, studies using different data sources, measures of volatility, outcome variables, and temporal scopes have concurred that households at higher risk of poverty are particularly likely to face higher levels of income volatility. For these households, a focus on annual income may misrepresent the intrayear volatility of their experience with poverty.

Agreeing on the merits of a sub-annual poverty measure leads to a natural follow-up question: Over how many months should we evaluate a household's income to determine if it is in poverty or not? We could make a case for a six-month, four-month, or two-month (and so on) accounting period with evidence that many low-income households can smooth consumption over multiple months, even if not over the entire year. This is a fair argument, but practical considerations lead us to settle on a one-month accounting period, which, unlike a four-month accounting period or another of similar length, can be produced using available, timely survey data and is consistent with the focus of past research on the intrayear volatility of earnings and incomes. Moreover, a one-month accounting period, by providing a monthly measure of poverty based on the income a household's members receive *in the given month*, offers an appropriate contrast (and supplement) to the traditional poverty measures based on a twelve-month accounting period.

There are conceptual shortcomings of a monthly poverty measure, however, that deserve elaboration. In certain contexts, a monthly measure of poverty may understate a household's ability to smooth consumption across months. In other words, a household experiencing a temporary loss of income may be able to maintain its normal consumption habits if it has built up savings in prior months or years. In the event of a large income loss (through the loss of a job, for example), households with more savings or wealth (or with greater ability to debt-finance their consumption) are more likely to maintain their standard consumption behavior despite having a low monthly income.[9] Therefore, a measure of monthly resources is likely to be less useful for households with high levels of savings or liquid assets, particularly if the resources used to smooth consumption are not in the form of interest, dividends, and rent, each of which is included in the resource measure used to determine poverty status.

In contrast, households with low levels of assets or savings engage in substantially less consumption smoothing after a job loss. When the members of a low-wealth household experience an income loss, they are less likely to be able to maintain their normal consumption habits relative to a high-wealth household experiencing income loss.[10] Consider that nearly half of U.S. residents, and more than half of Black residents, claim that they do not have money set aside to use for unexpected expenses or emergencies.[11] Low-income households not only have less wealth but also experience reduced access to credit cards and other ways to debt-finance their consumption.

The example given here focuses on consumption after income loss, but a focus on income received in a single month may also understate a household's consumption capabilities in the subsequent month or more after a large income *gain*. The onetime EITC payment, for example, provided around $2,500 to the average recipient in 2018.[12] Evidence suggests that the EITC modestly improves the ability of single mothers to maintain stable consumption across months.[13] Households receiving the EITC often use the payments to cover debt and outstanding expenses or to purchase durable goods (such as cars); they use it to build savings less frequently.[14] The lowest-income households are the least likely to keep the EITC intact for future needs.[15] Still, many households do see increases in consumption for multiple months after EITC receipt.[16] Thus, attributing the entire benefit value to a single month's resources, as our measure of monthly poverty does, is likely to understate many households' abilities to smooth their consumption of EITC benefits.

Ultimately, whether monthly poverty is strongly associated with monthly trends in consumption is a question we can answer with data. Later I demonstrate that the monthly measures of poverty better correspond with monthly variation in food hardship, housing hardship, and mental health relative to employment rates or other measures of poverty. In short, a measure of monthly poverty probably understates the ability of many households to smooth consumption across months, particularly high-wealth households and particularly in the initial months following large income transfers. For most months and most low-income households, however, the monthly poverty measure offers a useful supplement to an annual measure of poverty, and several validation tests corroborate this claim.

The Timeliness of Poverty Estimates

A final challenge relates to the timeliness of publicly provided poverty estimates. A particularly useful measure of monthly poverty, especially during crises such as the COVID-19 pandemic, is one that can be produced and made public in (close to) real time. The central challenge in providing more timely estimates of poverty is capturing month-to-month changes in demographic, labor market, and social policy conditions. If a framework for projecting monthly poverty rates is to be useful, it should, as much as possible, be able to account for new or altered income support programs introduced in prior months and to evaluate the effect of these programs on monthly poverty rates. The monthly poverty measure presented is able to incorporate these new income transfers with a short lag time.

A Few Words on Methods

To avoid turning this chapter into a dense description of methodology, I provide only a brief overview of the technical process for producing our monthly measures of poverty. Readers who want to get into the weeds of the methods can visit the appendix to this chapter or, even better, the underlying paper.[17]

Our framework uses two sources of data from the Current Population Survey: the Annual Social and Economic Supplement (ASEC) and the Basic Monthly files. The ASEC is released only once per year, but it features all the necessary income and poverty data to identify family units in poverty. The monthly files do not have the same income and poverty information but do feature more timely information on demographic characteristics and employment rates to project monthly updates of poverty. We construct our monthly poverty measure in the ASEC file. In doing so, we use the same components as in the annual SPM framework, but we convert each annual value into an estimated monthly value.

For our 2020 and 2021 projections, we include payments from CARES Act income transfers and subsequent COVID-related relief programs, such as the expanded Child Tax Credit from July 2021. The COVID-related income relief must be simulated within the ASEC data. When simulating income transfers such as the CARES Act's stimulus checks and unemployment benefits within our data, we closely follow administrative records on the number of beneficiaries for each program. For the stimulus checks, for example, we match Department of Treasury data on the timing and count of the stimulus checks distributed. For unemployment benefits, we match Department of Labor estimates of the number of beneficiaries in each state and month, matching also by the racial/ethnic and gender composition of beneficiaries in the states.

With the new measure of income in our ASEC file that takes into account current taxes and transfers, we create our measure of monthly poverty (monthly income relative to one-twelfth the annual poverty threshold). We then take what we know about the relationship between poverty and a full set of individual characteristics from our ASEC data (after bringing in our new income transfers), and we export the conditional likelihood of poverty to our monthly CPS file. Doing so provides us with an estimate of monthly poverty for each individual observed in each month of the data. The appendix to this chapter provides more detail on each step.

There are limitations to this methodology. In addition to the standard survey error present in all estimates of poverty, the procedure for estimating monthly poverty rates may generate three other sources of error. First, our process of converting annual income components to monthly income requires assumptions about how, for example, an individual's annual earnings are spread throughout the year. For individuals who are currently unemployed, we can reasonably estimate their earnings in the given month (often zero), but for those who are not we are forced to rely on an assumption that they earn one-twelfth of their annual earnings evenly across each month. Second, our simulation of new income transfers into the ASEC file is surely imperfect. Although we match administrative records to the extent possible in allocating new benefits in our sample, there is undoubtedly some simulation error in both the receipt level and benefit level of some income transfer simulations. Third, our imputation of poverty rates from the ASEC to monthly files relies on an assumption that the association of poverty with a set of observable characteristics does not change meaningfully over time. One example of when this assumption does not hold is when wages for a worker in a certain low-pay occupation (and with a set of other observable characteristics) grow faster than wages in other occupations, causing us to overstate the likelihood of poverty for households that include a person in that occupation.

Are Our Measurements Meaningful?

Given the number of technical procedures needed to create this monthly poverty measure, as well as the limitations in creating it, it is reasonable to question whether the measure is truly useful and whether it expands our knowledge beyond other indicators of economic well-being, such as employment rates.

A number of validation tests confirm the accuracy of our estimation procedure in producing reliable estimates of monthly poverty. We have shown in prior work that our framework matches monthly estimates of poverty from previous years of the Survey of Income and Program Participation (SIPP), including by racial/ethnic group. Moreover, the simulations of CARES Act benefits match several external benchmarks, such as administrative records from the IRS on how many stimulus checks were distributed.

Here I focus on a set of validation tests that might be particularly salient to readers: How does our measure of monthly poverty align with month-to-month trends in hardship and well-being? I present evidence at the national level—as well as for various subgroups—that our monthly measure of poverty outperforms a number of other indicators, including trends in employment, in aligning with trends in hardship.

Figure 5.1 compares trends in national monthly SPM rates (indexed to their values in April 2020) versus trends in food insufficiency (left panel)

Figure 5.1   Trends in the National Rate of Monthly Poverty Compared to Food and Housing Hardship, 2020–2022

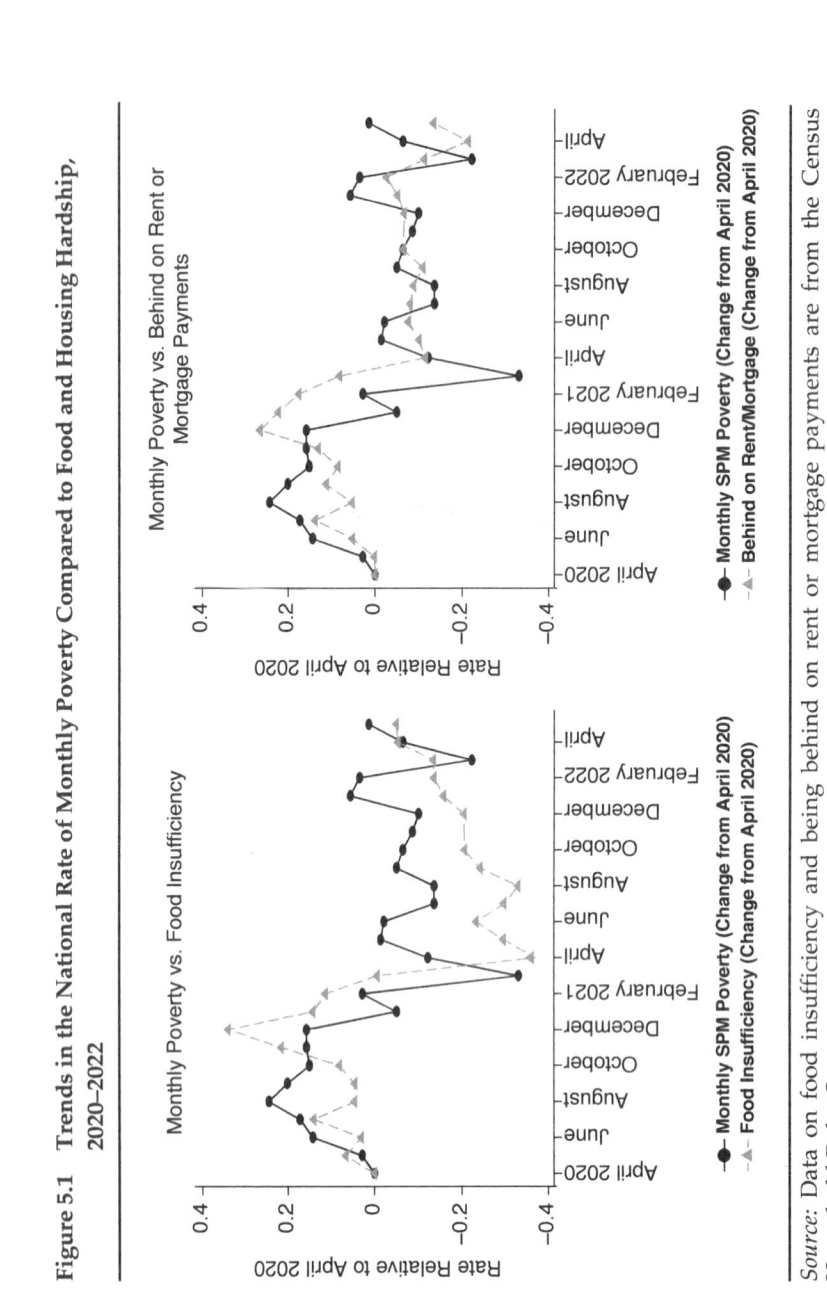

Source: Data on food insufficiency and being behind on rent or mortgage payments are from the Census Household Pulse Survey.

Note: The correlations are $r = 0.58$ for monthly poverty and food insufficiency, and $r = 0.48$ for monthly poverty and being behind on rent or mortgage payments. See subgroup analyses in subsequent tables and figures. The sharp declines in poverty in March of each year are due to the provision of refundable tax credits during these months.

and being behind on rent or mortgage payments (right panel). The two hardship measures are from the Census Household Pulse Survey (Pulse), which was introduced in April 2020 to collect regular estimates of material hardship, economic insecurity, and other indicators. The figure shows that trends in monthly poverty and the hardship measures generally evolve in the same direction. In early 2021, for example, stimulus checks and refundable tax credits pushed down the monthly poverty rates, and they also pushed down levels of food insufficiency and housing hardship. The monthly poverty rates ebbed and flowed as the monthly Child Tax Credit payments were distributed in July 2021, and when the $300 per week unemployment benefit supplements expired in September 2021, trends in the hardship measures generally followed. (Subsequent figures look in more detail at changes in poverty after these policy changes.) Overall, the monthly trends in poverty correlate relatively strongly with trends in food insufficiency ($r = 0.58$) and trends in falling behind on rent or mortgage payments ($r = 0.48$). How do these correlations compare to other indicators of interest, and how do they vary by subgroup? Table 5.2 provides evidence on these questions.

Specifically, table 5.2 provides correlation coefficients for three hardship indicators (food insufficiency, being behind on rent, and facing difficulty with expenses) with three economic indicators (the monthly poverty rate, a version of the monthly poverty rate before COVID-era taxes and transfers are included, and the group's non-employment rate). A larger number indicates a stronger relationship, on average, with a value of 1 indicating that changes in the poverty and hardship indicators are perfectly correlated. I present these relationships for five main subgroups of interest: White, Black, and Hispanic individuals; respondents with children; and adults ages sixty-five or older.

The first of these measures—rates of monthly poverty with all COVID-related transfers included—generally features the strongest relationship across each of the hardship indicators. Within-group variation in this measure of poverty aligns with variation in food insufficiency, for example, better than measures of poverty without COVID-era transfers or the employment rate. That better measures of poverty result from including the COVID-related transfers demonstrates that we must take into account the CARES Act, the ARP, and the other large policy interventions when attempting to understand how households across the country fared, at least economically, throughout the COVID-19 pandemic.

There are some notable differences across groups and indicators worth mentioning. Among older adults, each of the economic indicators more weakly predicts patterns of hardship compared to the relationships for the

Table 5.2   Correlation of Monthly Poverty Rates with Hardship Outcomes, by Race/Ethnicity, Age, and Children in the Household, April 2020 to May 2022

	Monthly SPM Poverty	Monthly SPM Poverty without COVID-19 Income Support	Group-Specific Non-Employment Rate
All individuals			
Food insufficiency	0.58	0.42	0.42
Behind on rent	0.48	0.48	0.43
Difficulty with expenses	0.35	−0.01	0.08
White individuals			
Food insufficiency	0.57	0.36	0.25
Behind on rent	0.44	0.53	0.44
Difficulty with expenses	0.31	−0.10	−0.11
Black individuals			
Food insufficiency	0.58	0.46	0.60
Behind on rent	0.50	0.60	0.47
Difficulty with expenses	0.51	0.25	0.30
Hispanic individuals			
Food insufficiency	0.54	0.34	0.42
Behind on rent	0.42	0.38	0.37
Difficulty with expenses	0.36	0.08	0.35
Children/respondents with children[a]			
Food insufficiency	0.63	0.38	0.50
Behind on rent	0.54	0.49	0.49
Difficulty with expenses	0.45	0.01	0.13
Age sixty-five or older			
Food insufficiency	0.33	0.05	−0.18
Behind on rent	0.18	−0.20	−0.49
Difficulty with expenses	0.02	−0.13	0.15
Mean, all groups and indicators	0.43	0.24	0.26

Source: Hardship and mental health data are from the Census Household Pulse Survey. Non-employment rates (1 minus the employment rate) are from the Current Population Survey and are calculated for the eighteen- to sixty-four-year-old populations in each group.

Note: Values represent the correlation of group-specific monthly poverty rates with group-specific hardship outcomes by group over the period April 2020 to May 2022 (*n* = 26 months per group).

[a] The poverty measures estimate child poverty rates, while the Pulse provides hardship outcomes (and the CPS for non-employment rates) for adults with children present in the home.

other subgroups examined, most likely for two related reasons: monthly variation in hardship was smaller for retirement-age adults than for other age groups, and retirement-age adults benefit from Social Security payments, which are included in both the poverty measures tested in table 5.2. Additionally, Black respondents are the only subgroup for whom employment trends rival trends in the monthly SPM poverty rate in aligning with food insufficiency, with both featuring strong correlations (0.58 and 0.60, respectively).

Some readers may be familiar with a separate monthly measure of poverty introduced by the work of Jeehoon Han, Bruce Meyer, and James Sullivan.[18] Their measure, unlike ours, is inversely aligned with monthly trends in hardship for most subgroups, particularly for Black adults, primarily because it does not adopt a full measure of household income. Specifically, replications of their measure demonstrate that the exclusion of CTC benefits from their measure of income strongly weakens the validity of their poverty measure.[19]

As one final validation test, we can assess the extent to which monthly poverty rates tend to accurately capture between-state variation in hardship or well-being. The answer, as presented in this chapter's appendix, is a clear yes: cross-state patterns of monthly poverty during 2020 and 2021 overlapped strongly with cross-state patterns in material hardship (and also in mental health outcomes). States with higher means of monthly poverty rates in 2020 and 2021 also tended to feature higher rates of food insufficiency ($r = 0.64$), missed rent or mortgage payments ($r = 0.75$), frequent anxiety ($r = 0.48$), feeling down ($r = 0.52$), lack of interest ($r = 0.59$), and frequent worrying ($r = 0.61$).

Trends in Monthly Poverty

With the conceptual case for a monthly poverty measure, as well as its construction, sufficiently covered, we can now turn to the observed trends in monthly poverty. I first present trends in the monthly SPM poverty rate for 2019—before the arrival of the COVID-19 pandemic—to illustrate the "typical" month-to-month variation in poverty rates revealed by our framework. I then show estimates of monthly poverty throughout 2020 and 2021—the years after the onset of COVID-19.

Figure 5.2 displays monthly poverty rates for each month in 2019 for the full population. The solid black line with circles includes all taxes and transfers, whereas the dashed gray line with triangles represents the pretax/transfer measure (a measure of poverty that excludes government taxes and transfers, compared to a post-tax/transfer measure that includes government taxes and transfers). In January 2019, 30.2 percent of all individuals lived with pretax/transfer incomes below the monthly

Figure 5.2 Trends in Monthly SPM Poverty in 2019

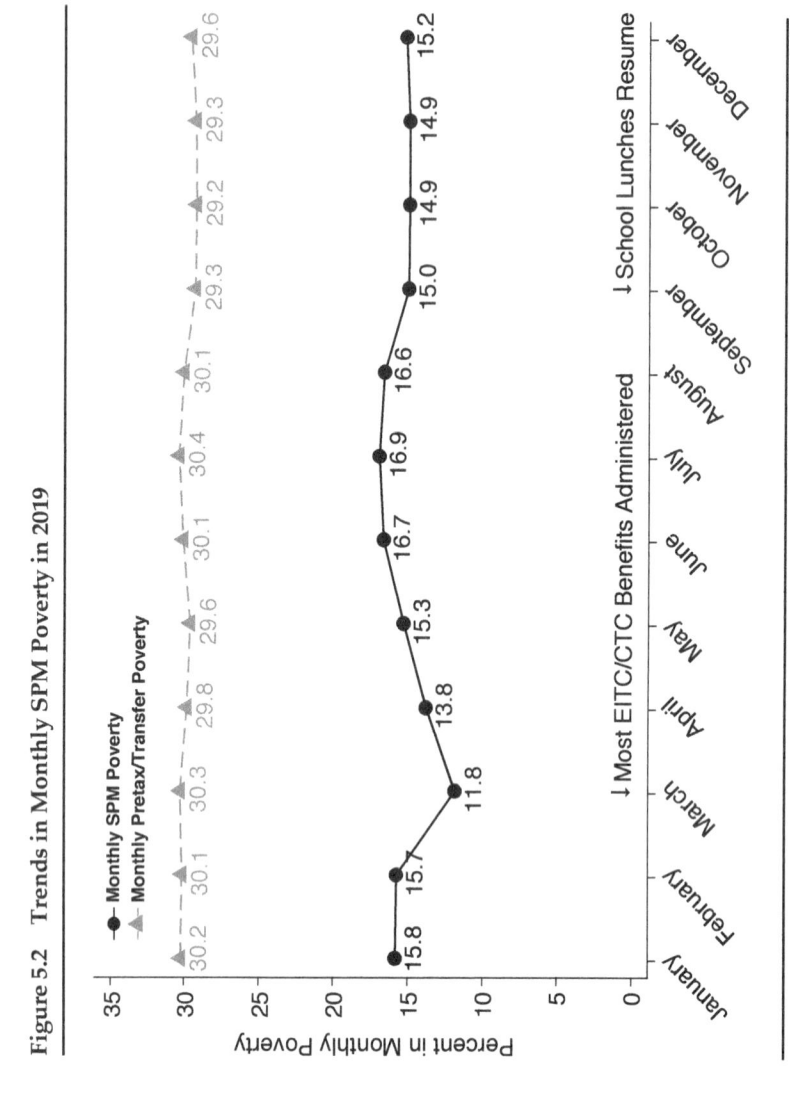

Source: Parolin, Curran, et al. 2022. Reprinted with permission.

poverty threshold, and 15.8 percent lived below this threshold when accounting for taxes and transfers. In March, a month when a large share of refundable tax credits were distributed, the monthly poverty rate fell to 11.8 percent, its lowest value of the year. April remained low compared to other months (13.8 percent) for similar reasons. By December 2019, the monthly poverty rate had fallen to 15.3 percent, slightly lower than the January 2019 rate. This decline can largely be attributed to the decline in the pretax/transfer poverty rate, which fell to 29.6 percent in December 2019. To put these rates into concrete numbers, we can say that around 51.7 million individuals across the United States lived in poverty in January 2019, though this number had declined to 49.7 million by December 2019. In the meantime, the count reached as low as 39.2 million in March 2019, but rose to as high as 55.2 million in July 2019.

Trends in Monthly Poverty in 2020 and 2021

Figure 5.3 turns toward estimates of monthly poverty throughout 2020 and 2021. Unlike figure 5.2, figure 5.3 features three lines running across each month: a pretax/transfer measure of poverty (dashed line with circles at the top); a measure of poverty that incorporates all taxes and transfers except for the COVID-related relief, such as transfers from the CARES Act and the ARP (middle line); and a monthly measure of poverty that includes all taxes/transfers, including COVID-related relief (bottom line).

In January and February 2020, the monthly poverty rate was similar to where it ended in 2019, at around 15 percent (or 50 million people in poverty). The COVID-19 pandemic began to affect employment rates in March 2020, though its largest consequences for employment rates came in April. Recall from chapter 3 that the April 2020 unemployment rate increased to around 15 percent (or up to 19 percent when accounting for misclassification errors).

Figure 5.3 shows that the pretax/transfer poverty rate climbed to 37.5 percent in April 2020 (the highest rate on record). In the same month, the monthly poverty rate that includes pre-pandemic income transfers but excludes the CARES Act (middle line in figure 5.3) likewise increased—from 15.5 percent in January to 19.9 percent in May 2020. Accounting for the CARES Act income transfers (the stimulus checks and the expanded unemployment benefits), however, changes the story. From January to April 2020, the monthly poverty rate accounting for all transfers actually *declined*, from 15.5 percent to 13.9 percent (bottom line of figure 5.3). To emphasize: despite a record-high rate of unemployment and a record-high pretax/transfer poverty rate, the monthly poverty rate when accounting for the CARES Act in April 2020 was *lower* than it was

Figure 5.3 Trends in Monthly SPM Poverty Rates in 2020 and 2021

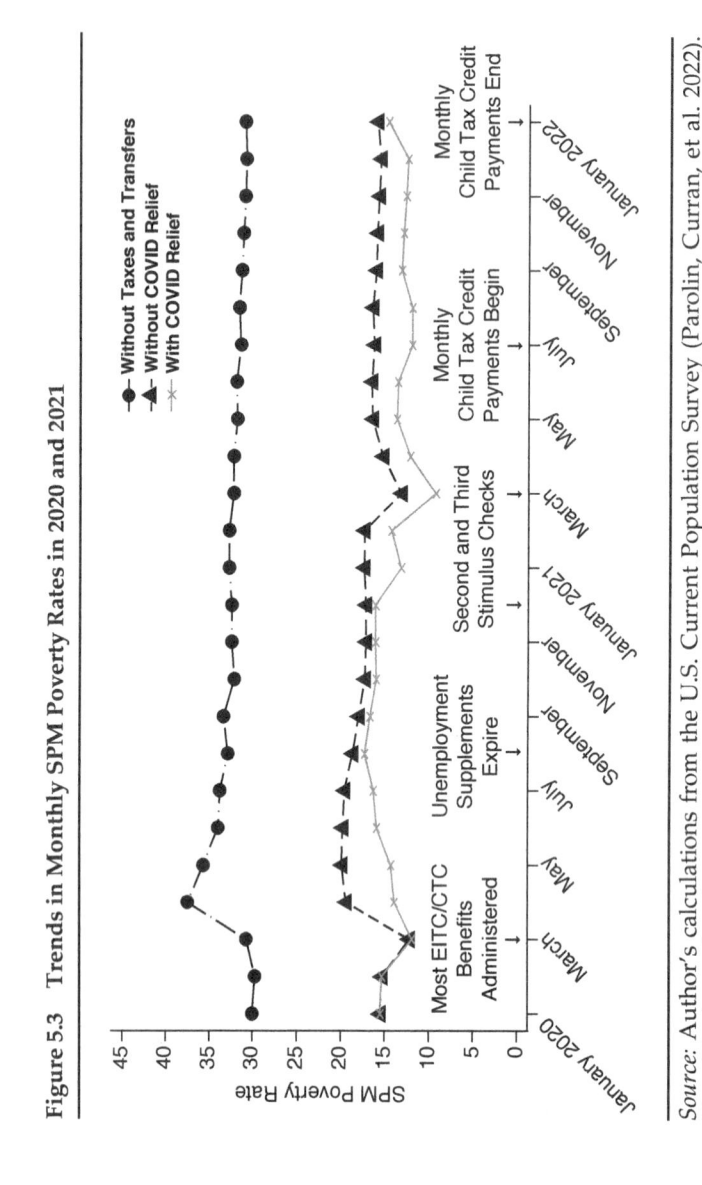

Source: Author's calculations from the U.S. Current Population Survey (Parolin, Curran, et al. 2022). *Note:* The large distribution of EITC benefits in March largely accounts for the observed drop in that month. Prior to accounting for the EITC, the pre-CARES monthly SPM rate was 16.1 percent in March 2020 and 21.4 percent in April 2020. The CARES Act's Economic Impact Payments and expanded unemployment benefits account for the declines from April through July 2020, when the Pandemic Emergency Unemployment Compensation expired. Pandemic Unemployment Assistance primarily accounts for the declines from August through December 2020. Stimulus checks provided in March 2021 and the expanded Child Tax Credit introduced in July 2021 contributed to declines in poverty in those months.

before the pandemic. In April 2020 alone, CARES Act transfers reduced the poverty rate by around 5.6 percentage points; in other words, around 18 million individuals were lifted out of poverty in April 2020.

In May 2020, the poverty rate remained lower than pre-crisis levels, thanks to the continuation of the $600 per week Pandemic Unemployment Compensation (PUC) supplement and to the receipt by some families of their stimulus checks during this month.

In June and July 2020, however, the post–CARES Act poverty rates began to rise relative to the levels in April and May. In June 2020, the monthly poverty rate with COVID relief taken into account had climbed to 15.9 percent, which was higher than the pre-pandemic rates observed in January and February 2020. The reduced poverty reduction effect of the CARES Act during this month is largely attributed to the fact that most of the stimulus checks had been distributed by this time. Thus, the early summer poverty rates climbed to higher than pre-crisis levels, even when taking the CARES Act's $600 per week unemployment supplement into account.

Rising employment rates contributed to a decline in the pre-CARES poverty rate from July to August 2020, but the post–CARES Act poverty rate nonetheless increased to 17.3 percent in August 2020 after the expiration of the $600 per week unemployment supplement at the end of July. Notably, this poverty rate was higher than the rates observed prior to the pandemic, and notably higher than the levels observed in April and May 2020. In August 2020, the CARES Act contributed only 1.4 percentage points to a reduction in the monthly poverty rate, primarily through the CARES Act's expansion of unemployment benefits (the Pandemic Unemployment Assistance program) to individuals who might not have qualified in the past. Put differently, the CARES Act lifted only around 4 million individuals out of poverty in August, down from 18 million in April 2020. Thus, while the combination of the stimulus checks and the $600 per week unemployment supplements blunted the rise in poverty in April and May 2020, their expiration subsequently contributed to a rise in poverty throughout the summer and autumn.

The slight recovery in employment rates throughout the remainder of 2020 contributed to steadily declining poverty rates from the level observed in August. At the end of 2020, the monthly poverty rate sat at 16.1 percent, representing around 53 million individuals in poverty. Thus, 3 million more people lived in poverty in December 2020 than in the previous February, just before COVID-19 made its mark, and around 9 million more people lived in poverty in December 2020 than in April of that year, when millions more adults were unemployed.

The policy and political changes at the end of 2020 promised to make 2021 just as eventful from a social policy perspective. The outgoing

Trump administration passed a second round of stimulus checks before departing, while the Biden administration introduced the American Rescue Plan and a new round of social spending. A third set of stimulus checks, a $300 federal supplement to weekly unemployment benefits, and the introduction of the monthly CTC payments in July 2021 further contributed to declines in poverty.

From December 2020 to January 2021, the monthly poverty rate fell from 16.1 percent to 13.2 percent, a decline driven by the second round of stimulus check payments. For context, 13.2 percent was an even lower rate than that observed in April 2020, as the stimulus check payments came on top of a pretax/transfer poverty rate (32.8 percent) that was nearly five percentage points lower than that of April 2020.

In March 2021, the rate fell yet again, this time to 9.3 percent—the lowest monthly poverty rate on record. March is always a peculiar time from a monthly poverty perspective, as once-per-year refundable tax credits are largely paid out in this month, leading to the temporary dips that are clearly visible in figure 5.3. In March 2021, however, the refundable tax credits were paired with the first of the ARP payments, including the third stimulus check payments and the $300 per week unemployment benefit bonuses. In March 2021, the ARP assistance cut the poverty rate by four percentage points (13 million people moved out of poverty), on top of the strong poverty reduction effects of the EITC and other tax credits.

The rates increased slightly in April, May, and June 2021, after the effects of the stimulus checks faded away. Yet the expanded unemployment benefits and SNAP benefit upgrades still made notable dents in the poverty rate: in June 2021, the monthly poverty rate, at 13.6 percent, was three percentage points lower than it would have been without the ARP support.

After the first monthly CTC payment in July 2021, however, the monthly poverty rate dropped to 12 percent, despite the fact that not all low-income families with children received the payment. To contextualize this rate, a 12 percent poverty rate in July 2021 was 4.3 percentage points lower than the poverty rate one year earlier, in July 2020. Moreover, the 12 percent poverty rate was lower than it had been in almost every month in 2020, with the slight exception of March 2020 (11.9 percent). What's more, the declines in poverty were relatively stable, for the most part, across months. In September 2021, the poverty rate ticked up slightly, to 13.2 percent, after the $300 unemployment supplement expired. Nonetheless, this level was lower than that observed prior to the onset of the COVID-19 pandemic, and poverty rates from October through December never climbed above 13 percent. In December 2021—at the close of the second year of the COVID-19 pandemic—the monthly poverty rate sat at 12.5 percent, a full three percentage points lower than the monthly poverty rate in January 2020. The monthly CTC payments ceased that month, however, and poverty increased to 15 percent in January 2022.

Trends by Race and Ethnicity

Despite the American welfare state's remarkable contributions to reducing poverty in 2020 and 2021, racial and ethnic gaps in poverty largely persisted. To be sure, all racial/ethnic groups benefited greatly from the CARES Act, the ARP, and the expanded CTC. Nevertheless, the persistent disparities despite this once-in-a-generation increase in social spending demonstrate just how entrenched these inequalities are in the United States. Figure 5.4 documents trends in post-tax/transfer poverty rates by race/ethnicity throughout 2020 and 2021. The lines for each racial/ethnic group show the poverty rate trends after CARES Act and ARP benefit distributions as well as all other transfers.

In January 2020, the monthly poverty rate for both Black and Hispanic individuals was just under 24 percent. Asian individuals had a poverty rate around 15 percent, and White individuals had the lowest rate of all groups: 11.2 percent. Black and Hispanic individuals were more than twice as likely as White individuals to live in poverty at the start of 2020, and this remained the case throughout 2020, with the exception of only one month, March. Notably, this is the month that sees the distribution of the majority of EITC benefits, which predominantly affect the incomes of low-wage workers (who, as we saw in chapter 3, are disproportionately likely to be Black or Hispanic).

Meanwhile, any progress gained from reducing monthly poverty rates for Black and Hispanic workers during the peak effectiveness of the CARES Act had faded by the end of 2020. In December 2020, the monthly poverty rate for Black individuals was 24.5 percent, 0.7 percentage points higher than the pre-pandemic January 2020 rate. In the same month, 25.3 percent of Hispanic individuals were in poverty, 1.6 percentage points higher than their January 2020 rate. White individuals, meanwhile, saw an increase of only 0.2 percentage points, rising from 11.2 to 11.4 percent from January to December 2020. Thus, despite the CARES Act's early success in reducing poverty, one in four Black and Hispanic residents lived in poverty at the end of 2020—more than twice the rate of White residents.

In 2021, the ARP again reduced poverty rates for all racial/ethnic groups, and with more consistency than the CARES Act in 2020. The expansion of the CTC in July 2021 was also particularly beneficial for Black and Hispanic individuals. By the end of the year, with the CTC expansion in place, the

Figure 5.4 Trends in Monthly SPM Poverty Rates (Post-tax/Transfer), by Race/Ethnicity, in 2020 and 2021

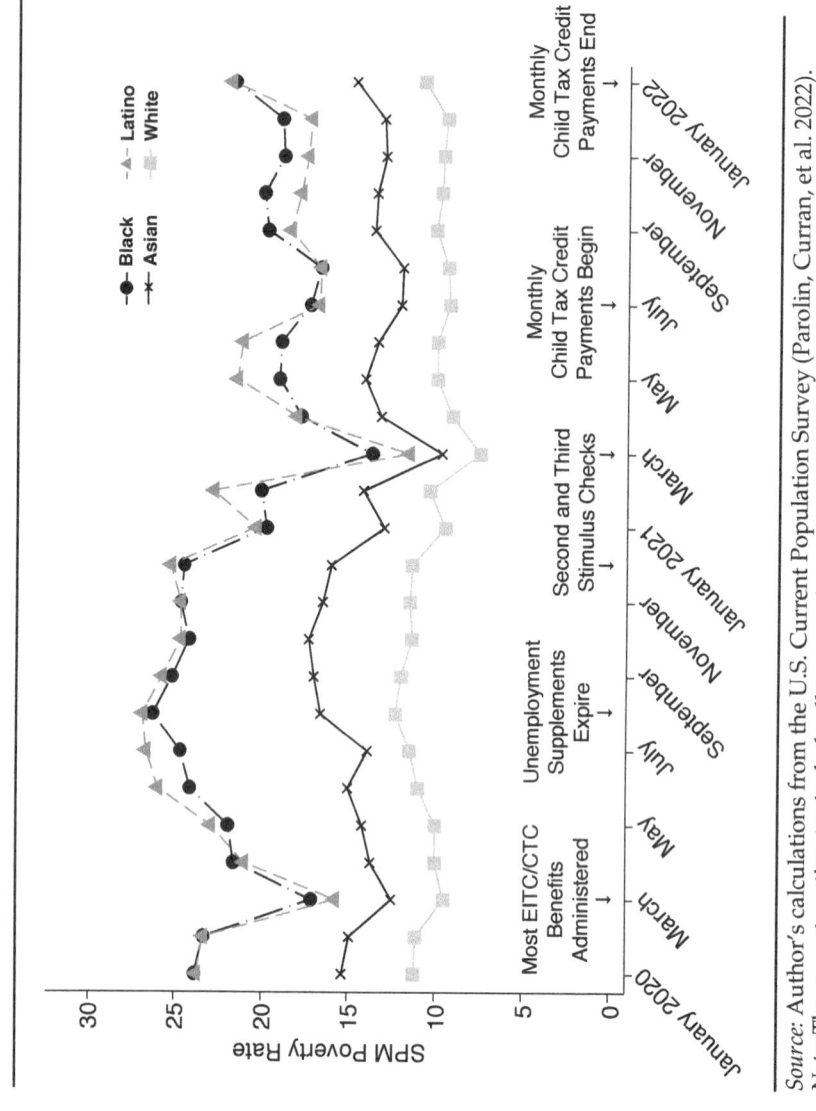

Source: Author's calculations from the U.S. Current Population Survey (Parolin, Curran, et al. 2022).
Note: The poverty estimates include all taxes and transfers, including COVID relief.

poverty rate for Black residents was 19 percent, more than five percentage points lower than the rate in December 2020. For Hispanic residents, the rate was 17.3 percent, down a full eight percentage points from their December 2020 rate. For White individuals, the rate in December 2021 was 9.5 percent, down from 11.4 percent at the end of 2020.

What should we make of these large declines toward the end of 2021? In short, they demonstrate that the expanded CTC in particular made three major contributions with respect to monthly poverty rates: it reduced levels of poverty for all groups, it closed racial/ethnic gaps in poverty rates, and it led to consistently low poverty rates—at least from July to December 2021.

Trends in Child Poverty

The consequences of the CTC expansion are even more visible when we narrow our focus to look at child poverty. Figure 5.5 presents trends in the monthly child poverty rate throughout 2020 and 2021.

Throughout 2020, the trends in monthly child poverty rates mostly mimic the shape of the trends for the population as a whole. Prior to the onset of the pandemic, monthly child poverty rates were 18.7 percent, and they closed the year in December 2020 at 19.7 percent. The most striking reductions in child poverty in 2020 came, as usual, in March with the distribution of EITC transfers, and then in 2021 after the expansion of the CTC in July. The solid black line in figure 5.5 that dips down in July 2021 shows just how impactful these payments were.

In June 2021, just prior to the first monthly CTC payment, the child poverty rate was 20.3 percent before accounting for COVID-related economic relief, and 15.8 percent after that accounting. In July 2021, the first month after the monthly CTC was distributed, the monthly child poverty rate fell from 15.8 percent to 11.9 percent—a 3.9-percentage-point (25 percent) decline from the prior month, or nearly 3 million fewer children living in poverty. This notable decline in child poverty occurred despite the fact that not all eligible children received the expanded CTC benefits. In the absence of all COVID-related relief (including the CTC), the monthly child poverty rate in July 2021 would have been 20 percent. Thus, the COVID-related economic relief, including the expanded CTC, contributed to an 8.1-percentage-point (40.6 percent) decline in monthly child poverty in July 2021 relative to what the July 2021 rate would have been in the absence of the added support.

Just as remarkable is the relative stability in low child poverty rates throughout the remainder of 2021. Though the rates increased slightly when the expanded unemployment benefits expired in September 2021, the monthly child poverty rate finished the year at 12.1 percent when

Figure 5.5   Trends in Monthly Child Poverty Rates, January 2020 to December 2021

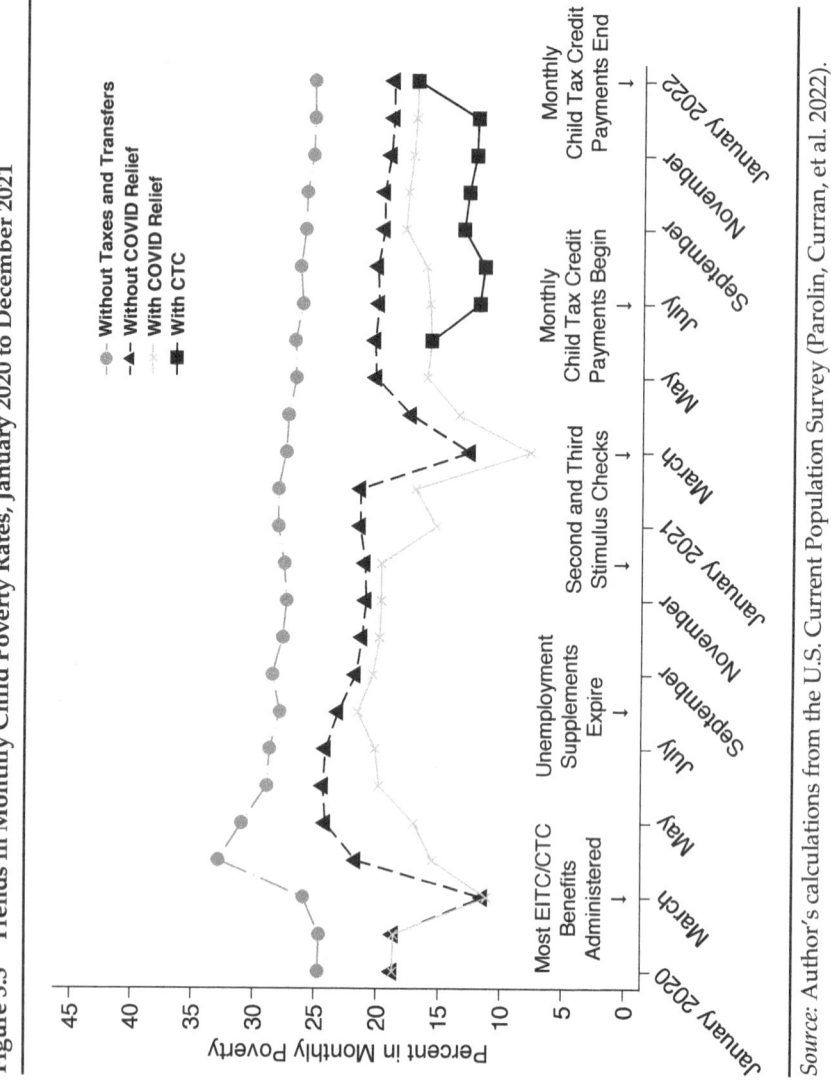

Source: Author's calculations from the U.S. Current Population Survey (Parolin, Curran, et al. 2022).

taking all transfers, including the CTC, into account. For context, this is 7.6 percentage points (or 39 percent, in relative terms) lower than the child poverty rate observed in December 2020. In other words, 5.5 million fewer children lived in poverty in December 2021 relative to the count in December 2020. In January 2022, however, child poverty rates increased again as the monthly CTC payments expired.

To put the reductions in child poverty into broader perspective, figure 5.6 compares the post-tax/transfer poverty rates to poverty rates for working-age adults (eighteen- to sixty-four-year-olds) and older adults (sixty-five and older). In a typical pre-pandemic month, the monthly child poverty rate was well above that of working-age and older adults. See January 2020, for example: at roughly 19 percent, the child poverty rate was higher than the rates for ages sixty-five and older (just under 16 percent) and ages eighteen to sixty-four (just above 14 percent). Over the next two years, monthly child poverty rates were far more volatile than the rates of the older two age groups, and particularly in contrast to rates for those sixty-five and older. This is no surprise: poverty rates for the older population are stable largely owing to the fact that most of this group is retired, not working (and thus not as exposed to the pandemic's employment consequences), and receiving a monthly cash payment (Social Security checks) to keep consumption stable. From January 2020 to December 2021, poverty rates for the older population fluctuated only between 14 and 16 percent.

Prior to the monthly CTC payments, child poverty rates dropped below rates for older adults only in March and April—the months when the lump-sum refundable tax credit payments are distributed. But during the six months in which the monthly CTC payments were distributed, child poverty rates were consistently lower than those of the older population and were largely comparable to the rates of the working-age population, unlike the months prior to the start of the pandemic.

The Annual Poverty Rate: The Lowest Poverty Rate in Recorded History

As emphasized at the start of this chapter, monthly poverty rates are a supplement to, not a substitute for, the annual measure of poverty. Thus far I have focused on monthly poverty rates because of the month-to-month volatility in poverty throughout 2020 and 2021. The remainder of this chapter focuses on standard annual poverty rates. Unlike the monthly poverty rates, which, for technical reasons, we can trace only back to 1994, the annual SPM poverty rate can be extended back to 1967, thanks to the work of Christopher Wimer and his colleagues.[20]

How do the annual poverty rates in 2020 and 2021 compare to those of the past? Figure 5.7 visualizes the long-run trends. The left panel

Figure 5.6   Trends in Post-tax/Transfer Monthly Poverty Rates among Children Compared to Poverty Rates of Other Age Groups, January 2020 to December 2021

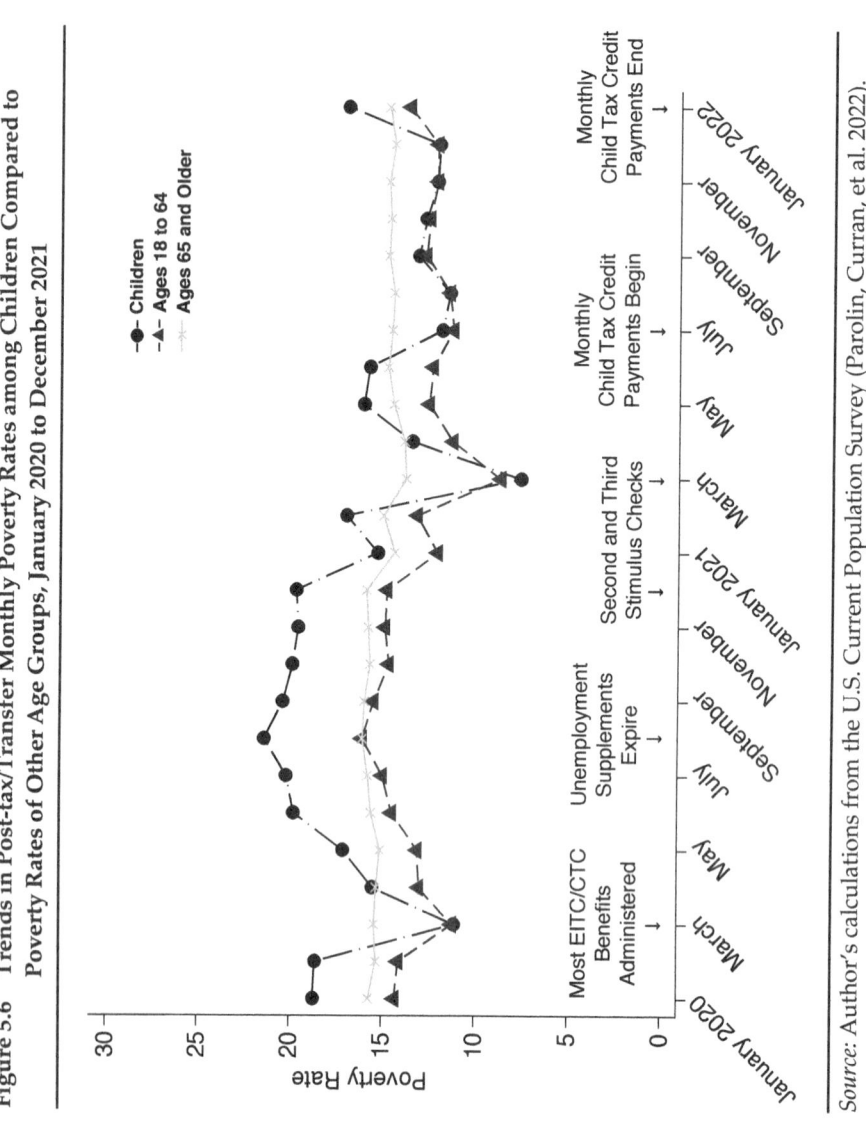

Source: Author's calculations from the U.S. Current Population Survey (Parolin, Curran, et al. 2022).

Figure 5.7   Annual SPM Poverty Rate, 1967 through 2021, and the Percentage-Point Decline in Annual SPM Poverty Attributable to Taxes and Transfers

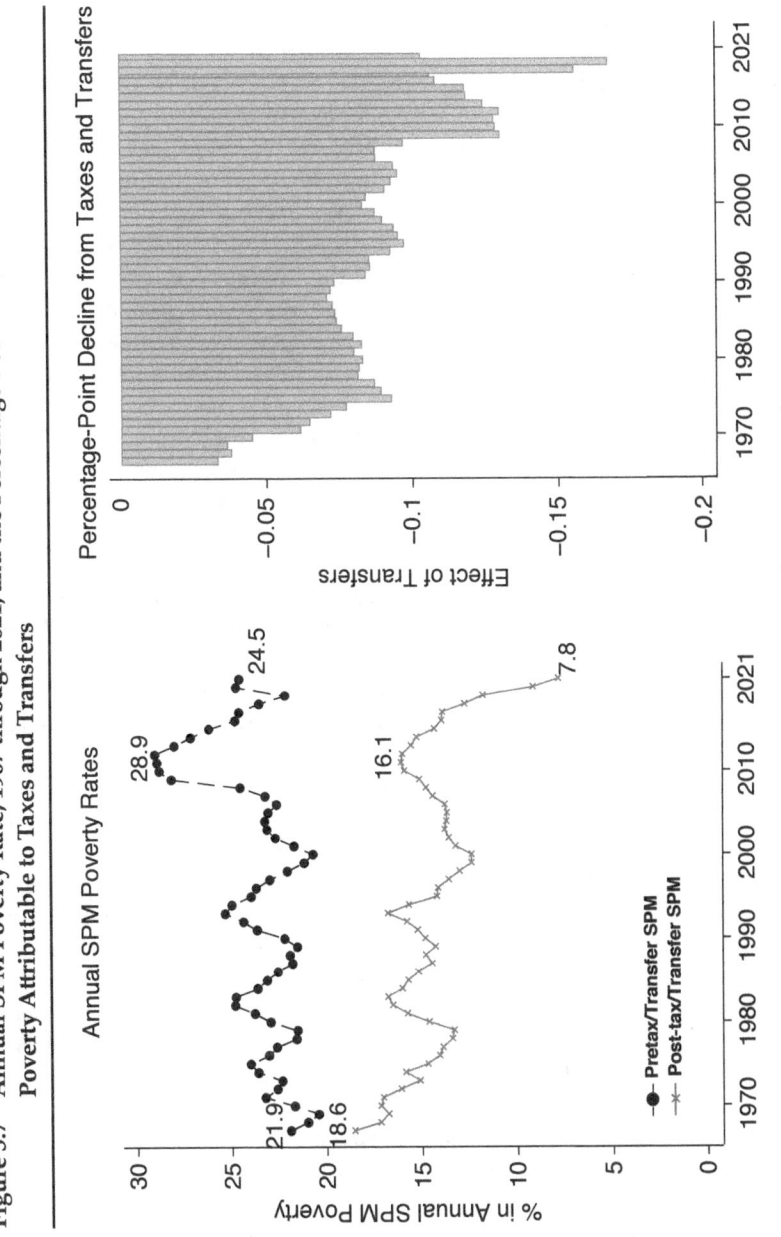

Source: Historical estimates of SPM poverty are from Wimer et al. 2016.

shows the pretax/transfer and the post-tax/transfer annual SPM poverty rates from 1967 through 2021. The right panel documents the poverty reduction effect attributed to taxes and transfers (simply the difference between the pretax/transfer and post-tax/transfer lines on the left). In 1967, the annual SPM poverty rate was 21.9 percent before taking into account taxes and transfers, but 18.6 percent after taxes and transfers. Thus, taxes and transfers directly reduced poverty by around 3.3 percentage points, as documented in the right panel of the figure.

In the decades following, two patterns stand out: first, we see ebbs and flows in poverty rates over this five-decade stretch. In 1979, the annual poverty rate declined to 13.3 percent, the lowest on record at the time. This rate increased in the 1980s, however, before falling below 13.3 percent in 1998, when the poverty rate fell to 13 percent. The spike in poverty during the Great Recession, starting in 2008, is clearly visible in the figure; poverty reached its local peak in 2011 at 16.1 percent, which at that time was the highest rate since the early 1990s. The long recovery carried on until 2019, when the poverty rate reached 11.8 percent—the lowest poverty rate on record at the time. But the sharp drops in 2020 and 2021 clearly stand out. From 2019 to 2020, the poverty rate declined from a then-low of 11.8 percent to a new low of 9.1 percent. In 2021, the poverty rate fell to another record low: 7.8 percent. The two years following the onset of COVID-19 pandemic were the only years since at least 1967 when the annual SPM poverty rate was below 10 percent.

This leads to the second pattern we see in figure 5.7: the widening gap between the pretax/transfer line and the post-tax/transfer line indicates that taxes and transfers are increasingly doing more to reduce poverty. This is best visualized in the right panel. By the early 1990s, for example, taxes and transfers cut the poverty rate by more than 7.5 percentage points—an effect three times greater than the effects in 1967. During the Great Recession, the welfare state cut the poverty rate by more than 12.5 percentage points.

The first two years of the COVID-19 pandemic, however, are in a league of their own: the welfare state cut the poverty rate by more than 15 percentage points in 2020. Taxes and transfers cut the poverty rate by 63 percent—nearly two-thirds—relative to the pretax/transfer poverty rate of 24.7 percent. The government's efforts in 2020 led to the largest reduction in poverty in U.S. history and the lowest poverty rate in modern U.S. history, all at a time when the unemployment rate temporarily climbed to its highest level on record. As discussed in chapter 4, the CARES Act and the second stimulus payment were certainly imperfect, but their net effects brought about the largest decline in U.S. poverty that we have ever seen. In 2021, the welfare state cut the poverty rate even more, by 17 percentage points, thanks in large part to the expanded CTC. Figures A5.3 and A5.4 in this chapter's appendix document even stronger effects of taxes and transfers, and the CTC in particular, on childhood poverty.

Table 5.3 provides more specific detail on which policies worked to reduce poverty in 2021 (and which did not), and for which age groups. Among children in 2021, the expanded CTC reduced poverty by 4.1 percentage points, or 44 percent; this effect was larger than the reduction effect of any other income transfer, and twenty times greater than the poverty reduction effect of cash assistance from TANF. TANF cut child poverty rates by only 0.2 percentage points (3 percent) in 2021 and also performed poorly in cutting child poverty rates in 2020 (0.3 percentage points, or 2.9 percent; not depicted), before the expanded CTC was implemented. In fact, state governments spent only 22 percent of their TANF budgets on cash support in 2020, a mere one percentage point higher than the pre-pandemic year of 2019.[21] Among working-age adults, the CTC reduced poverty by 1.2 percentage points (13.4 percent), second only to Social Security benefits (3.4 percentage points, or 30 percent). Social Security benefits, by far the strongest antipoverty tool for the older population, cut their poverty rate by 32 percentage points (or 75.1 percent) in 2021.

For further contextualization of the uniqueness of the poverty reduction effects of measures taken in 2020 and 2021 compared to the five previous decades, figure 5.8 visualizes the historical relationship between the annual unemployment rate and the annual SPM poverty rate.

Typically, when unemployment is higher, the poverty rate is higher. This makes sense: the primary source of income for most families is market earnings, so when jobs disappear, incomes tend to decline. From 1970 through 2019, this was clearly the case. Figure 5.8 shows a strong, positive relationship between unemployment and the poverty rate (a correlation of $r = 0.64$). But the figure also features two wild outliers: 2020 and 2021. If we place 2020 on the "best fit" line to naively project what the poverty rate might have been had 2020 followed historical precedent, its average unemployment rate of just over 8 percent would represent something close to a 17 percent annual SPM poverty rate, even with taxes and transfers. But 2020 was a large anomaly: with its low poverty rate, 2020 sits alone on the left side of the figure, a strong outlier in the midst of an otherwise strong relationship between annual unemployment and the annual poverty rate. The only other outlier is 2021.

The anomalies of 2020 and 2021 had important consequences, and first and foremost was their effect on the economic security of households across the country that, without additional financial support, would have been far less prepared to cope with the uncertainty of the pandemic. More broadly, the pandemic years ought to challenge conventional thinking among scholars regarding the role of unemployment in influencing poverty. Employment will always be (and generally should be) a strong predictor of an individual's poverty status.[22] But the extent to which that is true is clearly alterable by government policy decisions. In the months in which work was uniquely scarce, poverty

Table 5.3   Reduction in Poverty by Age Group and Income Transfer Program, 2021

Program	Percentage-Point Reduction (Percentage Reduction) among Children Ages Zero to Seventeen	Percentage-Point Reduction (Percentage Reduction) among Adults Ages Eighteen to Sixty-Four	Percentage-Point Reduction (Percentage Reduction) among Adults Ages Sixty-Five and Older
Child Tax Credit	4.1 pp (44.0%)	1.2 pp (13.4%)	0.2 pp (1.8%)
Earned Income Tax Credit	1.3 pp (19.9%)	0.8 pp (9.1%)	0.2 pp (1.7%)
SNAP	1.2 pp (19.4%)	0.8 pp (9.1%)	0.6 pp (5.2%)
Unemployment Insurance	0.7 pp (11.8%)	0.8 pp (8.9%)	0.4 pp (3.3%)
Social Security	1.4 pp (20.7%)	3.4 pp (30.0%)	32.0 pp (75.1%)
Supplemental Security Income	0.4 pp (7.1%)	0.9 pp (10.4%)	1.0 pp (8.9%)
TANF	0.2 pp (3.0%)	0.1 pp (1.0%)	0.0 pp (0.3%)

Source: Author's estimates from the 2022 Current Population Survey Annual Social and Economic Supplement, with calendar year 2021 as income reference.

Note: SNAP = Supplemental Nutrition Assistance Program. TANF = Temporary Assistance for Needy Families. Post-tax/transfer 2021 SPM poverty rates were 5.2 percent, 7.9 percent, and 10.6 percent, respectively, for children, working-age adults, and older adults. Reductions in poverty are relative to the poverty rate in the same year without the specified benefit.

Figure 5.8   Annual Average Unemployment Rate Compared to Annual SPM Poverty Rate, 1970–2021

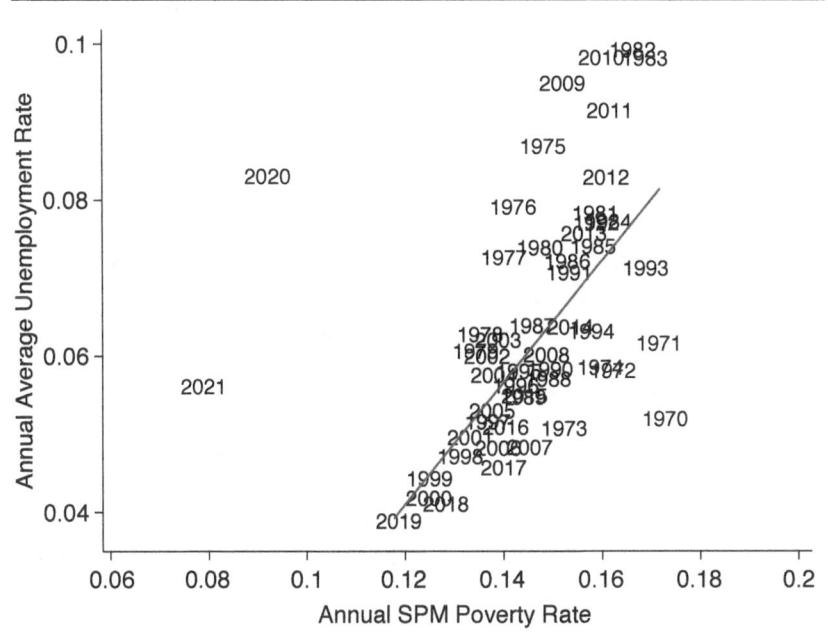

Source: Historical SPM poverty data are from Wimer et al. 2016. Annual unemployment rates are from U.S. Bureau of Labor Statistics 2020.

reached its all-time low. There are reasons to favor a work-first strategy—such as the consequences for long-term economic growth or for family well-being, or normative judgments around joblessness—but it remains evident that joblessness and poverty need not evolve perfectly in tandem. In 2020 and 2021, they certainly did not.

The Record-Low Child Poverty Rate in International Perspective

As a final contextualization of the record-low poverty rate in 2021, I close this chapter with a comparison of the recent low U.S. child poverty rate with rates in other advanced economies. The United States has generally had higher child poverty rates than these other countries.[23] The expanded CTC, however, contributed to the lowest child poverty rates in U.S. history, whether we apply the SPM or a "relative" measure of poverty (defined as having annual income below 50 percent of the national median household income, adjusted for family size) that is more commonly used in cross-national poverty research. Relative poverty measures carry limitations—namely, that they tend to capture income inequality as much as they capture economic deprivation; nonetheless, their use is widespread in comparative research. The *relative* child poverty rate in the United States fell from around 21 percent in 2019 to 12 percent in 2021.

Figure 5.9 compares the relative U.S. child poverty rates in 2019 and 2021 to levels in other countries for which we have comparable data. As detailed in the appendix to this chapter, I take the most recent level of child poverty for each country for which we have microdata after 2012. This includes both high-income and middle-income countries for which data are available, though I signal the categories through darker- versus lighter-colored bars in figure 5.9. (Darker bars indicate countries that the World Bank deems to be high-income countries.) In 2019, the relative child poverty rate in the United States ranked fortieth among the fifty-three country-years examined, comparable to levels observed in Bulgaria and Mexico. In 2021, however, the relative child poverty rate in the United States ranked twenty-first among the fifty-three country-years examined, comparable to levels in Switzerland and Germany.

The relative U.S. child poverty rate would have been 18 percent in the absence of CTC benefits in 2021 (see the chapter appendix); thus, the direct income gains due to the CTC contributed to the United States moving from the eightieth percentile of child poverty rates (with the top percentiles representing higher poverty rates) to the fortieth percentile of child poverty rates among the countries examined.

Figure 5.10 documents the percentage decline in poverty rates due to taxes and transfers, by country. In 2019, taxes and transfers reduced the U.S. relative child poverty rate by 21.5 percent, comparable to the reduction effect of Paraguay, Peru, and Brazil. In 2021, taxes and transfers reduced the U.S. relative child poverty rate by 57.5 percent, placing the United States amid the ranks of Norway and Belgium.

Although, among its international peers, the United States is generally an outlier with respect to child poverty rates, that changed in 2021, as figures 5.9 and 5.10 show. The CTC expansion's large effects on child poverty rates also align with cross-national evidence that an unconditional child allowance can reduce child poverty.[24] However, given that the program was implemented for only one year, U.S. child poverty rates will increase in 2022. Nonetheless, these findings demonstrate that policy changes in 2021 contributed to record-low child poverty rates in the United States, temporarily placing the country in line with the child poverty rates of peer countries.

Figure 5.9 Relative Child Poverty Rates in the United States and Child Poverty Rates in Fifty-One Other Countries, 2019 and 2021

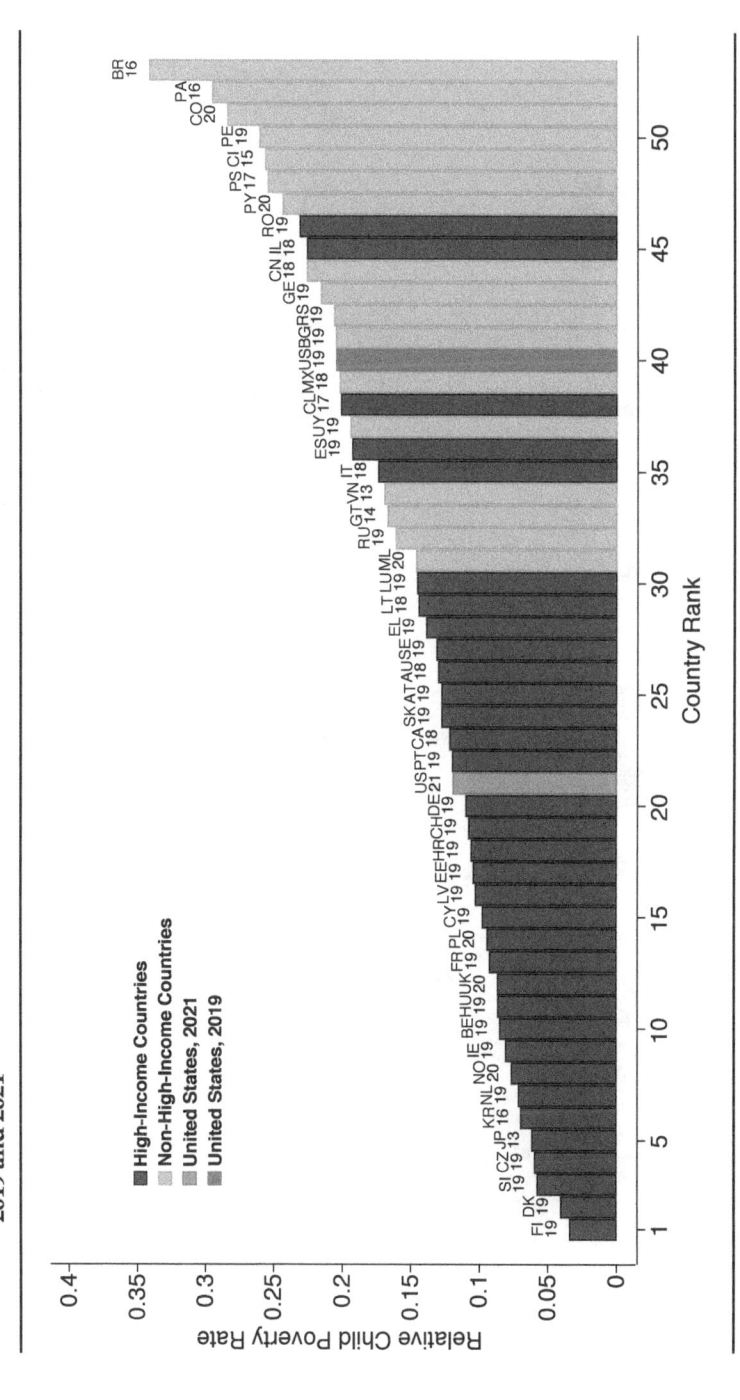

Source: U.S. estimates are from the U.S. Current Population Survey Annual Social and Economic Supplement. Data for other countries are from the European Union Statistics on Income and Living Conditions (EU-SILC) and from the Luxembourg Income Study (LIS) of the Cross-National Data Center in Luxembourg.
Note: The relative poverty measure assesses household resources compared to 50 percent of the national equivalized median household income. World Bank classifications of "high-income" countries are used.

Figure 5.10 Reduction in Relative Child Poverty Rates due to Taxes and Transfers in the United States and in Fifty-One Other Countries, 2019 and 2021

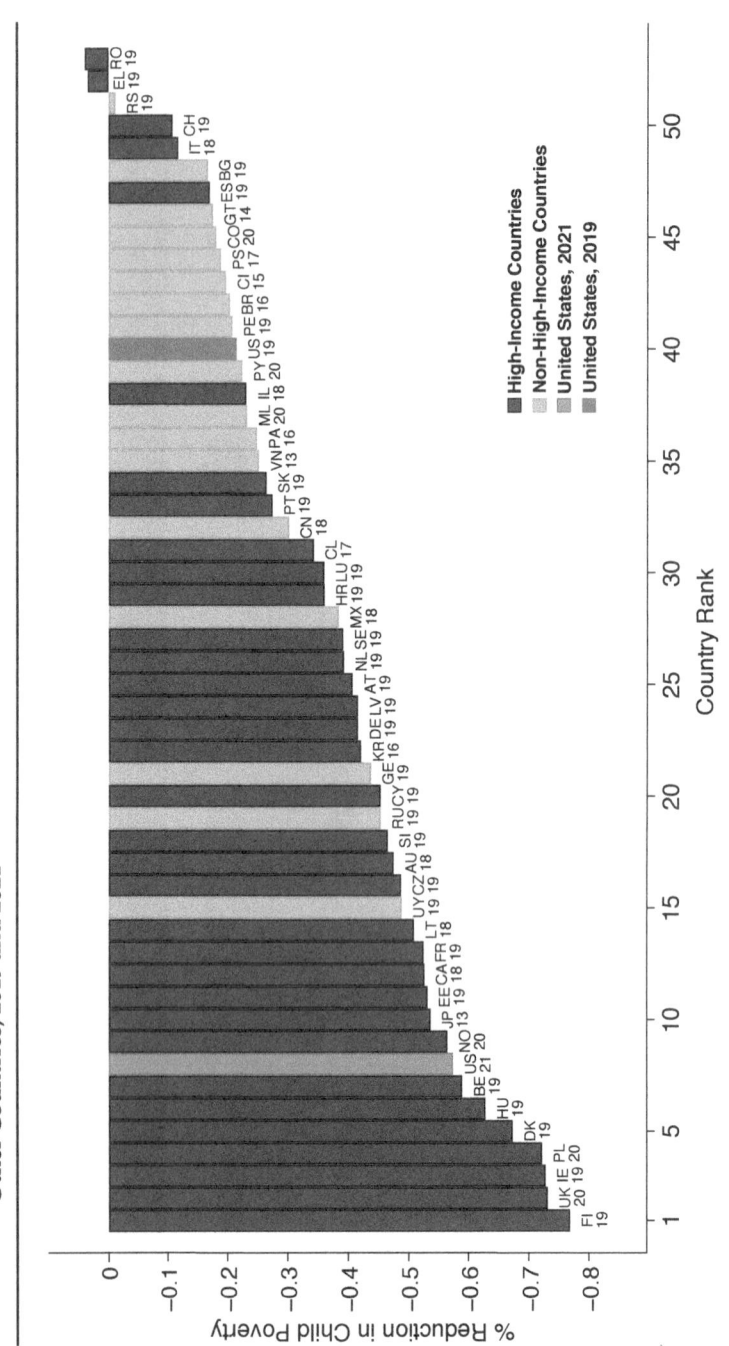

Source: U.S. estimates are from the Current Population Survey Annual Social and Economic Supplement. Data for other countries are from the EU-SILC and the LIS Cross-National Data Center in Luxembourg.

Note: The relative poverty measure assesses household resources compared to 50 percent of the national equivalized median household income. World Bank classifications of "high-income" countries are used.

What about Other Forms of Well-Being?

Poverty is only one indicator of economic well-being. Its focus on income offers a useful, but incomplete, portrait of how well a family can get by in tough times. Some argue that the SPM poverty thresholds are too low, while others maintain that the geographic adjustments to poverty thresholds are too harsh, or that some of the data we use to measure poverty are too full of holes to be reliable. I am sympathetic to these arguments and generally agree with calls for a multidimensional perspective of poverty. Consider that only one-third of individuals experiencing food insufficiency in 2020 were in SPM-level annual poverty, according to my estimates from the CPS. Particularly in a multifaceted crisis like the COVID-19 pandemic—when the collapse of the labor market was only one of several major concerns—we must move beyond income to also understand how the pandemic affected material hardship and mental health. The next chapter switches focus away from income and toward understanding the role of the CARES Act, the ARP, and the CTC in shaping food insufficiency, housing hardship, and mental health throughout the COVID-19 pandemic.

Chapter 5 Appendix

This appendix provides more details on the construction of the monthly version of the Supplemental Poverty Measure.

The Supplemental Poverty Measure

The SPM is the most widely used measure of poverty in the United States today. When counting a family unit's resources, Unlike the U.S. official poverty measure, it includes all taxes and transfers, including benefits from SNAP, the EITC, and the COVID-era stimulus checks. The poverty threshold for the SPM is based on how much typical households have spent in recent years on food, clothing, shelter, and utilities, plus a little more for extra necessities. The threshold also takes into account geographic differences in the cost of living. For instance, the poverty threshold in San Jose, California, where the median rental value for a two-bedroom home was above $3,000 in 2020, is higher than the threshold in rural Alabama, where the median rental value for a two-bedroom home was $612.[25] For a two-parent, two-child family renting a home in an average-cost city (Phoenix, Arizona, for example), the annual SPM poverty threshold is around $29,000, and the monthly poverty threshold is around $2,400.

Monthly Estimates of Income

We construct our monthly poverty measure in the CPS ASEC file. In doing so, we use the same components as in the annual SPM framework, but we convert each annual value into an estimated monthly value.

To do so we use five sets of assumptions regarding the annual-to-monthly conversions of income components in the ASEC (see table A5.1).

In short, the conversions make assumptions regarding the relationship of annual-to-monthly values based on current employment status, duration of unemployment, current month, and more. For individuals who report receiving earnings from employment during the year but also report being currently unemployed for more than four weeks, we set the monthly earnings to zero (see category 2 in table A5.1). We distribute refundable tax credits in the month in which low-income family units are most likely to file taxes, according to IRS data (see category 3). We include the value of subsidized school lunches only in the months in which children tend to attend schools (see category 5).

After converting our income components to monthly values within the ASEC, we create an indicator of whether the SPM unit's monthly income is below its monthly SPM poverty threshold. We then combine the ASEC monthly poverty estimates with up-to-date data on demographic, employment, and household characteristics from the monthly CPS files. To produce an estimate of poverty for January 2020, for example, we combine the January 2020 monthly file with the most recent ASEC file (2019), which measures incomes from the prior calendar year (2018). We treat the lack of poverty status in the monthly files as a missing data problem and use a procedure called combined-sample multiple imputation (CSMI) to generate the likelihood of poverty in the monthly files.

We estimate a monthly poverty measure from January 1994 onward. Our initial year of analysis is 1994 because data on the duration of unemployment is not consistently available in the monthly files prior to that year. For our 2020 and 2021 projections, we include payments from CARES Act income transfers and subsequent COVID-related relief programs, such as the expanded Child Tax Credit from July 2021. Unlike the conversion processes described here, which adjust observed annual values to projected monthly values, the COVID-related income relief must be simulated within the ASEC data. We follow the simulation framework introduced in our 2022 article "Estimating Monthly Poverty Rates in the United States."[26] For EIP payments (stimulus checks), we follow the distribution schedule of the Treasury Department and its assumptions on the share of tax units receiving payments through direct deposit (earlier receipt of payments) and the share receiving checks by mail (payments over several months depending on tax unit income).[27] This approach leads to the majority of EIP payments being distributed in April and May. We follow the Urban Institute's conservative estimate that participation rates among the eligible were around 70 percent.[28] In our assignment of the benefits within the CPS ASEC, we meet the 70 percent participation target (among those eligible) by assuming that

Table A5.1   Conversion of Annual Income Components to Monthly Income Components

1	*Income components divided by twelve to move from annual to monthly values*
Components	Social Security, income from retirement, SSI, worker's compensation, veteran's benefits, survivor's benefits, income from disability, income from dividends, child support, alimony, income from other sources, WIC, heating assistance, housing assistance, medical out-of-pocket expenses, state and federal taxes (excluding tax refunds)
Rule	Divide annual values by twelve and apply to each month.
2	*Income components that should be adjusted if members of SPM unit are not employed in the given month but were employed in prior months*
Components	(1) Income from wages, business, farm work, work-related expenses, FICA taxes; (2) standard (non–CARES Act) unemployment insurance benefits
Rule	(1) Income components are converted to zero for an individual who is unemployed for five or more weeks. For individuals unemployed for one to four weeks, we prorate the earnings to estimate a monthly value based on average hourly earnings and the number of weeks in the month employed (2) Unemployment insurance benefits are converted to zero if the individual is currently employed. If the individual is currently jobless and reports receiving unemployment benefits in the prior year, we prorate the benefits to match the weeks of unemployment in the month
3	*Income components that are distributed only in a single month*
Components	EITC, CTC (before July 2021), other refundable tax credits
Rule	We project the month of tax filing based on IRS data and allocate the refundable tax credits accordingly in the given month. This leads to the largest share of refundable tax credits being distributed in February and March, with the remaining benefits concentrated in April. For the monthly CTC payments introduced in July 2021, we provide the family unit's eligible benefit level, taking into account state-specific coverage rates from the IRS.

(Table continues on p. 128)

Table A5.1   (*Continued*)

4	*Means-tested transfer benefits typically dispersed unevenly throughout the year*
Components	SNAP, TANF
Rule	Among all SPM units reporting receipt of SNAP (or TANF) benefits in the CPS ASEC, we calculate the benefit value that the family is eligible for in a given month based on state policy rules, family size, monthly earnings. If the projected benefit value is greater than one-twelfth the annual value of SNAP/TANF but less than the reported annual SNAP/TANF value, we set the unit's monthly SNAP/TANF value as the projected benefit value. If the projected monthly benefit value is greater than the reported annual value, we designate the reported annual value as the monthly benefit. (By definition, this will be less than the maximum monthly benefit value.) If the SPM unit reports no annual benefits, we give no monthly benefits, even if the unit appears to be eligible.
5	*Education-related income support*
Components	School lunches and income from education, including Pell Grants and other aid from government sources, nongovernmental scholarships, and grants
Rule	These income components are divided by nine and applied to non-summer months to account for their typical distribution during the school year.

Source: Author's summary of Parolin, Curran, et al. (2022).

lower-income families and non-tax-filers are less likely to receive the benefits than higher-income individuals, since lower-income individuals are less likely to have filed taxes and provided direct deposit information to the IRS. We follow the work of George Borjas to identify immigrants who are likely to be undocumented and thus are ineligible to receive the EIPs.[29]

For the CARES Act unemployment benefit expansions (PUC, PUA, and PEUC), we follow the work of Marianne Bitler and her colleagues in measuring the share of recently unemployed individuals who receive unemployment benefits by taking the cumulative number of initial UI payments over the cumulative number of individuals who lost jobs from March 1, 2020, onward.[30] We produce this participation rate by state and month using state-month data on cumulative initial UI claims and cumulative job loss. We assign the benefits in our CPS ASEC data using state-level data on the race/ethnicity and sex composition of the unemployed individuals receiving the benefits. This information comes from the Century Foundation's Unemployment Insurance Data Dashboard, a compilation of Department of Labor data.[31] Our simulation of the monthly CTC payments starting in July 2021 directly follows the IRS's distribution of payments by month and state. We assume that non-tax-filers and the lowest-income SPM units are, again, the least likely to receive the benefits in state-months with imperfect coverage.

In the summer months, for all states with P-EBT payments activated, we apply the typical value of school lunches to the same individuals who normally receive them. For states without P-EBT activated, we do not provide the value of school lunch benefits in the summer months. We start with USDA reports of which states have activated P-EBT, but we also scanned the websites of states that are unlisted to confirm their details. New York State, for example, was not listed by the USDA as a state that had activated P-EBT payments in 2022, but it did provide P-EBT benefits that year, funded through its 2021 P-EBT, so we include it as a P-EBT state in our calculations. For some school districts that went with remote learning more often during the year, P-EBT benefits could have been larger, or they could have been provided at different points in the year. We cannot reach that level of granularity in the CPS ASEC, however, so we simply provide uniform P-EBT benefits within states, a potential shortcoming.

After converting our income components to monthly values within the ASEC, we create a binary monthly poverty indicator equal to one if the SPM unit's monthly income is below one-twelfth the value of its annual SPM poverty threshold. Because projecting new poverty thresholds requires more timely consumption data and introduces the possibility of new sources of measurement error, we use observed SPM thresholds from the ASEC file. Recall that SPM poverty thresholds vary based on family unit size, geographic location of residence, and whether the family owns or rents its residence.

Producing Monthly Updates to Estimates of Poverty

To produce our estimates of poverty on a monthly basis, we combine our ASEC monthly poverty estimates with up-to-date data on demographic, employment, and household characteristics from the monthly CPS files. To produce an estimate of poverty for January 2020, for example, we combine the January 2020 monthly file with the most recent ASEC file (2019). We apply CSMI to impute poverty rates from the annual CPS file into the monthly CPS file.[32] To apply the CSMI, we merge the two samples and construct a common set of indicators that are likely to be useful in estimating a family unit's poverty status. Table A5.2 provides the list of indicators.

Table A5.2   Indicators Included in Models for Imputing Poverty Rates from the Annual CPS File into the Monthly CPS File

Indicator	Operationalization
Age	Five-year age bins from zero to eighty-five
Sex	Female or male
Education	Low (high school or less), medium (more than high school, less than college), or high (college degree) education, measured for those age eighteen or older in the family unit
Race/ethnicity	Indicators for White, Black, Asian, Hispanic, or other race/ethnicity
Citizenship and origin	Indicators for citizenship and whether born outside the United States
Family structure	Dummies for single with no kids, single with kids, two adults with no kids, two adults with kids, three or more adults with no kids, three or more adults with kids, and retirement-age adults only; indicator of whether more than one family lives in the unit; and count variables of number of working-age adults in the unit, number of individuals age sixty-five or older in the unit, and number of children in the unit (top-coded at five)
Marital status	Indicator of whether the head of the family unit is currently married
Employment	Indicators of the share of working-age adults in the unit who are currently employed, whether in labor force, and household work intensity (hours worked per week by working-age adults in the unit relative to the number of working-age adults in the unit); one-digit occupation codes for employed adults (eleven binary indicators, including an indicator for unemployed)
Unemployment	Number of weeks unemployed; set to zero if not unemployed
Disability status	Indicator of whether at least one working-age person in the unit has any physical or cognitive disability related to hearing or vision, difficulty with memory, physical difficulty, personal care limitation, or disability limiting mobility
State of residence	Dummy variables for all states
Metropolitan central city status	Indicators of whether the unit is not in a metropolitan area, is in a central city, or is outside a central city; and if central city status is unknown (but in metro area) or metro status is missing or unknown

Table A5.2   (*Continued*)

Indicator	Operationalization
Interaction terms	Interactions of household employment rate with: household work intensity; duration of unemployment; household type; household education, age, sex, race/ethnicity, disability, and citizenship characteristics; and state of residence. Additional interactions of duration of unemployment with: household type; household education, age, sex, race/ethnicity, disability, and citizenship characteristics; and state of residence. Additional interactions of household work intensity with household type and with household education, age, sex, race/ethnicity, disability, and citizenship characteristics.

Source: Author's summary of Parolin, Curran, et al. (2022).
Note: All indicators except unit-level count variables (the number of children in the unit, the number of weeks unemployed, and so on) are operationalized as mean values at the family-unit level to ensure that each family unit receives the same predicted likelihood of poverty.

We then apply multiple imputation using chained equations to estimate SPM poverty status in the monthly data. In addition to the indicators identified in table A5.2, we apply a large number of interaction effects to increase the predictive power of the model. The CSMI estimates run ten iterations of the model. We take the mean of ten separate imputations to compute the likelihood of poverty for each family unit and, in turn, an average poverty rate for the country as a whole. The results are robust when using an alternative approach that estimates the conditional likelihood of poverty using logistic regression in the ASEC and subsequently producing out-of-sample predictions in the basic monthly files.

An Additional Reliability Test

This book and the research on which it is based present a number of validity tests to demonstrate the reliability of the monthly poverty measure. Figure A5.1 presents one additional test: comparisons of state-level means in monthly poverty with state-level means of hardship and well-being indicators.

The hardship and well-being indicators are from the Census Household Pulse Survey. The cross-state patterns of monthly poverty during 2020 and 2021 overlap strongly with cross-state patterns in material hardship (and also with mental health indicators). States with higher mean

Figure A5.1   Relationship of Mean State-Level Monthly SPM Poverty Rate and Mean State Levels of Food Insufficiency, Missed Rent Payments, and Well-Being Indicators, April 2020 to September 2021

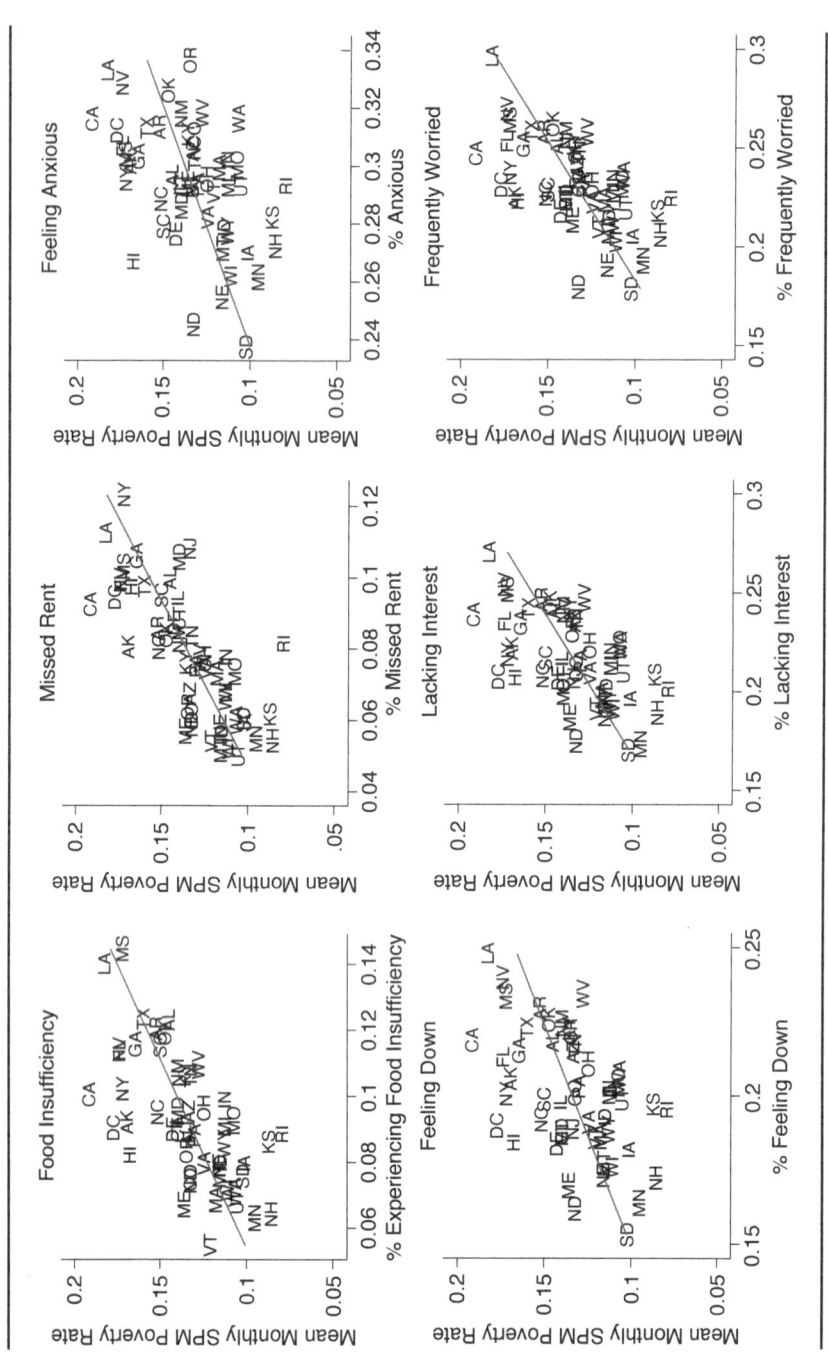

Source: Author's calculations from the U.S. Current Population Survey and Census Household Pulse Survey.

monthly poverty rates in 2020–2021 also tended to feature higher rates of food insufficiency ($r = 0.64$), missed rent or mortgage payments ($r = 0.75$), frequent anxiety ($r = 0.48$), feeling down ($r = 0.52$), lacking interest ($r = 0.59$), and frequent worrying ($r = 0.61$).

Are Trends in Hardship and Well-Being from the Pulse Reliable?   A potential objection to the comparisons to the Pulse data is that the Pulse survey may be unreliable in some contexts. The Census Bureau introduced the Census Household Pulse Survey in April 2020 to provide high-frequency data on the economic and social well-being of individuals across the United States. As a web-based survey with low response rates (averaging 5.9 percent response across waves 1 through 47), the Pulse is prone to measurement error. Cross-sectional point estimates from any wave of the Pulse tend to suggest, for example, that vaccine uptake is higher than observed in reality.[33] Moreover, point estimates of food insufficiency are not comparable to other surveys, given different sampling methods and question designs.[34]

The important question for comparing trends in monthly poverty from the CPS to trends in hardship from the Pulse, however, is the internal consistency of the Pulse across survey waves. The Pulse has consistently employed the same broad survey strategy since its inception in April 2020. There is no compelling evidence that wave-to-wave trends in estimates of material hardship or mental health suffer from measurement error that would bias the trends toward being comparable with our estimates of monthly poverty.[35]

That said, there are some differences in sampling strategy across Pulse waves (or its three "phases") that could affect the internal consistency of the Pulse estimates. Between phase 1 (April to July 2020) and phase 2 (August to October 2020) of the Pulse, the survey was changed from a weekly to a biweekly format; at the same time, response rates increased from around 3 percent in week 12 to 10 percent in week 13. To address the possibility that these changes to the Pulse sampling strategy bias the conclusions reached in this study, table A5.3 repeats the associations provided in chapter 5, but excluding Pulse phase 1.

Narrowing the scope to phases 2 and 3, which had higher response rates and consistent biweekly sampling periods, leads to the same conclusions reached before. These findings reinforce the fact that changes in response rates, or any persistent bias in estimates due to sampling frame or response rate concerns, do not strongly affect our conclusions.[36]

As a separate test of the Pulse's internal consistency, figure A5.2 compares monthly variation in employment rates according to the Pulse with monthly variation in employment rates according to the CPS from

Table A5.3   **Comparison of Associations of Mean State-Level Monthly SPM Poverty Rate with Mean State Levels of Food Insufficiency, Missed Rent Payments, and Well-Being Indicators When Excluding Pulse Phase 1, April to July 2020**

	Monthly Poverty Rate: All Pulse Phases, April 2020 to May 2022	Monthly Poverty Rate: Without Pulse Phase 1 (without April to July 2020)
Food insufficiency	0.58	0.48
Behind on rent	0.48	0.36
Frequent anxiety	0.52	0.41
Feeling down	0.48	0.44
Lacking interest	0.47	0.40
Frequent worrying	0.54	0.45
Worried about rent	0.48	0.60
Difficulty with expenses	0.35	0.36

Source: Author's calculations from the U.S. Current Population Survey and Census Household Pulse Survey.

April 2020 through May 2022. The upper-left panel shows strong consistency in the employment trends observed in the Pulse compared to employment trends in the CPS ($r = 0.83$). Although the Pulse generally features lower employment rates for any given month, month-to-month changes in unemployment nonetheless track well with the changes observed in the CPS. The other panels show that the two surveys' employment trends are more closely aligned for White adults ($r = 0.88$) than for Black adults ($r = 0.63$) or Hispanic adults ($r = 0.50$). Thus, it may be that the Pulse sampling design affects the consistency of results for Black and Hispanic respondents more than for White respondents. Overall, there is no reliable evidence to suggest that the conclusions reached in comparing monthly trends in poverty to hardship outcomes are due to any wave-to-wave inconsistencies in Pulse sampling procedures or response rates.

Comparing Poverty Rates across Countries

The cross-national comparison of child poverty rates applies two different measures of poverty: the Supplemental Poverty Measure, which is exclusively producible for the United States, and a "relative" measure of poverty, a percent-of-median poverty measure commonly applied outside of the United States and in internationally comparable estimates of poverty. Table A5.4 outlines the core differences in these two measures of poverty.

Figure A5.2   Comparison of Variation in the Current Population Survey (CPS) and Census Household Pulse Survey (Pulse) Monthly Employment Rates of Adults Ages Eighteen to Sixty-Four, April 2020 to May 2022

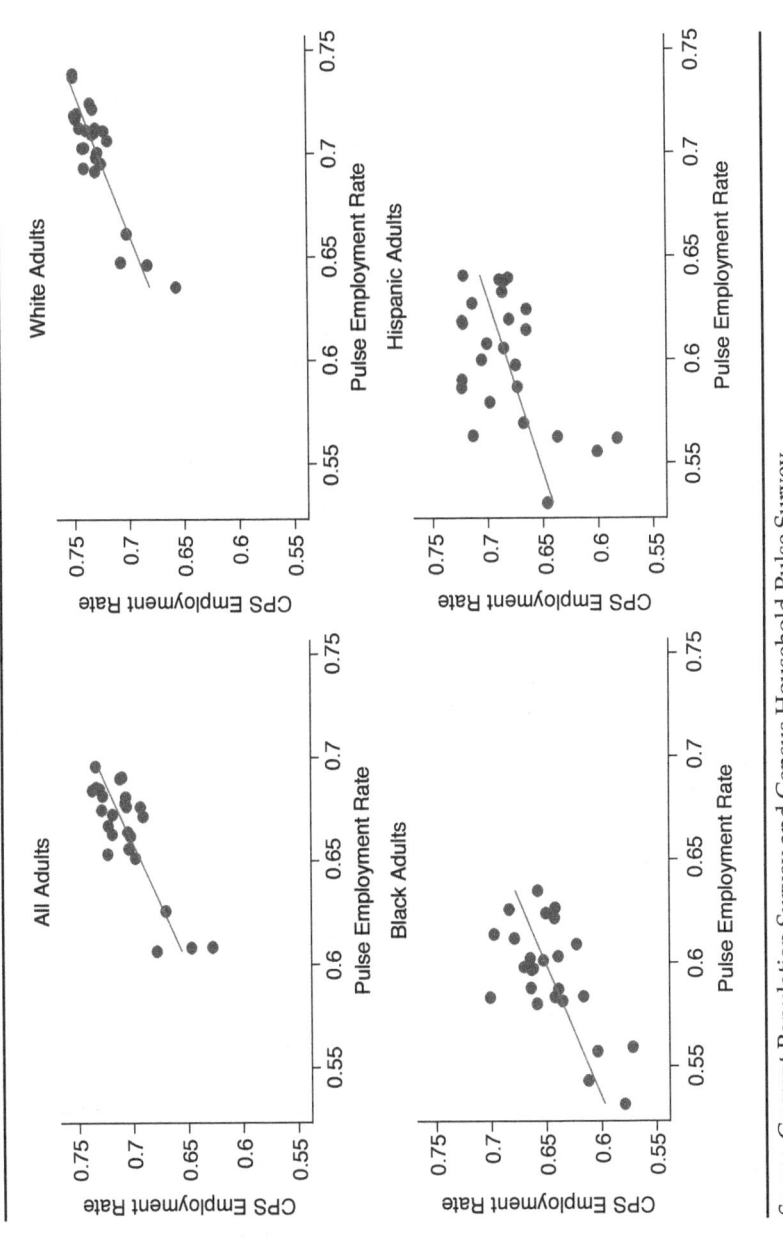

Source: Current Population Survey and Census Household Pulse Survey.
Note: The Pulse survey asks: "In the last 7 days, did you do ANY work for either pay or profit?" The CPS employment measure also captures employment status in the prior week.

Table A5.4   Differences between Poverty Measures

	Supplemental Poverty Measure	Relative Poverty Measure
Country and period	United States, 1967–2021	All countries and years
Measurement of resources	All taxes and transfers, minus out-of-pocket expenses related to work, medical care, and child support paid to other households	All taxes and transfers
Poverty threshold	Set based on a five-year moving average of expenditures on food, clothing, shelter, and utilities; varies regionally based on local housing costs	Set at 50 percent of the national equivalized median household income in a given year
Unit of analysis	Resource-sharing units (in 95 percent of cases or more, this unit is equivalent to the household, but some households have multiple units)	Household
Equivalence scale	Poverty thresholds vary by family size, so an equivalence scale is not directly applied to household incomes	Square root equivalence scale applied to household income
Income accounting period	Annual income received during the calendar year	Annual income received during the calendar year

Source: Author's compilation.

The relative poverty measure, which is commonly used in internationally comparative research, sets the poverty threshold at 50 percent of the national equivalized median income for the country and year. Income is measured at the household level. I apply a square root equivalence scale that accounts for economies of scale by dividing household income by the square root of the number of household members. The relative poverty threshold in the United States was $39,793 before equivalizing household incomes, and $23,365 after equivalizing household incomes.

The data follow established practice in international poverty measurement in primarily presenting post-tax/transfer measures of poverty.[37] The post-tax/transfer measures of poverty include near-cash benefits such as food and nutrition support (primarily relevant for the United States), but they do not include the monetary value of publicly provided services, such as education or health care, following common practice in the literature. The pre-tax/transfer measures include all private income, such as earnings from employment, but also capital income gross of income taxes or Social Security contributions. The difference between the post-tax/transfer and pre-tax/transfer estimates in a given year is commonly used in assessing the relative strength of a country's tax and transfer system; this is an accounting exercise, however, and does not take into account behavioral differences should the tax and transfer system be altered.[38]

Data Sources

For the U.S. measures of poverty, the analysis relies exclusively on the Current Population Survey's Annual Social and Economic Supplement, the data set commonly applied to estimates of poverty and household income. The non-U.S. estimates come from either the Luxembourg Income Study (LIS) of the Cross-National Data Center in Luxembourg or the European Union Statistics on Income and Living Conditions (EU-SILC) survey. The LIS and EU-SILC both provide harmonized micro-data across a wide range of countries. The LIS collects data from national statistical agencies and includes middle-income and non-European countries (in addition to high-income European countries), while the EU-SILC provides data for all EU member states.

The analysis prioritizes poverty estimates from 2019, the year prior to the onset of the COVID-19 pandemic. However, applying poverty rates from 2020 (for the countries available) does not meaningfully alter the cross-national comparisons. For countries observed in both the LIS and EU-SILC data sets in 2019, we prioritize the LIS estimates for convenience; by definition, the estimates do not vary meaningfully for most countries observed in the EU-SILC and LIS. (Rare exceptions are European countries in which the EU-SILC is not the data used in the LIS). Table A5.5 provides the data source used for each of our estimates and also clarifies the country abbreviations used in the study's primary results.

Table A5.5   Data Sources and Country Abbreviations in Figures 5.9 and 5.10 (Cross-National Variations in Child Poverty Rates)

Country	Abbreviation	Data Source
Australia	AU	Survey of Income and Housing (via LIS)
Austria	AT	EU-SILC
Belgium	BE	EU-SILC
Brazil	BR	National Continuous Household Sample Survey (via LIS)
Bulgaria	BG	EU-SILC
Canada	CA	Canadian Income Survey (via LIS)
Chile	CL	National Socio-Economic Characterization Survey (via LIS)
China	CN	Chinese Household Income Survey (via LIS)
Colombia	CO	Great Integrated Household Survey (via LIS)
Croatia	HR	EU-SILC
Cyprus	CY	EU-SILC
Czechia	CZ	EU-SILC
Denmark	DK	EU-SILC
Estonia	EE	EU-SILC
Finland	FI	EU-SILC
France	FR	EU-SILC
Georgia	GE	Household Income and Expenditure Survey (via LIS)
Germany	DE	German Socio-Economic Panel (via LIS)
Greece	EL	EU-SILC
Guatemala	GT	National Survey of Living Conditions (via LIS)
Hungary	HU	EU-SILC
Ireland	IE	EU-SILC
Israel	IL	Household Expenditure Survey (via LIS)
Italy	IT	EU-SILC
Ivory Coast	CI	Household Living Standards Survey (via LIS)
Japan	JP	Japan Household Panel Survey (via LIS)
Latvia	LV	EU-SILC
Lithuania	LT	EU-SILC
Luxembourg	LU	EU-SILC
Mali	ML	Modular and Permanent Household Survey (via LIS)
Mexico	MX	Household Income and Expenditure Survey (via LIS)
Netherlands	NL	EU-SILC
Norway	NO	Household Income Statistics (via LIS)
Palestine	PS	Palestine Expenditure and Consumption Survey (via LIS)
Panama	PA	Continuous Household Survey (via LIS)
Paraguay	PY	Continuous Household Survey (via LIS)
Peru	PE	National Household Survey (via LIS)

Table A5.5 (*Continued*)

Country	Abbreviation	Data Source
Poland	PL	Household Budget Survey (via LIS)
Portugal	PT	EU-SILC
Romania	RO	EU-SILC
Russia	RU	Survey of the Population Income and Participation in Social Programs (via LIS)
Serbia	RS	EU-SILC
Slovakia	SK	
Slovenia	SI	EU-SILC
South Korea	KR	Household Income and Expenditure Survey and Farm Household Income and Expenditure Survey (via LIS)
Spain	ES	EU-SILC
Sweden	SE	EU-SILC
Switzerland	CH	EU-SILC
United Kingdom	UK	Family Resources Survey (via LIS)
United States	US	CPS ASEC
Uruguay	UY	Continuous Household Survey (via LIS)
Vietnam	VN	Vietnam Household Living Standards Survey (via LIS)

Source: Author's compilation.
Note: LIS = Luxembourg Income Study, which harmonizes input data from national statistical agencies. EU-SILC = European Union Statistics on Income and Living Conditions. CPS ASEC = Current Population Survey Annual Social and Economic Supplement.

Figure A5.3   U.S. Child Poverty Rates Using the Supplemental Poverty Measure and the Relative Poverty Measure, 1967 to 2021

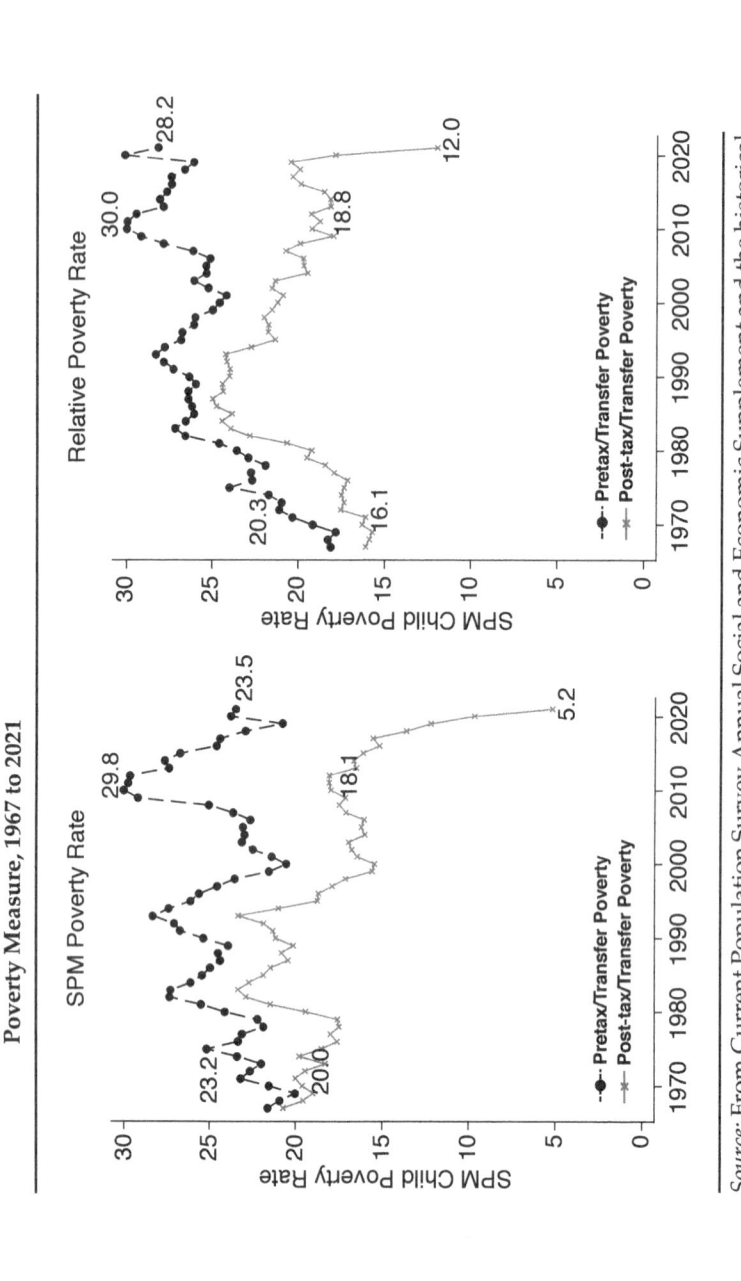

Source: From Current Population Survey Annual Social and Economic Supplement and the historical SPM data series from Fox et al. (2015).
Note: The relative poverty measure assesses household resources compared to 50 percent of the national equivalalized median household income.

Figure A5.4   U.S. Child Poverty Rates before and after Accounting for the Child Tax Credit, 2019 and 2021

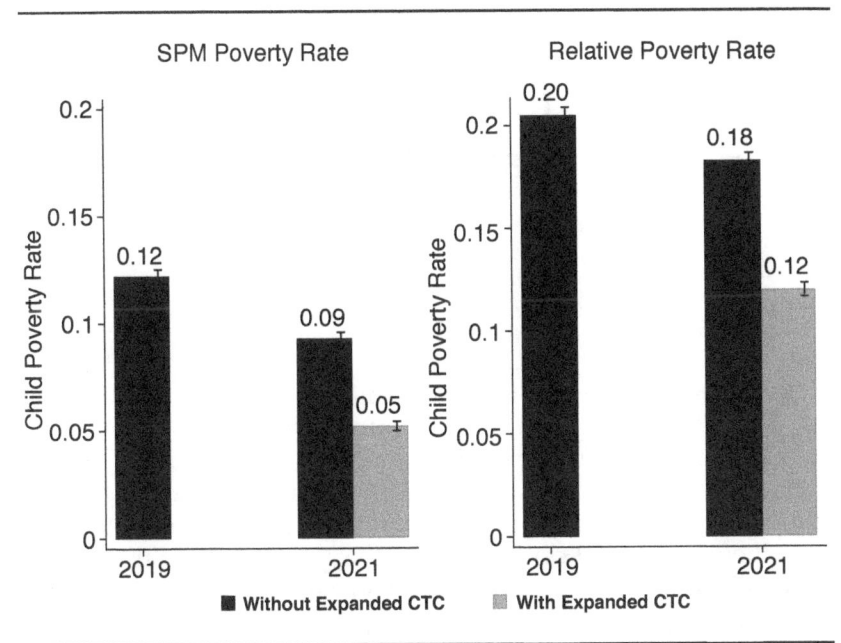

Source: From the Current Population Survey Annual Social and Economic Supplement.
Note: The relative poverty measure assesses household resources compared to 50 percent of the national equivalized median household income. Error bars represent 95 percent confidence intervals.

Chapter 6

Beyond Income: Material Hardship and Mental Health

$\mathbf{A}$s discussed in chapter 4, policymakers often face challenges in finding the right balance between the timeliness and precision of benefit distribution during times of crisis. Policy research in times of economic and social crisis is similar. When the COVID-19 pandemic began, many researchers paused their usual work to focus on gathering data and evidence about the pandemic's multiple crises. Academics often prepublish their work in working paper series before they go through the lengthy peer review process, and these papers were quickly filled with analyses of new data on how U.S. households were coping with the pandemic. This rapid shift was important for generating new knowledge to guide ongoing policy responses, but it occasionally meant producing results that later findings would contradict.

For instance, several high-profile media reports and academic papers in 2020 pointed to record increases in levels of food hardship during the first year of the pandemic. According to a *Washington Post* article published in November 2020, "It is likely that there's more hunger in the United States today than at any point since 1998, when the Census Bureau began collecting comparable data about households' ability to get enough food."[1] A story in the *New York Times* similarly wrote that food insecurity in the United States in early 2020 was "without modern precedent."[2] These two news accounts were based on separate academic studies that made comparisons to the same pre-pandemic data set in suggesting that food hardship had doubled or tripled from 2019 to 2020.[3] With time, however, it became clear that these claims were not accurate.

Each of these studies had compared results from new COVID-era surveys conducted online to pre-pandemic estimates of food hardship from a separate source of data, the Current Population Survey Food Security Supplement (FSS), which uses different sampling methods.

The official estimates of food insecurity for 2020 released by the U.S. Department of Agriculture (USDA) showed that food insecurity neither doubled nor tripled from its levels in 2019: in fact, the rate of food insecurity did not change from 2019 to 2020.[4] Other nationally representative data had reached similar conclusions: an Urban Institute study found in April 2021, for example, that food insecurity slightly *declined* during the first year of the pandemic.[5] Evidence from the Panel Study of Income Dynamics, in contrast, pointed to a slight increase in food hardship from 2019 to 2021, though it amounted to nothing near a two- or threefold increase from pre-pandemic levels.[6]

In this chapter, I sift through the large body of rapid pandemic-era research to provide an overview of, and original analysis on, patterns of "material hardship"—a term that refers to challenges such as inability to pay for food, rent, or other basic necessities—and mental health during the first two years of the pandemic. Like chapter 5, this one is concerned with the second of the three perspectives on poverty detailed in chapter 1: a focus on poverty as *the state of lacking adequate resources in the here and now*. This chapter provides some cause for optimism: fewer households than originally reported reduced their food intake, a sign of the success of the government's rapid policy response. But even if food hardship was mostly kept in check, many other social indicators point to cause for concern: more than one-third of low-income families reported frequently feeling anxious or worried throughout 2020 and 2021. Given the many complexities of COVID-19—fearing for one's health and the health of friends and family, juggling new care responsibilities, facing severe work disruptions, enduring long stretches of isolation, and managing the uncertainty of the virus—individuals' *subjective* well-being was more likely to be detached from their *financial* well-being. Though government income transfers can help put food on the table, they cannot buy peace of mind when day-to-day life is so disrupted.

The evidence presented in this chapter allows me to make four primary claims. First, *levels of material hardship were persistently high in the United States before COVID-19 struck, and they remained high during the pandemic*. Before we get into a discussion of trends in hardship—such as whether food hardship increased during the pandemic or not—it is important to establish that pre-pandemic levels of hardship in the United States were not great to begin with. Thus, even if hardship had remained at pre-pandemic levels a year after the start of COVID, this would not have indicated that "all is fine," but only that things could have been much worse. Prior to the onset of COVID-19, more than one in ten households faced food insecurity, according to the U.S. Department of Agriculture.[7] Rates of housing instability were likewise high, as evidenced by the 1.4 million children in public schools in 2018–2019 who were identified as facing homelessness or severe housing instability.[8] Maintaining "baseline" levels of hardship, in short, is better than seeing a situation become much worse, but it is no cause for celebration.

Second, I demonstrate that *levels of material hardship increased during some months of COVID-19, declined in others, and were mostly stable from 2019 to 2020.* Food and housing hardships were volatile throughout 2020 and 2021. By the end of 2020, rates of food and housing hardship had climbed higher than the rates observed in the initial months of the pandemic. In 2021, they fluctuated again, climbing high initially and then declining dramatically (especially for food hardship) in the second half of 2021. But did food hardship increase from 2019 to 2020, or from 2019 to 2021? The USDA estimates suggest not. This chapter presents new findings to demonstrate that little or no change in food hardship was evident all along in the same data set that scholars were using to project a doubling or tripling of hardship. At the same time, evidence shows that visits to food pantries probably increased across the United States, and that the sources of families' concerns regarding food availability became more varied than before. Even if average rates of food hardship remained stable, there was a lot of turmoil beneath the surface that challenged households' ability to cope during COVID-19.

Third, I demonstrate that *the CARES Act and the American Rescue Plan were largely responsible for both the month-to-month fluctuations in hardship and the general stability in hardship from 2019 to 2020.* Just as the stimulus checks, unemployment benefits, increases in SNAP benefits, and CTC expansions had a major impact on keeping poverty in check, they also played a large role in preventing material hardship from getting worse. This chapter offers causal evidence that the expanded CTC, for example, strongly reduced food insufficiency for low-income families with children.

Fourth, I present an important caveat to all these findings: though material hardship ebbed and flowed, *mental health remained concerningly poor throughout the pandemic, and it often worsened even when material hardship was alleviated.* The trends serve as an important reminder that, particularly during a crisis like a pandemic, financial hardship is not the only threat to personal well-being. The complexity of the COVID-19 crisis left many adults frequently worried and severely anxious—problems that cannot be resolved by temporary income transfers.

Persistently High Material Hardship

Given that much of this chapter focuses on changes in material hardship over time, it is important to start with a portrait of hardship and well-being on the eve of the pandemic. In other words, what is the pre-pandemic base from which we can evaluate changes in hardship and well-being during the COVID-19 pandemic? The answer is not particularly heartening: levels of material hardship were high prior to the arrival of COVID-19.

Take food insecurity, for example. The USDA defines a household as food-insecure if the respondent reports being "uncertain of having, or unable to acquire, enough food to meet the needs of all their members because they had insufficient money or other resources for food." In 2019, before the arrival of the pandemic, 10.5 percent of households were food-insecure at some point during the year. Around 38 million individuals, including 6 million children, lived in households that, for financial reasons, struggled to put food on the table.[9] Food insecurity rates in 2019 were higher for Black and Hispanic individuals, for families with children (especially single mothers with children), and for families with lower incomes.

The 2019 rates were not the highest in recent decades. During the Great Recession, for example, average rates of food security hovered around 15 percent.[10] Such widespread exposure to food hardship can have considerable long-term consequences. In their review of the literature, Craig Gundersen and James Ziliak document evidence that food insecurity during childhood can lead to worse health outcomes in adulthood.[11] Analysis of students' exam performance, meanwhile, suggests that food insecurity strongly reduces learning outcomes and scores on standardized tests.[12] Other studies have documented the contribution of programs like SNAP not only to reductions in food hardship over time[13] but also to long-run benefits for children who receive the extra income support.[14] But the rise in SNAP benefits alone was unable to make up for the simultaneous decline in cash benefits from programs such as Temporary Assistance for Needy Families (TANF), and thus rates of food hardship remained high on the eve of the COVID-19 pandemic.

Housing hardship was also high in 2019, a fact well captured in the number of public school students who experienced homelessness or severe housing instability in a given year. In 2018–2019, an estimated 1.4 million children in kindergarten through twelfth grade were either unsheltered or living in homeless shelters, in hotels or motels, or with other families.[15] This is likely an undercount, as the estimates rely on teachers or school officials learning and reporting that their students were experiencing homelessness. In New York City alone, the number of such students exceeded 100,000 in 2019–2020.[16] Thus, even if student homelessness did not increase in New York City from 2019 to 2020 (and available evidence suggests that it did not), the fact that one-tenth of the city's students continued to lack stable housing was nothing to celebrate.

Other indicators of housing hardship point to similarly bleak conditions. In 2019, more than 20 million renters paid more than 30 percent of their income on housing costs.[17] Nearly two-thirds of families with incomes under $25,000, meanwhile, paid more than half of their annual income in rent.[18] In a given year, roughly 4 million households face the threat of eviction.[19]

Several studies suggest that high rates of hardship for families in poverty are largely due to the decline of the cash-based safety net that, prior to the mid-1990s, offered a floor of support for adults (particularly those with children) who lost their jobs or could not find work.[20] The shift to a work-based safety net placed the "deep poor" and the "nearly poor" on divergent paths. For those who could access the labor market and find at least poorly paid jobs, federal and state governments offered SNAP benefits, EITC and CTC payments, and more to subsidize the worker's low pay and increase their take-home pay. Able-bodied adults who did not find work received very little support, especially after the introduction of TANF in the mid-1990s. The reforms may have contributed to higher employment rates, a key aim of the welfare reform advocates of the 1980s and 1990s; however, they also made the hardships experienced by those left behind even more severe.[21]

Regardless of the precise cause of the difficulties, however, the rates of food and housing hardship on the eve of the pandemic were concerningly high. It is important to remember these facts when we switch to the discussion of changes in hardship from 2019 to 2020 and beyond.

Hardship before and throughout the COVID-19 Pandemic

Given the large spike in joblessness in 2020, it would be reasonable to expect a correspondingly large increase in material hardship. The evidence on changes in material hardship from before the pandemic to during the pandemic, however, is mixed. I first walk through some of the evidence on year-to-year changes (for example, from 2019 to 2020) in food and housing hardship before getting into the details of month-to-month changes in hardship throughout 2020 and 2021.

To begin, table 6.1 clarifies the definitions of "material hardship" and "mental health." The first three indicators capture forms of food hardship, but with slightly different definitions. To measure food insecurity, as defined by the USDA, members of a household are asked whether they "were uncertain of having" or "unable to acquire" enough food owing to financial constraints. This definition includes an element of uncertainty lacking in the next two indicators, severe food insecurity and food insufficiency. Instead, these two measures more strictly capture whether food intake was reduced or whether the household did not have enough to eat in the prior week. Being behind on rent or mortgage

Table 6.1   Definitions and Primary Data Sources for Material Hardship and Mental Health Indicators

Hardship or Mental Health Indicator	Definition	Primary Data Source
Food insecurity	Uncertainty at times during the year about having or being able to acquire enough food to meet the needs of all household members, owing to insufficient money or other resources	CPS Food Security Supplement
Severe food insecurity	Disruption to normal eating patterns of one or more household members and reduction in food intake at times during the year, owing to insufficient money or other resources	CPS Food Security Supplement
Food insufficiency	One or more household members "sometimes" or "often" not having enough to eat in the prior week	Census Household Pulse Survey
Behind on rent or mortgage payments	Not currently caught up on rent or mortgage payments	Census Household Pulse Survey
Frequent anxiety	Feeling anxiety "more than half the days" or "nearly every day" over the previous two weeks	Census Household Pulse Survey
Frequent worrying	Being unable to stop worrying "more than half the days" or "nearly every day" over the previous two weeks	Census Household Pulse Survey

Source: Author's compilation.

is the primary indicator of housing hardship used in this chapter, while the mental health indicators capture frequent anxiety and frequent worrying, as defined in the table.

Year-to-Year Changes in Food Hardship

Figure 6.1 documents annual trends in levels of food insecurity from the CPS Food Security Supplement. Recall from table 6.1 that food insecurity includes whether insufficient resources had caused an individual to be uncertain of having, or being unable to acquire, enough food at some point during the year. The solid black line with Xs in figure 6.1

Figure 6.1   Households Experiencing Food Insecurity and Severe Food Insecurity, 2000–2020

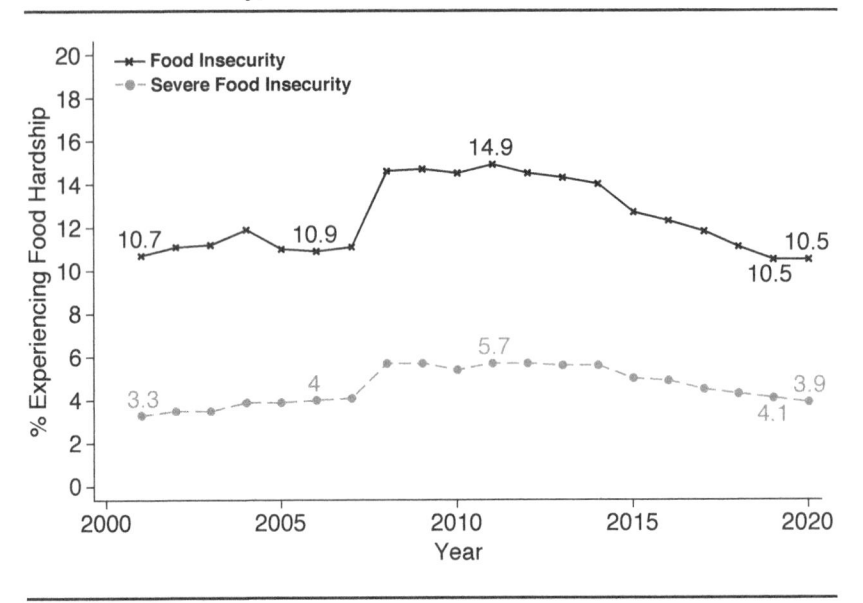

Source: Author's visualization of data from Coleman-Jensen et al. 2021.

plots the trends in household food insecurity. The dashed gray line with circles visualizes the share of households with "severe food insecurity," a measure of whether food intake was reduced.[22] All those who faced this more extreme version of food insecurity are included, by definition, in the less extreme conceptualization of food insecurity.

In 2001, 10.7 percent of households faced food insecurity, while 3.3 percent faced the more severe form of food insecurity. These numbers remained relatively stable through the lead-up to the Great Recession. In 2008, however, household food insecurity spiked from 11 percent to around 15 percent, where it hovered until around 2014. Similarly, the more severe form of food insecurity climbed to just under 6 percent. From 2014 to 2019, the rates gradually declined: 10.5 percent of households reported food insecurity in 2019, while 4.1 percent reported severe insecurity. For context, the rate of food insecurity in 2019 was the lowest rate observed since at least 2001. This aligns closely with trends in annual poverty rates: 2019 also saw the lowest level of poverty in U.S. history (until the subsequent decline in 2020, of course).

However, even as poverty declined from 2019 to 2020, food insecurity simply remained flat, at 10.5 percent. Despite a record-high rate of unemployment in March 2020, and despite the imperfections of the CARES Act, the share of households reporting financial difficulties in putting food on the table did not triple, double, or even increase; instead, that share remained steady at the lowest rate on record since the turn of the century. The share of households with severe food insecurity, meanwhile, declined from 4.1 percent in 2019 to 3.9 percent in 2020. The official estimates of trends in food hardship thus do not contradict the poverty estimates presented in chapter 5 but instead corroborate them.

Though overall rates of food hardship were flat from 2020 to 2021, it is important to point out that there are disparities in the direction of changes across race/ethnicity: among White individuals, food insecurity declined slightly, from 7.9 percent to 7.1 percent; among Black individuals, however, food insecurity increased from 19.1 percent in 2019 to 21.7 percent in 2020, a 2.6 percentage point (14 percent) increase.[23] Similarly, Hispanic individuals saw a jump in food insecurity from 15.6 percent to 17.2 percent, marking a 1.6-percentage-point (10 percent) increase. Though these levels are still far lower than those observed during the Great Recession, the different directions of the trends for White and non-White respondents point to a concerning exacerbation of inequalities in food hardship and probably reflect the unequal access to the CARES Act's income transfers.

Consistent with the USDA estimates, other surveys also find overall stability in food hardship. The Urban Institute's Well-Being and Basic Needs Survey (WBNS) (a nationally representative survey of adults ages eighteen to sixty-four) finds a decline in food insecurity from 23.9 percent in 2019 to 20.5 percent in 2020.[24] Panel data from the PSID reports a slight increase in food hardship, though over the period from 2019 to 2021 (rather than 2020). The PSID estimates suggest a 2.8-percentage-point increase (from 15.5 percent to 18.3 percent) in the share of families who "often" or "sometimes" did not have enough to eat and lacked money to get more food. The fact that each of these surveys uses slightly different sampling techniques and definitions of food hardship helps to explain the mismatches in the pre-pandemic levels of food hardship that they report. Importantly, however, each survey used the same sampling techniques for its pre-pandemic estimates and its estimates during the pandemic; as a result, they report trends that are likely to be more reliable than analyses that compare estimates across two or more surveys. Those trends suggest that food hardship might have declined slightly (WBNS), might have increased slightly (PSID), or might have remained the same (USDA), but that it probably did not change dramatically from the prior year.

Findings from the Pulse help to clarify the complex nature of food hardship during the COVID-19 pandemic. Unlike the WBNS and the PSID, the Pulse began collecting data in April 2020, after the onset of the pandemic, so it lacks a reliable estimate of food hardship in 2019. Nonetheless, it does offer several important data points that help us understand the sources and direction of food insufficiency during the pandemic. For example, the Pulse not only includes an indicator of food insufficiency (whether the respondent sometimes or often did not have enough to eat in the prior week) but also asks why the respondent answered positively. A respondent reporting food insufficiency could indicate whether that was due to a lack of money or a fear of traveling to the supermarket during a global pandemic. Such distinctions are important, as they lead to different understandings of the nature of food hardship during the pandemic and the impact of a given policy response on food hardship. For example, although extra income support is essential to reducing food insufficiency, it is not enough if food insufficiency stems from nonfinancial sources (such as a fear of contracting the virus at the grocery store).

Throughout 2020, around 20 percent of respondents reporting food insufficiency cited nonfinancial reasons (rather than a lack of income) as the primary source of their hardship. Nonfinancial reasons could include concerns about visiting the store during a pandemic or dissatisfaction with the types of food available at the store. The other 80 percent of respondents facing food insufficiency, in contrast, did point to a lack of income as the source of their food hardship. Recall that the WBNS, the PSID, and the USDA survey, in showing modest changes in food hardship from 2019 to 2020–2021, applied a definition of food insecurity that emphasized *not being able to afford* food items. The Pulse definition's inclusion of nonfinancial sources of food hardship may explain a small share of the mismatch between levels of food hardship reported in the Pulse relative to levels reported in preexisting surveys. When focusing on the group that specifically reported financial difficulties in meeting food and nutrition needs, however, the Pulse had evidence all along that food hardship attributable to lack of money might not be on the rise.

The Pulse explicitly asked respondents whether they experienced food insufficiency prior to the onset of the pandemic. From April through December 2020, the average share of respondents who answered that they had experienced food insufficiency prior to the pandemic consistently hovered around 9 percent. Using this indicator and respondents' *current* food insufficiency status, we can separate all respondents into four groups based on their experience of food insufficiency *before* the pandemic and their experience *during* the first year of the pandemic. At

Figure 6.2   Food Insufficiency prior to the Onset of the COVID-19 Pandemic Relative to Food Insufficiency during 2020

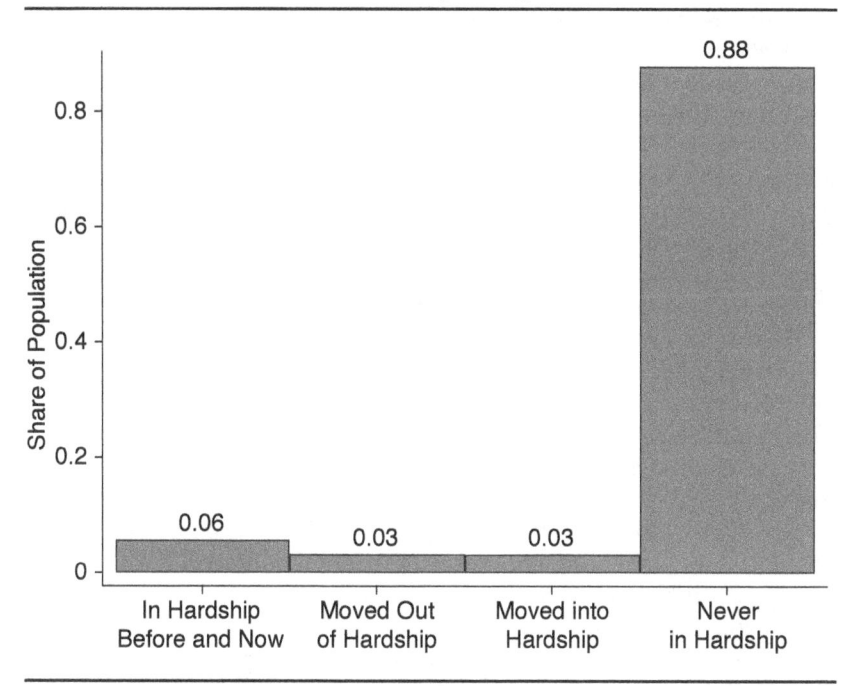

Source: Author's calculations from the Census Household Pulse Survey.

the two extremes, we have the "never in hardship" group, which experienced food insufficiency neither before nor during the pandemic, and the "in hardship before and now" group, which reported food insufficiency both before and during the pandemic. The two groups in the middle are those who reported experiencing food hardship before the pandemic but not when answering the Pulse survey in 2020 ("moved out of hardship") and those who did not face food hardship before the pandemic but were experiencing it when they answered the Pulse survey in 2020 ("moved into hardship"). Figure 6.2 plots how these four groups contributed to the overall levels of food insufficiency from April to December 2020. (The values are averages over this time period.)

For food insufficiency to increase, we would need to see an increase in the number of those in the "moved into hardship" group (who did not experience food hardship prior to the pandemic but did during the pandemic) compared to the "moved out of hardship" group. In other words, if the number of people moving into food hardship is the same as, or fewer than, the number of those moving out of food hardship, it is unlikely that food hardship is increasing. Yet the findings from the Pulse suggested that this is exactly what was happening in 2020.

An average of 6 percent of respondents reported that they were in food hardship both before the pandemic and when surveyed during the pandemic. For context, this figure represents about two-thirds of individuals who experienced food hardship over the course of the pandemic. An estimated 3 percent of respondents were in the "moved out of hardship" group, and another 3 percent were in the "moved into hardship" group. The vast majority (88 percent) experienced food hardship neither before nor during the pandemic.

There are two important takeaways from these findings. First, those experiencing food hardship during the pandemic were primarily those who experienced it prior to the onset of the pandemic. The mean rate of food insufficiency in 2020 among those who had experienced food insufficiency before the pandemic, at 64.7 percent, was eighteen times higher than the rate among those who had not experienced prior food insufficiency (3.5 percent). This finding echoes a prevalent theme in this book: the high rates of poverty and hardship prior to the arrival of COVID-19 directly contributed to poor levels of economic, physical, and subjective well-being during the pandemic. The second takeaway is that the share of respondents moving into food insufficiency was nearly identical to the share moving out of food insufficiency, suggesting no net change in food insufficiency due to financial challenges. These results align pretty well with the official estimates of food hardship that the USDA reported a few months later: the approximately 10.5 percent of the country experiencing food hardship represented no statistically significant change between 2019 to 2020. In other words, the USDA's conclusions in late 2021 that there had been few if any changes in financially induced food hardship were evident in the Pulse as early as spring 2020.

There are several important addenda, however, to the trends reported in the Pulse and the USDA data. Even though average rates of food hardship remained relatively unchanged, some surveys point to a large increase in the use of charitable food services during 2020. The same WBNS study that points to a decline in food hardship, for example, finds an increase in the share of those receiving free groceries or meals, from 13.2 percent in 2019 to 19.7 percent in 2020. Similarly, evidence from New York City suggests that visits to food pantries increased from 12 percent in January/February 2020 (before the pandemic) to 32 percent in September/October 2020.[25] Estimates from the Pulse suggest that 9 percent of respondents in 2020 received either free groceries or a free meal in the week prior to completing the survey. Moreover, only

20 percent of respondents in the Pulse who reported receiving free meals or groceries also said that they experienced food insufficiency. It is likely that the generosity of food pantries and other local organizations that offered free meals contributed meaningfully to the lack of a strong increase in food hardship from 2019 to 2020.

It is worth emphasizing again that a focus on *trends* is different from a focus on *levels*. Even if food hardship changed little from 2019 to 2020, levels were high to begin with, particularly among low-income families with children and Black and Hispanic families of all types. Large inequalities by race/ethnicity, gender, family type, and education levels in food hardship persisted throughout the pandemic, a natural consequence *not* of the COVID-19 pandemic itself but of the historic unwillingness in the United States to build welfare state and labor market institutions that sufficiently and inclusively support the financial well-being of all.

Year-to-Year Changes in Housing Hardship

Consistent evidence on housing hardship generally points to a story similar to the trends in food hardship. The Urban Institute's WBNS survey, for example, found declines across several dimensions of housing hardship. The share of respondents reporting problems with paying utility bills declined from 12.3 percent in 2019 to 10.8 percent in 2020, and utility shutoffs declined from 3.8 percent to 2.6 percent. Problems with paying the rent or mortgage declined from 10.3 percent to 9.3 percent.

The Urban Institute study was not alone in its findings: the Federal Reserve found that delinquencies on home mortgages declined during the COVID-19 pandemic, in contrast to the large increases observed during the Great Recession.[26] Delinquencies were particularly low, the study found, when the CARES Act was distributing the $600 per week unemployment benefits in the first half of 2020. Additionally, Luke Shaefer and his colleagues have documented evidence that nonpayment of rent and evictions remained close to pre-pandemic levels well after the onset of the pandemic.[27] In fact, from April to June 2020, rates of nonpayment of rent were lower than rates observed in April 2019. The authors also point to data from the Federal Reserve Bank of Cleveland, which finds that rates of eviction were lower in 2020 than in 2019.[28]

Eviction moratoria at the national, state, and local levels are likely to have played an important role in reducing eviction rates during the COVID-19 pandemic.[29] In September 2020, the Centers for Disease Control and Prevention (CDC) issued a nationwide halt on most evictions, largely to reduce mobility and prevent the spread of COVID-19. This measure was extended for the vast majority of rents through late

2021. The National Low Income Housing Coalition estimates that 6.5 million households that were behind on rent payments may have benefited from the moratorium.[30] Most of these households were headed by Black and Latino individuals. Researchers from Princeton's Eviction Lab similarly have found that the eviction moratoria prevented more than 1 million evictions throughout the pandemic.[31]

Beyond trends in food and housing hardship, a number of other data points support a general stability in financial security, or even increases, from 2019 to 2020. In June 2020, for example, 70 percent of adults were able to cover a $400 emergency expense in cash, up from 63 percent in October 2019.[32] Credit card data demonstrated that the lowest-income households saw the largest relative increases in the balance of their bank accounts thanks to the stimulus checks and unemployment payments. By October 2020, the average low-income cardholder had 50 percent more cash on hand than at the same time in 2019.[33]

Month-to-Month Fluctuations in Food and Housing Hardship during 2020–2021

Despite modest year-to-year changes in food and housing hardship from 2019 to 2020, there were notable month-to-month changes during the COVID-19 pandemic that align closely with changes to income support programs throughout 2020 and 2021. Figure 6.3 documents monthly trends in food insufficiency (left panel) and missed rent or mortgage payments (right panel) from April 2020 through December 2021. The dashed gray line in both panels represents levels for lower-income respondents (incomes below $35,000), while the solid black line with circles represents the trends for respondents with incomes above $35,000.

In April 2020, the month when COVID-19 sent unemployment to a record high, an estimated 17 percent of respondents with income below $35,000 reported food insufficiency, while 4 percent of respondents with incomes above $35,000 faced food insufficiency. For both groups, however, the levels gradually increased throughout the year. By December 2020, an estimated 25 percent of the lower-income respondents were experiencing food insufficiency. The data show a spike after the expiration of the $600 per week unemployment benefits in July 2020, consistent with evidence that these benefits contributed to lower levels of food hardship than would have been observed in their absence.[34]

From December 2020 to March 2021, food insufficiency declined steeply for the lower-income respondents, dropping from 25 percent to 18 percent. The decline coincided with two stimulus check payments and the payout of many refundable tax credits, demonstrating again

Figure 6.3   Trends in Food Insufficiency and Missed Rent or Mortgage Payments, April 2020 to December 2021

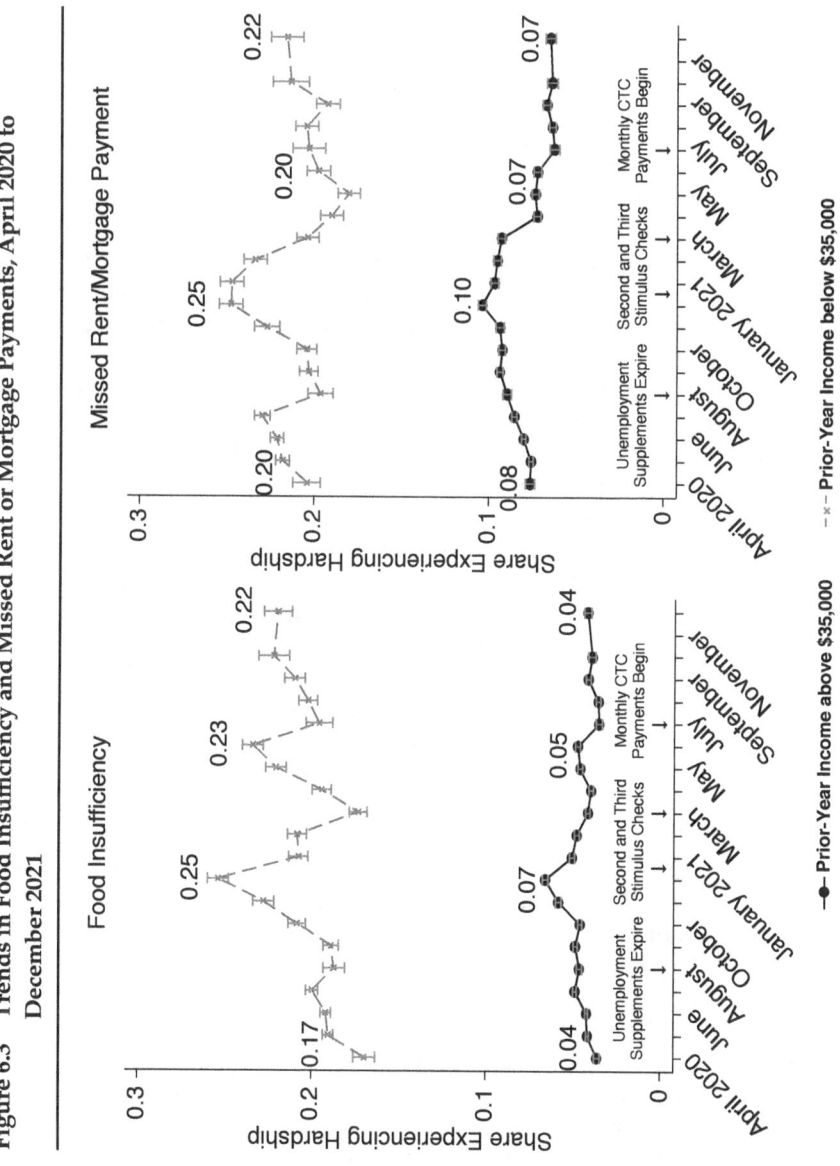

Source: Author's calculations from respondents to the Census Household Pulse Survey.

the likely effect of income transfers on fluctuations in hardship. From March through June 2021, food hardship again climbed, but dropped down in July 2021, when the refundable CTC was introduced; it then increased slightly after September 2021, when the $300 per week unemployment supplement expired. In other words, food hardship went up and down throughout 2020 and 2021, largely coinciding with increases and decreases in income support.

Housing hardship (right panel) shows some volatility from month to month, though not to the same extent as food hardship. In April 2020, 20 percent of lower-income respondents reported missing a rent or mortgage payment—a concerningly high level. The April 2020 rate was 8 percent for respondents with incomes over $35,000. Similar to food hardship, both income groups reached peak levels of housing hardship in December 2020—25 percent for lower-income respondents and 10 percent for higher-income respondents—with large increases coinciding with declining support from unemployment benefits. Missed rent and mortgage payments then declined again when the two stimulus checks and refundable tax credits were distributed; 2021 closed with housing hardship rates at 22 percent and 7 percent for lower- and higher-income respondents, respectively.

These patterns reveal notable month-to-month volatility in hardship, even if year-to-year changes were relatively minor. Moreover, the month-to-month changes corresponded closely with increases and decreases in the provision of cash support: the increases in food and housing hardship after the $600 per week unemployment benefits expired in July 2020 are evident in figure 6.3, as are the declines when the early 2021 stimulus checks and refundable tax credits were distributed.

The Impact of the Policy Response

To what extent are the CARES Act, the ARP, and the expanded CTC responsible for the patterns of food and housing hardship documented here? Much of the evidence is clear from a simple examination of the timing of hardship increases and declines: that food insufficiency declined after stimulus checks were paid out, for example, is surely no coincidence. Several studies have offered compelling descriptive evidence drawing a link between policy and hardship.[35]

Some studies have also worked to produce plausibly causal evidence of the role of policy changes in reducing hardship, using variation in policy rules across place, time, and family type to assess the effect of extra cash on food challenges. For example, Lauren Bauer and her colleagues have found that the Pandemic EBT (P-EBT) benefits (vouchers similar to SNAP benefits that compensated for students' lost access to school breakfasts and lunches due to school closures) lowered levels of food insecurity for families with children.[36]

In a separate study, I worked with several colleagues—Elizabeth Ananat, Sophie Collyer, Megan Curran, and Christopher Wimer—to produce evidence of the impact of the expanded CTC payments on food and housing hardship in 2021.[37] Recall from prior chapters that the monthly CTC payments were first distributed in July 2021 and then paid out through December 2021; then a lump-sum payment (half the total benefit value) was made in the early spring of 2022 (tax time). Given that only families with children received the benefits, and also that families received different levels of benefits depending on how many children they had and their ages, we were able to reliably estimate how the CTC affected food and housing hardship. Readers interested in the results from our difference-in-differences estimates can see the chapter appendix. Here, figure 6.4 visualizes the descriptive trends in food and housing hardship for families with children relative to families without children throughout 2021; these trends align with the pattern of results observed in our regression estimates. The first shaded area represents the time of the monthly CTC payments, and the second represents the lump-sum payments. The upper panel presents results for all respondents; the lower panel shows results for low-income respondents (less than $35,000 in pretax income).

Food insufficiency among all households with children increased from 9.8 percent in April 2021 to 13.4 percent at the end of June 2021, before the first CTC payment. Childless families saw a similar increase in food insufficiency, from 6.1 percent to 7.2 percent during this period. After the first CTC payment, however, food insufficiency remained relatively stable for childless households (7.2 percent to 7.1 percent) but declined for families with children, from 13.4 percent to 9.4 percent. Among low-income families with children, the decline was even larger: food insufficiency fell from 29.8 percent in June to 20.8 percent in July 2021, while the rate for low-income childless households fell only from 19.5 percent to 19.0 percent.

Throughout the rest of 2021, levels of food insufficiency ticked up slightly for both family types, reflecting the withdrawal of expanded unemployment benefits, the early withdrawal in some states of emergency SNAP allotments, and rising food prices.[38] Despite the lump-sum CTC payments in March 2022, food hardship increased for both family types during this time.

For both income levels and household types, trends in falling behind on rent or mortgage payments showed very little change from before the monthly CTC payments to afterwards. Roughly 20 percent of low-income households with children were behind on rent or mortgage

Figure 6.4   Trends in Food and Housing Hardship by Household Type, 2021–2022

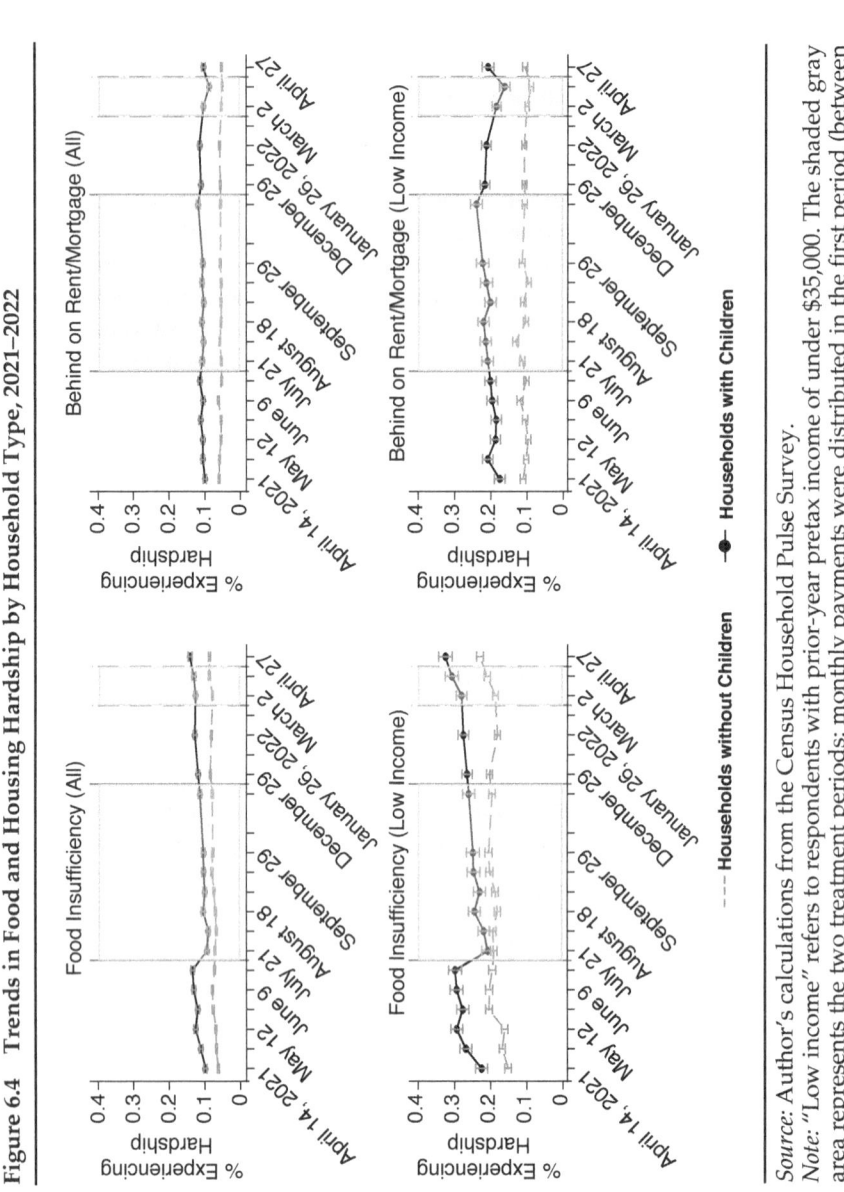

Source: Author's calculations from the Census Household Pulse Survey.
Note: "Low income" refers to respondents with prior-year pretax income of under $35,000. The shaded gray area represents the two treatment periods: monthly payments were distributed in the first period (between the solid lines) and the lump-sum payment was distributed in the second period (between the dashed lines).

payments throughout 2021. A monthly payment of up to $300 per child can go a long way toward increasing food consumption, but it may be too little to have any significant impact on housing hardship. Moreover, the small effect sizes may have been partly driven by the eviction moratoria, which temporarily eased monthly housing cost burdens for some residents. Upon receipt of the lump-sum CTC payments in March 2022, however, housing hardship declined for families with children, while remaining stable for childless households.

These general patterns align with what we see when we use our econometric tools to estimate the differential effects of the monthly versus lump-sum payments. Specifically, we find that the monthly CTC payments reduced food insufficiency among families with children by at least 2.3 percentage points (19 percent reduction). We are not the only researchers to have found evidence of declining food hardship: using a different data set and a different set of respondents, Natasha Pilkauskas and her colleagues similarly find that the monthly CTC payments contributed to declines in food hardship. Moreover, they see "some evidence that the credit reduced medical hardships, reduced reliance on friends and family for food, and improved respondents' ability to pay utility bills."[39] Both their study and ours have also found slightly stronger reductions in food hardship for Black parents with children than for White parents with children.

Though the monthly payments reduced food hardship, we find no significant reductions from the effects of the lump-sum payment (aligning with the trend presented in figure 6.4). Instead, the lump-sum payment reduced the likelihood that families with children would fall behind on rent payments by at least 1.2 percentage points (10 percent). Additional analyses of the Pulse data confirm that families receiving the CTC benefits reported being more likely to use the lump-sum payment on debt and housing payments, while the monthly benefits were more likely to be spent on food and other everyday items. The differential use of the two payment types is consistent with past evidence on spending from the EITC.[40]

Moreover, the results are consistent with analyses of 2021–2022 consumption data. My colleagues Giulia Giupponi, Emma Lee, Sophie Collyer, and I used debit and credit card spending data to show that the monthly CTC payments increased spending on items at grocery stores and general stores to a greater extent than the lump-sum payments— a finding consistent with the food hardship results presented earlier. Instead, the lump-sum payment uniquely contributed to more spending at children's clothing stores, while both payment types increased consumption at formal childcare centers.[41] Evidence from multiple studies thus points to differential consumption responses from the monthly and lump-sum

CTC payments, with the former doing more to increase spending on food items and reduce food insufficiency. Given this evidence, should most or all refundable tax credits be distributed monthly rather than in lump-sum form moving forward? I return to this question and elaborate on the pros and cons of such a change in this book's concluding chapter.

Though the CTC was able to reduce poverty and hardship, it could not resolve all of parents' worries during the pandemic. Multiple studies suggest that unconditional cash payments to families with children in 2021 had no significant effects on mental health or subjective well-being.[42] For all families, worry and anxiety persisted and remained high throughout the pandemic, even when material hardship declined.

What Income Transfers Can't Buy: Subjective Well-Being and Mental Health

Material hardship and mental health often go hand in hand, as we know from research showing that adults who report financial difficulties are more likely to experience higher levels of stress and anxiety.[43] This was true to some extent in the midst of the pandemic, when lower-income families were more likely to report frequent anxiety and frequent worrying than were higher-income families. Perhaps more than in nonpandemic times, however, even higher-income households reported facing persistently high levels of anxiety and worrying. This finding suggests that the complexity of the crisis left many adults in a state of elevated anxiety and worry that temporary income transfers could not fix on their own.

Figure 6.5 documents some of these trends by showing levels of frequent worrying (left panel) and frequent anxiety (right panel) from April 2020 through December 2021. As before, the solid black line with circles plots trends for respondents with prior-year incomes above $35,000, while the dashed gray line represents trends for respondents with prior-year incomes under $35,000. At the onset of the COVID-19 pandemic, 31 percent of the lower-income respondents and 20 percent of the higher-income respondents reported frequent worrying. These figures gradually increased throughout 2020 as COVID-19 cases spread throughout the country, peaking at 39 percent of lower-income respondents and 25 percent of higher-income respondents in December 2020. Rates declined as the pandemic slowed slightly in early 2021, although lower-income respondents' level of frequent worrying remained at around 30 percent in December 2021—nearly the same rate as in April 2020.

The patterns are similar when we look at frequent anxiety (right panel). In April 2020, 37 percent of lower-income respondents reported frequent

Figure 6.5 Trends in Frequent Worrying and Frequent Anxiety by Income, April 2020 to December 2021

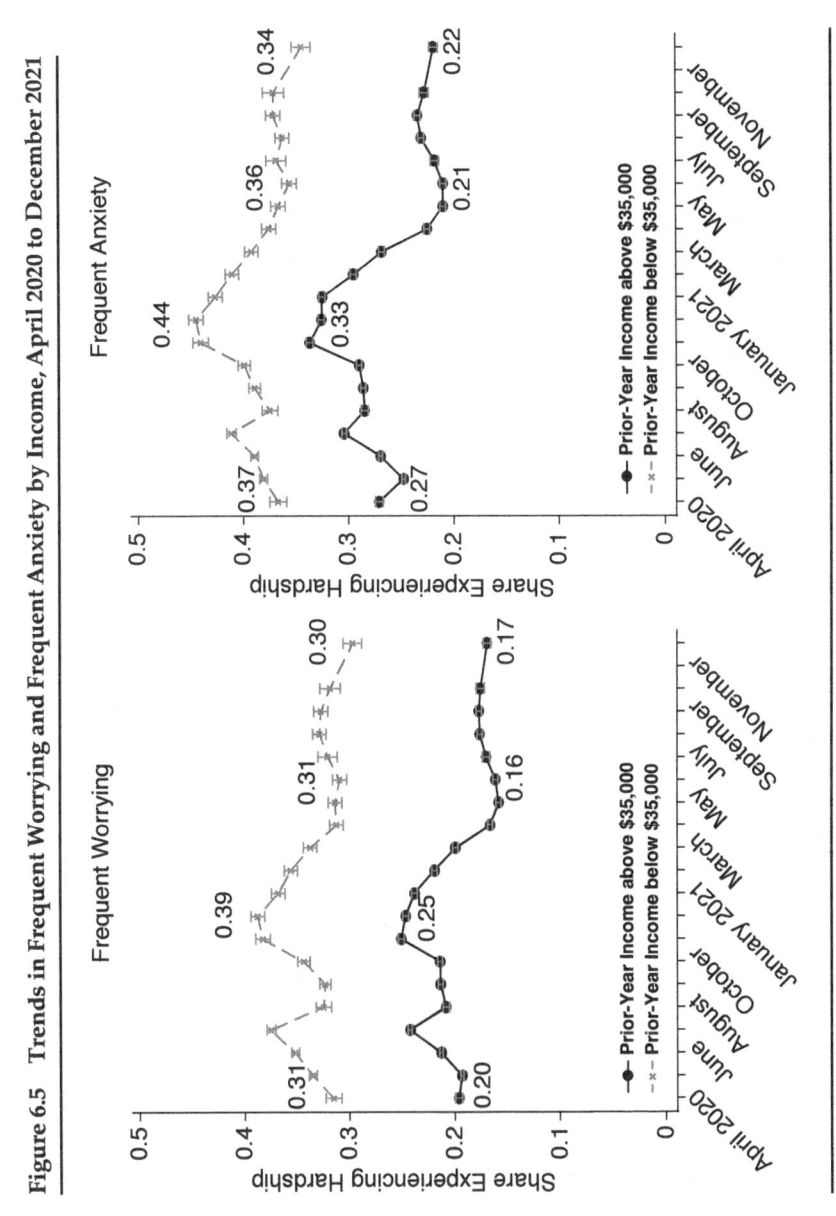

Source: Author's calculations from respondents to the Census Household Pulse Survey.

anxiety. Though this figure fluctuated some from month to month, there was no point at which fewer than one-third of lower-income families reported frequent anxiety throughout 2020 and 2021. For respondents with incomes above $35,000, frequent worrying declined from 27 percent in April 2020 to 22 percent in December 2021; it never fell below 20 percent during that time.

The consistently high levels of worrying and anxiety indicate that, particularly in the context of COVID-19, all was not well, even with reductions in poverty and stable levels of hardship. Despite the unarguable success of the CARES Act and the ARP in promoting economic security, the unprecedented influx of income transfers from these programs could not do much to provide peace of mind.

Other empirical evidence corroborates these findings from the Pulse. Beyond anxiety and worrying, for example, one study found that depression-like feelings increased dramatically after the onset of COVID-19.[44] Google searches related to loneliness and sadness similarly increased.[45] A phone-based survey conducted before and during the COVID-19 pandemic similarly found that parents experienced more negative moods after the onset of the pandemic, and parents facing challenges related to income loss also experienced declining sleep quality and more uncooperative behavior by their children.[46] Indeed, it is not only parents who faced challenges related to mental health and well-being after the pandemic arrived, but children as well.[47]

Qualitative research likewise finds that families faced immense stress in adapting to the day-to-day changes in everyday life resulting from the pandemic.[48] For families with young children in particular, levels of stress and hardship were often higher than for families with older children or no children.[49] Each of these findings serves as an important reminder that, particularly during the COVID-19 pandemic, personal well-being could not be boiled down to financial hardship.

It is not overly difficult to make sense of these facts. Consider that, first, families benefiting from the income transfers throughout 2020 and 2021 probably knew that these were temporary income supports and that, while temporarily useful in making ends meet, these transfers alone were not going to provide long-run economic security. Second, and perhaps more importantly, the complexities of COVID-19 obviously evoked concerns beyond the strictly economic. After all, as a previously unknown virus spread throughout the country and the world, too many families experienced serious health consequences rather than simply economic losses (see chapter 2). Beyond the health consequences, families with children also had to manage during widespread closures of schools and childcare centers—the focus of the next chapter.

Chapter 6 Appendix

The difference-in-differences estimates in table A6.1 follow a model specified as:

$$y_i = \beta_1 \text{Children}_i + \beta_2 \text{MonthlyCTC}_i + \beta_3 \text{LumpsumCTC}_i$$
$$+ \beta_4 (\text{Children} * \text{MonthlyCTC})_i + \beta_5 (\text{Children} * \text{LumpsumCTC})_i$$
$$+ \beta_6 X_i + \varepsilon_i$$

The outcome variable is one of the hardship indicators (separate models for each). *MonthlyCTC* and *LumpsumCTC* are binary indicators of whether the survey occurred during the monthly payment period (July to December 2021) or lump-sum payment period (March to May 2022), respectively. The model also interacts the treatment indicator (*Children*) with a dummy covering the partially treated months of January and February 2022, during which many families had leftover funds from the monthly payments and some began receiving the lump-sum payment. Given this interaction, the reference period for both our monthly and lump-sum treatment effects is April to June 2021. We operationalize a binary treatment indicator measured as whether the household has children (value set to 1) or is childless (value set to 0). Childless households, which do not directly benefit from the reform, form our control group.

Table A6.1   Difference-in-Differences Estimates: Effect of the 2021 CTC Expansion on Hardship Outcomes, 2021 and 2022

	Food Insufficiency, All Incomes	Behind on Rent or Mortgage, All Incomes	Food Insufficiency, Low Income	Behind on Rent or Mortgage, Low Income
Monthly Payments, July to December 2021 relative to January to June 2021				
Household with children	0.031*** (0.003)	0.039*** (0.003)	0.048*** (0.009)	0.052*** (0.008)
Household with children X CTC months	−0.023*** (0.006)	−0.004 (0.005)	−0.058** (0.018)	0.008 (0.016)

(*Table continues on p. 164*)

Table A6.1   (*Continued*)

	Food Insufficiency, All Incomes	Behind on Rent or Mortgage, All Incomes	Food Insufficiency, Low Income	Behind on Rent or Mortgage, Low Income
Lump-Sum Payment, March to May 2022 relative to January to June 2021				
Household with children X CTC months	−0.005 (0.007)	−0.012+ (0.007)	−0.009 (0.023)	−0.009 (0.020)
Pretreatment mean among members of the treated group	0.119	0.107	0.276	0.192

Source: Census Household Pulse Survey.
Note: "X" indicates that we have interacted the two terms within our regression model. All estimates are from the same model with a sample size of 937,990 (all incomes) and 181,404 (low income). "Low income" refers to having prior-year household income below $35,000. All models include state fixed effects; week fixed effects; controls for age, education, and sex of household head; an interaction of household with children and whether expanded unemployment benefits were provided in the given state-month; and an interaction of households with children and whether SNAP emergency allotments were provided in the given state-month. Robust standard errors are in parentheses.
$^+ p < 0.10$; * $p < 0.05$; ** $p < 0.01$; *** $p < 0.001$

Chapter 7

Poverty as a Stratifying Feature: School and Childcare Closures

THE LINGERING consequences of poverty contributed to greater direct exposure to the health and employment risks of COVID-19, as chapters 2 and 3 documented. But entering the pandemic in or near poverty had another set of consequences as well, especially for families with children: it became more challenging to adjust to the school and childcare closures brought on as pandemic-related restrictions were put in place. Here the book's third perspective on poverty becomes particularly relevant: *poverty as a stratifying feature that moderates the short- and long-run consequences of a life disruption*. Recall from chapter 1 that this perspective acknowledges that even when poverty does not directly increase the likelihood of facing a life disruption, persistent exposure to poverty nonetheless amplifies the challenges of adapting to a life disruption when it occurs.

This chapter explores this third perspective on poverty through the lens of a life disruption that affected families with younger children in particular: school and childcare center closures during the COVID-19 pandemic.[1] In April 2020, nearly all states mandated a temporary closure of schools and a shift to distance learning.[2] Meanwhile, childcare centers throughout the country either temporarily closed or reduced their in-take capacity, sometimes by choice but also owing to declining demand from parents who were hesitant to send in their children. The closures, many people would have argued, were justified, particularly during the first spring of the pandemic, when access to COVID tests was scarce, vaccines were out of sight, and much about the virus was still unknown. But the closures nonetheless came with side effects: learning losses for students exposed to remote schooling, immense social and psychological challenges for the nation's youth, and greater difficulties for parents in their attempt to balance work and care responsibilities.

This chapter shows that it was not always the lowest-income places that were most exposed to school and childcare closures. However, it was often the lowest-income families who faced greater costs from such exposure. The consequences for the educational performance of students from families in poverty, for example, were greater than they were for the highest-income students, particularly in districts that spent more time in distance or hybrid learning.

Wealthy families were generally able to adapt to the new reality with greater ease: they were more likely to form learning pods with other students in the neighborhood, to have access to reliable internet access and a dedicated laptop for their children's learning, and to supplement any potential learning loss with after-hours tutoring or online resources. Children from lower-income families, meanwhile, were likely to be preoccupied with a more fundamental concern: more than 22 million low-income students had benefited from free or reduced-price school lunches on an average school day.[3] Beyond food and nutrition concerns, children from lower-income families were less likely to have a dedicated space to work from in their home, or a reliable internet connection. This is evidence of the stratifying feature of poverty on which this third perspective focuses: entering the pandemic with fewer resources made it more challenging to adapt to school closures, with the consequence that income-based gaps in educational performance and economic opportunity might widen for years to come.

Against this backdrop, this chapter asks two questions. First, which groups and places were most exposed to school and childcare center closures? This is a surprisingly difficult question to answer, as no public, nationwide database existed on school and childcare closures in the United States during the first year of the pandemic. As a result, we have to get creative in order to measure the scale of these closures. To do so, I present results based on anonymized, aggregated mobility records from more than 40 million cell phones across the United States—a surprisingly reliable source of secure data with which to track the total number of monthly visits to schools and childcare centers during the pandemic relative to before the pandemic. Combined with school-specific data on the demographics of students from the U.S. Department of Education, this chapter provides a comprehensive set of evidence on the socioeconomic, geographic, and demographic disparities in exposure to school and childcare closures.

After addressing trends and differential exposure to school and childcare closures, this chapter addresses a second question: What have been the consequences of school and childcare closures, particularly for lower-income families and their children?

Tracking School and Childcare Closures

Unfortunately, there is no government-administered database on the opening and closing decisions of all schools or childcare centers in the United States. We would be lucky to even find a centralized database of the names, locations, and quantity of formal childcare centers across the country. To track the opening decisions of schools, some researchers relied on the websites of the largest school districts in the country, while others turned to a select group of districts to report whether they were, say, operating with distance learning for a particular week.[4] These efforts were useful, but because they covered only the largest school districts, they missed the majority of schools across the country, and rural schools in particular. Information on childcare closures, meanwhile, was nearly nonexistent.

The data presented in this chapter instead cover nearly all schools and formal childcare centers in the United States, with monthly estimates on the likely opening or closure status of these schools and centers. Rather than tracking 100,000 school websites each month, this evidence relies on aggregated, anonymized, and monthly data from more than 40 million cell phones across the country. Each month we can see a count of the number of cell-phone users who visited a given school or childcare center, and we can compare that number to the total number of visits in the same month in 2019, before the onset of the pandemic.[5] If a school goes from 50,000 visits in April 2019 to 5,000 visits in April 2020, we can be pretty sure that this is a school that has closed or turned to some form of distance learning. Using this logic, Emma Lee and I have compiled two databases that track the decline in in-person visits to schools and childcare centers.[6]

In the results presented throughout this chapter, we identify a school as "closed or mostly closed" if it had a decline in visits of at least 50 percent relative to the visit count in the same month in 2019. For example, if Park Hill South High School in Riverside, Missouri, goes from 50,000 visits in April 2019 to 5,000 visits in April 2020, we would call this a 90 percent decline in visits in April 2020. By our definition, the school was closed or mostly closed. Some students could still have been attending in person, and many could have been engaged in distance learning, but the indicator clearly captures that the school was not functioning the same as it was back in April 2019. We then repeat this measure for May and each subsequent month: if visits to Park Hill South numbered 48,000 in May 2019 and 40,000 in May 2020, we would identity this as a 17 percent decline in May 2020. The school may not have been fully back to normal, but these numbers are not aberrant enough to call it "closed or mostly closed." The threshold of a 50 percent decline in visits as an indication that a school or childcare center was closed or mostly closed is somewhat arbitrary, but we show in our work that this cutoff works well to identify schools that in fact were operating under a hybrid or fully remote learning situation.[7]

I should note that when we measure visits to a school, we cannot see any information about the actual cell-phone users in the data; the only information made available is how many phones entered the proximity of a given school or childcare center over the course of a month. The data are secure and provided free for academic researchers to use through a company called SafeGraph. To measure which students were exposed to distance learning, we combine the SafeGraph data with a large set of school-level indicators from the Department of Education that inform us of each school's third-grade math performance, the share of students who experienced homelessness, the share who had limited English proficiency, the share who were eligible for free or reduced-price school lunch, and the share who were racial/ethnic minorities.

Trends in School Closures and Distance Learning

Figure 7.1 presents national trends in school closures from January 2020 through December 2021. In April 2020, a month when COVID-19 was rapidly spreading across the country, forty-eight states and Washington, D.C., mandated or recommended the closure of schools. We estimate that 89.6 percent of all schools, including 92 percent of middle and high schools, turned to distance learning in April (see figure 7.1).[8] This rate remained high in May 2020, the final month of the school year for most districts in the country.

Beginning in September 2020, the start of the new academic year for most schools, state and local governments adopted vastly different approaches to distance learning. As a result, school closures were distributed much more unevenly across the country from September through December 2020 in comparison to the previous spring. In September 2020, an estimated 40.2 percent of all schools were closed or mostly closed. This figure subsequently climbed to 56.1 percent of schools in December 2020, the month when the Alpha variant of COVID-19 spread throughout the country. Middle and high schools were about 6.6 percentage points more likely than elementary schools to be engaged in distance learning in December, consistent with many schools' desire to prioritize in-person learning for younger students.

Throughout 2021, school closures steadily declined, most likely driven by a combination of greater access to vaccines, the ebbs and flows of the virus, and more pressure from parents and communities to put students back in schools. In January 2021, an estimated 42.1 percent of schools

Figure 7.1   Trends in the Share of Closed or Mostly Closed Schools, January 2020 to December 2021

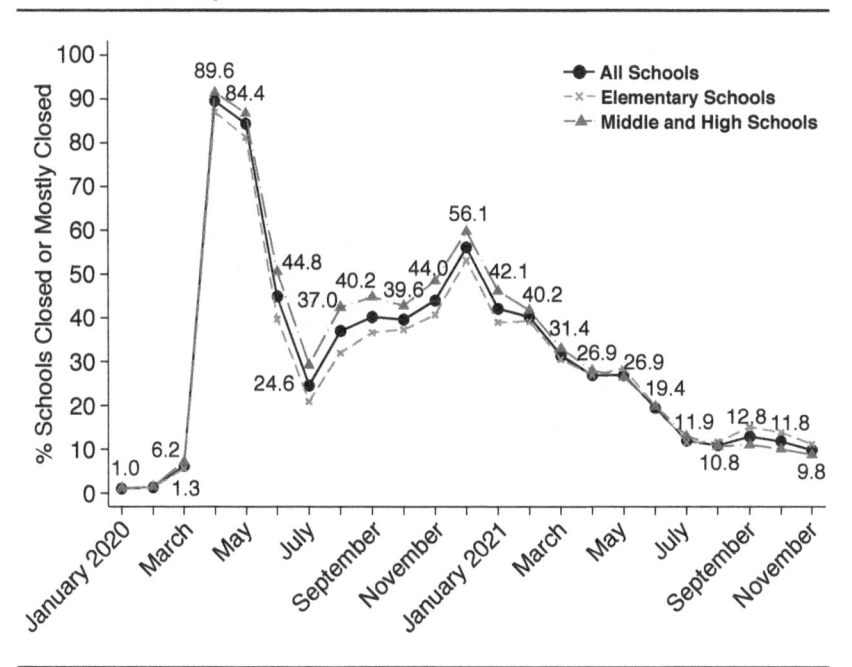

Source: Author's calculations from SafeGraph data (Parolin and Lee 2021a).

were still at less than half their January 2019 capacity, but this percentage gradually declined to 9.8 percent of schools in November 2021.[9]

The November 2021 rate might come as a surprise to some. How were the in-person attendance rates of one in ten schools still under half their November 2019 attendance rates? There are a few likely answers. First, some schools had continued to offer remote learning or hybrid options to students, particularly given that the pandemic had not subsided by the end of 2021. Second, many parents decided during the pandemic to remove their children from public schools and to either homeschool them or send them to a private school. (Private schools were less likely to switch to distance learning at the peak of the pandemic.) A study of Michigan schools in 2021 found, for example, that around 10 percent of the parents of kindergartners decided against public school enrollment in the fall of 2020; instead, homeschooling rates and private school options increased considerably, particularly elementary school students.[10] Third, there may be some measurement error in the counts; notice that even in January 2020, prior to the onset of the pandemic, our

**Figure 7.2   Geographic Disparities in School Closures from September
2020 to December 2020 by the Relative Decline in Total Visits
Compared to the Same Month in 2019**

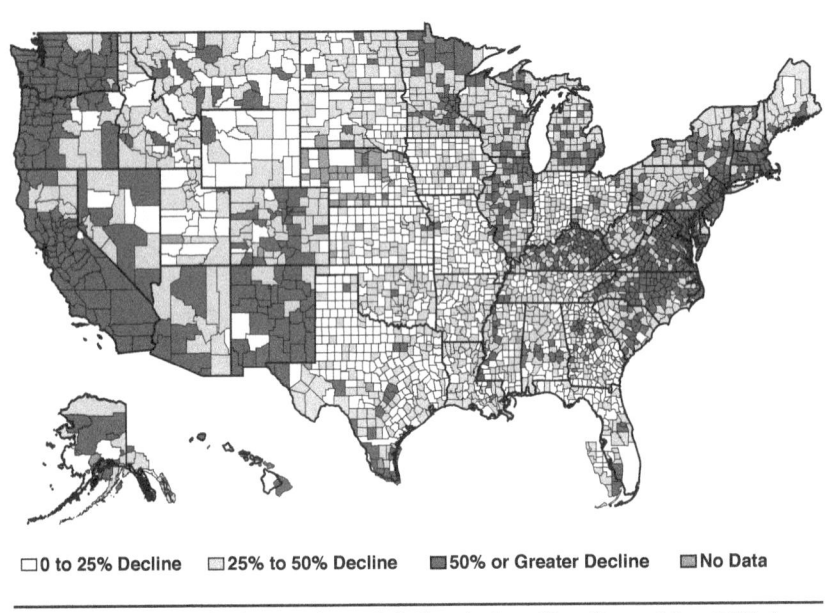

☐0 to 25% Decline   ☐25% to 50% Decline   ■50% or Greater Decline   ▣No Data

Source: Author's calculations from SafeGraph data (Parolin and Lee 2021a).

data registered 1 percent of schools already experiencing a 50 percent
decline in visits relative to January 2019.

Nonetheless, our findings make clear that during the spring and
autumn of 2020, school closures and distance learning were in widespread use across the United States. Particularly in the latter period,
however, closures were concentrated in particular parts of the country.

School Closures across Place

Figure 7.2 visualizes the geographic disparities in school closures across
the country. Specifically, it shows variation in the average year-over-
year decline of in-person visits to schools in nearly every U.S. county.
The figure presents averages from September through December 2020—
the period when school closures were still high but not universal (as in
April 2020).

The darkest-shaded counties are those where schools, on average,
saw declines of at least 50 percent in in-person visits from 2019 to 2020.
These counties are concentrated in the West in Washington, Oregon,

Figure 7.3   Trends in Exposure to Closed or Mostly Closed Schools, by Students' Race/Ethnicity, January 2020 to December 2021

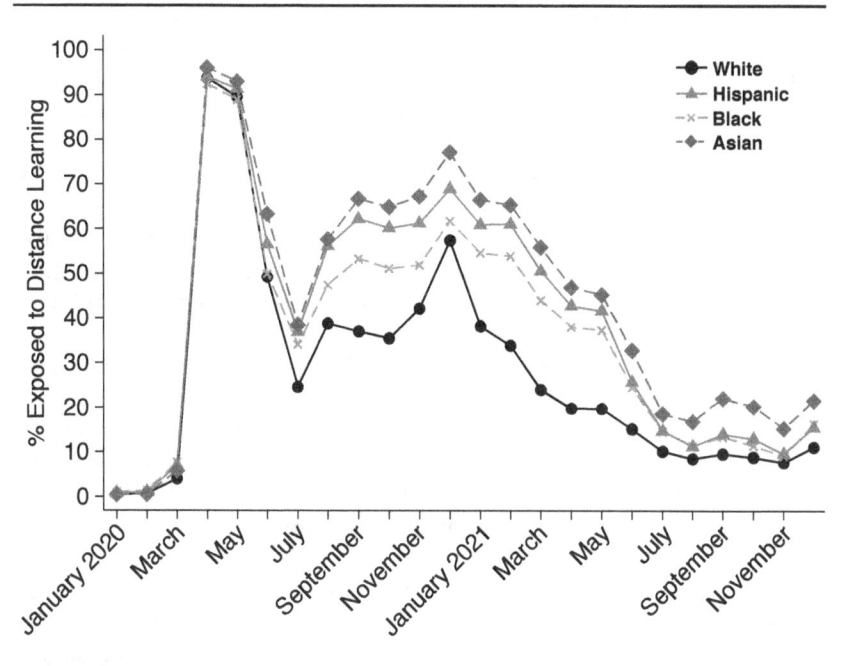

Source: Author's calculations from SafeGraph data (Parolin and Lee 2021a).

California, Nevada, and New Mexico, as well in the East, especially in Washington, D.C., Maryland, Massachusetts, and New York. The counties with the smallest year-over-year declines in in-person visits tend to be concentrated in states across the Midwest and upper Midwest, such as South Dakota, North Dakota, Wyoming, Montana, Iowa, and Kansas.

Although we are not particularly interested here in what drove schools' decisions to turn to remote learning, most of the recent work asking that question has pointed to three factors: local and state politics, population density (which reflects how easily COVID-19 can spread throughout a community), and local COVID-19 case rates.[11]

Which Students Were Most Exposed to School Closures?

Just as some *places* had a higher prevalence of school closures relative to others, some *groups of students* were also more likely than others to be exposed to closures and distance learning. Figure 7.3 presents trends in exposure to school closures by race/ethnicity (White, Black, Hispanic, and Asian—the four groups we can focus on with adequate precision). Though students in each of these racial/ethnic categories faced similar rates of distance learning in April 2020, disparities set in and widened throughout the following autumn. In October 2020, an estimated 35.4 percent of White students were exposed to distance learning, compared to 51.2 percent of Black students, 60.2 percent of Hispanic students, and 64.9 percent of Asian students. These disparities would remain relatively persistent throughout the end of 2021.

While the levels of exposure for each group varied in line with the national trends shown in figure 7.1, Asian students were consistently the most exposed to school closures and distance learning, probably because a large share of Asian students lived in California, a state that, as figure 7.2 depicts, generally led the nation in closure rates. Black and Hispanic students consistently faced higher rates of closures than did White students. To be clear, these patterns do not suggest that race or ethnicity was a driving factor behind schools' decisions to close, but rather that the many factors that led schools to shift to distance learning impacted more non-White students than White students.

Why might these findings be concerning? Owing to both large racial/ethnic differences before the onset of the pandemic and the association of more exposure to distance learning with larger learning loss during the pandemic, racial/ethnic gaps in learning are likely only to have widened—a claim to which I return momentarily.

While figure 7.3 looks at exposure to school closures by students' race/ethnicity, figure 7.4 provides insight into links between schools' socioeconomic characteristics and their likelihood of closure. Specifically, the figure examines patterns of school closure over the 2020–2021 school year (September 2020 through May 2021) across several characteristics: race, income, language, third-grade math scores, student homelessness, and family structure. Specifically, the figure groups schools according to their decile rank on the given characteristic (x-axis) and the share of schools closed within that decile rank (y-axis).

The upper-left panel, for example, shows school closure rates across the distribution of schools' shares of White students. (The schools with the smallest share of White students are on the left, and those with the highest share are on the right.) Among schools with the smallest share of White students, schools were closed or in distance learning for an average of 60 percent of the 2020–2021 school year. The subsequent deciles show a linear relationship between school closures and the share of White students at these schools: the higher the share of White students in the school's population, the more likely it was to be open. In schools with the highest share of White students, the rate of school closure was only

Figure 7.4 Full or Partial School Closures by Students' Economic or Demographic Characteristics, September 2020 to May 2021

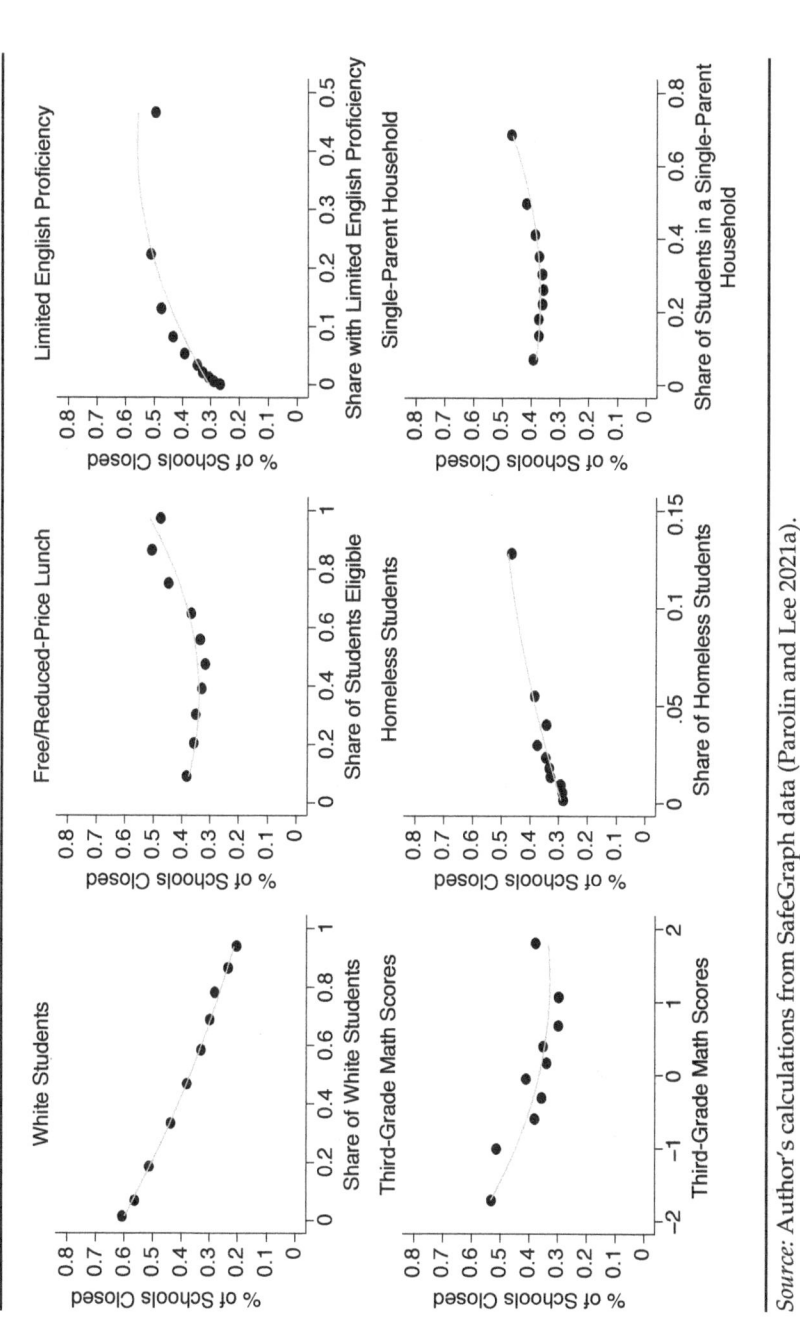

Source: Author's calculations from SafeGraph data (Parolin and Lee 2021a).
Note: The figure is a binned scatterplot in which each dot represents the decile of the characteristic (x-axis). The y-axis position is the share of closed schools in the given decile of schools.

20 percent, or one-third the rate for the schools with very few White students.

The upper-middle panel shows rates of school closure depending on the share of a school's students who were eligible for free or reduced-price lunch. This measure is often used as a proxy for a school's poverty rates. The pattern is nonlinear: among the 70 percent of schools with the lowest shares of students who were eligible for free or reduced-price lunch (the first seven deciles), school closures rates did not vary by much. However, among the top 30 percent—those schools with higher shares of students eligible for free or reduced-price lunch—we see slightly higher closure rates, hovering just around 50 percent. In other words, the poorest schools experienced more closures and more distance learning than the schools with the smallest share of students eligible for free or reduced-price lunch; the relationship between the two indicators, however, was not constant across the distribution of eligibility for free or reduced-price lunch.

The upper-right panel documents closures with respect to the share of students with limited English proficiency. With the exception of the final decile, the share of school closures increased monotonically with the school's share of non-native English speakers. The schools with the highest share of students with limited English proficiency were more than twenty percentage points more likely to be closed than schools with the lowest share of such students.

The lower-left panel looks at the relationship between school closures and students' third-grade math scores.[12] This panel, perhaps more than others, provides direct insight into whether exposure to closures was highest among schools that were already behind academically. The findings show that this was indeed the case. An estimated 50 percent of the schools with the lowest math scores (bottom decile) were closed or in distance learning, on average, during the 2020–2021 school year. This rate was around fifteen percentage points higher than for schools with average math score levels.

The bottom-middle panel presents school closures across the distribution of shares of K-12 students experiencing homelessness. Just under 30 percent of schools with the lowest rates of student homelessness (bottom decile) were closed or in distance learning, on average. But among schools with the highest rates of student homelessness, nearly 50 percent were closed or in distance learning.

Finally, the lower-right panel shows more muted variation across the distribution of shares of students from single-parent households across census tracts, though there is some evidence that the places with the highest share of students with single parents were more exposed to school closures and distance learning.

Consequences of School Closures and Distance Learning

The findings presented in figures 7.3 and 7.4 reveal large disparities in exposure to distance learning by race/ethnicity and pre-pandemic educational performance that could exacerbate regional, racial, and class-based divides in the educational performance of U.S. students. Consider that, even prior to the pandemic, income-based gaps in educational performance had been widening for nearly half a century. Among children from higher- versus lower-income families who were born in 2001, the achievement gap was around one-third larger than for children born twenty-five years earlier.[13] Moreover, the income-based achievement gap was twice as large as Black-White achievement gaps, a reversal from previous decades. If greater exposure to distance learning was associated with greater learning loss, and if those losses were even larger for low-income students exposed to distance learning, then it would follow that pandemic-related education disruptions have worsened these income-based differences in learning outcomes. Available evidence suggests that this is precisely the case.

Several studies have now demonstrated that students learned far less through distance learning than they do in a traditional face-to-face setting. In one of the earliest high-quality studies on the topic, a group of researchers used Dutch exam data before and during the pandemic to track learning losses among students in the Netherlands.[14] Though the Netherlands should be considered a best-case scenario in terms of being prepared to mitigate COVID-related learning losses—it has relatively low levels of inequality, equitable school funding, and widespread access to broadband internet, and its lockdown period was relatively brief— Dutch students exposed to distance learning made "little or no progress" in their educational performance.[15]

Relative to the Netherlands, the United States has a much more unequal system of school funding and larger baseline gaps in educational outcomes across different income groups. If Dutch students experienced unequal learning losses during the pandemic, then American students are likely to have experienced the same—or worse.

One of the most convincing studies in the United States was conducted by researchers at the Center for Education Policy Research at Harvard University who used testing data from 2.1 million students across ten thousand U.S. schools to evaluate whether remote learning widened gaps in achievement by income and race/ethnicity.[16] Their findings point to large disparities in learning losses: among schools that prioritized remote learning, achievement growth was lower for all students, but especially for students at high-poverty schools. Among schools that engaged in remote learning for most of 2020–2021, high-poverty schools suffered 50 percent more learning loss in mathematics than low-poverty schools. In contrast, math achievement gaps between high- and low-poverty schools did not widen among the schools that remained open and with in-person instruction.[17]

These researchers' findings demonstrate that it was more difficult for families in poverty to adjust to remote learning; as a result, students from these families suffered the greatest learning losses when schools shifted to distance learning. Poverty acted as a *stratifying feature* that amplified the consequences of the shift to remote learning for families with lower incomes at the start of the pandemic.

It is not challenging to understand *why* the lowest-income students suffered the most with the turn to distance learning. To start, school closures put greater pressure on low-income parents, many of whom had lost jobs in the pandemic, to address their children's nutrition needs: more than 22 million low-income students had benefited from free or reduced-price school lunches on an average school day.[18] Though the federal government provided additional cash support to families with children who had received free or reduced-price lunch at school, the distribution of the funds was delayed in many states, and even after it was received the burden of food provision was still shifted from the school cafeteria to the low-income parent.[19]

Beyond food challenges, students in low-income families were far less likely to have a dedicated room, desk, or computer from which to engage in virtual school activities.[20] Moreover, higher-income families had greater capacity to invest time and resources into extracurricular learning activities, whether additional tutoring, summer education camps, or even visits to the library.[21] The families who entered the pandemic in poverty were far less able to adapt to the challenges posed by school closures and distance learning. The lowest-income students experienced the largest learning losses as a result, further exacerbating income-based divides in educational performance.

Federal Policy Efforts to Close Learning Gaps

To counteract learning losses and improve the ability of schools to remain open during the pandemic, the federal government's Elementary and Secondary School Emergency Relief (ESSER) program invested more than $190 billion in support for schools across the country. The largest tranche of funding ($120 billion) came from the American Rescue Plan Act passed in March 2021; this funding amounted to $30,000 spent per student in some low-income districts, more than double the federal per-student support in a normal year.[22] The funds need to be spent by the end of 2024 but are otherwise provided to school districts to use with broad discretion.[23] One mandate requires schools to spend at least 20 percent of these funds on academic recovery efforts, for example, but provides little specification on which academic recovery efforts they should fund.[24]

Brookings Institution researchers have identified high-quality tutoring programs as one intervention with the greatest potential to reverse the math and reading losses of 2020–2021.[25] In fact, this is one of the services for which districts expect to increase spending the most from 2022 to 2025.[26] Summer learning and extended school days are among the other interventions to which districts expect to allocate more resources, though parents' and teachers' resistance to extensions of the school year have largely inhibited the extra schooling that is likely necessary to meaningfully offset learning losses.[27] However, spending plans are different from districts' actual allocations of resources, data on which are scarce. Few mechanisms are in place to evaluate districts' spending, let alone the efficacy of their spending; I return to this shortcoming in the book's concluding chapter.

We probably will not know until standardized test scores are released in the future whether progress has been made in reducing income-based disparities in learning loss. Initial projections are not optimistic. Dan Goldhaber and his colleagues, for example, estimate that high-poverty districts that went remote during the pandemic will need to spend nearly all of the ESSER funds—rather than just the mandated 20 percent—on academic recovery efforts in order to fully offset their pandemic learning losses.[28]

Childcare Center Closures

Like schools across the country that shut their doors during the peak of the pandemic, childcare centers were also forced to adapt to the realities of COVID-19. Unlike schools, however, distance learning had little relevance for childcare centers; for the most part, they were either open or closed, providing their essential in-person care services or not. In the spring of 2020, most childcare centers were closed or at reduced capacity.

The closure of childcare centers hurt not only parents and children but also the broader economy. Childcare centers provide working parents with reliable supervision and physical care of their children—including feeding, playing, and maintaining hygiene—throughout the workday.[29] Prior to the arrival of COVD-19, the majority of children under the age of five participated in some form of nonparental care arrangement.[30] Childcare centers provide an environment that promotes the social and cognitive development of young children. For the broader economy, childcare centers facilitate many thousands of jobs, not only for care workers themselves but also for the working parents who send their children there.[31]

Prior to the arrival of COVID-19, access to childcare centers was already largely unequal by race/ethnicity and income. Research has shown, for example, that childcare deserts (geographic locations with inadequate childcare supply) vary from state to state and disproportionately impact rural communities, low- and middle-income families, and Black and Hispanic families.[32] And even those families with plenty of care options nearby can face prohibitively high costs. The cost of infant care in New York, for example, averages more than $15,000 per year. Even with the state's higher minimum wage ($15 per hour), a minimum-wage worker would have to pay nearly two-thirds of her annual salary to cover the average cost of infant care.[33]

The wrench thrown into the daily operations of formal childcare centers by the pandemic affected most working parents with young children. Like schools, different childcare centers in different places across the United States imposed different capacity restrictions on attendance. As a result, inequalities in exposure to care closures were vast throughout 2020 and 2021, with potential consequences for inequalities in child outcomes, parental employment, and family well-being.

To track childcare center closures, we again turn to our SafeGraph data, which provide information on in-person visits to more than eighty-five thousand childcare centers across more than two thousand counties in the United States. Importantly, the data used here capture only formal, center-based childcare; we cannot account for home-based care or care provided in other informal settings.[34] And as this chapter discusses later, many of the apparent declines in visits to formal childcare centers could simply reflect a COVID-era substitution of informal childcare environments for formal ones. In other words, rather than sending four-year-old Lucie to the KinderCare down the road, as Mom and Dad did before the pandemic, perhaps Lucie now goes to Grandma Edith's house between 9:00 AM and 3:00 PM each day, allowing her parents to continue working as before. Lucie is still receiving some type of daily care, but this arrangement is not discernible in our data set, except as it contributes to a decline in visits to formal childcare institutions.

Just as for schools, the data presented here identify a childcare center as closed or at strongly reduced capacity if it experiences a 50 percent decline in monthly visits relative to the same month in 2019. Particularly for childcare centers, where attendance is not mandatory (unlike in schools), the declines we identify probably reflect a combination of parental choice (like the choice made by Lucie's parents) and capacity restrictions (being able to take in only so many children each day to adhere with proper distancing regulations). The data on total visits here cannot distinguish between these two factors, but some studies do provide insight on their relative contribution. A study of close to one thousand children ages three to five showed that, by the beginning of June 2020, preschool enrollment had dropped from the pre-pandemic rate of 61 percent of all children in the United States to 8 percent.[35] This drop in enrollment was primarily due to childcare center closures, which affected 74 percent of children previously enrolled, but also to the voluntary decisions of parents: an estimated 11.7 percent of families chose to remove their children from preschool programs that remained open.[36] It is possible, however, that these relative shares changed over the course of the pandemic.

Trends in Childcare Center Closures

Figure 7.5 displays the share of U.S. childcare centers that either closed or strongly reduced capacity in each month from January 2020 through December 2021. In addition to showing the total share of childcare centers meeting the 50 percent decline cutoff, the figure also visualizes the share of centers with reduced capacity at varying levels above that cutoff: a 50 to 60 percent decline, a 60 to 70 percent decline, and so on.

Just as for schools, the first major peak in childcare center closures is observed in April 2020, when an estimated 70 percent of childcare centers were closed or operating at reduced capacity by at least half. This rate declined to 59 percent in May and to 27.5 percent in July 2020. In November 2020, however, the rate increased to 35 percent and climbed further to 42 percent in December 2020, perhaps owing in part to the new wave of COVID-19 cases sweeping over the United States that month.

Throughout 2021, the share of childcare centers at reduced capacity gradually declined, but it remained at around 20 percent even in November 2021, the post-pandemic month when the share of centers at reduced capacity was at its smallest. Looking more deeply into the severity of capacity reduction in November, figure 7.5 shows that very few of these centers were experiencing a 90 to 100 percent reduction in capacity; instead, the majority of them were seeing 50 to 70 percent fewer visits compared to the same month in 2019.

To gain more insight on the characteristics of places with higher closure rates, and to learn who is more exposed to care closures, figure 7.6 shows the association of race/ethnicity, poverty, and family structure with care closure rates. Here the demographic characteristics represent those of the census tract in which the care center is based. The upper-left panel of figure 7.6 shows the same negative relationship with race that we observed for schools: childcare centers in census tracts with more White families were far less likely to be at reduced capacity, whereas areas

Figure 7.5 Trends in the Share of Childcare Facilities That Closed or Operated at Very Reduced Capacity, January 2020 to December 2021

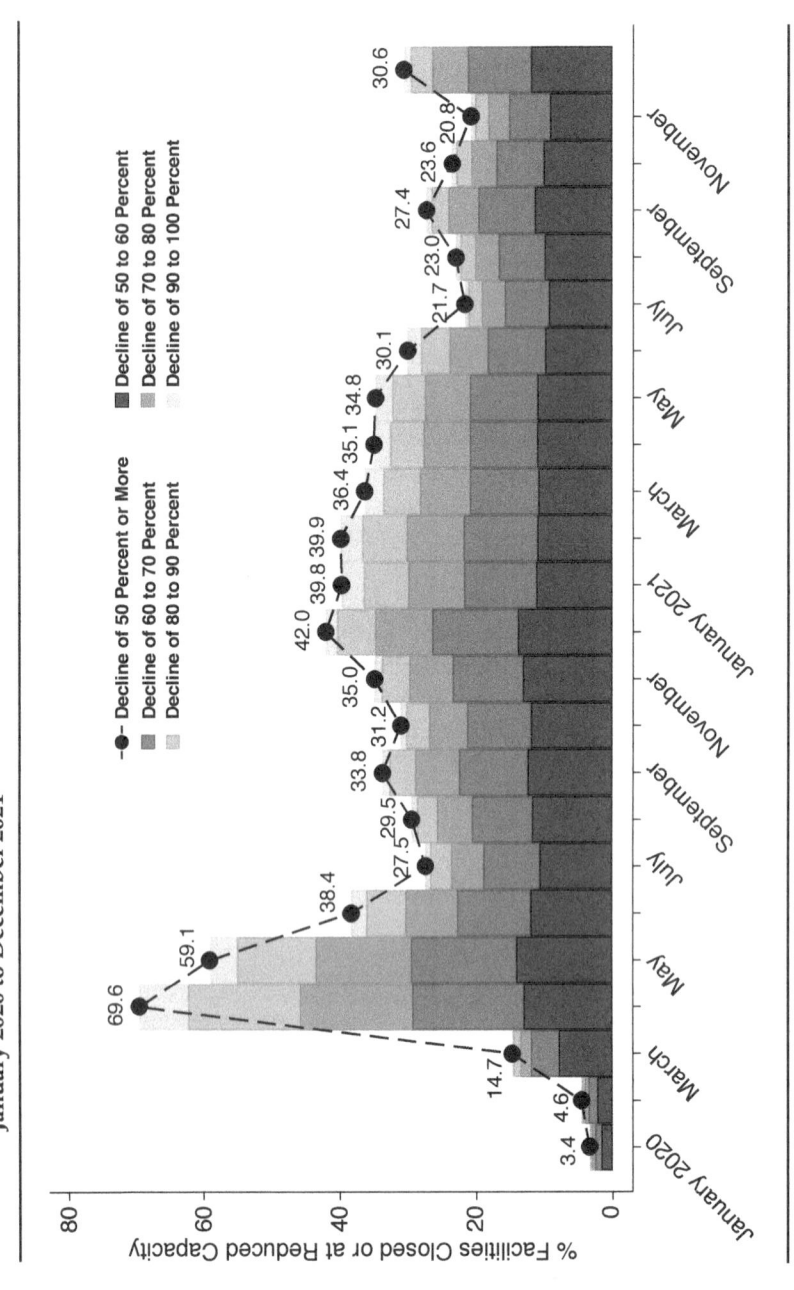

Source: Author's analysis of data from SafeGraph (Lee and Parolin 2021).

Figure 7.6   Share of Childcare Facilities That Closed or Operated at Very Reduced Capacity, by Census Tract Demographic Characteristics, January 2020 to December 2021

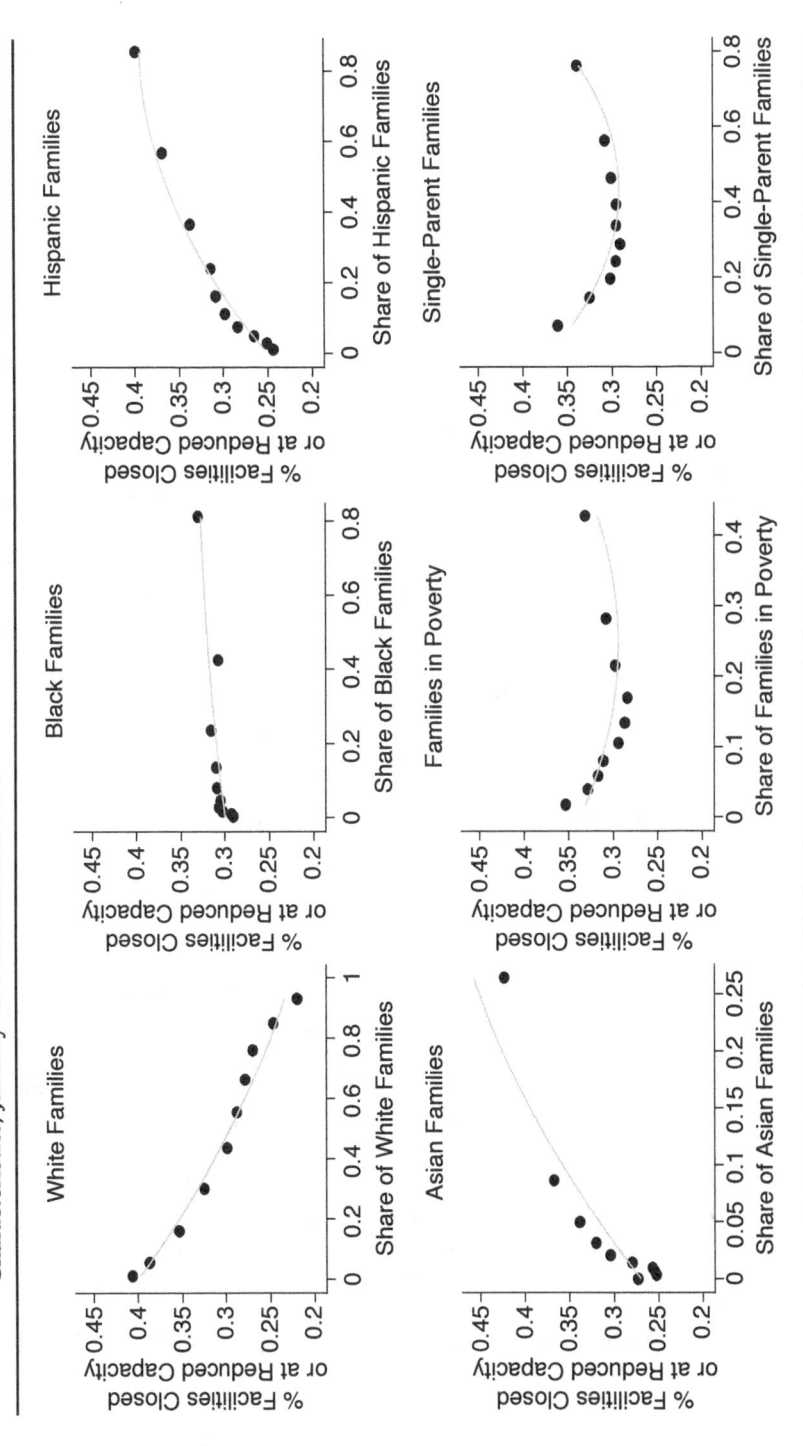

Source: Author's analysis of data from SafeGraph (Lee and Parolin 2021).

with fewer White families faced much higher closure rates. Specifically, the census tracts with the highest shares of White families faced a mean closure rate of around 20 percent, while tracts with the lowest shares of White residents faced a closure rate of around 40 percent.

The upper-middle panel shows that the share of Black families in a census tract is not strongly associated with closure rates. In contrast, the upper-right panel shows a positive association between closure rates and the share of Hispanic families in a census tract. The childcare centers serving the greatest share of Latino families show a 40 percent closure rate, whereas those with the lowest share of Latino families show only a 25 percent closure rate. A similar trend can be seen in the lower-left panel, which shows an increase in childcare closures as the share of Asian families increases in a census tract. Again, a variety of factors influenced these racial/ethnic differences in exposure, the most important probably being population density, population size, and local COVID-19 case counts.

The lower-middle and lower-right panels show a slight U-shaped relationship between the share of families in poverty (middle) and the share of single-parent families (right) and closure rates. In other words, families in poverty and single-parent families were not necessarily exposed to childcare center closures at a higher rate than other families, but when they did experience a closure, they were likely to face greater difficulties in adapting to the loss of care support.

The Consequences of Childcare Center Closures and Capacity Reductions

Parents, children, and childcare staff alike have been challenged by the closures and capacity reductions of childcare centers. For working parents, the extra barriers to childcare center access have shifted responsibility for care back to the family. Balancing work and care responsibilities was already difficult enough in the United States, a country that lacks the paid leave provisions and public childcare investments of many peer nations. Although evidence is mixed on the effect of school and care center closures on mothers' employment outcomes during the pandemic (see chapter 3), there is no arguing that these closures have made life far more difficult for working parents, and for working mothers in particular.[37] Mothers have taken on a disproportionate share of unpaid childcare work compared to men during the pandemic, and mothers were more likely than fathers to experience depression, feelings of isolation, and stress.[38]

Young children, particularly those from lower-income families, have also paid a price: those not enrolled at a childcare center have often lacked daily participation in at-home learning activities, such as reading with an adult, physical exercise, and engaging with music.[39] Parental engagement at home, meanwhile, varies widely based on income and class, and the fact that parents with lower levels of education often have less time to read and play with their children contributes to differential development outcomes.[40]

Finally, the consequences of care center closures and declines in capacity (or demand) for care services also have direct consequences for childcare staff. In a March 2020 survey of six thousand childcare providers, 49 percent reported that they experienced a loss of income due to reduced enrollment. In the same survey, only 11 percent of childcare providers reported confidence that their program would be able to survive an indeterminate length of closure without financial assistance.[41]

Poverty as a Stratifying Feature in the Pandemic

The consequences of poverty are not limited to a point-in-time calculation of income, nor to the ways in which poverty directly exposes a household to a set of risk factors. Instead, experiencing poverty over one's life also makes it far more difficult to adapt to a given life disruption, whether it be losing a job, experiencing the addition or loss of a family member, or facing the closure of schools and childcare centers.

School and childcare center closures were among the COVID-related challenges that left no family with young children unaffected. As this chapter has demonstrated, the vast majority of schools and care centers shut their doors in April 2020, and many of them either remained closed or operated at reduced capacity or in a hybrid format throughout 2020 and 2021. Especially during the 2020–2021 school year, schools with lower third-grade math scores and schools with more non-White students spent more time in distance learning. Moreover, the lowest-income students at these schools suffered the greatest learning losses, portending a widening of income-based gaps in educational performance, as well as economic opportunity, in the years ahead. Likewise, the hit to the childcare industry may translate into more inequalities in access to formal care moving forward.

Low-income families were not necessarily exposed to more childcare closures or capacity reductions, but they faced particularly large challenges in navigating work and care responsibilities when formal care centers closed. This is the stratifying effect of exposure to poverty: when a life disruption hits, it is the lowest-income households that tend to pay the highest price.

Chapter 8

Ten Policy Lessons for Improving Economic Well-Being after the COVID-19 Pandemic

A T THE start of this book, I posed four questions that the subsequent chapters would go on to explore: How did poverty influence the consequences of the COVID-19 pandemic? What was the role of government income support in reducing poverty during the pandemic? What lessons does the COVID-19 pandemic offer for how we measure and conceptualize poverty in the United States? And finally, what policy lessons from the pandemic should we apply to efforts to improve the economic well-being of households in the future? In this concluding chapter, I reflect on what the evidence presented in the intervening chapters—covering the health disparities, the unemployment shock, the government's policy response, poverty rates, material hardship, school closures, and childcare-center closures—offers to those four questions.

Poverty and the Consequences of COVID-19

The three perspectives on poverty identified in chapter 1—understanding poverty as a risk factor, as a measure of current resources, and as a stratifying feature—offer a useful framework for summarizing how poverty influenced the consequences of the COVID-19 pandemic, as well as how the federal government's actions affected poverty during the pandemic.

Unequal exposure to poverty was central to the economic, health, and social consequences of the pandemic. Building on the first of our three perspectives on poverty, this book has shown pre-pandemic exposure to poverty to have been a central risk factor increasing the likelihood of facing the many life disruptions that COVID-19 imposed. At the onset of the pandemic, more than 40 million U.S. residents had incomes below the poverty line, and a disproportionate share of them were Black or Hispanic. Worse, the average Black adult in poverty in 2019 had spent 57 percent of her childhood in poverty, compared to 34 percent for the average Hispanic adult in poverty and 20 percent for the average White adult in poverty. These disparate experiences of poverty, accumulating from birth onward, contributed directly to unequal health and employment outcomes at the onset of the COVID-19 pandemic. As chapter 2 documented, the COVID-related death rate in the highest-poverty counties in the United States, around four hundred for every hundred thousand residents, was nearly twice the rate of the lowest-poverty counties. A county's poverty rate more strongly aligned with its COVID case rates and death rates than health insurance rates, residents' ages, racial/ethnic composition, or population density. At the individual level, the average adult with an income below half the poverty line was around three times more likely to die of COVID-related causes than the average adult with an income more than three times the poverty line.[1]

Unsurprisingly, given their lower pre-pandemic incomes, Black and Hispanic workers also faced the brunt of the unemployment spike. As chapter 3 documented, one in three adults who entered the pandemic in poverty were unemployed in April 2020. Moreover, adults whose income put them just below the poverty line in 2019 experienced a twenty-four-percentage-point increase in unemployment—twice the magnitude of the increase in unemployment for those with 2019 incomes nearly four times the poverty line. More than gender, age, or parenthood, pre-pandemic poverty status was the dominant factor shaping employment disparities. At the same time, low-wage workers who managed to hang on to their jobs were at increased risk of encountering COVID on the job in part because they were the least likely to be able to work from home (see chapter 3).

Viewed through the lens of poverty as the immediate state of lacking adequate resources to meet needs—the second of the three perspectives—the government's policy response after the onset of the COVID-19 pandemic was undoubtedly successful at reducing poverty rates. Despite the record-high unemployment rate, new income support policies brought the U.S. poverty rate down to 9.1 percent in 2020, an all-time low. The CARES Act's income transfers put more than $900 billion directly into the pockets of U.S. adults in 2020, doubling the size of non-retirement, non-health-care support. As a result, taxes and transfers cut the annual poverty rate by more than fifteen percentage points, a record performance. In 2021, the expansion of the Child Tax Credit brought the nation's child poverty rate to another record low: at 5.1 percent, the child poverty rate was less than half of what it had been in 2019. Internationally, the U.S. child poverty rate in 2021 put the country on par with Germany, and the U.S. tax and transfer system was temporarily reducing poverty as effectively as the Norwegian welfare state. For a country generally known for its high poverty rates compared to its international peers, the federal government's ability to reduce poverty to this extent is nothing short of historic. As chapter 6 discussed, the policy response also generally kept food insecurity at its lowest recorded level since at least 2000.

The third perspective viewed poverty as a stratifying feature that exacerbated the challenges of low-income households in adapting to the pandemic's disruptions. Even when life disruptions hit low- and high-income households alike, it is generally those in poverty who face the greatest challenges in adapting. This was certainly the case with school closures and distance learning. After nearly all schools temporarily shut down in April 2020, between 40 and 56 percent continued to operate at very reduced capacity (measured as at least a 50 percent year-over-year decline in attendance) throughout 2020. As chapter 7 documented, lower-income students were not necessarily more exposed to school closures than higher-income students, but they did face greater costs when schools closed: students in high-poverty schools that primarily turned to distance learning suffered 50 percent more learning loss than students in low-poverty schools engaged in distance learning. In contrast, math achievement gaps between high- and low-poverty schools did not widen among schools that stayed open.[2] As a stratifying feature, poverty amplified the consequences of the shift to remote learning for families who entered the pandemics with lower incomes.

These three perspectives on poverty offer evidence on two of this book's research objectives; moreover, they help to reconcile the competing narratives regarding patterns of inequality throughout the pandemic. While some scholars argue that "COVID Increased Inequality in America"[3] and others argue that inequality declined throughout the pandemic,[4] this book shows that either claim can be confirmed, depending on which of the three perspectives on poverty one adopts. An appropriately comprehensive account should recognize all three perspectives simultaneously.

The three perspectives, as emphasized in chapter 1, are an organizing device that builds on past poverty research; in turn, they can also be applied in future work to increase our understanding of how point-in-time poverty status interacts with exposure to, and ability to recover from, life disruptions related to employment changes, health shocks, the birth or loss of family members, and more.

What Does the COVID-19 Pandemic Teach Us about Poverty?

The third aim of this book was to extract lessons from the COVID-19 pandemic to help us conceptualize poverty. Studies of poverty tend to focus on one of three themes: the sources (or determinants) of poverty, the measurement of poverty, and the consequences of poverty. As previewed in the opening chapter, the pandemic offers lessons we can bring to each area of study.

The pandemic added to our understanding of the *determinants* of poverty by providing perhaps the strongest proof to date that *poverty is not simply a product of individual characteristics or behaviors*. There is a strong tradition in American poverty of focusing on individual behavior when identifying the sources of high poverty among certain groups. As Michael Katz, an eminent historian of poverty in the United States, writes in *The Undeserving Poor*, "the idea that poverty is a problem of persons—that it results from personal moral, cultural, or biological inadequacies—has dominated discussions of poverty for well over 200 years."[5] In the past half-century, individualist perspectives on poverty have largely narrowed their focus to family structure and employment as two dominant drivers of poverty rates.[6] For example, to explain why some groups of people are more likely to live in poverty than others, researchers often derive their answers from behavioral characteristics: if more members of group X would find full-time work, then maybe they would have the same poverty rate as group Y, the argument goes. While the average working person should of course have a higher income than the average jobless person, the American welfare state penalizes joblessness far more than other high-income countries do.[7]

Scholars who view poverty solely through this behavior-centered lens often take the *context*—such as the prevailing welfare state in a country and its labor market institutions—as fixed. This line of thinking can be useful if the purpose is to inform an eighteen-year-old American about the steps she should take to increase her chances of achieving economic security in adulthood. It is less useful for understanding why young adults in the United States are poorer than other age groups, why Black Americans of any age are more likely than White Americans to live in poverty, or why Americans face higher poverty rates than do those who live in other high-income countries.

In the context of the COVID-19 pandemic, the behavioral perspective is at odds with what we have observed: record-high unemployment leading to record-low poverty rates. The federal government's intervention severely weakened the relationship between unemployment and

Figure 8.1   Annual SPM Poverty Rates among Adults by Whether They Were Unemployed for at Least Four Weeks during the Year, 1975–2020

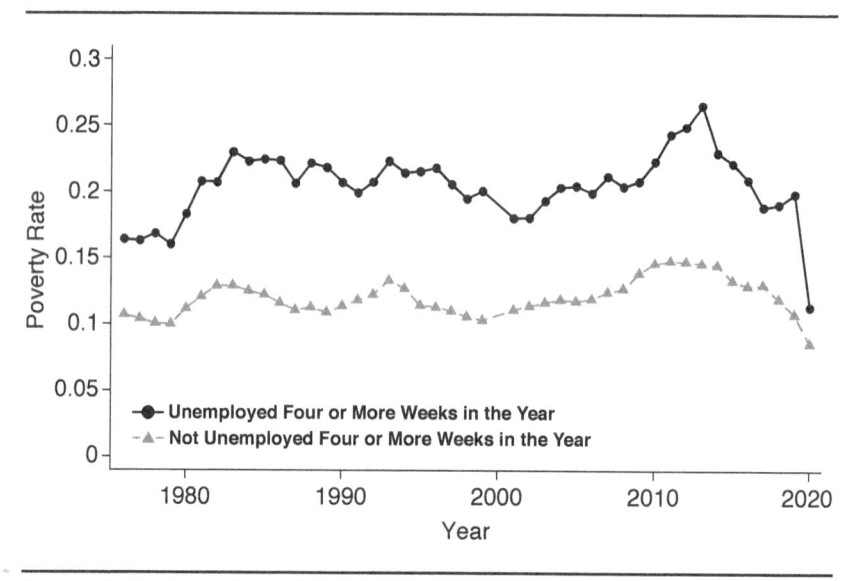

Source: Author's analysis of CPS ASEC data.
Note: Sample limited to adults ages eighteen to sixty-four. See the chapter 8 appendix (figure A8.1) for estimates of the conditional likelihood of poverty among the unemployed.

poverty. Figure 8.1 visualizes this relationship by documenting poverty rates from 1975 through 2020 for working-age adults who spent at least four weeks in the year unemployed (solid black line with circles) and for those who did not spend at least four weeks in the year unemployed (dashed gray line with triangles). From 1975 through 2019, the poverty rate among those who experienced unemployment spells never dropped below 15 percent, and it reached as high as 26 percent in the years of the Great Recession. In contrast, the poverty rate among those who had no unemployment spells hovered between 10 and 15 percent, generally remaining five to ten percentage points below that of the unemployed group. In 2020, however, the poverty rate among those who were unemployed for at least four weeks fell to 12 percent—the lowest level on record.[8] Moreover, the gap in poverty rates between the groups fell to 2.7 percentage points, which was the smallest gap on record.

In nonpandemic years, how large should the gap be between those two lines? The answer to this question depends partially on one's value judgments and policy priorities. Reducing the "penalty" for being unemployed reduces the incentive for jobless adults to return to work; reducing poverty rates for both groups through taxes and transfers can keep the employment disincentives in check while benefiting all, but at the cost of greater government spending. Meanwhile, the American public is not particularly fond of providing generous support for jobless able-bodied adults, and especially for those without children.[9] Trade-offs and constraints are hard to avoid. Politics aside, the patterns in figure 8.1 document the clear ability of the state to alter the relationship between unemployment and poverty. Researchers of poverty cannot ignore the role of the political and institutional context when studying the determinants of poverty across time, place, or groups, and they no longer need to look abroad to imagine a counterfactual context: the policy environment in the United States in 2020 and 2021 proved that the country is capable of sharply reducing the association of poverty with individual risk factors such as unemployment.

For understanding the *measurement* of poverty, the pandemic demonstrated that *the way scholars measure and conceptualize poverty can, in certain contexts, misrepresent the burdens of poverty for low-income households*. Lee Rainwater and Tim Smeeding open their influential book *Poor Kids in a Rich Country* with a call for "Taking the Definition of Poverty Seriously."[10] They advance a set of thoughtful perspectives on how and where to draw the poverty line, building on the works of Robert Hunter, W.E.B. Du Bois, and Peter Townsend, as well as the more U.S.-oriented works of Mollie Orshansky, Connie Citro, and others.[11] Moreover, their effort to take seriously the definition of poverty has been followed by two decades of continued (and productive) debate on the most appropriate conceptualization of poverty. Nearly all of this debate, however, has focused on the counting of resources (what do we count as income?) and on drawing the poverty threshold (how much income does a given family type need to be out of poverty?).

This book has argued that three other considerations ought to be taken into account when developing estimates of poverty: Over how many months should we count a family unit's resources when determining its poverty status? How frequently should poverty estimates be released? And how quickly can and should poverty estimates be made available? Chapter 5 put forth a framework for producing a monthly poverty rate that is based on a household's resources in a single month, that can be released each month, and that can be made available as early as one or two weeks after the end of a month. By contrast, the Census Bureau's annual measure of poverty focuses on income received over a twelve-month period and is generally released nine months after the reference year ends (for example, 2020 poverty rates were released in September 2021).

The added value of the monthly poverty measure is likely to depend on the social and economic context. In times of rapid employment or income fluctuations, the timeliness and shorter accounting period of a monthly poverty measure can be particularly useful for documenting in close to real time the economic conditions of households across the country. For example, as shown in chapter 5, monthly poverty measures more accurately tracked monthly trends in hardship than the employment rate, not only at the national level but also for subgroups defined by age, family status, state, or race/ethnicity. In nonpandemic years, does the monthly poverty measure still add value? Yes, I would argue, albeit less than it did in the context of COVID-19. Month-to-month volatility in earnings and incomes predated the pandemic, as Chapter 5 demonstrated, especially for recipients of once-per-year refundable tax credits and adults navigating the low-wage labor market. Even in 2019, the national monthly poverty rate ranged from 12 percent to 16.9 percent, and within-year variability in poverty rates for families with children generally matched across-year variability in the past two decades.

As chapter 5 emphasized, however, a monthly measure of poverty has its own limitations and should be understood as a supplement to, rather than a substitute for, the standard annual measures of poverty. The monthly poverty measure requires the simulation of new income transfers and the imputation of poverty status into the monthly CPS files, and it poses other technical challenges that increase potential measurement error. Although the monthly poverty measure performed well in tracking other real-world indicators throughout the pandemic, there is no guarantee that, without adaptations, this success would continue in future years.

Ignoring resource constraints, the most notable improvement to the monthly poverty measure would be to replace all of its current simulations and imputations with a monthly representative survey question on household resources. The idea is not far-fetched: the Bureau of Labor Statistics (BLS) surveys a representative sample of households each month for the Basic Monthly CPS file. The only income question in this monthly survey, however, is a categorical indicator of "money from jobs; net income from business, farm or rent; pensions; dividends; interest; Social Security payments; and any other monetary income received by family members" over the prior twelve months. This income definition is not meant to capture near-cash benefits, such as those from SNAP, or tax-based credits, such as the expanded CTC payments. As such, the current income question cannot produce reliable estimates of annual poverty, let alone monthly poverty.[12] Moreover, a respondent is more likely to err when trying to accurately recall income received over the prior year than if asked to recall income received over the prior month. Adding one item to the Basic Monthly CPS files asking respondents to report the income that their household members (or family unit) received in the prior month, inclusive of all in-kind and tax-based transfers, would be a minimally invasive way to improve our ability to track monthly poverty rates. Such data improvements would strongly improve the Census Bureau's ongoing efforts to institutionalize a sub-annual poverty measure.

Beyond improvements to sub-annual poverty measurement, poverty researchers should continue to critically assess whether frequently applied measures of poverty (annual or otherwise) appear to align with reality and when they do not, to investigate why. For example, how should we comprehend the fact that in 2019 the average Black family *not* in SPM poverty experienced levels of food insecurity comparable to those of the average White family *in* poverty? Or how should we reconcile the fact that most families experiencing food insecurity do not have annual incomes below the SPM poverty line? As chapter 5 discussed, the SPM is a large improvement over the official poverty measure (OPM) and, in recent years, the (standard, non-anchored) SPM better tracks other economic measures of well-being, such as food and housing hardship, than the OPM. Calls to re-prioritize the OPM are misguided; this would be true on conceptual grounds even if the OPM were to out-perform the SPM in some contexts in aligning with hardship trends. That said, there are opportunities to improve the SPM, and a more fruitful path forward for debates over poverty measurement would be to consider (1) the appropriate benchmarks for determining a "better" poverty measure and (2) which technical modifications to a conceptually sound measurement framework can feasibly lead to that "better" measure.

Finally, evidence from the COVID-19 pandemic has implications for how we consider the *consequences* of poverty. This evidence reinforces the fact that poverty is not merely a point-in-time state but a condition that, once experienced, often permeates the rest of an individual's life. Efforts to improve the economic prospects of low-income Americans must start with that fact in mind. Viewing poverty through a cross-sectional (point-in-time) lens may conceal the fact that, for example, the average Black adult currently in poverty spent 57 percent of her childhood in poverty, which is much longer than the childhood poverty experience of the average White adult currently in poverty (20 percent). Moreover, reducing point-in-time estimates, though an important policy achievement, is far different than eliminating the disadvantages associated with cumulative poverty exposure, as was evident during the pandemic. Recall from chapter 1 that the rate of *childhood* poverty of the average employed adult working in a high-risk occupation in the context of the pandemic was 1.8 times the rate of *childhood* poverty of working adults who were not in those high-risk jobs. Moreover, we saw in chapter 6 that the strongest predictor of current hardship, such as food insufficiency, was past hardship. Specifically, an adult who entered the pandemic having experienced food insufficiency sometime before the onset of the pandemic was eighteen times more likely to experience food insufficiency during the pandemic (compared to those who had not experienced food insufficiency before).

Reducing disadvantage, then, is not a singular act, but an outcome of persistent policy choices that ought to begin with targeting disparate exposure to poverty in childhood. This point directly connects to the growing body of research investigating the long-run benefits of policies that reduce poverty rather than (or in addition to) investigating their short-term costs.[13]

Ten Lessons for Policy

The fourth aim of this book has been to identify policy lessons from the COVID-19 pandemic. A skeptical take on this question might argue that not many lessons can be drawn from the pandemic that would apply to a calmer, post-pandemic era. The pandemic was, after all, a once-in-a-generation health crisis that was met with a set of policy interventions that were specific to the moment. What that skeptical take does not consider, however, is that the life-altering events experienced by a large share of Americans during the pandemic—losing a job, navigating the paperwork to acquire government income support, experiencing a health scare, panicking upon discovering that their health insurance plan may not cover the needed treatment, managing the closure of schools for an extended period of time, and more—are regularly experienced by a smaller subset of U.S. residents, even in the absence of an economic recession or a global pandemic. The pandemic expanded the reach and accelerated the pace at which households experienced these life disruptions. Although these types of life disruptions or challenges are less likely to make headlines in calmer years and carry fewer of the macroeconomic consequences of 2020, the pain and turmoil experienced by individuals facing these hardships are no less real.

Job loss, for example, is relatively common even in less volatile economic times. Christina Cross, Rourke O'Brien, and I have shown that, in a given year between 1990 and 2019, around 7 percent of adults had at least one household member who lost a job during the year.[14] The rate is higher among Black and Hispanic adults: in 2019, for example, around 10 percent of Black and Hispanic adults shared a home with someone who had been employed in 2018 but was no longer working (and was not retired or studying) in 2019. Sometimes other members of the household increased their work hours or secured wage increases to offset the earnings losses of the newly unemployed adult, but more often household income declined sharply.

Health challenges, needless to say, arise outside of pandemics. As do disruptions to health care coverage and lack of access to affordable and high-quality health insurance more generally. Recall that around 29 million individuals lacked access to health insurance on the eve of the pandemic.[15] Food and housing hardship were also prevalent in the United States well before COVID arrived. Recall that more than 1.4 million children in the nation's public schools experienced homelessness or severe housing instability in 2018–2019, while one in ten households across the United States experienced food insecurity.[16] On this front, the pandemic's policy lessons have already translated into longer-term solutions: in December 2022, Congress approved a permanent version of the Pandemic EBT (P-EBT) program, under the name of Summer EBT, to provide nutrition support to low-income families with school-age children during the summer.[17] Lessons can be (and have already been) learned.

Caution, of course, is necessary in extracting policy lessons from a context as atypical as a pandemic and applying them to other contexts. But, as I argue, the policy experiments from 2020 and 2021 nonetheless point to ten lessons that policymakers should consider moving forward. Some relate to the provision of support during calmer post-pandemic years, and others offer guidance for preparing the policy infrastructure to more efficiently respond to future economic downturns.

Before jumping into these policy lessons, I would offer a couple of caveats. First, there are certain policy domains that this book's evidence cannot inform. Scholars of public health, epidemiology, and related health sciences are far more equipped than I am to discuss the appropriate health measures to slow the spread of transmissible viruses and prevent pandemics in the first place. Similarly, macroeconomists are far more knowledgeable than I am about the role of monetary policy in addressing economic downturns. This book cannot speak to those policy areas other than to say that, to the extent that economic and health crises are preventable, it would certainly be preferable to enlist the tools and expertise of these disciplines in doing so. Another caveat: these ten lessons are not meant to be a generic wish list of policy reforms but instead a set of policy changes suggested by the evidence offered in this book. None of the proposed changes are free of trade-offs, and all deserve scrutiny.

Lesson 1: Learn from the PUA and Expand Access to Unemployment Insurance among Jobless Adults

As chapter 4 documented, the CARES Act's reforms expanded access to unemployment benefits through the Pandemic Unemployment Assistance (PUA), supplemented benefit levels up to $600 per week through the Pandemic Unemployment Compensation (PUC), and also extended the maximum duration of benefit receipt. The PUC benefits in particular elevated the replacement rates of unemployment benefits to more than 100 percent of prior wages for a large share of unemployed adults.[18] As figure 8.1 documents, these benefits effectively severed the relationship between longer-term unemployment and poverty.

In nonpandemic contexts, however, benefit levels that exceed wages are, of course, unsustainable; moreover, current benefit levels are not the greatest weakness of states' Unemployment Insurance systems. Instead, the central takeaway from the pandemic's UI changes should be the importance of expanding access to benefits through mechanisms similar to the PUA, which allowed self-employed workers and other individuals who do not typically qualify for UI to gain access to the support.

Much of the focus on the UI expansions has been on what went wrong: application processes were difficult for jobless adults to navigate, benefit payments were often delayed, many eligible applicants did not receive benefits, and many ineligible applicants did receive benefits. These short-comings need to be addressed, and researchers have already written at length on how to undergo broader reforms of states' UI systems. Josh Bivens and his colleagues provide a blueprint that would lead to universal minimum standards for benefit eligibility, duration, and amounts across all states.[19] Till von Wachter has similarly outlined plans to enforce minimum standards and improve state financing schemes.[20] Others have focused on technical improvements for more efficient benefit distribution.[21]

Where the expansions were successful, however, was in improving access to unemployment support in a progressively targeted manner. Barriers to benefit access have long been a concern of policy research: in a typical year prior to 2020, a minority of unemployed adults received UI benefits.[22] Access improved notably in 2020 and 2021: the share of unemployed adults receiving unemployment support was likely twice as high as observed during the Great Recession, as chapter 4 documented. PUA beneficiaries represented 40 percent of overall UI claims during 2020, and the program's benefits disproportionately went to lower-income adults and those "more marginally attached to the labor market."[23] The success of the PUA should be built on, albeit in a modified form, beyond the pandemic.

In continuing a PUA-like program, state governments, either independently or through incentives or mandates from the federal government, would need to define the expanded eligibility criteria and benefit levels. The minimum benefit during the 2020–2021 expansion—defined as one-half of the state's average weekly benefit, or around $150 per week in many states—would serve as a precedent and a realistic base-line. In the post-pandemic period, however, modifications to eligibility criteria would be necessary. In 2020 and 2021, PUA access could be granted to unemployed adults who reported that they were not eligible for standard UI benefits and were unable to work owing to the conse-quences of the pandemic. The program could be modified to incorporate slightly stricter post-pandemic eligibility guidelines while still accom-modating part-time, self-employed, and other workers whose employ-ment is more precarious. Bivens and his colleagues propose a minimum eligibility standard based on prior hours worked rather than the current standard based on prior earnings.[24] In this scenario, adults who worked at least three hundred hours in approximately the past year—for example, fifteen hours per week for twenty weeks—and who worked during at least two quarters of the year would be eligible.[25] This proposal is among many different pathways that could achieve expanded UI access and reduce poverty rates among the unemployed.

To illustrate the importance of expanding benefit access to UI (in general and relative to increasing benefit values), I have simulated poverty rates among the unemployed (over 2016 to 2019 to achieve large enough sample sizes in a nonpandemic period) in two alterna-tive policy scenarios: one in which state-level UI expansions increase access to 90 percent of unemployed adults while applying a benefit level of one-half the state's median weekly benefit level; and one in which a $300 per week supplement is added to UI benefits, while keeping participation in UI as observed. In this simplified simulation, neither scenario accounts for possible behavioral effects. Nonetheless, the dif-ferences between these two alternative policy environments in poverty reduction effects are vast and illustrative. The first scenario (which focuses on expanding benefit access) contributes to a decline in the annual SPM poverty rate from 20.9 percent to 16.5 percent among the unemployed, a 4.4-percentage-point decline. This would be the lowest rate of poverty among the unemployed in a nonpandemic year since at least 1980. The second scenario (which focuses on improving benefit levels) reduces poverty only from 20.9 percent to 20.4 percent, a 0.5-percentage-point decline.[26]

There are costs to expanding benefit access: state governments would need additional revenues through payroll taxes or the federal UI trust fund to accommodate the new expenditures (which would vary in amount by state and year), and expanded benefit eligibility would reduce incentives for marginally employed workers to pursue more sustained employment. Nonetheless, if policymakers are interested in reducing poverty among unemployed adults, expanding eligibility criteria and reducing barriers to UI benefits are necessary reforms.

Lesson 2: Reduce Early Exposure to Poverty through a Permanent Expansion of the Child Tax Credit

A clear pattern throughout this book has been the link between childhood poverty and adult disadvantages during the pandemic. Its findings sit atop a much broader set of evidence that poverty during childhood has direct effects on child development, as well as lasting effects on socioeconomic outcomes throughout adulthood.[27] The children most exposed to poverty tend to complete fewer years of schooling, work fewer hours, and earn lower wages than young adults who did not experience poverty during childhood.[28] Meanwhile, Black children's much greater likelihood of growing up in poverty compared to White children leads directly to their disadvantages in adulthood.[29]

As Jordan Matsudaira, Jane Waldfogel, Christopher Wimer, and I have shown in our collaborative work, racial differences in exposure to childhood poverty explain more of the racial differences in young adult poverty rates than racial differences in employment, education, or marriage.[30] The lack of welfare state and labor market institutions to reduce exposure to poverty for Black children, or to sever the link between childhood poverty and economic opportunity in adulthood, contributed to the particular vulnerability of this population to the pandemic's consequences.

One clear strategy for reducing exposure to poverty during childhood is to provide families with children, especially those with young children, unconditional payments to support the basic needs of the child and the family. Indeed, this was a central recommendation of the National Academy of Science's report on cutting child poverty in half in the United States.[31] Most wealthy countries in the world offer some type of child allowance like this; the United States does not, with the exception of the expanded CTC benefits paid out to most families with children from July to December 2021. Recall from chapter 3 that the expanded CTC payments, introduced as part of the American Rescue Plan, provided monthly cash support of up to $300 per child to nearly all families with children regardless of their current or recent employment status. This policy stood in stark contrast to the standard CTC policy: making payments only once a year to parents with sufficient earnings, leaving out the most vulnerable families.[32] Chapters 4 and 5 presented evidence on the consequences of the expanded CTC: it immediately cut monthly child poverty rates by around one-third,[33] reduced the annual child poverty rate in 2021 to the lowest rate in U.S. history,[34] brought the U.S. child poverty rate in line with Germany's,[35] cut child poverty at a rate comparable to Norway's,[36] cut food hardship among low-income families with children by around one-fourth,[37] had no meaningful short-run consequences for employment,[38] and increased consumption at child-care centers and grocery stores.[39]

It is possible that the consequences of the program could look different should it be made permanent; some have argued, for example, that the negative employment consequences of a CTC expansion could offset some of its potential poverty reduction effects.[40] Though these employment effects did not manifest in the six months of payments in 2021, we cannot rule out that a permanent version of the program could evoke different behavioral responses.[41] Any such effects, of course, would need to be tracked should the program be made permanent. Prognostications about future employment effects aside, there is little debate that the one-year expansion of the CTC in 2021 brought massive, albeit temporary, success in the country's fight against child poverty. Making its expansion permanent—including the credit's full refundability—should be a policy priority if the United States wishes to consistently maintain low levels of child poverty.

Lesson 3: If Necessary, Trade in Part or All of the TANF Program to Help Fund a Fully Refundable Child Tax Credit at 2021 Benefit Levels

Ideally, an expanded CTC could be achieved through cross-party negotiations on tax reform rather than by substituting it for other social programs, as has been the case with modifications to refundable tax credits in prior decades.[42] If additional revenues are needed to politically justify a permanent CTC expansion, Congress would be wise to go after state and local tax deductions, which primarily benefit high-income taxpayers, before cutting from social spending programs. But compromise on social programs may be necessary, as suggested by recent right-of-center proposals.[43] In that event, the takeaways from the COVID-19 pandemic suggest that the Temporary Assistance for Needy Families program is worth trading on the condition that the trade results in a fully refundable CTC at the 2021 expansion's benefit levels.

In all but a few states, the TANF program did little to directly support families in need during the pandemic (see chapter 5). In the past, TANF (and especially Aid to Families with Dependent Children, its predecessor program) was largely a cash assistance program targeted at low-income families with children, and at single parents in particular. In 1997, the year of the program's transition to TANF, state governments spent an average of 84 percent of their TANF budgets on cash assistance.[44] In 2020, the first year of the pandemic, the average state instead spent 22 percent of its TANF budget on cash support—one percentage point higher than 2019, though still lower than in 2017 (23 percent). Cash support from TANF reduced child poverty rates in 2020 by a mere 2.9 percent (0.3 percentage points), as documented in chapter 5. Recall that the expanded CTC cut child poverty rates by 44 percent (4.1 percentage points) the next year—fifteen times the effect of TANF. After the program's implementation, state governments allocated their TANF budgets, with relatively little accountability, toward a wide range of other purposes, such as work-supporting activities (12.4 percent of the average budget), childcare subsidies (16.6 percent), pre-K and Head Start (8.5 percent), program management (10 percent), tax credits (9 percent), child welfare services (8.3 percent), and a catchall "other" category (13.1 percent).[45]

Federal and mandated state spending amounts to approximately $31 billion, $7 billion of which was allocated to cash support. The remaining $24 billion, if distributed as cash support to families in need, is greater than the amount that is theoretically necessary to lift all single-parent families in the United States out of poverty.[46] However, TANF's overall level of funding, as well as its trade-in value, is declining by the year. That funding for TANF is not indexed to inflation means that the size of the program, in real terms, declines annually, and has already fallen by more than 40 percent overall since the program's 1997 introduction. In another decade, the real value of TANF funding will be more than 60 percent below its 1997 levels (assuming, for simplicity, an annual average inflation rate of 3 percent). Should the political balance of Congress require that it need to identify cost savings in order to fund an expanded CTC, and should TANF's elimination create conditions for a CTC expansion in line with the refundability and benefit levels of the 2021 expansion, then now is a good time to pursue the trade.

There are benefits and costs to such a swap. Among the benefits of trading TANF for the CTC would be reducing not only exposure to early child poverty but also the between-state disparities in benefit provision that contribute to racial/ethnic gaps in poverty. Consider that at present the states with the most Black residents are less likely to use their TANF programs to offer cash support for families in need.[47] For example, one-fourth of Alabama residents are Black, and the state uses only 8 percent of its TANF budget on cash assistance for low-income families, one of the smallest shares in the nation.[48] A CTC expansion similar to that of 2021, in contrast, would equalize benefit levels and access across all states. Any barriers to accessing the expanded CTC (presumably still run by the IRS, as I discuss later) would still be more surmountable than the barriers to accessing TANF cash support.

Politically, there are some ways that conservatives could sell the CTC-for-TANF swap as a win. Under TANF, benefit values generally decline as working parents increase their earnings, effectively generating a tax on more work; under the expanded CTC, at least as structured in the 2021 expansion, the average low-income parent receives the same benefit even if they increase their earnings. Ending "welfare" to reduce taxes on working families (albeit while also extending income support to nonworking families) could at least be more politically palatable than implementing the CTC without the TANF trade-in. Moreover, TANF was in the news in 2020–2021 primarily because of obscene examples of fraud in the program. The most publicized case of late was in Mississippi, where the state knowingly funneled $1.1 million to Brett Favre—a former National Football League quarterback who made millions during his playing career—for a set of speeches that he never gave.[49] (More broadly, the state is accused of improperly spending more than $70 million of TANF funds, including money that went to build a volleyball court at the University of Southern Mississippi and money used for a Malibu-based drug rehabilitation center for a professional wrestler who went by the stage name "The Million Dollar Man.") These are only the high-profile examples.[50] Given the widespread misuse of this poorly functioning social program, perhaps voters would be amenable to replacing it with a more effective one.

Politics aside, such a trade would come with costs for state governments and for some current TANF and SNAP recipients. The majority of states (forty-four of the fifty) offer broad-based categorical eligibility (BBCE) rules that grant access to SNAP benefits on the condition of qualifying for any TANF program or service (not limited to TANF cash assistance).[51] For example, offering TANF-funded childcare services to a family would qualify them for BBCE access to SNAP benefits. The use of BBCE allows states to lift the income requirement for SNAP eligibility from 130 percent to 200 percent of the poverty line, effectively extending access to a larger share of low-income families. Thus, eliminating TANF would also remove access to SNAP for this specific group of families above 130 percent of the poverty line. All in all, the elimination of BBCE would affect between 5 percent and 8 percent of SNAP participants.[52] However, families with children who receive BBCE access to SNAP would also benefit from the CTC expansion, at least if it is structured similar to the 2021 policy rules. The net gain for most families with children would outweigh any small losses in income for the 5 to 8 percent of BBCE-enabled SNAP participants whose incomes are already above the federal poverty line.

The other potential harms are to the budgets of state governments and to the various important programs to which non-cash TANF resources are allocated. If TANF were eliminated, states would lose around $16.5 billion in annual resources (an average of $330 million per state) that they currently use to fund everything that is not cash support, as listed earlier. The programs and services that states fund with federal TANF resources can (and do) operate apart from TANF; state-funded support for pre-K and Head Start, for example, is not tied to TANF. In 2020, twenty-eight states used TANF resources to fund pre-K and Head Start, though only eight used federal funds (rather than state TANF funds to fulfill maintenance-of-effort requirements).[53] All states, meanwhile, have pre-K and Head Start programs. Substituting the expanded CTC for TANF would force the eight states using federal TANF funds to either use their general revenues (or resources from other sources, such as the Child Care and Development Block Grant) to replace the lost TANF funding for pre-K and Head Start. In some circumstances, such programs may see declines in funding. The twenty states that use state rather than federal TANF funds on pre-K and Head Start could continue to do so; though federal TANF funds would be eliminated, the money that states currently spend on TANF in order to receive the federal support would be untouched. However, there is no guarantee that states would continue to spend their own TANF funds in this manner, and if they do not, this could carry negative consequences for families currently benefiting from TANF-funded childcare, state supplements to the EITC, and more. While most families would gain, on average, from receiving the fully refundable CTC at higher benefit levels, some working families may lose out if states cut back on childcare subsidies or their state EITCs.

Thus, an alternative resolution would be to trade in half of the current spending on TANF, including all the resources currently going toward cash assistance, while freezing and transferring the remaining half of current TANF spending to supplement the Child Care and Development Block Grant and Social Services Block Grant. At present, most states currently transfer TANF resources to these alternative block grants, through which states can invest in services, and childcare support especially, for low-income families with children. Such an alteration would generate a smaller level of potential offsets for the expanded CTC but would do more to ensure that fewer working families lose out in the transition. And to emphasize: an even better outcome for low-income families would be for Congress to achieve the refundable CTC through tax negotiations rather than cuts to existing spending programs.

Others are more optimistic than I am that TANF can be productively reformed into a program that better serves low-income families.[54] Favorable evidence on reform, however, simply isn't there: championed by a Democratic administration in the mid-1990s, the program has remained dysfunctional through successive Republican and Democratic administrations alike as the provision of cash assistance, as well as the overall size of the block grants, has consistently trended downward.[55]

Should Congress develop the political capacity to make major improvements in its assistance to low-income families, it should not use that capital in an attempt to reform TANF. Instead, if trading in the program helps to achieve a permanent version of a refundable CTC at the 2021 benefit levels, Congress should strongly consider the deal and establish a durable, federalized provision of unconditional cash support for families with children.

Lesson 4: Convert the Lump-Sum, Refundable CTC Benefits, and Possibly EITC Benefits, to Monthly Payments

Chapter 6's analyses of the expanded CTC revealed that recipients use the monthly payments differently than they use the lump-sum payment that they receive at tax time. Results from two separate studies, using two separate data sources, found that monthly CTC payments reduced food insufficiency and increased credit/debit card spending at grocery stores to a greater extent than the lump-sum payment. Instead, recipients were more likely to use the higher-value lump-sum payment to catch up on rent payments or purchase higher-cost items, such as children's clothing.[56] These findings are consistent with past work looking at consumption responses to the EITC.[57] Analysis of the expanded CTC is unique, however, in that it has identified different consumption patterns when the same policy is administered in two different ways in the same twelve-month span.

The findings suggest that the timing of payments affects whether the policy achieves its purported goals; if policymakers want these tax credits to reduce families' food hardship, the evidence suggests that shifting to monthly payment would make for a stronger policy tool. (To be clear, the formally stated goal of the CTC is not reducing food hardship, but rather reducing families' tax burdens; indeed, reducing food hardship may not even be the primary objective of policymakers who support the CTC's expansion.) Moreover, should the monthly payments be made permanent, they would probably help reduce the debt and rent arrears toward which the lump-sum payment, including the CTC, tends to be put. At the least, monthly payments would give recipients the opportunity to decide for themselves whether to use the payments for day-to-day items or save them up to cover debt, durables, or emergencies.[58]

Another major benefit of monthly payments would be a reduction in the intrayear volatility of poverty rates, particularly for families with children. Recall from chapter 5 that families with children receive, on average, one-third of their annual income transfers in a single lump-sum payment; as a consequence, monthly child poverty rates dip around tax time, then spike and remain at higher levels throughout the year. In a 2021 report, Christal Hamilton and her colleagues at Columbia University envision what monthly poverty rates in the past would have looked like in 2019 if EITC and CTC benefits had been distributed monthly rather than in lump-sum form.[59] They find that child poverty rates would be consistently lower by around seven percentage points for the average month compared to delivering the benefits only at tax time. In other words, monthly payments would have cut child poverty by around one-third in each month. Moreover, they find that the monthly payments could have kept around 10 percent of children from experiencing a spell of poverty at some point in the year, compared to the rate observed with the lump-sum payment.

Two caveats and conditions apply to this policy takeaway, however. First, there is mixed evidence on whether low-income households prefer the lump-sum or more frequent payments. On the one hand, recipients of the EITC had this option until 2010 with the Advance EITC (AEITC), but they rarely used it: only about 3 percent of recipients opted for monthly payments.[60] On the other hand, families with children receiving the CTC payments had the option to opt out of the monthly payments and receive all the benefits as a lump-sum payment instead, but only 5.8 percent chose to do so.[61] Rather than revealing a preference one way or the other, the lack of opt-outs from both the lump-sum EITC and the monthly CTC most likely represents bias toward the default option. Opting out of a given payment type requires being aware of that option and having the mental bandwidth to calculate the costs and benefits of doing so—neither of which is abundant in time- and resource-strapped households. A U.S. Government Accountability Office (GAO) analysis of the AEITC's low participation rate confirms this conclusion: fewer than half of eligible employees knew that the EITC existed at all, and fewer than one-quarter of that group knew that it was possible to receive an EITC payment in advance.[62]

Conflicting evidence on preferences for the lump-sum EITC also can be found in city-specific fieldwork and interventions. In one qualitative study, Jennifer Sykes and her colleagues interviewed 115 EITC recipients in the Boston area to understand how low-income families perceived the credit compared with other income transfers.[63] They found that their interviewees highly valued the lump-sum EITC and looked forward to the large payment with the approach of tax time. At the same time, both the researchers and their interviewees were primarily comparing the lump-sum EITC to monthly TANF payments, which were distributed by a program that not only had different rules and a different policy logic but was associated with stigma. Moreover, Sykes and her team found that 90 percent of their sample carried unpaid credit card debt or were behind on utilities and rent payments; the parents in their sample made "paying down debt a priority at tax time, as they see it as the first step on the path toward upward mobility."[64] Presumably, monthly provision of EITC payments would reduce the accumulation of that debt (and its interest payments) in the first place.

A Chicago-based EITC intervention in 2014 provides a contrasting example. Participants who had been assigned quarterly EITC payments were compared to a proper control group — 164 respondents who did not receive the quarterly payments. Among the treatment group of 343 individuals, 90 percent reported a preference for the switch to the quarterly, rather than annual, payment. The group receiving the quarterly payments also reported less stress and a greater ability to meet monthly expenses, consistent with the quantitative evidence to date on the monthly CTC expansion in 2021.[65]

The desirability of monthly payments of refundable tax credits also depends in part on the outcomes that policymakers hope to achieve. Should policymakers' intention be to protect against large income shocks, then the "Rainy Day EITC" reform proposed by Sarah Halpern-Meekin and her colleagues might be a better fit than the conversion to monthly payments.[66] The "Rainy Day" reform would allow EITC recipients to defer one-fifth of their lump-sum payment to be received in a second lump-sum payment (with a savings match from the federal government) later in the year. The policy goal underlying the proposal is to provide low-income adults with a stockpile of emergency savings to promote financial security. In contrast, the policy goal underlying the provision of monthly payments is to reduce immediate hardship, most notably the inability to afford sufficient food for all members of the household.

Calls for a more frequent distribution of lump-sum credits are not new. Back in 2008, for example, Steve Holt proposed a reform that would have provided EITC recipients with half their benefit values in four installments throughout the year, in addition to the lump-sum payment at tax time.[67] Michelle Lyon Drumbl's 2019 book *Tax Credits for the Working Poor* similarly calls for year-round EITC delivery.[68] Consistent in these proposals are two major administrative challenges: the process of distributing monthly payments and procedures for altering benefit levels when a tax unit's income situation changes. The first of these challenges is no longer a serious concern: between July and December 2021 during the pandemic, the IRS proved capable of distributing monthly cash payments (as well as three rounds of stimulus checks) to most families with children. The IRS also gave recipients the option of opting out of the monthly payments, as detailed earlier; thus, low-income families who placed particularly high value on the lump-sum payments could still choose to receive those. To consistently maintain the capacity to administer monthly payments without scaling back other operations, the IRS may need the resources to hire additional staff. There is now no doubt, however, regarding its technical capabilities for distributing monthly payments.

The second major challenge, and the second condition of this proposal for monthly benefit distribution, relates to the IRS's ability to accurately estimate benefit levels of advance CTC and EITC payments. For payments to be distributed in advance of tax filing, the IRS must be able to produce a reliable estimate of the benefit levels that a family should receive based on the structure of its tax unit and its income during the tax year. For a fully refundable CTC in line with the 2021 policy parameters, this is, for most families with children, relatively straightforward: the benefit levels are fixed and easily estimable for most families. Exceptions to the rule include families undergoing a change in size or structure (the addition of a child or the separation of a partner or spouse), and changes in earnings among higher-income families with children, who are either on or exceeding the benefit's phaseout.

For the EITC, however, the challenge is greater: given that EITC benefits phase in as earnings rise, accurate estimates of benefits are conditional on accurate estimates of earnings. However, earnings tend to be more volatile, and thus more difficult to predict in advance, for workers in many low-income households. When estimated benefit levels for advance EITC payments exceed what the tax unit should receive based on its subsequent tax filing, (1) the tax unit can be held liable to repay the excess benefits, a heavy burden for low-income families; and (2) the EITC's error and overpayment rates increase, contributing to greater political challenges in sustaining and strengthening the program.[69] Consider that high error rates in the AEITC were among the reasons that the advance payments were disbanded. This explains the "possibly the EITC" caveat in this policy recommendation to convert refundable tax credits to monthly payments; improvements to benefit estimation and reductions in error rates would need to accompany any transition from lump-sum to monthly EITC payments. In the absence of such improvements, the EITC could remain in its lump-sum form while advance CTC payments, ideally at 2021 benefit levels (or higher), could be distributed monthly.

To be sure, safeguards can be implemented to protect low-income families against EITC/CTC overpayments, but they carry additional costs (financially and politically). The ARP's CTC expansions, for example, included a "safe harbor" rule to protect low- and median-income tax filers (for example, under $60,000 of adjusted gross income for joint tax filers) from needing to repay any tax credit overpayments.[70] However, the safe harbor provisions increase the costs of the program in ways that are difficult to predict in advance and increase political opposition to the program.[71] These costs should motivate further research on how the IRS can distribute advance payments in a manner that reduces overpayment and error rates. As a recent sign of optimism, a Tax Policy Center analysis finds that in most cases the IRS can now accurately predict the value of the refundable tax credit benefits that a tax unit should be eligible for over the following year using just three months of a family's income information.[72]

The 2021 expansion of the CTC offers a successful precedent for the distribution of monthly rather than once-per-year refundable tax credit payments, even if there are technical processes to sort out. Given the negative consequences of food insecurity and insufficiency for children in particular, as well as evidence that monthly payments are more effective at reducing everyday hardships related to food and nutrition, shifting to monthly distributions of CTC benefits is warranted. Converting the EITC into monthly payments, however, is conditional on first improving the IRS's ability to more accurately anticipate families' annual benefit values.

Lesson 5: Keep the IRS in Charge of Distributing Refundable Tax Credit Payments and Increase Its Capacity to Reach Non-Tax-Filers

As chapter 4 detailed, a key limitation of the CARES Act's and the ARP's income support programs was incomplete access to their benefits, particularly for low-income households that were not required to file taxes in prior years. In trying to balance the timeliness, targeting, and duration of pandemic income support, the federal government opted for the trade-off of not ensuring that all low-income households likely to be eligible for such support were targeted. As chapter 4 documented, around one-third of low-income adults with children reported not receiving the monthly CTC payments. One reason is surely the underreporting of benefits in the survey data, but even IRS records suggest that 3 to 5 million children may have missed out on receiving the advance CTC payments. Access to benefits is also a problem in normal times: an estimated 20 percent of potential EITC recipients miss out on the benefits.[73]

The goal of achieving higher participation rates, as well as more frequent payments, has led to discussion of whether a future version of the CTC should fall under the purview of the Social Security Administration (SSA).[74] The SSA has experience in distributing monthly payments to a specific age group (Social Security retirement benefits), with near-perfect coverage rates, and so it would seem a particularly appropriate agency to administer regular payments to families with children as well. Removing the CTC from the IRS out of targeting concerns, however, would be a mistake; instead, Congress should focus on improving the ability of the IRS to successfully reach its missing targets (non-tax-filers in particular).

The IRS's performance with the advance CTC payments was actually more impressive than the SSA's performance with Supplemental Security Income (SSI), a program that distributes monthly payments to adults and children who have low income and are blind or disabled. The SSI participation rate is around 61 percent, lower than that of the CTC.[75] Put differently, there is no guarantee that the SSA would achieve higher take-up rates or be better equipped to identify adults who are currently missing out on CTC benefits. Meanwhile, there are other risks from transferring the CTC to the SSA: as a cash benefit administered by the SSA rather than a tax reduction under the IRS, the CTC payments would count, unless legislated otherwise, as income when low-income adults apply for SNAP or TANF benefits, reducing what they could receive from those programs. No such risk is involved when the IRS distributes the CTC as a tax credit. Additionally, as Robert Greenstein notes, transfers framed as tax reductions rather than as direct cash payments are more politically sustainable.[76] The public is generally more willing to support tax relief than programs framed as direct social spending.[77] The same is true within Congress: expansions of the EITC and CTC in prior decades have primarily succeeded "as part of the horse trading that occurs when lawmakers assemble tax legislation," as Greenstein writes.[78]

Rather than jettisoning the IRS's involvement in distributing CTC and EITC benefits, the federal government should help the agency improve its ability to reach eligible non-tax-filers (even if the CTC is not made fully refundable). First, the IRS should expand its free online filing tools. During the pandemic, the IRS offered an online portal for tax units with sufficiently low income (below the amount that requires tax filing) to file simplified claims in order to receive the CTC payments and/or stimulus checks. The rollout was not perfect; for example, a Spanish-language version of the CTC portal was not available until the end of November 2021, just before the final monthly CTC payment was paid. But the change nonetheless created a pathway for resource-constrained tax units to file with the IRS without reporting their incomes or having to navigate the full labyrinth of U.S. tax rules. Moving forward, the agency should expand such tools to also cover those eligible for EITC benefits. More broadly, the IRS should use its considerable resources and data to generate a free, easy-to-use tax filing system designed with low-income tax filers in mind. Work from Code for America during the pandemic shows just how powerful such a tool can be: more than 100,000 families used the group's accessible and user-friendly web portal to claim more than $400 million in CTC benefits in 2021.[79]

Second, the federal government should facilitate more checks of cross-program eligibility. For example, in April 2020, at the beginning of the pandemic, the Department of the Treasury, the IRS, and Veterans Affairs (VA) worked together to ensure that recipients of VA benefits, who generally do not earn enough to file a tax return, would automatically receive their stimulus checks without needing to take further action.[80] Placing the burden on the resource- and information-rich state rather than each individual to properly distribute benefits to eligible individuals ought to be the baseline rather than the exception, and the collaboration across these three departments is progress toward that aim. Moving forward, federal and state governments should identify further data-sharing opportunities so that state governments providing SNAP or Medicaid benefits, for example, could trigger secure and direct CTC enrollment (with consent) through the transfer of information to the federal government.[81] Providing evidence of the potential benefits of communication across programs, Chuck Marr and his colleagues estimate that three in four low-income adults who were unlikely to automatically receive IRS-administered stimulus check payments participated in SNAP or Medicaid.[82] The IRS could thus greatly improve its targeting of non-tax-filers if secure mechanisms were in place for the federal and state governments' programs to work together.

There are other pathways toward increasing access to refundable tax credits, such as reducing the complexity of tax filing and improving efforts to share information in non-English languages. The federal government would be wise to investigate further any steps that could increase access to benefits distributed through the tax system, but it should not rush to take the distribution of these benefits away from the purview of the IRS.

Lesson 6: Institutionalize Automatic Stabilizers for UI and SNAP to Reduce the Trade-offs in the Timeliness, Targeting, and Duration of Income Support

In 2019, before the impending pandemic, the policy professionals Heather Boushey, Ryan Nunn, and Jay Shambaugh published the edited volume *Recession Ready: Fiscal Policies to Stabilize the American Economy.*[83] The purpose of the book was to offer a blueprint for a federal policy response should an economic recession hit the United States. As it turned out, the country would be staring down a potential recession merely a year after the book went to press.

The book's proposed policy solutions were largely designed to reduce the pressure on the three major trade-offs faced by policymakers in a crisis era: balancing the timeliness, targeting, and duration of benefit payments. Timeliness and duration can largely be addressed through the use of automatic stabilizers, a policy design that is central to the contributions in *Recession Ready*. Stabilizers would trigger automatic benefit distributions when the first strong signs of economic decline become evident. Claudia Sahm provides one example of how such automatic triggers could work: when the three-month average unemployment rate rises by at least half a percentage point relative to its lowest point in the past year, expanded unemployment benefits (or a stimulus check) could be activated to mitigate the financial pain among those facing joblessness and to stimulate a floundering economy.[84] This type of automatic support could increase the timeliness of benefit payments, which would be triggered automatically rather than only after renewed rounds of congressional action. Moreover, an automatic trigger could address, to some extent, the duration of benefit distribution, as the benefit enhancement could be set to expire (or taper out) as objective economic conditions improve, such as the unemployment rate declining.

Hilary Hoynes and Diane Whitmore Schanzenbach have also detailed a plan to automatically increase both access to SNAP benefits and their generosity during economic downturns.[85] The pandemic again provides a useful case study on why institutionalizing this type of automatic stabilizer can be particularly important: rather than waiting for the end of December 2020 (nine months after COVID-19 swept across the country) to increase SNAP benefits by 15 percent, the change could have been made several months sooner had it been legislated to kick in automatically after a labor market collapse.

What might have been the impact of this type of automatic stabilizer on poverty rates throughout 2020? Building on the Hoynes and Schanzenbach's proposal, I have simulated alternative monthly poverty rates in 2020 for a scenario in which the 15 percent increase in the SNAP maximum benefit and in SNAP Emergency Allotments (EAs) was automatically activated in April 2020, when the unemployment rate spiked. In April 2020, the SNAP changes would have lifted an additional 2 million U.S. residents out of poverty, for a 0.6-percentage-point reduction in poverty. Barring any strong behavioral responses to the SNAP benefits, this expansion would have continued to lift around 2 million people out of poverty each month through the end of the year, contributing to a combined 14.8 million person-months of poverty avoided throughout 2020. In December 2020, the monthly poverty rate for the full population would have been an estimated 15.5 percent (similar to the rate just before the pandemic arrived) rather than the observed 16.1 percent. Aside from lower poverty rates, the earlier SNAP activation would most likely have contributed to lower rates of food hardship. Evidence on some states' early expiration of the SNAP Emergency Allotments in 2022 shows that the withdrawal of SNAP benefits increased food insufficiency.[86]

This simulation accounts only for the automatic expansion of SNAP benefits. If the automatic stabilizer had also extended some version of the weekly unemployment supplements (through the PUC) from August 2020 to December 2020, perhaps millions more would have pulled from poverty; instead, the PUC was not expanded again until March 2021. To prepare for the next crisis, Congress should learn its lesson from the pandemic (and the Great Recession): reduce the crisis-era pressure on policymakers as they seek to balance the timeliness, targeting, and duration of income supports by implementing income support benefits that are triggered as soon as an economic downturn begins.

Lesson 7: Build the Federal Administrative Capacity to Convert the Paycheck Protection Program into a Targeted Work-Sharing Program

In the midst of economic recession, should the government work to insure workers or should it insure jobs? This question, which forms the title of a 2021 paper by Giulia Giupponi, Camille Landais, and Alice Lapeyre, simplifies the primary difference in policymaking during recessions between the United States and countries like Germany and the United Kingdom: in the United States firms tend to lay off workers but newly jobless adults are supported through unemployment benefits, while other countries tend to financially support firms on the condition that they maintain their employees, even if at reduced work intensity.[87] Germany's use of short-time work-sharing schemes during the Great Recession, for example, contributed to its more stable employment and poverty rates from 2009 to 2011 compared to many other high-income countries.[88] After the pandemic hit, the U.S. government attempted to pursue both aims at once: its expanded unemployment benefits provided ample income support for jobless adults, while the newly created Paycheck Protection Program provided financial support to firms on the condition that they preserve their employees' wages and employment.

The PPP provided more than $800 billion (roughly eight times the cost of the 2021 CTC expansion) in support to firms with fewer than five hundred employees. The policy was *timely* in that the Small Business Administration was able to disperse funds as early as April 2020, but the PPP was hardly *targeted*. The SBA lacked the infrastructure to adequately identify eligible firms and to vet the firms applying for support, in amounts potentially up to $10 million; it also lacked the accountability mechanisms to ensure that its loans (nearly all of which were forgivable) were primarily used to support workers' wages. As a result, about two-thirds of the funds went to business owners and shareholders, and only $13.2 billion of the $510 billion in PPP loans provided in 2020 made it to households in the bottom fifth of the income distribution (the workers most likely to be in poverty). The policy was expensive, regressive, and plagued by abuse.[89]

It would be tempting to advocate for the elimination of PPP-style policies altogether and redouble efforts to provide direct income support for adults after they lose their jobs. But this would be a mistake. Had the policy infrastructure of a wage subsidy or work-sharing scheme been developed after the onset of the Great Recession, when the success of similar programs was evident in other high-income countries, it is possible that millions more jobs could have been spared after the onset of the pandemic (while still keeping employees temporarily away from in-person work). Back-of-the-envelope estimates suggest that if three-fourths of the overall 2020 allocation of PPP funds (around $600 billion) had been spent on wage subsidies for workers with average annual salaries (around $55,000), the program could have saved the equivalent of more than 10 million job-years—or three to four times the rate of job-years actually preserved in 2020. Such preservation of jobs, in turn, would have reduced the pressure on income support programs and decreased the psychological toll that often accompanies job loss. Thus, rather than disbanding the PPP, the federal government should simply learn from what went wrong: it should begin now to establish the administrative capacity to avoid a rushed and untargeted distribution of funds and ensure that future PPP resources end up in the pockets of low- and middle-wage workers rather than high-income owners and shareholders.

Lesson 8: Better Monitor the Use of ESSER Funds and Be Prepared to Invest Better-Targeted Resources in Schools Experiencing the Greatest Learning Losses

A central finding of chapter 7 was that students in high-poverty schools that engaged primarily in distance learning during 2020 (of necessity, many would argue) experienced disproportionate learning losses. Given the centrality of educational performance in later-life outcomes, from high school graduation rates to college attendance and adult poverty status, it is critical that these educational gaps be addressed in order to avoid widening income-based inequalities in economic opportunity moving forward.

As part of COVID-era spending packages (primarily the ARP), the federal government allocated around $190 billion in Elementary and

Secondary School Emergency Relief (ESSER) funds to schools to enable them to address COVID-related security concerns and begin tackling learning loss and students' mental health concerns. The resources were allocated according to Title I spending rules, meaning that public schools with more lower-income students received relatively more support. School districts were tasked with spending the largest one-time investment in the nation's education system, by 2025, to improve student well-being and learning outcomes, upgrade facilities and school technologies, and improve teacher retention and development. In 2020, districts largely used the resources to address safety concerns, such as upgrading school air ventilation systems.[90] In 2021, around 28 percent of the ESSER resources were allocated to academic recovery efforts, just over the mandated 20 percent minimum.[91] Goldhaber and his colleagues estimate, however, that high-poverty districts that went remote during the pandemic will need to spend nearly all of the ESSER funds on academic recovery efforts if they are to recover their learning losses.[92]

What works in reducing those losses? High-quality tutoring programs is one evidence-backed intervention with potential to reverse the math and reading losses of 2020–2021,[93] and tutoring is one of the services for which districts expect to increase spending the most from 2022 to 2025, according to a survey of districts' ESSER spending plans (which must be submitted in order to receive the funds).[94] Summer learning and extended school days are among the other interventions to which districts expect to allocate more resources. Spending plans are different, however, from actual allocations of the resources, for which data are scarce.[95] In 2022, fewer than half of state governments published public information on how they spent ESSER resources.[96] Those that did generally offered only broad levels of detail. California, for example, reported that 78 percent of its ESSER expenditures fell into the "other" category—a rather unhelpful indication of whether its ESSER distributions were working well to offset learning loss.[97] The federal government does collect and publish data from state expenditure reports, but after a notable lag and again with only broad information on expenditure categories.

There is reasonable fear that the lack of accountability could lead to challenges similar to those that arise with the TANF program: state governments (and in this case, school districts) have broad discretion on how to spend the funds, so long as the allocations can be slotted into one of six broadly defined categories (including the "other" option).[98] Early examples of questionable spending include the reconstruction of track and field facilities at a Kentucky high school and an upgrade to sports facilities at an Iowa school—justified, according to the district, given that the expansion to the bleachers allowed for more social distancing among spectators.[99] In Texas, the McAllen Independent School District, where three-fourths of the students are identified as economically disadvantaged, opted to spend $4 million of its relief funds to build an outdoor learning environment to be completed in December 2024.[100] Although perhaps these represent important long-run investments to improve the schools' learning opportunities, it is fair to wonder how students who suffered learning losses during the pandemic will benefit from them. Even if these examples are outliers compared with more productive uses of the federal spending, they point to the need for stricter guidelines in using the ESSER funds, as well as stronger mechanisms for tracking the use of funds.

Greater federal oversight of districts' spending would improve the ability to track and evaluate the efficacy of ESSER spending, albeit at a cost: school districts would need to allocate extra personnel time (and thus greater resources) to comply with the additional reporting mandates. But this extra demand would be worth the cost, particularly in the context of a $190 billion investment in school districts' operational capabilities.

In short, the mechanisms in place to evaluate districts' spending are scarce. State governments and school districts are essentially running thousands of experiments with public money at this moment, yet federal and state governments lack a cohesive data infrastructure to monitor where the money is being spent, let alone to evaluate how effectively these investments are improving student outcomes. Developing this data infrastructure as well as more seamless information sharing between states, school districts, and the national U.S. Department of Education ought to be a priority moving forward. We will likely be able to assess whether progress has been made in reducing income-based disparities in learning loss only after future standardized test scores have been released. Helping to close the COVID-era education gaps would mark a notable policy success for ESSER spending but would also leave largely open one important question: Which investments of public resources actually succeeded in closing those gaps?

Moreover, if the education disparities persist in spite of these interventions, the federal government's loosely targeted spending will reasonably be questioned. In that event, the challenges would be doubled and the federal government would have to act again, as the COVID-driven learning gaps and their consequences for economic opportunity would be too large to ignore. In renewing its efforts, Congress should allocate resources that are more directly targeted at schools that experienced the largest learning losses (rather than basing funding levels solely on existing formulas, including Title I), and it should more narrowly limit the allocation of these resources to evidence-driven solutions to improve the learning performance of students at lower-performing (and lower-income) schools.

Lesson 9: Promote Greater Access to Affordable, High-Quality Health Care Coverage

The ninth recommendation—to work toward more accessible and higher-quality health care coverage—is necessarily vague. The evidence presented here has suggested, rather logically, that lower health insurance coverage rates go hand in hand with higher COVID case rates and fatality rates (see chapter 2). Even in a full-coverage scenario, however, many of the income-based health disparities documented in this book would probably have persisted. County-level poverty rates were more strongly aligned with case and fatality rates than health insurance coverage, and income-based gaps in health outcomes persisted even in states with high insurance coverage.[101] On balance, however, the evidence is clear that the insured fared better during the pandemic, consistent with a much broader set of causal evidence of the individual benefits to having access to health care coverage.[102]

There are many pathways to improving access to health care coverage as well as its quality.[103] The debate over which pathway is optimal, however, is largely beyond the scope of this book's evidence base. The evidence presented in chapter 2 does suggest the benefits of state Medicaid expansion: the twelve non-expansion states (Alabama, Florida, Georgia, Kansas, Mississippi, North Carolina, South Carolina, South Dakota, Tennessee, Texas, Wisconsin, and Wyoming) have some of the highest uninsured rates in the country, and they also experienced higher shares of what are likely to have been COVID deaths in 2020.[104] For these twelve states, expanding Medicaid might be a good place to start toward improving health outcomes. In fact, South Dakota and North Carolina are, at time of writing, in the process of doing so, bringing the number of non-expansion states down to 10. Voters in South Dakota approved Medicaid expansion in November 2022, while legislators in North Carolina agreed to a deal in March 2023 to expand Medicaid by 2024.

Estimates from the Urban Institute suggest that if these states had expanded Medicaid before the pandemic, the number of insured adults in the country would drop by around 4 million, or close to a 30 percent decline in the share of uninsured.[105] Around 650,000 uninsured workers in "essential" occupations would have been covered if these states had expanded Medicaid prior to the pandemic, with Black and Hispanic workers benefiting the most.[106] Expanding Medicaid comes at a cost, of course: though the federal government covers most of the bill, spending in the non-expansion states would increase by $2.7 billion, though some of that would be offset by savings on uncompensated care.[107]

Even if we are fortunate enough to never again see a pandemic on the scale of COVID-19, the pandemic's consequences reaffirm the nation's need for equitable access to health services. Improving access to affordable health care coverage—whether through Medicaid expansion in the holdout states or more ambitious reforms at the federal and state levels—ought to remain a goal of U.S. policymaking.

Lesson 10: Invest More Resources in the Census Bureau's Data Collection Capabilities

The final policy lesson relates to the need for greater investment in the nation's public data infrastructure. This book has relied on data from many sources; some were well established prior to the pandemic (such as the Current Population Survey), some were introduced during the pandemic (Census Household Pulse Survey), and some were private-sector data sources that filled information gaps in the federal government's data infrastructure (for example, cell-phone data to track school closures). All these data sources carry lessons for improving the federal government's data collection in nonpandemic years.

The CPS data form the backbone of contemporary poverty and inequality research, yet this data source has limitations that could be rectified with greater government investment. I discussed the monthly income components earlier; other limitations include the lack of material hardship data in the CPS samples and the lack of timely (sub-annual) indicators of economic well-being.

The Pulse largely made up for those shortcomings during the pandemic. As an experimental, web-based survey, however, the Pulse had clear limitations, including a participation rate in the initial waves of data of less than 5 percent. Without its own pre-pandemic reference point, the Pulse faced the challenge of comparing its estimates of, say, material hardship and mental health to estimates from other surveys. Nonetheless, the survey's internal validity (that is, the ability to make comparisons across Pulse waves, even if not from the Pulse to other samples) was largely consistent and of tremendous use for tracking near-real-time changes in social and economic conditions. The Pulse in its current form will be discontinued, but its best components should be directly integrated into the Basic Monthly CPS files.

Specifically, the Pulse's questions on food insufficiency, difficulty staying caught up on rent or mortgage payments, and extensive worrying and anxiety ought to be directly embedded into the monthly CPS. There would be two major benefits of such an addition. First, it would give the United States a single high-quality source of data to evaluate poverty, hardship, and mental health. The European Union has already implemented such a data source: poverty *and* material hardship can be officially estimated from the same sample of respondents to the EU Statistics on Income and Living Conditions (EU-SILC) survey. The U.S. Census Bureau and the BLS should follow suit and incorporate these three elements of the Pulse into the CPS. Second, incorporating these indicators into the monthly surveys would address the issue of timeliness: unlike the annual ASEC survey, which is released once a year after a considerable lag, the monthly files are processed and publicly released quickly. Combined with the monthly income question, my modest proposal is to add four indicators to the Basic Monthly CPS files: food hardship, difficult with rent or mortgage payments, and the extent of worrying. To avoid increasing the burden on respondents, the BLS could identify four less relevant indicators to remove.

This modest change would go a long way toward improving the monitoring of the scale and intensity of poverty in the United States. In addition to providing more timely estimates of economic well-being, it would allow researchers to more appropriately investigate whether our indicators of poverty accurately reflect households' economic and social well-being. The COVID-19 pandemic has taught us the importance of having timely and comprehensive data to guide policy responses, and this change would allow for that beyond the pandemic.

Lessons Still to Learn

We have many lessons yet to learn, and points of progress to make, if we are to improve living conditions for the nation's lowest-income residents.

As I finished writing this book, inflation had surged and then receded in the span of just one year, altering the consumption power of household incomes. Such price volatility underscores the need for intrayear measures of household economic well-being. As prices rise and fall, changes in poverty may correspond less with changes in well-being, emphasizing the importance of combining income-based indicators of poverty with measures of material hardship, mental health, and subjective well-being.

Certain themes that this book did not address in detail deserve to be acknowledged. Community- and faith-based organizations often play a more significant role in providing support in economic downturns, and the pandemic was no exception.[108] Although the focus here has been on providing evidence on the public policy response to the pandemic, it is important not to ignore the important role of community organizations in providing local support. Moreover, two other topics that have gone unaddressed here deserve elaboration in future research: the role of informal networks and the role of wealth in buffering COVID-era income shocks.

Relatedly, this book's evidence base is not conducive to broad take-aways in regard to post-COVID labor market policies, parental and sick leave programs, higher education, and other policy areas that affect the well-being of low-income households in pandemics and normal times alike. The role of policy in influencing higher wages, paid leaves, more accessible education, and more affordable housing is, of course, of high importance; I have omitted these topics from this book's policy recommendations simply because the COVID-era evidence presented here cannot speak as directly to post-COVID reforms in these areas.

The COVID-19 pandemic offered many lessons for improving economic well-being in the United States beyond the pandemic. We witnessed the coexistence of a record-high unemployment rate with a record-low poverty rate. We witnessed how expanding the generosity of, and access to, unemployment benefits can protect incomes in times of job loss. And we witnessed reductions in food hardship through monthly cash payments to low-income families with children. We witnessed the consequences of the state not doing more to reduce economic vulnerability, particularly among racial/ethnic minorities, prior to the onset of the pandemic. We witnessed the impact of prior exposure to poverty on the livelihoods of adults during the crisis, as well as the impact of current exposure to childhood poverty on students' learning outcomes during the shift to distance learning.

In short, we witnessed the menacing consequences of poverty but also the enormous power and capability of the state to reduce poverty and improve well-being among households going through difficult times. We owe it to all those who happen to experience life in low-income America to apply the lessons learned during the pandemic as we move forward.

Chapter 8 Appendix

Figure A8.1   **Conditional Increase in the Likelihood of Poverty among Adults from Being Unemployed for at Least Four Weeks during the Year**

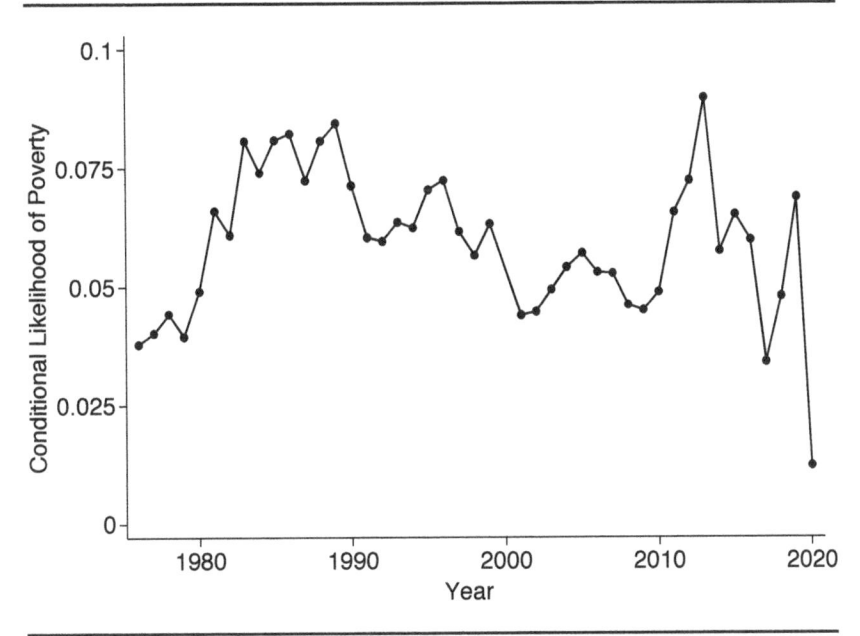

Source: Author's analysis of Current Population Survey Annual Social and Economic Supplement data.

Note: The sample is limited to adults ages eighteen to sixty-four. The figure controls for age, gender, race/ethnicity, number of children in the household, number of working-age adults in the household, number of household members age sixty-five or older, marital status, whether foreign-born, and whether a citizen. The results corroborate figure 8.1's conclusion: the relative "penalty" for being unemployed in 2020 was the lowest penalty on record.

Notes

Chapter 1: Three Perspectives on Poverty in the Context of COVID-19

1. National Center for Homeless Education 2021.
2. Coleman-Jensen et al. 2020.
3. Gornick and Meyers 2005; Hardy and Park 2022; Mattingly, Schaefer, and Carson 2016.
4. Keisler-Starkey and Bunch 2020.
5. Fox 2020.
6. Wright, Hubbard, and Darity 2022.
7. Blanchet, Saez, and Zucman 2022.
8. Fox 2020; Short 2012.
9. Edwards and Smith 2020.
10. Moffitt 2015.
11. Parolin 2021b; Shaefer and Edin 2013.
12. Shrivastava and Thompson 2022.
13. Fox 2020.
14. Tolbert, Drake, and Damico 2022.
15. Khullar and Chokshi 2018.
16. See "Union Membership, Coverage, and Earnings from the CPS" database, constructed by Barry Hirsch and David Macpherson and available at: www.unionstats.com.
17. Organization for Economic Cooperation and Development 2019.
18. Hertel-Fernandez et al. 2020.
19. Goldstein and McKinley 2020.
20. Ferré-Sadurní 2020.
21. Congressional Research Service 2021c.
22. Lee and Parolin 2021.

23. Parolin and Lee 2021a.
24. Schreiber 2022.
25. Atkinson 2019.
26. The unit of analysis in U.S. poverty measurement is often the resource sharing unit, which may exclude unrelated members of a household. For example, between 3 and 5 percent of U.S. households have multiple resource sharing units to be examined in calculations of the Supplemental Poverty Measure. I use "household" as shorthand, as it is more intuitive and less cumbersome than "resource sharing unit."
27. Fox and Burns 2021.
28. Citro and Michaels 1995; Wimer et al. 2016.
29. Desmond and Western 2018.
30. Duncan et al. 1998.
31. Badgett 1994; Couch and Fairlie 2010.
32. National Academy of Sciences 2019.
33. Mazurenko et al. 2018.
34. The Panel Study of Income Dynamics microdata is available at the Institute for Social Research website, https://simba.isr.umich.edu/Zips/EarlyRelease.aspx.
35. Duncan, Ziol-Guest, and Kalil 2010; McLoyd 1990; Ziol-Guest et al. 2012.
36. Another way of interpreting this evidence is to compare childhood poverty exposure based on adult outcomes. With respect to adult occupation, this analysis reveals that the average employed adult working in a high-risk occupation was exposed to 1.8 times the rate of poverty in childhood compared to working adults not in a high-risk job.
37. Parolin and Lee 2022.
38. Atkinson 2019.
39. Bailey and Duquette 2014; Jenkins 2020; Waldfogel 2013.
40. Fox 2020.
41. Hoynes, Page, and Stevens 2006; Rainwater and Smeeding 2005; Wimer et al. 2016.
42. Fox 2020.
43. Morduch and Schneider 2017.
44. Fox and Burns 2021.
45. O'Connor 2001.
46. Aizer, Hoynes, and Lleras-Muney 2022.
47. Brady 2019; National Academy of Sciences 2019; Townsend 1979.
48. Brady, Finnigan, and Hübgen 2017; Katz 1990.
49. Parolin, Curran, and Wimer 2020.
50. Parolin, Collyer, et al. 2021b.
51. Elmendorf and Furman 2008.
52. I exclude the Lost Wages Assistance (LWA) program from this simplified overview of the timing of unemployment supplements, as the LWA depleted its funds in less than a month (early August to early September 2020) and was not as accessible as the Pandemic Unemployment Assistance benefits.
53. Finkelstein et al. 2022.
54. Goldhaber et al. 2022, 6.

Chapter 2: Poverty as a Risk Factor, Part 1: The Unequal Health Consequences of COVID-19

1. Amin 2022.
2. King 1967.
3. The poverty rate cited here is an estimate of county-level OPM poverty from Opportunity Insights in 2010. The rate is equivalent to two standard deviations above the mean among all counties. The data on death rates are also from Opportunity Insights.
4. Johns Hopkins University & Medicine 2021.
5. These estimates are not weighted by counties' population sizes, leading to lower average vaccination coverage rates than were observed nationally.
6. Centers for Disease Control and Prevention 2023.
7. Li et al. 2021.
8. For ease of interpretation, all outcomes are presented as standard deviations.
9. See also evidence from Chen et al. 2021; and Finch and Finch 2020.
10. Finkelstein et al. 2022; Quan et al. 2021.
11. Finkelstein et al. 2022.
12. Goyal et al. 2020.
13. Gershengorn et al. 2021; Gross et al. 2020; Mahajan and Larkins-Pettigrew 2020.
14. Andrasfay and Goldman 2021.
15. Goldman and Andrasfay 2022.
16. Katz 1990.
17. Gilens 1999.
18. Krimmel and Rader 2017.
19. Parolin 2019b.
20. Michener 2018.
21. Currie 2011; Torche 2014.
22. Centers for Disease Control and Prevention 2022; Blackwell, Lucas, and Clarke 2014.
23. Koma et al. 2020.
24. Ibid.
25. McLoyd 1998.
26. Freytas-Tamura, Hu, and Rogers Cook 2020.
27. Tolbert, Drake, and Damico 2022.
28. Gaffney et al. 2020.
29. National Conference of State Legislatures 2021.
30. Council of Economic Advisers 2022.
31. Gaffney et al. 2020.
32. Centers for Disease Control and Prevention 2021a.
33. Schnake-Mahl and Bilal 2021.
34. Institute for Children, Poverty and Homelessness 2016.
35. Lofquist 2012.
36. Pew Research Center 2013.
37. Tobolowsky et al. 2020.

38. Ahmad et al. 2020.
39. Berenbrok et al. 2021.
40. Press, Huisingh-Scheetz, and Arora 2021.
41. Parolin 2019b; Western and Rosenfeld 2011.
42. Centers for Disease Control and Prevention 2021b.
43. Borjas 2020; Rho et al. 2020.
44. Gabrell, Yeung, and Jameel 2020.
45. Schneider and Harknett 2020.
46. Hertel-Fernandez et al. 2020.
47. Chen et al. 2021; Hawkins, Davis, and Kriebel 2021.
48. Rothwell and Smith 2021.
49. Chen and Krieger 2021; Hawkins, Davis, and Kriebel 2021.
50. Hawkins, Davis, and Kriebel 2021.
51. New York State Department of Labor 2021; Officer of Governor Gavin Newsom 2021.
52. Finkelstein et al. 2022.

Chapter 3: Poverty as a Risk Factor, Part 2: Disparities in Job Loss and Job Quality

1. Johnson and Fritz 2020; Mervosh, Lu, and Swales 2020.
2. Matraji and Leung 2020.
3. Congressional Research Service 2021c.
4. Gupta 2021.
5. Hardy and Logan 2020.
6. Gould 2021.
7. Hardy and Logan 2020.
8. Anyamele, McFarland, and Fiakofi 2021; Couch, Fairlie, and Xu 2020; Holder, Jones, and Masterson 2021.
9. The author's calculations from the Current Population Survey.
10. U.S. Bureau of Labor Statistics 2020.
11. The author's estimates from the 2020 Current Population Survey's Annual Social and Economic Supplement (ASEC) (incomes in calendar year 2019).
12. U.S. Bureau of Labor Statistics 2021.
13. Ibid.
14. An adult who is both out of work and actively pursuing work is "unemployed." "Non-employment," in contrast, refers only to whether a non-retired adult is working or not, regardless of whether they are looking for work (or are "active" in the labor market). To address misclassification error, I include adults who are jobless, not unemployed, but who report being absent for "other reasons" as in fact being unemployed.
15. Gould and Kassa 2020.
16. Rothstein 2019.
17. Schwandt and Wachter 2019.
18. Gould 2021.
19. Centers for Disease Control and Prevention 2022.

20. Gould 2021.
21. Ibid.
22. Goldin 2022; Furman, Kearney, and Powell 2021a.
23. Goldin 2022, 13.
24. Cited in Goldin 2022.
25. Ibid.
26. Furman, Kearney, and Powell 2021b.
27. Badgett 1994; Couch and Fairlie 2010.
28. Darity and Mason 1998.
29. Consider Nevada, one of the states hit hardest given its reliance on the service and tourism sectors. The unemployment rate for Nevadans who were in poverty in 2019 climbed to 49 percent for the period from April to June 2020 (up from 13 percent in the period from January to February), compared to 25.4 percent for Nevadans who were not in poverty before the pandemic (up from 4.4 percent in the January to February period). This within-state gap between the poor and the nonpoor was larger than the changes between Nevada and most other states.
30. Congressional Research Service 2021c.
31. Cajner et al. 2020.
32. Bateman and Ross 2021; Gould and Kassa 2021.
33. Gould and Shierholz 2020.
34. Chen et al. 2021; Hawkins, Davis, and Kriebel 2021; Rho et al. 2020.
35. Gupta 2021.
36. Yeung and Hofferth 1998.
37. Gassman-Pines and Gennetian 2020; Gotlib et al. 2020; Latino Decisions 2020; Patrick et al. 2020.
38. Fox et al. 2015.
39. Coleman-Jensen et al. 2012; Nord, Andrews, and Carlson 2008.
40. Parolin and Wimer 2020.

Chapter 4: The Policy Response: The CARES Act, the American Rescue Plan Act, and the Child Tax Credit

1. Congressional Budget Office 2020; Congressional Research Service 2021b.
2. Wachter 2019.
3. Greig et al. 2022.
4. This estimate excludes Social Security spending, which is primarily but not exclusively targeted at retirement-age adults.
5. Congressional Research Service 2020.
6. Author's calculations of spending data from The White House 2008; Council of Economic Advisers 2014; U.S. Department of Labor 2022; and Internal Revenue Service 2022. Great Recession spending included a 2008 stimulus check, the Making Work Pay tax credit, payroll tax cuts, UI unemployment insurance benefits, COBRA health insurance subsidies, SNAP expansions, $250 payments to select individuals of retirement age or with a disability, and the Wounded Warrior Tax Credit.

7. Wachter 2019.
8. This estimate is from the CPS ASEC for the 2020 reference year. It is the number of adults reporting receipt of UI benefits relative to the total number of current or recently unemployed adults.
9. Iacurci 2020.
10. Ganong et al. 2020.
11. We could argue that such preparations should have been made after the Great Recession a decade before, particularly given that other high-income countries had successfully applied work-sharing schemes to mitigate the damage of the financial crisis, but no such steps were taken in the United States.
12. Autor et al. 2022, 6.
13. Ibid.
14. Dalton 2021.
15. Autor et al. 2022.
16. Curran and Collyer 2020.
17. Marr et al. 2020.
18. Chishti and Bolter 2020.
19. Migration Policy Institute 2019.
20. Parolin and Brady 2018.
21. Marr et al. 2020.
22. Holtzblatt and Karpman 2020. The Urban Institute survey is "a nationally representative, internet-based survey of nonelderly adults designed to assess the impact of the COVID-19 pandemic on adults and their families and how those impacts change over time." The authors report a sample size of 4,352 adults ages eighteen to sixty-four.
23. Marr et al. 2020.
24. Murphy 2021.
25. Herd and Moynihan 2018.
26. Carey, Groen, and Jensen 2021.
27. Ibid.
28. Forsythe 2021.
29. Meyer, Mok, and Sullivan 2009; Parolin 2019a.
30. See Forsythe 2021; Moffitt and Ziliak 2020.
31. Bell et al. 2020; Bell et al. 2021.
32. Henderson 2020.
33. Ibid.
34. U.S. Secret Service 2022.
35. Parolin, Collyer, et al. 2021b.
36. Congressional Research Service 2021b.
37. Davis et al. 2019.
38. Curran and Collyer 2020.
39. Hoynes 2019; Pac et al. 2017.
40. Shaefer et al. 2018; Shaefer and Edin 2013.
41. Goodman-Bacon and McGranahan 2008; Mendenhall et al. 2012; Michelmore and Jones 2015.

42. Parolin, Collyer, et al. 2021b.
43. U.S. Department of the Treasury 2021.
44. Fox 2020.
45. Bitler, Hoynes, and Kuka 2017.
46. Bitler, Hoynes, and Schanzenbach 2023.
47. Bauer et al. 2020.

Chapter 5: Tracking Poverty in the Here and Now

1. Parolin, Curran, et al. 2022
2. Morduch and Schneider 2017.
3. Atkinson 2019, 63–64.
4. U.S. Department of Health, Education, and Welfare 1976, 30.
5. Bania and Leete 2009; Hill et al. 2013; Morris et al. 2015.
6. Morduch and Siwicki 2017.
7. Bania and Leete 2009; Morris et al. 2015.
8. LaBriola and Schneider 2020.
9. Meyer and Sullivan 2006.
10. Fisher et al. 2019; Ganong et al. 2020.
11. Ganong et al. 2020.
12. Congressional Research Service 2021a; U.S. Department of Agriculture 2017.
13. Athreya, Reilly, and Simpson 2014.
14. Goodman-Bacon and McGranahan 2008.
15. Smeeding, Ross Phillips, and O'Connor 1999.
16. Baugh et al. 2018.
17. Parolin, Curran, et al. 2022.
18. Han, Meyer, and Sullivan 2020. I do not discuss their measure here, but readers curious about the differences can see Parolin, Collyer, et al. 2022.
19. Parolin, Collyer, et al. 2022.
20. Wimer et al. 2016.
21. Azevedo-McCaffrey and Safawi 2022.
22. Iceland 2019.
23. Gornick and Jäntti 2012; National Academy of Sciences 2019; Rainwater and Smeeding 2005.
24. Rainwater and Smeeding 2005.
25. Parolin, Curran, et al. 2022.
26. Ibid.
27. U.S. Department of the Treasury 2020.
28. Holtzblatt and Karpman 2020.
29. Borjas and Cassidy 2019.
30. Bitler, Hoynes, and Schanzenbach 2020.
31. Century Foundation 2021.
32. Capps et al. 2018; Rendall et al. 2013; Royston 2004; Van Hook et al. 2015.

33. Bradley et al. 2021.
34. Winship and Rachidi 2020.
35. Parolin, Collyer, et al. 2022.
36. Ibid.
37. Atkinson 2019.
38. Gornick and Jäntti 2012.

Chapter 6: Beyond Income: Material Hardship and Mental Health

1. Frankel et al. 2020.
2. DeParle 2020.
3. A number of such studies could be cited, all of which, though well intentioned, point to the challenges inherent in rapidly interpreting data from new surveys. For higher-profile examples, see Schanzenbach and Pitts 2020; Ziliak 2021.
4. Coleman-Jensen et al. 2021.
5. Karpman and Zuckerman 2021.
6. Microdata from the Institute for Social Research Survey Research Center's Panel Study of Income Dynamics, available at: https://simba.isr.umich.edu /Zips/EarlyRelease.aspx.
7. Coleman-Jensen et al. 2020.
8. National Center for Homeless Education 2021.
9. U.S. Department of Agriculture, Economic Research Service, "Key Statistics & Graphics," available at: https://www.ers.usda.gov/topics/food-nutrition -assistance/food-security-in-the-u-s/key-statistics-graphics/. I emphasize "for financial reasons" here, as the USDA explicitly defines "hardship" as having "insufficient money or other resources." However, one-fifth of respondents reporting food hardship during COVID-19 indicated that their challenges were not related to money.
10. Ibid.
11. Gundersen and Ziliak 2015.
12. Bond et al. 2021.
13. Gundersen and Ziliak 2015.
14. Hoynes, Schanzenbach, and Almond 2016.
15. National Center for Homeless Education 2021.
16. Evelly 2021.
17. Joint Center for Housing Studies of Harvard University 2020b.
18. Joint Center for Housing Studies of Harvard University 2020a.
19. Eviction Lab, "Eviction Tracking System," available at: https://evictionlab .org/eviction-tracking/.
20. Parolin 2021a; Shaefer et al. 2019.
21. Shaefer et al. 2019.
22. USDA Economic Research Service, "Key Statistics & Graphics."
23. Bitler, Hoynes, and Schanzenbach 2023; Coleman-Jensen et al. 2021.

24. Karpman and Zuckerman 2021.
25. Collyer et al. 2020.
26. Dettling and Lambie-Hanson 2021.
27. Shaefer et al. 2020.
28. As also documented by Princeton's Eviction Lab in its "Eviction Tracking System."
29. Fish et al. 2020.
30. Aurand and Threet 2021.
31. Fish et al. 2020.
32. Board of Governors of the Federal Reserve System 2020.
33. Bachas et al. 2020; JPMorgan Chase Institute 2020.
34. Shaefer et al. 2020.
35. Cooney and Shaefer 2021; Shaefer et al. 2020.
36. Bauer et al. 2020; Bauer, Ruffini, and Schanzenbach 2021.
37. Parolin, Ananat, et al. 2021.
38. Schanzenbach 2023.
39. Pilkauskas et al. 2022, 1.
40. Goodman-Bacon 2018; Smeeding, Ross Phillips, and O'Connor 1999.
41. Parolin, Giupponi, et al. 2022.
42. Glasner et al. 2022; Jacob et al. 2022.
43. Lorant et al. 2003.
44. Ettman et al. 2020.
45. Brodeur et al. 2021.
46. Gassman-Pines and Gennetian 2020.
47. Patrick et al. 2020.
48. Waxman and Gupta 2021.
49. Sandstrom, Adams, and Pyati 2019.

Chapter 7: Poverty as a Stratifying Feature: School and Childcare Closures

1. This chapter is based on Parolin and Lee 2021a and Parolin and Lee 2021b.
2. Education Week 2020.
3. Mendoza 2020.
4. See the COVID-19 School Data Hub (https://www.covidschooldatahub.com/) and the "Enrollment Tracker: 2020–2022" at Return to Learn Tracker (https://www.returntolearntracker.net/2020-22-enrollment-changes/). See also Education Week 2020.
5. Selection into the cell-phone data that we have access to could in theory be a problem, particularly given that lower-income families are less likely to have cell phones. We partially account for this possibility by examining year-over-year change, under an assumption that selection effects do not worsen from one year to the next. Moreover, the SafeGraph sample of cell phones closely corresponds to U.S. census population counts by state and county, suggesting broad coverage across the country.

6. Parolin and Lee 2021a; Lee and Parolin 2021.
7. Parolin and Lee 2021a.
8. This estimate corresponds closely with findings from the Census House-hold Pulse Survey that 93 percent of families with children had engaged in distance learning by summer.
9. The December 2021 rate ticked up slightly, to 15.3 percent, but this could have been due to changes in winter holiday schedules during the COVID era from what they had been in December 2019, contributing to a slight bump in the share of schools with smaller monthly visit counts.
10. Musaddiq et al. 2021.
11. Grossmann et al. 2021.
12. The only subject and grade combination available in the Opportunity Insights data was third-grade math scores.
13. Reardon 2011.
14. Engzell, Frey, and Verhagen 2021.
15. Ibid.
16. Goldhaber et al. 2022.
17. Ibid.
18. Mendoza 2020.
19. Bauer et al. 2020.
20. McElrath 2020.
21. Jæger and Blaabæk 2020.
22. Locke 2022.
23. Malkus 2021.
24. Goldhaber et al. 2022.
25. Kuhfeld et al. 2022.
26. McKinsey and Company 2022.
27. Locke 2022.
28. Goldhaber et al. 2022.
29. England and Folbre 1999; Hook 2006; Rindfuss et al. 2007.
30. RegionTrack 2019.
31. Bernal 2015; Harding Weaver 2002; Koh and Neuman 2009.
32. Malik et al. 2018.
33. Economic Policy Institute 2020.
34. We estimate the coverage rate of the SafeGraph data to be around 78 per-cent of all licensed childcare centers, the broadest among available data sets. This estimate is based on the number of childcare centers in our database relative to the 109,414 total licensed childcare institutions in the United States (Lee and Parolin 2021).
35. Barnett, Jung, and Nores 2020.
36. Ibid.
37. Furman, Kearney, and Powell 2021a.
38. Zamarro and Prados 2021.
39. Barnett, Jung, and Nores 2020.
40. Tomopoulos et al. 2010; Waller et al. 2021.
41. National Association for the Education of Young Children 2020.

Chapter 8: Ten Policy Lessons for Improving Economic Well-Being after the COVID-19 Pandemic

1. Finkelstein et al. 2022.
2. Goldhaber et al. 2022.
3. Wright, Hubbard, and Darity 2022.
4. Blanchet, Saez, and Zucman 2022.
5. Katz 1990, 269.
6. Townsend 1979.
7. Brady, Finnigan, and Hübgen 2017.
8. For those worried about how the changing composition of the (un)employed affects these patterns, figure A8.1 presents the increase in the conditional likelihood of poverty for the unemployed, adjusting for age, gender, race/ethnicity, number of children in the household, number of working-age adults in the household, number of household members age sixty-five or older, whether the individual is married, whether the adult is foreign-born, and whether the adult is a citizen. The conclusions are similar.
9. Greenstein 2022.
10. Rainwater and Smeeding 2005.
11. See Hunter 1904; Du Bois 1967; Townsend 1979; Fisher 1992; and Citro and Michaels 1995.
12. For a counterperspective, see Han et al. 2022; for an argument that their counterperspective is incorrect, see Parolin, Collyer, et al. 2022.
13. Aizer, Hoynes, and Lleras-Muney 2022.
14. Parolin, Cross, and O'Brien 2023.
15. Keisler-Starkey and Bunch 2020.
16. Coleman-Jensen et al. 2020; National Center for Homeless Education 2021.
17. Neuberger and Bergh 2022.
18. Ganong, Noel, and Vavra 2020.
19. Bivens et al. 2021.
20. Von Wachter 2019.
21. Burke et al. 2021.
22. Blank and Card 1991; Forsythe 2021; von Wachter 2019.
23. Greig et al. 2022, 1.
24. Bivens et al. 2021.
25. By "approximately the past year" I am referring to the base period used for UI benefit determination. A base period is a set of prior working months—often defined as the first four of the five quarters preceding job loss—over which earnings are evaluated to determine UI eligibility and benefit values. Bivens et al. (2021) also propose expanding the base period for determining eligibility to six quarters of work, so that workers with sufficient hours from one of the six quarters preceding job loss could qualify for UI benefits.
26. Underreporting of unemployment benefits in the CPS ASEC is likely to bias both of these estimates but should not alter the general conclusion.

The 10 percent of unemployed adults who do not receive UI benefits in this simulation are randomly selected among the broader pool of unemployed adults. Applying a PUA-like benefit of $300 per week reduces poverty from 20.9 percent to 14.1 percent among the unemployed, a decline of 6.8 percentage points.

27. Corcoran 1995; Duncan and Magnuson 2013; Hill and Duncan 1987.
28. Hill and Duncan 1987; Levy and Duncan 2000; McLanahan and Sandefur 1994.
29. McLoyd 1990; Nolan et al. 2016.
30. Parolin, Matsudaira, et al. 2022.
31. National Academy of Sciences 2019.
32. Collyer, Harris, and Wimer 2019.
33. Parolin, Collyer, et al. 2021a.
34. Creamer et al. 2022.
35. Parolin and Filauro 2022.
36. Ibid.
37. Parolin, Ananat, et al., forthcoming.
38. Ananat et al. 2022.
39. Parolin, Giupponi, et al. 2022.
40. Corinth et al. 2021.
41. Ananat et al. 2022.
42. Greenstein 2022.
43. York and Watson 2021.
44. Schott, Pavetti, and Floyd 2018.
45. Azevedo-McCaffrey and Safawi 2022.
46. Parolin 2021a.
47. Parolin 2019b.
48. Schott, Pavetti, and Floyd 2018.
49. Wolfe 2022.
50. A few other examples include "funding for overnight camps, textbook subsidies for college students, scholarships for college students from well-off families, [and] the imputed value of Girl Scouts' volunteer time" (Parolin 2021a 1136).
51. Rosenbaum 2019.
52. Ibid.
53. Azevedo-McCaffrey and Safawi 2022.
54. Dutta-Gupta 2019.
55. Parolin 2021a.
56. Parolin, Ananat, et al., forthcoming; Parolin, Giupponi, et al. 2022.
57. Drumbl 2019; Goodman-Bacon and McGranahan 2008; Sykes et al. 2014.
58. Hammond and Orr 2016.
59. Hamilton et al. 2022.
60. U.S. Government Accountability Office 2007. As potential reasons for the low participation rates, the GAO notes that the monthly advances at the time were small ($140 per month was the *maximum* allowance in 2010) and that the administration of the payments was left to businesses to manage and distribute rather than the IRS.

61. U.S. Government Accountability Office 2022. This estimate is based on the cited GAO's report that an average of 36.1 million monthly payments were distributed, while 2.1 million tax filers opted out of the monthly payments.
62. Drumbl 2019.
63. Sykes et al. 2014.
64. Ibid., 245.
65. Drumbl 2019.
66. Halpern-Meekin et al. 2018.
67. Holt 2008, 2015.
68. Drumbl 2019.
69. Wancheck and Greenstein 2011.
70. Hammond and Maag 2021.
71. Wancheck and Greenstein 2011.
72. Maag et al. 2022.
73. Jones and Ziliak 2019.
74. See the discussion in Greenstein (2022) and Hammond and Maag (2021).
75. Greenstein 2022.
76. Ibid.
77. Ellis and Faricy 2021; McCabe 2018.
78. Greenstein 2022, 2.
79. Newville and Zucker 2021.
80. Internal Revenue Service 2020.
81. Greenstein 2022.
82. Marr et al. 2020.
83. Boushey, Nunn, and Shambaugh 2019.
84. Sahm 2019.
85. Hoynes and Whitmore Schanzenbach 2019.
86. Schanzenbach 2023.
87. Giupponi, Landais, and Lapeyre 2022.
88. Brenke, Rinne, and Zimmermann 2011.
89. Autor et al. 2022.
90. Locke 2022.
91. Goldhaber et al. 2022.
92. Ibid.
93. Kuhfeld et al. 2022.
94. McKinsey and Company 2022.
95. Malkus 2021; Waldman and Fortis 2021.
96. Roza and Silberstein 2022.
97. Ibid.
98. Malkus 2021.
99. Waldman and Fortis 2021.
100. Ibid.
101. Finkelstein et al. 2022.
102. Mazurenko et al. 2018.

103. Linke Young et al. 2020.
104. Council of Economic Advisers 2022.
105. Buettgens and Ramchandani 2022.
106. Cross-Call and Broaddus 2020.
107. Buettgens and Ramchandani 2022.
108. Roels et al. 2022.

References

Ahmad, Khansa, Sebhat Erqou, Nishant Shah, Umair Nazir, Alan R. Morrison, Gaurav Choudhary, and Wen-Chih Wu. 2020. "Association of Poor Housing Conditions with COVID-19 Incidence and Mortality across U.S. Counties." *PLoS ONE* 15(11, November 2): e0241327. DOI: https://doi.org/10.1371/journal .pone.0241327.

Aizer, Anna, Hilary W. Hoynes, and Adriana Lleras-Muney. 2022. "Children and the U.S. Social Safety Net: Balancing Disincentives for Adults and Benefits for Children." Working Paper 29754. National Bureau of Economic Research, February. DOI: https://doi.org/10.3386/w29754.

Amin, Reema. 2022. "Nearly 10% of NYC Students Were Homeless Last Year, According to Report." *Chalkbeat*, October 26. https://ny.chalkbeat.org/2022 /10/26/23423652/nyc-homeless-students-pandemic-shelter-transportation-bus.

Ananat, Elizabeth, Benjamin Glasner, Christal Hamilton, and Zachary Parolin. 2022. "Effects of the Expanded Child Tax Credit on Employment Outcomes: Evidence from Real-World Data from April to December 2021." Working Paper 29823. National Bureau of Economic Research, March. DOI: https:// doi.org/10.3386/w29823.

Andrasfay, Theresa, and Noreen Goldman. 2021. "Reductions in 2020 U.S. Life Expectancy Due to COVID-19 and the Disproportionate Impact on the Black and Latino Populations." *Proceedings of the National Academy of Sciences* 118 (5, January 14): e2014746118. DOI: https://doi.org/10.1073/pnas.2014746118.

Anyamele, Okechukwu D., Saundra M. McFarland, and Kenneth Fiakofi. 2021. "The Disparities on Loss of Employment Income by U.S. Households during the COVID-19 Pandemic." *Journal of Economics, Race, and Policy* 5(July 15): 115–33. DOI: https://doi.org/10.1007/s41996-021-00086-1.

Athreya, Kartik, Devin Reilly, and Nicole Simpson. 2014. "Single Mothers and the Earned Income Tax Credit: Insurance without Disincentives?" Discussion

Paper 8114. Institute for the Study of Labor (IZA), April. https://ftp.iza.org/dp8114.pdf.

Atkinson, Anthony B. *Measuring Poverty around the World*. Princeton, N.J.: Princeton University Press.

Aurand, Andrew, and Daniel Threet. 2021. "The Road Ahead for Low Income Renters." National Low Income Housing Coalition, July 21. https://nlihc.org/sites/default/files/The-Road-Ahead-for-Low-Income-Renters.pdf.

Autor, David, David Cho, Leland D. Crane, Mita Goldar, Byron Lutz, Joshua Montes, William B. Peterman, David Ratner, Daniel Villar, and Ahu Yildirmaz. 2022. "The $800 Billion Paycheck Protection Program: Where Did the Money Go and Why Did It Go There?" *Journal of Economic Perspectives* 36(2, Spring): 55–80. DOI: https://doi.org/10.1257/jep.36.2.55.

Azevedo-McCaffrey, Diana, and Ali Safawi. 2022. "To Promote Equity, States Should Invest More TANF Dollars in Basic Assistance." Center on Budget and Policy Priorities, January 12. https://www.cbpp.org/research/family-income-support/to-promote-equity-states-should-invest-more-tanf-dollars-in-basic.

Bachas, Natalie, Peter Ganong, Pascal J. Noel, Joseph S. Vavra, Arlene Wong, Diana Farrell, and Fiona E. Grieg. 2020. "Initial Impacts of the Pandemic on Consumer Behavior: Evidence from Linked Income, Spending, and Savings Data." Working Paper 27617. National Bureau of Economic Research, July. https://www.nber.org/papers/w27617.

Badgett, M. V. Lee. 1994. "Rising Black Unemployment: Changes in Job Stability or in Employability?" *Review of Black Political Economy* 22(3, March): 55–75. DOI: https://doi.org/10.1007/bf02689973.

Bailey, Martha J., and Nicolas J. Duquette. 2014. "How Johnson Fought the War on Poverty: The Economics and Politics of Funding at the Office of Economic Opportunity." *Journal of Economic History* 74(2, June): 351–88. DOI: https://doi.org/10.1017/S0022050714000291.

Bania, Neil, and Laura Leete. 2009. "Monthly Household Income Volatility in the U.S., 1991/92 vs. 2002/03." *Economics Bulletin* 29(3, August 25): 2100–2112. https://EconPapers.repec.org/RePEc:ebl:ecbull:eb-08i30028.

Barnett, Steven, Kwanghee Jung, and Milagros Nores. 2020. "Young Children's Home Learning and Preschool Participation Experiences during the Pandemic. NIEER 2020 Preschool Learning Activities Survey: Technical Report and Selected Findings" (technical report). National Institute for Early Education Research, August. https://nieer.org/wp-content/uploads/2020/11/NIEER_Tech_Rpt_July2020_Young_Childrens_Home_Learning_and_Preschool_Participation_Experiences_During_the_Pandemic-AUG2020.pdf.

Bateman, Nicole, and Martha Ross. 2021. "The Pandemic Hurt Low-Wage Workers the Most—and So Far, the Recovery Has Helped Them the Least." Brookings Institution, July 28. https://www.brookings.edu/research/the-pandemic-hurt-low-wage-workers-the-most-and-so-far-the-recovery-has-helped-them-the-least/.

Bauer, Lauren, Abigail Pitts, Krista Ruffini, and Diane Whitmore Schanzenbach. 2020. "The Effect of Pandemic EBT on Measures of Food Hardship." Hamilton Project, July. https://www.hamiltonproject.org/assets/files/P-EBT_LO_7.30.pdf.

Bauer, Lauren, Krista Ruffini, and Diane Whitmore Schanzenbach. 2021. "An Update on the Effect of Pandemic EBT on Measures of Food Hardship." Brookings Institution, September 29. https://www.brookings.edu/research/an-update-on-the-effect-of-pandemic-ebt-on-measures-of-food-hardship/.

Baugh, Brian, Itzhak Ben-David, Hoonsuk Park, and Jonathan A. Parker. 2018. "Asymmetric Consumption Smoothing." Working Paper 25086. National Bureau of Economic Research, September. DOI: https://doi.org/10.3386/w25086.

Bell, Alex, Thomas J. Hedin, Roozbeh Moghadam, Geoffrey Schnorr, and Till von Wachter. 2021. "10 Key Trends from the Unemployment Crisis in California and Their Implications for Policy Reform." California Policy Lab, April 29. https://www.capolicylab.org/publications/10-key-trends-from-the-unemployment-crisis-in-california-and-implications-for-policy-reform/.

Bell, Alex, Thomas Hedin, Geoffrey Schnorr, and Till von Wachter. 2020. "An Analysis of Unemployment Insurance Claims in California during the COVID-19 Pandemic" (report). California Policy Lab, December 21. https://www.capolicylab.org/wp-content/uploads/2020/12/Dec-21st-Analysis-of-CA-UI-Claims-during-the-COVID-19-Pandemic.pdf.

Berenbrok, Lucas A., Shangbin Tang, Kim C. Coley, Cristina Boccuti, Jingchuan Guo, Utibe R. Essien, Sean Dickson, and Immaculada Hernandez. 2021. "Access to Potential COVID-19 Vaccine Administration Facilities: A Geographic Information Systems Analysis." University of Pittsburgh School of Pharmacy and Westhealth Policy Center, February 2. https://www.westhealth.org/wp-content/uploads/2021/02/Access-to-Potential-COVID-19-Vaccine-Administration-Facilities-2-2-2021.pdf/.

Bernal, Raquel. 2015. "The Impact of a Vocational Education Program for Childcare Providers on Children's Well-Being." *Economics of Education Review* 48(October): 165–83. DOI: https://doi.org/10.1016/j.econedurev.2015.07.003.

Bitler, Marianne, Hilary Hoynes, and Elira Kuka. 2017. "Child Poverty, the Great Recession, and the Social Safety Net in the United States." *Journal of Policy Analysis and Management* 36(2): 358–89. DOI: https://doi.org/10.1002/pam.21963.

Bitler, Marianne, Hilary W. Hoynes, and Diane Whitmore Schanzenbach. 2020. "The Social Safety Net in the Wake of Covid-19." Working Paper 27796. National Bureau of Economic Research, September. DOI: https://doi.org/10.3386/w27796.

———. 2023. "Suffering, the Safety Net, and Disparities during COVID-19." *RSF: The Russell Sage Foundation Journal of the Social Sciences* 9(3): 32–59. DOI: https://doi.org/10.7758/RSF.2023.9.3.02.

Bivens, Josh, Melissa Boteach, Rachel Deutsch, Francisco Díez, Rebecca Dixon, Brian Galle, Alix Gould-Werth, Nicole Marquez, Lily Roberts, Heidi Shierholz, and William Spriggs. 2021. *Reforming Unemployment Insurance: Stabilizing a System in Crisis and Laying the Foundation for Equity.* Joint report of the Center for American Progress, Center for Popular Democracy, Economic Policy Institute, Groundwork Collaborative, National Employment Law Project, National Women's Law Center, and Washington Center for Equitable Growth, June. https://www.epi.org/publication/unemployment-insurance-reform/.

Blackwell, Debra L., Jacqueline W. Lucas, and Tainya C. Clarke. 2014. *Summary Health Statistics for U.S. Adults: National Health Interview Survey, 2012. Vital and Health Statistics* 10(260). National Center for Health Statistics, February. https://www.cdc.gov/nchs/data/series/sr_10/sr10_260.pdf.

Blanchet, Thomas, Emmanuel Saez, and Gabriel Zucman. 2022. "Real-Time Inequality." Working Paper 30229. National Bureau of Economic Research, July. http://www.nber.org/papers/w30229.

Blank, Rebecca M., and David E. Card. 1991. "Recent Trends in Insured and Uninsured Unemployment: Is There an Explanation?" *Quarterly Journal of Economics* 106(4, November): 1157–89. DOI: https://doi.org/10.2307/2937960.

Board of Governors of the Federal Reserve System. 2020. "Update on the Economic Well-Being of U.S. Households: July 2020 Results." September 17. http://www.publicnow.com/view/3D8F91EF550F9D37D89B0F296E081BD38 FDE9672.

Bond, Timothy N., Jillian B. Carr, Analisa Packham, and Jonathan Smith. 2021. "Hungry for Success? SNAP Timing, High-Stakes Exam Performance, and College Attendance." Working Paper 28386. National Bureau of Economic Research, January. DOI: https://doi.org/10.3386/w28386.

Borjas, George J. 2020. "Demographic Determinants of Testing Incidence and COVID-19 Infections in New York City Neighborhoods." Faculty Research Working Paper RWP20-008. Harvard Kennedy School, April. DOI: http://dx.doi.org/10.2139/ssrn.3572329.

Borjas, George J., and Hugh Cassidy. 2019. "The Wage Penalty to Undocumented Immigration." *Labour Economics* 61:101757. DOI: https://doi.org/10.1016/j.labeco.2019.101757.

Boushey, Heather, Ryan Nunn, and Jay Shambaugh, eds. 2019. *Recession Ready: Fiscal Policies to Stabilize the American Economy.* Hamilton Project, May. https://www.brookings.edu/wp-content/uploads/2019/05/AutomaticStabilizers_FullBook_web_20190508.pdf.

Bradley, Valerie C., Shiro Kuriwaki, Michael Isakov, Dino Sejdinovic, Xiao-Li Meng, and Seth Flaxman. 2021. "Unrepresentative Big Surveys Significantly Overestimated US Vaccine Uptake." *Nature* 600(7890): 695–700. DOI: https://doi.org/10.1038/s41586-021-04198-4.

Brady, David. 2019. "Theories of the Causes of Poverty." *Annual Review of Sociology* 45(1): 155–75. DOI: https://doi.org/10.1146/annurev-soc-073018-022550.

Brady, David, Ryan M. Finnigan, and Sabine Hübgen. 2017. "Rethinking the Risks of Poverty: A Framework for Analyzing Prevalences and Penalties." *American Journal of Sociology* 123(3, November): 740–86. DOI: https://doi.org/10.1086/693678.

Brenke, Karl, Ulf Rinne, and Klaus F. Zimmermann. 2011. "Short-Time Work: The German Answer to the Great Recession." Discussion Paper 5780. Institute for the Study of Labor (IZA), June. http://ftp.iza.org/dp5780.pdf.

Brodeur, Abel, Andrew E. Clark, Sarah Fleche, and Nattavudh Powdthavee. 2021. "COVID-19, Lockdowns, and Well-Being: Evidence from Google Trends." *Journal of Public Economics* 193(January): 104346. DOI: https://doi.org/10.1016/j.jpubeco.2020.104346.

Buettgens, Matthew, and Urmi Ramchandani. 2022. "3.7 Million People Would Gain Health Coverage in 2023 if the Remaining 12 States Were to Expand Medicaid Eligibility." Urban Institute, August 3. https://www.urban.org/research/publication/3-7-million-people-would-gain-health-coverage-2023-if-remaining-12-states-were.

Burke, Ryan, Mikey Dickerson, Lauren Lockwood, Tara Dawson McGuinness, Marina Nitze, Ayushi Roy, and Emily Wright-Moore. 2021. "A Playbook for Improving Unemployment Insurance Delivery." New America, June 22. https://www.newamerica.org/new-practice-lab/playbook/improve-unemployment/.

Cajner, Tomaz, Leland D. Crane, Ryan A. Decker, John Grigsby, Adrian Hamins-Puertolas, Erik Hurst, Christopher Kurz, and Ahu Yildirmaz. 2020. "The U.S. Labor Market during the Beginning of the Pandemic Recession." Working Paper 2020-58. Becker Friedman Institute, July. https://bfi.uchicago.edu/wp-content/uploads/HurstBFI_WP_202058_Revision.pdf.

Capps, Randy, James D. Bachmeier, and Jennifer Van Hook. 2018. "Estimating the Characteristics of Unauthorized Immigrants Using U.S. Census Data: Combined Sample Multiple Imputation." *ANNALS of the American Academy of Political and Social Science* 677(1): 165–79. DOI: https://doi.org/10.1177/0002716218767383.

Carey, Patrick, Jeffrey A. Groen, and Bradley A. Jensen. 2021. "Applying for and Receiving Unemployment Insurance Benefits during the Coronavirus Pandemic." U.S. Bureau of Labor Statistics, *Monthly Labor Review* (September). https://www.bls.gov/opub/mlr/2021/article/pdf/applying-for-and-receiving-unemployment-insurance-benefits-during-the-coronavirus-pandemic.pdf.

Centers for Disease Control and Prevention. 2021a. "Vaccines and Immunizations: How to Talk to Your Patients about COVID-19 Vaccination." July 28. https://www.cdc.gov/vaccines/covid-19/hcp/engaging-patients.html.

———. 2021b. "Vaccines and Immunizations: Interim List of Categories of Essential Workers Mapped to Standardized Industry Codes and Titles." March 29. https://www.cdc.gov/vaccines/covid-19/categories-essential-workers.html.

———. 2022. "Risk for COVID-19 Infection, Hospitalization, and Death by Race/Ethnicity." Updated December 28, 2022. https://www.cdc.gov/coronavirus/2019-ncov/covid-data/investigations-discovery/hospitalization-death-by-race-ethnicity.html.

———. 2023. "Risk for COVID-19 Infection, Hospitalization, and Death by Age Group." Updated February 6, 2023. https://www.cdc.gov/coronavirus/2019-ncov/covid-data/investigations-discovery/hospitalization-death-by-age.html.

The Century Foundation. 2021. "Unemployment Insurance Data Dashboard." The Century Foundation, August 18. https://tcf.org/content/data/unemployment-insurance-data-dashboard.

Chen, Jarvis T., and Nancy Krieger. 2021. "Revealing the Unequal Burden of COVID-19 by Income, Race/Ethnicity, and Household Crowding: U.S. County versus Zip Code Analyses." *Journal of Public Health Management and Practice* 27(suppl. 1, January/February): S43–56. DOI: https://doi.org/10.1097/phh.0000000000001263.

Chen, Yea-Hung, Maria Glymour, Alicia Riley, John Balmes, Kate Duchowny, Robert Harrison, Ellicott Matthay, and Kirstin Bibbins-Domingo. 2021. "Excess Mortality Associated with the COVID-19 Pandemic among Californians 18–65 Years of Age, by Occupational Sector and Occupation: March through October 2020." *PLoS ONE* 16(6): e0252454. DOI: https://doi.org/10.1371/journal.pone.0252454.

Chishti, Muzaffar, and Jessica Bolter. 2020. "Vulnerable to COVID-19 and in Frontline Jobs, Immigrants Are Mostly Shut Out of U.S. Relief." Migration Policy Institute, April 24. https://www.migrationpolicy.org/article/covid19-immigrants-shut-out-federal-relief.

Citro, Constance F., and Robert T. Michaels, eds. 1995. *Measuring Poverty: A New Approach.* Washington, D.C.: National Academies Press.

Coleman-Jensen, Alisa, Mark Nord, Margaret Andrews, and Steven Carlson. 2012. "Household Food Security in the United States in 2011." Economic Research Report 141. U.S. Department of Agriculture Economic Research Service, September. https://www.ers.usda.gov/publications/pub-details/?pubid=45021.

Coleman-Jensen, Alisa, Matthew P. Rabbitt, Christian A. Gregory, and Anita Singh. 2020. "Household Food Security in the United States in 2019." Economic Research Report 275. U.S. Department of Agriculture, Economic Research Service, September. https://www.ers.usda.gov/webdocs/publications/99282/err-275.pdf?v=9263.7.

———. 2021. "Household Food Security in the United States in 2020." Economic Research Report 298. U.S. Department of Agriculture, Economic Research Service, September. https://www.ers.usda.gov/publications/pub-details/?pubid=102075.

Collyer, Sophie, Chantal Bannerman, Rebecca Charles, Katherine Friedman, and Christopher Wimer. 2020. "Spotlight on Hunger: Food Hardship in New York City Is Rising as New Yorkers Wait for a Second Federal Stimulus Bill." Columbia University, Center on Poverty and Social Policy, November. https://static1.squarespace.com/static/610831a16c95260dbd68934a/t/61f401afbd1069619ff4770f/1643381167245/POVERTY_TRACKER_REPORT22.pdf.

Collyer, Sophie, David Harris, and Christopher Wimer. 2019. "Left Behind: The One-Third of Children in Families Who Earn Too Little to Get the Full Child Tax Credit." *Poverty & Social Policy Brief* 3(6, May 13). Columbia University, Center on Poverty and Social Policy. https://static1.squarespace.com/static/610831a16c95260dbd68934a/t/61154a19cce7cb59f8660690/1628785178307/Who-Is-Left-Behind-in-the-Federal-CTC-CPSP-2019.pdf.

Congressional Budget Office (CBO). 2020. Phillip L. Swagel (CBO director) to Senator Mike Inzi (chairman of Committee on the Budget), "re: Preliminary Estimate of the Effects of H.R. 748, the CARES Act, Public Law 116-136, Revised, with Corrections to the Revenue Effect of the Employee Retention Credit and to the Modification of a Limitation on Losses for Taxpayers Other than Corporations," April 27. https://www.cbo.gov/system/files/2020-04/hr748.pdf.

Congressional Research Service. 2020. "Comparing the Congressional Response to the Great Recession and the COVID-19-Related Recession: Unemployment Insurance (UI) Provisions." CRS Report 46472, July 30. https://crsreports.congress.gov/product/pdf/R/R46472.

———. 2021a. "The Earned Income Tax Credit (EITC): How It Works and Who Receives It." CRS Report 43805, January 12. https://sgp.fas.org/crs/misc /R43805.pdf.

———. 2021b. "Federal Spending on Benefits and Services for People with Low Income: FY2008–FY2020." CRS Report 46986, December 8. https://crsreports .congress.gov/product/pdf/R/R46986.

———. 2021c. "Unemployment Rates during the COVID-19 Pandemic." CRS Report 46554, August 20. https://sgp.fas.org/crs/misc/R46554.pdf.

Cooney, Patrick, and H. Luke Shaefer. 2021. "Material Hardship and Mental Health Following the COVID-19 Relief Bill and American Rescue Plan Act." *Michigan Poverty Solutions* (University of Michigan), May. http://sites.fordschool .umich.edu/poverty2021/files/2021/05/PovertySolutions-Hardship-After -COVID-19-Relief-Bill-PolicyBrief-r1.pdf.

Corcoran, Mary. 1995. "Rags to Rags: Poverty and Mobility in the United States." *Annual Review of Sociology* 21(1): 237–67. DOI: https://doi.org/10.1146 /annurev.so.21.080195.001321.

Corinth, Kevin, Bruce D. Meyer, Matthew Stadnicki, and Derek Wu. 2021. "The Anti-Poverty, Targeting, and Labor Supply Effects of Replacing a Child Tax Credit with a Child Allowance." Working Paper 29366. National Bureau of Economic Research, October. DOI: https://doi.org/10.3386/w29366.

Couch, Kenneth A., and Robert Fairlie. 2010. "Last Hired, First Fired? Black-White Unemployment and the Business Cycle." *Demography* 47(1, February 1): 227–47. DOI: https://doi.org/10.1353/dem.0.0086.

Couch, Kenneth A., Robert W. Fairlie, and Huanan Xu. 2020. "Early Evidence of the Impacts of COVID-19 on Minority Unemployment." *Journal of Public Economics* 192(December): 104287. DOI: https://doi.org/10.1016/ j.jpubeco.2020.104287.

Council of Economic Advisers. 2014. "The Economic Impact of the American Recovery and Reinvestment Act Five Years Later." Chapter 3 in *2014 Economic Report of the President* (Washington: U.S. Government Printing Office, March 14). https://obamawhitehouse.archives.gov/sites/default/files/docs/erp_2014 _chapter_3.pdf.

———. 2022. "Excess Mortality during the Pandemic: The Role of Health Insurance" (issue brief). The White House, July 12. https://www.whitehouse .gov/cea/written-materials/2022/07/12/excess-mortality-during-the-pandemic -the-role-of-health-insurance/.

Creamer, John, Emily A. Shrider, Kalee Burns, and Francis Chen. 2022. "Poverty in the United States: 2021." Report P60-277. U.S. Census Bureau, September 13. https://www.census.gov/library/publications/2022/demo/p60-277.html.

Cross-Call, Jesse, and Matt Broaddus. 2020. "States That Have Expanded Medicaid Are Better Positioned to Address COVID-19 and Recession." Center on Budget and Policy Priorities, July 14. https://www.cbpp.org/research/health/states -that-have-expanded-medicaid-are-better-positioned-to-address-covid-19 -and.

Curran, Megan A., and Sophie Collyer. 2020. "Teenage and Young Adult Dependents Left Out of Cash Payments in the COVID-19 Crisis." *Policy & Social Brief* 4

(7, May 21). https://static1.squarespace.com/static/5743308460b5e922a25a6dc7 /t/5ed5264a0e59687e73ee827a/1591027279060/Dependents-CARESAct -COVID19-CPSP-2020.pdf.

Currie, Janet. 2011. "Inequality at Birth: Some Causes and Consequences." *American Economic Review* 101(3, May): 1–22. http://www.jstor.org/stable/29783707.

Dalton, Michael. 2021. "Putting the Paycheck Protection Program into Perspective: An Analysis Using Administrative and Survey Data." Working Paper 542. U.S. Bureau of Labor Statistics, November 5. https://www.bls.gov/osmr /research-papers/2021/pdf/ec210080.pdf.

Darity, William A., and Patrick L. Mason. 1998. "Evidence on Discrimination in Employment: Codes of Color, Codes of Gender." *Journal of Economic Perspectives* 12(2, Spring): 63–90. DOI: https://doi.org/10.1257/jep.12.2.63.

Davis, Aidan, Meg Wiehe, Sophie Collyer, David Harris, and Christopher Wimer. 2019. *The Case for Extending State-Level Child Tax Credits to Those Left Out: A 50-State Analysis.* Institute on Taxation and Economic Policy, April. https://itep.sfo2.digitaloceanspaces.com/041719-Child-Tax-Credit_ITEP -CPSP.pdf.

DeParle, Jason. 2020. "As Hunger Swells, Food Stamps Become a Partisan Flash Point." *New York Times*, May 6. https://www.nytimes.com/2020/05/06/us/politics /coronavirus-hunger-food-stamps.html.

Desmond, Matthew, and Bruce Western. 2018. "Poverty in America: New Directions and Debates." *Annual Review of Sociology* 44(1): 305–18. DOI: https:// doi.org/10.1146/annurev-soc-060116-053411.

Dettling, Lisa, and Lauren Lambie-Hanson. 2021. "Why Is the Default Rate So Low? How Economic Conditions and Public Policies Have Shaped Mortgage and Auto Delinquencies during the COVID-19 Pandemic." Board of Governors of the Federal Reserve System, March 4. https://www.federalreserve.gov /econres/notes/feds-notes/why-is-the-default-rate-so-low-20210304.htm.

Drumbl, Michelle Lyon. 2019. *Tax Credits for the Working Poor: A Call for Reform.* Cambridge: Cambridge University Press.

Du Bois, W.E.B. 1967. *The Philadelphia Negro: A Social Study.* New York: Schocken Books.

Duncan, Greg J., and Katherine Magnuson. 2013. "The Long Reach of Early Childhood Poverty." In *Economic Stress, Human Capital, and Families in Asia: Research and Policy Challenges,* edited by Wei-Jun Jean Yeung and Mui Teng Yap. Dordrecht: Springer.

Duncan, Greg J., W. Jean Yeung, Jeanne Brooks-Gunn, and Judith R. Smith. 1998. "How Much Does Childhood Poverty Affect the Life Chances of Children?" *American Sociological Review* 63(3, June): 406–23. DOI: https:// doi.org/10.2307/2657556

Duncan, Greg J., Kathleen M. Ziol-Guest, and Ariel Kalil. 2010. "Early-Childhood Poverty and Adult Attainment, Behavior, and Health." *Child Development* 81(1, January/February): 306–25. https://www.jstor.org/stable/40598980.

Dutta-Gupta, Indivar. 2019. "Improving TANF's Countercyclicality through Increased Basic Assistance and Subsidized Jobs." Brookings Institution, May 19. https://www.brookings.edu/research/improving-tanfs-countercyclicality -through-increased-basic-assistance-and-subsidized-jobs/.

Economic Policy Institute. 2020. "Child Care Costs in the United States." Updated October 2020. https://www.epi.org/child-care-costs-in-the-united-states/#/NY.

Education Week. 2020. "The Coronavirus Spring: The Historic Closing of U.S. Schools." *Education Week,* July 1. https://www.edweek.org/ew/section /multimedia/the-coronavirus-spring-the-historic-closing-of.html.

Edwards, Roxanna, and Sean M. Smith. 2020. "Job Market Remains Tight in 2019, as the Unemployment Rate Falls to Its Lowest Level since 1969." U.S. Bureau of Labor Statistics, April. https://www.bls.gov/opub/mlr/2020/article /job-market-remains-tight-in-2019-as-the-unemployment-rate-falls-to-its -lowest-level-since-1969.htm#:~:text=The%20U.S.%20labor%20market%20 remained,rate%20increased%20over%20the%20year.

Ellis, Christopher, and Christopher Faricy. 2021. *The Other Side of the Coin: Public Opinion toward Social Tax Expenditures.* New York: Russell Sage Foundation.

Elmendorf, Douglas W., and Jason Furman. 2008. "Three Keys to Effective Fiscal Stimulus." *Brookings,* January 26. https://www.brookings.edu/opinions /three-keys-to-effective-fiscal-stimulus/.

England, Paula, and Nancy Folbre. 1999. "The Cost of Caring." *Annals of the American Academy of Political and Social Science* 561(1, January): 39–51. DOI: https://doi.org/10.1177/000271629956100103.

Engzell, Per, Arun Frey, and Mark D. Verhagen. 2021. "Learning Loss Due to School Closures during the COVID-19 Pandemic." *Proceedings of the National Academy of Sciences* 118(17, April 7): e2022376118. DOI: https://doi.org /10.1073/pnas.2022376118.

Ettman, Catherine K., Salma M. Abdalla, Gregory H. Cohen, Laura Sampson, Patrick M. Vivier, and Sandro Galea. 2020. "Prevalence of Depression Symptoms in U.S. Adults before and during the COVID-19 Pandemic." *JAMA Network Open* 3(9, September 2): e2019686. DOI: https://doi.org/10.1001 /jamanetworkopen.2020.19686.

Evelly, Jeanmarie. 2021. "Number of Homeless NYC Students Surpasses 100K for 6th Consecutive School Year." *City Limits,* November 8. https://citylimits .org/2021/11/08/number-of-homeless-nyc-students-surpasses-100k-for-6th -consecutive-school-year/.

Ferré-Sadurní, Luis. 2020. "New York City Schools, Restaurants, and Bars Are Shut Down over Coronavirus." *New York Times,* March 15. https://www .nytimes.com/2020/03/15/nyregion/coronavirus-nyc-shutdown.html.

Finch, W. Holmes, and Maria E. Hernández Finch. 2020. "Poverty and Covid-19: Rates of Incidence and Deaths in the United States during the First 10 Weeks of the Pandemic." *Frontiers in Sociology* 5(June 15): 1–10. DOI: https://doi.org /10.3389/fsoc.2020.00047.

Finkelstein, Amy, Geoffrey Kocks, Maria Polyakova, and Victoria Udalova. 2022. "Heterogeneity in Damages from a Pandemic." Working Paper 30658. National Bureau of Economic Research, November. DOI: https://doi.org /10.3386/w30658.

Fish, Joe, Emily Lemmerman, Renee Louis, and Peter Hepburn. 2020. "Eviction Moratoria Have Prevented over a Million Eviction Filings in the U.S. during the COVID-19 Pandemic." Eviction Lab, December 15. https://evictionlab.org /missing-eviction-filings/.

Fisher, Gordon M. 1992. "The Development and History of the Poverty Thresholds." *Social Security Bulletin* 55(4, Winter): 3–14. https://www.ssa.gov/policy/docs/ssb/v55n4/v55n4p3.pdf.

Fisher, Jonathan, David Johnson, Timothy Smeeding, and Jeffrey P. Thompson. 2019. "Estimating the Marginal Propensity to Consume Using the Distributions of Income, Consumption, and Wealth." Working Paper 19-4. Federal Reserve Bank of Boston, Research Department, February. DOI: https://doi.org/10.29412/res.wp.2019.04.

Forsythe, Eliza. 2021. "Understanding Unemployment Insurance Coverage in Early 2021." University of Illinois at Urbana-Champaign, February 1. http://publish.illinois.edu/elizaforsythe/files/2021/02/understanding-unemployment-insurance-coverage-in-early-2021-version-feb-1-2021.pdf.

Fox, Liana. 2020. "The Supplemental Poverty Measure: 2019." *Current Population Reports* 60-272. U.S. Census Bureau, September. https://www.census.gov/content/dam/Census/library/publications/2020/demo/p60-272.pdf.

Fox, Liana E., and Kalee Burns. 2021. "The Supplemental Poverty Measure: 2020." *Current Population Reports* P60-275. U.S. Census Bureau, September. https://www.census.gov/content/dam/Census/library/publications/2021/demo/p60-275.pdf.

Fox, Liana, Christopher Wimer, Irwin Garfinkel, Neeraj Kaushal, and Jane Waldfogel. 2015. "Waging War on Poverty: Poverty Trends Using a Historical Supplemental Poverty Measure." *Journal of Policy Analysis and Management* 34(3, Summer): 567–92. DOI: https://doi.org/10.1002/pam.21833.

Frankel, Todd C., Brittney Martin, Andrew Van Dam, and Alyssa Fowers. 2020. "A Growing Number of Americans Are Going Hungry." *Washington Post*, November 25. https://www.washingtonpost.com/graphics/2020/business/hunger-coronavirus-economy/.

Freytas-Tamura, Kimiko de, Winnie Hu, and Lindsey Rogers Cook. 2020. "'It's the Death Towers': How the Bronx Became New York's Virus Hot Spot." *New York Times*, May 26. https://www.nytimes.com/2020/05/26/nyregion/bronx-coronavirus-outbreak.html.

Furman, Jason, Melissa S. Kearney, and Wilson Powell III. 2021a. "How Much Have Childcare Challenges Slowed the U.S. Jobs Market Recovery?" Peterson Institute for International Economics, May 17. https://www.piie.com/blogs/realtime-economic-issues-watch/how-much-have-childcare-challenges-slowed-us-jobs-market.

———. 2021b. "The Role of Childcare Challenges in the U.S. Jobs Market Recovery during the COVID-19 Pandemic." Working Paper 28934. National Bureau of Economic Research, June. DOI: https://doi.org/10.3386/w28934.

Gabrell, Michael, Bernice Yeung, and Maryam Jameel. 2020. "Millions of Essential Workers Are Being Left Out of COVID-19 Workplace Safety Protections, Thanks to OSHA." *ProPublica*, April 16. https://www.propublica.org/article/millions-of-essential-workers-are-being-left-out-of-covid-19-workplace-safety-protections-thanks-to-osha.

Gaffney, Adam W., Laura Hawks, David H. Bor, Steffie Woolhandler, David U. Himmelstein, and Danny McCormick. 2020. "18.2 Million Individuals at

Increased Risk of Severe COVID-19 Illness Are Un- or Underinsured." *Journal of General Internal Medicine* 35(8, August): 2487–89. DOI: https://doi.org/10.1007/s11606-020-05899-8.

Ganong, Peter, Damon Jones, Pascal J. Noel, Fiona E. Greig, Diana Farrell, and Chris Wheat. 2020. "Wealth, Race, and Consumption Smoothing of Typical Income Shocks." Working Paper 27552. National Bureau of Economic Research, July. DOI: https://doi.org/10.3386/w27552.

Ganong, Peter, Pascal J. Noel, and Joseph S. Vavra. 2020. "U.S. Unemployment Insurance Replacement Rates during the Pandemic." Working Paper 27216. National Bureau of Economic Research, August. https://www.nber.org/papers/w27216.

Gassman-Pines, Anna, and Lisa A. Gennetian. 2020. "COVID-19 Job and Income Loss Jeopardize Child Well-Being: Income Support Policies Can Help." Child Evidence Brief 9. Society for Research in Child Development, December. https://www.srcd.org/sites/default/files/resources/FINAL_SRCDCEB-JobLoss.pdf.

Gershengorn, Hayley B., Samira Patel, Bhavarth Shukla, Prem R. Warde, Monisha Bhatia, Dipen Parekh, and Tamira Ferreira. 2021. "Association of Race and Ethnicity with COVID-19 Test Positivity and Hospitalization Is Mediated by Socioeconomic Factors." *Annals of the American Thoracic Society* 18(8, August): 1326–34. DOI: https://doi.org/10.1513/AnnalsATS.202011-1448OC.

Gilens, Martin. 1999. *Why Americans Hate Welfare: Race, Media, and the Politics of Antipoverty Policy.* Chicago: University of Chicago Press.

Giupponi, Giulia, Camille Landais, and Alice Lapeyre. 2022. "Should We Insure Workers or Jobs during Recessions?" *Journal of Economic Perspectives* 36(2, Spring): 29–54. https://www.jstor.org/stable/27123973.

Glasner, B., Oscar Jiménez-Solomon, Sophie M. Collyer, Irwin Garfinkel, and Christopher T. Wimer. 2022. "No Evidence the Child Tax Credit Expansion Had an Effect on the Well-Being and Mental Health of Parents." *Health Affairs* 41(11, November): 1607–15. DOI: https://doi.org/10.1377/hlthaff.2022.00730.

Goldhaber, Dan, Thomas K. Kane, Andrew McEachin, Emily Morton, Tyler Patterson, and Douglas O. Staiger. 2022. "The Consequences of Remote and Hybrid Instruction during the Pandemic." Working Paper 30010. National Bureau of Economic Research, May. DOI: 10.3386/w30010.

Goldin, Claudia. 2022. "Understanding the Economic Impact of COVID-19 on Women." Working Paper 29974. National Bureau of Economic Research, April. DOI: https://doi.org/10.3386/w29974.

Goldman, Noreen, and Theresa Andrasfay. 2022. "Life Expectancy Loss among Native Americans during the COVID-19 Pandemic." *Demographic Research* 47(9, July 27): 233–46. DOI: 10.4054/demres.2022.47.9.

Goldstein, Joseph, and Jesse McKinley. 2020. "Coronavirus in N.Y.: Manhattan Woman Is First Confirmed Case in State." *New York Times*, March 1. https://www.nytimes.com/2020/03/01/nyregion/new-york-coronvirus-confirmed.html.

Goodman-Bacon, Andrew. 2018. "Difference-in-Differences with Variation in Treatment Timing." Working Paper 25018. National Bureau of Economic Research, September. DOI: https://doi.org/10.3386/w25018.

Goodman-Bacon, Andrew, and Leslie McGranahan. 2008. "How Do EITC Recipients Spend Their Refunds?" *Economic Perspectives* 32(2nd quarter): 17–32. https://EconPapers.repec.org/RePEc:fip:fedhep:y:2008:i:qii:p:17-32:n :v.32no.2.

Gornick, Janet C., and Markus Jäntti. 2012. "Child Poverty in Cross-National Perspective: Lessons from the Luxembourg Income Study." *Children and Youth Services Review* 34(3, March): 558–68. DOI: https://doi.org/10.1016 /j.childyouth.2011.10.016.

Gornick, Janet C., and Marcia K. Meyers. 2005. *Families That Work: Policies for Reconciling Parenthood and Employment.* New York: Russell Sage Foundation.

Gotlib, Ian H., Lauren R. Borchers, Rajpeet Chahal, Anthony Gifuni, and Tiffany Ho. 2020. "Early Life Stress Predicts Depressive Symptoms in Adolescents during the COVID-19 Pandemic: The Mediating Role of Perceived Stress." May 18. https://papers.ssrn.com/sol3/papers.cfm?abstract_id=3606441.

Gould, Elise. 2021. "Older Workers Were Devastated by the Pandemic Downturn and Continue to Face Adverse Employment Outcomes." Economic Policy Institute, April 29. https://www.epi.org/publication/older-workers -were-devastated-by-the-pandemic-downturn-and-continue-to-face-adverse -employment-outcomes-epi-testimony-for-the-senate-special-committee-on -aging/.

Gould, Elise, and Melat Kassa. 2020. "Young Workers Hit Hard by the COVID-19 Economy." Economic Policy Institute, October 14. https://www.epi.org /publication/young-workers-covid-recession/.

——. 2021. "Low-Wage, Low-Hours Workers Were Hit Hardest in the COVID-19 Recession." Economic Policy Institute, May 20. https://files.epi.org/uploads /224913.pdf.

Gould, Elise, and Heidi Shierholz. 2020. "Not Everybody Can Work from Home: Black and Hispanic Workers Are Much Less Likely to Be Able to Telework." Economic Policy Institute, March 19. https://www.epi.org/blog/black-and -hispanic-workers-are-much-less-likely-to-be-able-to-work-from-home/.

Goyal, Monika K., Joelle N. Simpson, Meleah D. Boyle, Gia M. Badolato, Meghan Delaney, Robert McCarter, and Denice Cora-Bramble. 2020. "Racial and/or Ethnic and Socioeconomic Disparities of SARS-CoV-2 Infection among Children." *Pediatrics* 146(4, October 1): e2020009951. DOI: https:// doi.org/10.1542/peds.2020-009951.

Greenstein, Robert. 2022. "Next Steps on the Child Tax Credit." Hamilton Project, November. https://www.brookings.edu/wp-content/uploads/2022 /11/20221129_THP_GreensteinCTC_EA.pdf.

Greig, Fiona, Daniel M. Sullivan, Samantha Anderson, Peter Ganong, Pascal J. Noel, and Joseph Vavra. 2022. "Lessons Learned from the Pandemic Unemployment Assistance Program during COVID-19." JPMorgan Chase & Co., April. https://www.jpmorganchase.com/institute/research/household-income -spending/lessons-learned-pandemic-unemployment-assistance-program-covid.

Gross, Cary P., Utibe R. Essien, Saamir Pasha, Jacob R. Gross, Shi-yi Wang, and Marcella Nunez-Smith. 2020. "Racial and Ethnic Disparities in Population-Level Covid-19 Mortality." *Journal of General Internal Medicine* 35(10, August 4): 3097–99. DOI: https://doi.org/10.1007/s11606-020-06081-w.

Grossmann, Matt, Sarah Reckhow, Katharine O. Strunk, and Meg Turner. 2021. "All States Close but Red Districts Reopen: The Politics of In-Person Schooling during the COVID-19 Pandemic." *Educational Researcher* 50(9, December): 637–48. DOI: https://doi.org/10.3102/0013189x211048840.

Gundersen, Craig, and James P. Ziliak. 2015. "Food Insecurity and Health Outcomes." *Health Affairs* 34(11, November): 1830–39. DOI: https://doi.org/10.1377/hlthaff.2015.0645.

Gupta, Alisha Haridasani. 2021. "Why Some Women Call This Recession a 'Shecession'." *New York Times*, May 9. https://www.nytimes.com/2020/05/09/us/unemployment-coronavirus-women.html.

Halpern-Meekin, Sarah, Sara Sternberg Greene, Ezra Levin, and Kathryn Edin. 2018. "The Rainy Day Earned Income Tax Credit: A Reform to Boost Financial Security by Helping Low-Wage Workers Build Emergency Savings." *RSF: The Russell Sage Foundation Journal of the Social Sciences* 4(2, February): 161–76. DOI: https://doi.org/10.7758/RSF.2018.4.2.08.

Hamilton, Christal, Christopher Wimer, Sophie Collyer, and Laurel Sariscsany. 2022. "Monthly Cash Payments Reduce Spells of Poverty across the Year." *Poverty & Social Policy Brief* 6(5, May 9). Columbia University, Center on Poverty and Social Policy. https://static1.squarespace.com/static/610831a16c95260dbd68934a/t/627ad342bc1db246690cdcf0/1652216643360/Monthly-Cash-Payments-Reduce-Spells-of-Poverty-CPSP-2022.pdf.

Hammond, Samuel, and Elaine Maag. 2021. "Issues in Child Benefit Administration in the United States." Tax Policy Center, December 2. https://www.taxpolicycenter.org/publications/issues-child-benefit-administration-united-states/full.

Hammond, Samuel, and Robert Orr. 2016. "Toward a Universal Child Benefit." Niskanen Center, October 25. https://www.niskanencenter.org/universal-child-benefit/.

Han, Jeehoon, Bruce D. Meyer, James X. Sullivan. 2020. "Income and Poverty in the COVID-19 Pandemic." Working Paper 27729. National Bureau of Economic Research, August. DOI: https://doi.org/10.3386/w27729.

———. 2022. "Real-Time Poverty, Material Well-Being, and the Child Tax Credit." Working Paper 30371. National Bureau of Economic Research, August. DOI: https://doi.org/10.3386/w30371.

Harding Weaver, Ruth. 2002. "Predictors of Quality and Commitment in Family Child Care: Provider Education, Personal Resources, and Support." *Early Education and Development* 13(3, July): 265–82. DOI: https://doi.org/10.1207/s15566935eed1303_2.

Hardy, Bradley L., and Trevon D. Logan. 2020. "Racial Economic Inequality amid the COVID-19 Crisis." Hamilton Project, August 13. https://www.hamiltonproject.org/papers/racial_economic_inequality_amid_the_covid_19_crisis.

Hardy, Erin, and Ji Eun Park. 2022. "2019 NSECE [National Survey of Early Care and Education] Snapshot: Child Care Cost Burden for U.S. Households with Children under Age 5." OPRE Report 2022-05. Washington: U.S. Department of Health and Human Services, Administration for Children and Families, Office of Planning, Research, and Evaluation (January). https://www.acf

.hhs.gov/sites/default/files/documents/opre/opre-2019-nsece-cost-of-care
-jan2022.pdf.

Hawkins, Devin, Letitia Davis, and David Kriebel. 2021. "COVID-19 Deaths
by Occupation, Massachusetts, March 1–July 31, 2020." *American Journal
of Industrial Medicine* 64(4, April): 238–44. DOI: https://doi.org/10.1002
/ajim.23227.

Henderson, Tim. 2020. "Unemployment Payments Weeks Late in Nearly Every
State." Pew Stateline, December 2. https://www.pewtrusts.org/en/research
-and-analysis/blogs/stateline/2020/12/02/unemployment-payments-weeks
-late-in-nearly-every-state.

Herd, Pamela, and Donald P. Moynihan. 2018. *Administrative Burden: Policymaking
by Other Means.* New York: Russell Sage Foundation.

Hertel-Fernandez, Alexander, Suresh Naidu, Adam Reich, and Patrick
Youngblood. 2020. "Understanding the COVID-19 Workplace: Evidence from
a Survey of Essential Workers" (issue brief). Roosevelt Institute, June. https://
rooseveltinstitute.org/wp-content/uploads/2020/07/RI_SurveryofEssential
Workers_IssueBrief_202006-1.pdf.

Hill, Heather D., Pamela Morris, Lisa A. Gennetian, Sharon Wolf, and Carly
Tubbs. 2013. "The Consequences of Income Instability for Children's Well-
being." *Child Development Perspectives* 7(2, June): 85–90. DOI: https://doi.org
/10.1111/cdep.12018.

Hill, Martha S., and Greg J. Duncan. 1987. "Parental Family Income and the
Socioeconomic Attainment of Children." *Social Science Research* 16(1, March):
39–73. DOI: https://doi.org/10.1016/0049-089X(87)90018-4.

Holder, Michelle, Janelle Jones, and Thomas Masterson. 2021. "The Early Impact
of Covid-19 on Job Losses among Black Women in the United States." *Feminist
Economics* 27(1/2): 103–16. DOI: https://doi.org/10.1080/13545701.2020.1849766.

Holt, Steven D. 2008. "Periodic Payment of the Earned Income Tax Credit."
Brookings Institution, June 5. https://www.brookings.edu/research/periodic
-payment-of-the-earned-income-tax-credit/.

———. 2015. "Periodic Payment of the Earned Income Tax Credit Revisited."
Brookings Institution, Metropolitan Policy Program, December. https://www
.brookings.edu/wp-content/uploads/2016/07/HoltPeriodicPaymentEITC121515
.pdf.

Holtzblatt, Janet, and Michael Karpman. 2020. "Who Did Not Get the Economic
Impact Payments by Mid-to-Late May, and Why?" Urban Institute, July.
https://www.urban.org/sites/default/files/publication/102565/who-did-not
-get-the-economic-impact-payments-by-mid-to-late-may-and-why.pdf.

Hook, Jennifer L. 2006. "Care in Context: Men's Unpaid Work in 20 Countries,
1965–2003." *American Sociological Review* 71(4, August): 639–60. DOI: https://
doi.org/10.1177/000312240607100406.

Hoynes, Hilary. 2019. "The Earned Income Tax Credit." *Annals of the American
Academy of Political and Social Science* 686(1, November): 180–203. https://journals
.sagepub.com/doi/full/10.1177/0002716219881621?journalCode=anna.

Hoynes, Hilary W., Marianne E. Page, and Ann Huff Stevens. 2006. "Poverty
in America: Trends and Explanations." *Journal of Economic Perspectives* 20
(1, Winter): 47–68. http://www.jstor.org/stable/30033633.

Hoynes, Hilary, and Diane Whitmore Schanzenbach. 2019. "Strengthening SNAP as an Automatic Stabilizer." Brookings Institution, May 16. https://www.brookings.edu/wp-content/uploads/2019/05/HoynesSchanzenbach_web_20190506.pdf.

Hoynes, Hilary, Diane Whitmore Schanzenbach, and Douglas Almond. 2016. "Long-Run Impacts of Childhood Access to the Safety Net." *American Economic Review* 106(4, April): 903–34. DOI: https://doi.org/10.1257/aer.20130375.

Hunter, Robert. 1904. *Poverty.* London: Macmillan & Co.

Iacurci, G. 2020. "There Are More People Getting Unemployment Benefits than There Are Unemployed Workers." *CNBC*, June 16. https://www.cnbc.com/2020/06/16/there-are-more-people-getting-unemployment-benefits-than-there-are-unemployed-workers.html.

Iceland, John. 2019. "Racial and Ethnic Inequality in Poverty and Affluence, 1959–2015." *Population Research and Policy Review* 38(5, October): 615–54. DOI: https://doi.org/10.1007/s11113-019-09512-7.

Institute for Children, Poverty, and Homelessness. 2016. "Overcrowding in New York City Community Districts." In *On the Map: The Dynamics of Family Homelessness in New York City* (report), April 1, 2016, 38–39. https://www.icphusa.org/wp-content/uploads/2016/04/Overcrowding.pdf.

Internal Revenue Service. 2020. "Veterans Affairs Recipients Will Receive Automatic Economic Impact Payments; Step Follows Work between Treasury, IRS, VA." IR-2020-75, April 17. https://www.irs.gov/newsroom/veterans-affairs-recipients-will-receive-automatic-economic-impact-payments-step-follows-work-between-treasury-irs-va

———. 2022. "SOI Tax Stats—Coronavirus Aid, Relief, and Economic Security Act (CARES Act) Statistics." Updated June 15, 2022. https://www.irs.gov/statistics/soi-tax-stats-coronavirus-aid-relief-and-economic-security-act-cares-act-statistics.

Jacob, Brian, Natasha Pilkauskas, Elizabeth Rhodes, Katherine Richard, and H. Luke Shaefer. 2022. "The COVID-19 Cash Transfer Study II: The Hardship and Mental Health Impacts of an Unconditional Cash Transfer to Low-Income Individuals." *National Tax Journal* 75(3, September): 597–625. DOI: https://doi.org/10.1086/720723.

Jæger, Mads Meier, and Ea Hoppe Blaabæk. 2020. "Inequality in Learning Opportunities during Covid-19: Evidence from Library Takeout." *Research in Social Stratification and Mobility* 68(August): 100524. DOI: https://doi.org/10.1016/j.rssm.2020.100524.

Jenkins, Stephen P. 2020. "Perspectives on Poverty in Europe: Following in Tony Atkinson's Footsteps." *Italian Economic Journal* 6(1, March): 129–55. DOI: https://doi.org/10.1007/s40797-019-00112-0.

Johns Hopkins University & Medicine, Coronavirus Resource Center. "COVID-19 Dashboard by the Center for Systems Science and Engineering (CSSE) at Johns Hopkins University (JHU)." 2021. https://coronavirus.jhu.edu/map.html.

Johnson, Thomas, and Angela Fritz. 2020. "You're under a Stay-at-Home Order? Here's What That Means in Your State." *Washington Post*, May 5. https://www.washingtonpost.com/health/2020/04/06/coronavirus-stay-at-home-by-state/.

Joint Center for Housing Studies of Harvard University. 2020a. "America's Rental Housing 2020" (report). https://www.jchs.harvard.edu/sites/default /files/Harvard_JCHS_Americas_Rental_Housing_2020.pdf.

——. 2020b. "The State of the Nation's Housing 2020." https://www.jchs.harvard .edu/sites/default/files/reports/files/Harvard_JCHS_The_State_of_the_Nations _Housing_2020_Report_Revised_120720.pdf.

Jones, Maggie R., and James P. Ziliak. 2019. "The Antipoverty Impact of the EITC: New Estimates from Survey and Administrative Tax Records." Working Paper 19-14. U.S. Census Bureau, Center for Economic Studies, April. https:// www2.census.gov/ces/wp/2019/CES-WP-19-14R.pdf.

JPMorgan Chase Institute. 2020. "Household Cash Balances during COVID-19: A Distributional Perspective." December. https://www.jpmorganchase.com /institute/research/household-income-spending/household-cash-balances -during-covid-19-a-distributional-perspective.

Karpman, Michael, and Stephen Zuckerman. 2021. "Average Decline in Material Hardship during the Pandemic Conceals Unequal Circumstances: Findings from the December 2020 Well-Being and Basic Needs Survey." Urban Institute, April 14. https://www.urban.org/research/publication/average-decline -material-hardship-during-pandemic-conceals-unequal-circumstances.

Katz, Michael B. 1990. *The Undeserving Poor: From the War on Poverty to the War on Welfare.* New York: Pantheon Books.

Keisler-Starkey, Katherine, and Lisa N. Bunch. 2020. "Health Insurance Coverage in the United States: 2019." *Current Population Reports* 60-271. U.S. Census Bureau, September. https://www.census.gov/content/dam/Census/library /publications/2020/demo/p60-271.pdf.

Khullar, Dhruv, and Dave A. Chokshi. 2018. "Health, Income, and Poverty: Where We Are and What Could Help" health policy brief). *Health Affairs: Culture of Health* (October). https://www.healthaffairs.org/do/10.1377 /hpb20180817.901935/.

King, Martin Luther, Jr. 1967. "The Other America," speech delivered April 14, 1967, at Stanford University. https://www.rev.com/blog/transcripts/the-other -america-speech-transcript-martin-luther-king-jr.

Koh, Serene, and Susan B. Neuman. 2009. "The Impact of Professional Development in Family Child Care: A Practice-Based Approach." *Early Education and Development* 20(3, May): 537–62. DOI: https://doi.org/10.1080/10409280902908841.

Koma, Wyatt, Samantha Artiga, Tricia Neuman, Gary Claxton, Matthew Rae, Jennifer Kates, and Josh Michaud. 2020. "Low-Income and Communities of Color at Higher Risk of Serious Illness if Infected with Coronavirus" (brief). Kaiser Family Foundation, May 7. https://www.kff.org/coronavirus-covid-19 /issue-brief/low-income-and-communities-of-color-at-higher-risk-of-serious -illness-if-infected-with-coronavirus/#.

Krimmel, Katherine, and Kelly Rader. 2017. "The Federal Spending Paradox: Economic Self-Interest and Symbolic Racism in Contemporary Fiscal Politics." *American Politics Research* 45(5, September): 1532673X17701222. DOI: https:// doi.org/10.1177/1532673x17701222.

Kuhfeld, Megan, Jim Soland, Karyn Lewis, and Emily Morton. 2022. "The Pandemic Has Had Devastating Impacts on Learning. What Will It Take

to Help Students Catch Up?" Brookings Institution, March 3. https://www
.brookings.edu/blog/brown-center-chalkboard/2022/03/03/the-pandemic
-has-had-devastating-impacts-on-learning-what-will-it-take-to-help-students
-catch-up/.

LaBriola, Joe, and Daniel Schneider. 2020. "Worker Power and Class Polarization
in Intra-Year Work Hour Volatility." *Social Forces* 98(3, March): 973–99. DOI:
https://doi.org/10.1093/sf/soz032.

Latino Decisions. 2020. "Latino Parent Voices: What Our Families Need Now."
https://nationalsurvey.ap-od.org/wp-content/uploads/2020/08/LatinoParent
Voices_Report.pdf.

Lee, Emma K., and Zachary Parolin. 2021. "The Care Burden during COVID-19:
A National Database of Child Care Closures in the United States." *Socius*
7(July). https://journals.sagepub.com/doi/full/10.1177/23780231211032028.

Levy, Dan Maurice, and Greg J. Duncan. 2000. "Using Sibling Samples to
Assess the Effect of Childhood Family Income on Completed Schooling."
Working paper. Northwestern University and University of Chicago
Joint Center for Poverty Research, April 27. https://EconPapers.repec.org
/RePEc:wop:jopovw:168.

Li, Daniel, Sheila M. Gaynor, Corbin Quick, Jarvis T. Chen, Briana J. K.
Stephenson, Brent A. Coull, and Xihong Lin. 2021. "Identifying U.S. County-
Level Characteristics Associated with High COVID-19 Burden." *BMC Public
Health* 21(1, May 28): 1007. DOI: https://doi.org/10.1186/s12889-021-11060-9.

Linke Young, Christen, James C. Capretta, Stan Dorn, David Kendall, and Joseph R.
Antos. 2020. "How to Boost Health Insurance Enrollment: Three Practical
Steps That Merit Bipartisan Support." *Health Affairs*, August 17. https://www
.healthaffairs.org/do/10.1377/forefront.20200814.107187/full/.

Locke, Charley. 2022. "American Schools Got a $190 Billion Covid Windfall.
Where Is It Going?" *New York Times Magazine*, September 8. https://www
.nytimes.com/2022/09/08/magazine/covid-aid-schools.html.

Lofquist, Daphne A. 2012. "Multigenerational Households: 2009–2011."
American Community Survey Briefs 11-03. U.S. Census Bureau, October.
https://www2.census.gov/library/publications/2012/acs/acsbr11-03.pdf.

Lorant, V., D. Deliège, W. Eaton, A. Robert, P. Philippot, and M. Ansseau. 2003.
"Socioeconomic Inequalities in Depression: A Meta-Analysis." *American
Journal of Epidemiology* 157(2): 98–112. DOI: https://doi.org/10.1093/aje/kwf182.

Maag, Elaine, H. Elizabeth Peters, Nikhita Airi, and Karen E. Smith. 2022. "How
Well Can Limited Data Predict Annual Tax Credits?" Tax Policy Center,
October 17. https://www.taxpolicycenter.org/publications/how-well-can
-limited-data-predict-annual-tax-credits.

Mahajan, Uma V., and Margaret Larkins-Pettigrew. 2020. "Racial Demographics
and COVID-19 Confirmed Cases and Deaths: A Correlational Analysis of
2,886 U.S. Counties." *Journal of Public Health* 42(3, September): 445–47. DOI:
https://doi.org/10.1093/pubmed/fdaa070.

Malik, Rasheed, Katie Hamm, Leila Schochet, Cristina Novoa, Simon Workman,
and Steven Jessen-Howard. 2018. "America's Child Care Deserts in 2018."
Center for American Progress, December. https://cdn.americanprogress.org

/content/uploads/2018/12/06100537/AmericasChildCareDeserts20182.pdf? _ga=2.226401882.1514283490.1620677656-148317000.1618016842.

Malkus, Nat. 2021. "The $200 Billion Question: How Much of Federal COVID-19 Relief Funding for Schools Will Go to COVID-19 Relief?" American Enterprise Institute, August 4. https://www.aei.org/research-products/report /the-200-billion-question-how-much-of-federal-covid-19-relief-funding-for -schools-will-go-to-covid-19-relief/.

Marr, Chuck, Kris Cox, Kathleen Bryant, Stacy Dean, Roxy Caines, and Arloc Sherman. 2020. "Aggressive State Outreach Can Help Reach the 12 Million Non-Filers Eligible for Stimulus Payments." Center on Budget and Policy Priorities, October 14. https://www.cbpp.org/research/federal-tax/aggressive-state -outreach-can-help-reach-the-12-million-non-filers-eligible.

Matraji, Laura, and Tiffany Leung. 2020. "Evaluating the Effectiveness of Social Distancing Interventions to Delay or Flatten the Epidemic Curve of Coronavirus Disease." *Emerging Infectious Diseases* 26(8, August): 1740–48. DOI: 10.3201/eid2608.201093.

Mattingly, Marybeth J., Andrew Schaefer, and Jessica A. Carson. 2016. "Child Care Costs Exceed 10 Percent of Family Income for One in Four Families." National Issue Brief 109(Fall). University of New Hampshire, Carsey School of Public Policy. https://scholars.unh.edu/cgi/viewcontent.cgi?article=1287& context=carsey.

Mazurenko, Olena, Casey P. Balio, Rajender Agarwal, Aaron E. Carroll, and Nir Menachemi. 2018. "The Effects of Medicaid Expansion under the ACA: A Systematic Review." *Health Affairs* 37(6): 944–50. DOI: https://doi.org/10.1377 /hlthaff.2017.1491.

McCabe, Joshua T. 2018. *The Fiscalization of Social Policy: How Taxpayers Trumped Children in the Fight against Child Poverty.* New York: Oxford University Press.

McElrath, Kevin. 2020. "Nearly 93% of Households with School-Age Children Report Some Form of Distance Learning during COVID-19." U.S. Census Bureau, August 26. https://www.census.gov/library/stories/2020/08/schooling -during-the-covid-19-pandemic.html.

McKinsey and Company. 2022. "Halftime for the K–12 Stimulus: How Are Districts Faring?" November 2. https://www.mckinsey.com/industries/education /our-insights/halftime-for-the-k-12-stimulus-how-are-districts-faring.

McLanahan, Sara, and Gary D. Sandefur. 1994. *Growing Up with a Single Parent: What Hurts, What Helps.* Cambridge, Mass.: Harvard University Press.

McLoyd, Vonnie C. 1990. "The Impact of Economic Hardship on Black Families and Children: Psychological Distress, Parenting, and Socioemotional Development." *Child Development* 61(2, April): 311–46. DOI: https://doi.org /10.1111/j.1467-8624.1990.tb02781.x.

———. 1998. "Socioeconomic Disadvantage and Child Development." *American Psychologist* 53(2, February): 185–204. DOI: https://doi.org/10.1037/0003-066x .53.2.185.

Mendenhall, Ruby, Kathryn Edin, Susan Crowley, Jennifer Sykes, Laura Tach, Katrin Kriz, and Jeffrey R. Kling. 2012. "The Role of Earned Income Tax Credit in the Budgets of Low-Income Households." *Social Service Review* 86(3): 367–400. DOI: https://doi.org/10.1086/667972.

Mendoza, Gilberto Soria. 2020. "Feeding Hungry Children: A Guide for State Policy-Makers." National Conference of State Legislatures. https://bestpractices .nokidhungry.org/sites/default/files/feeding-hungry-children--a-guide-for -state-policymakers_0.pdf.

Mervosh, Sarah, Denise Lu, and Vanessa Swales. 2020. "See Which States and Cities Have Told Residents to Stay at Home." *New York Times*, April 20. https:// www.nytimes.com/interactive/2020/us/coronavirus-stay-at-home-order .html.

Meyer, Bruce D., Wallace K. C. Mok, and James X. Sullivan. 2009. "The Under-Reporting of Transfers in Household Surveys: Its Nature and Consequences." Working Paper 15181. National Bureau of Economic Research, July. DOI: 10.3386/w15181.

Meyer, Bruce D., and James X. Sullivan. 2006. "Consumption, Income, and Material Well-Being after Welfare Reform." Working Paper 11976. National Bureau of Economic Research, January. DOI: https://doi.org/10.3386/w11976.

Michelmore, Katherine, and Lauren Jones. 2015. "Timing Is Money: Does Lump-Sum Payment of Tax Credits Induce High-Cost Borrowing?" Annual conference on taxation and minutes of the annual meeting of the National Tax Association. *Proceedings* 108: 1–41. https://www.jstor.org/stable/90023231.

Michener, Jamila. 2018. *Fragmented Democracy: Medicaid, Federalism, and Unequal Politics.* Cambridge: Cambridge University Press.

Migration Policy Institute. 2019. "Profile of the Unauthorized Population: United States." https://www.migrationpolicy.org/data/unauthorized-immigrant -population/state/US.

Moffitt, Robert A. 2015. "The Deserving Poor, the Family, and the U.S. Welfare System." *Demography* 52(3, June 6): 729–49. DOI: https://doi.org/10.1007 /s13524-015-0395-0.

Moffitt, Robert A., and James P. Ziliak. 2020. "COVID-19 and the U.S. Safety Net." *Fiscal Studies* 41(3, September): 515–48. DOI: https://doi.org/10.1111 /1475-5890.12243.

Morduch, Jonathan, and Rachel Schneider. 2017. *The Financial Diaries: How American Families Cope in a World of Uncertainty.* Princeton, N.J.: Princeton University Press.

Morduch, Jonathan, and Julie Siwicki. 2017. "In and Out of Poverty: Episodic Poverty and Income Volatility in the U.S. Financial Diaries." *Social Service Review* 91(3, September): 390–421. DOI: https://doi.org/10.1086/694180.

Morris, Pamela A., Heather D. Hill, Lisa A. Gennetian, Chris Rodrigues, and Sharon Wolf. 2015. "Income Volatility in U.S. Households with Children: Another Growing Disparity between the Rich and the Poor?" Discussion Paper 1429-15. Institute for Research on Poverty, July. https://www.irp.wisc .edu/wp/wp-content/uploads/2018/05/dp142915.pdf.

Murphy, Dan. 2021. "Economic Impact Payments: Uses, Payment Methods, and Costs to Recipients." Brookings Institution, February. https://www.brookings .edu/wp-content/uploads/2021/02/20210216_Murphy_ImpactPayments_Final -4.pdf.

Musaddiq, Tareena, Kevin Strange, Andrew Bacher-Hicks, and Joshua Goodman. 2021. "The Pandemic's Effect on Demand for Public Schools, Homeschooling, and Private Schools." Working Paper 29262. National Bureau of Economic Research, September. DOI: 10.3386/w29262.

National Academy of Sciences. 2019. *A Roadmap to Reducing Child Poverty.* Washington, D.C.: National Academies Press.

National Association for the Education of Young Children. 2020. "Am I Next? Sacrificing to Stay Open, Child Care Providers Face a Bleak Future without Relief." December. https://www.naeyc.org/sites/default/files/globally-shared /downloads/PDFs/our-work/public-policy-advocacy/naeyc_policy_crisis _coronavirus_december_survey_data.pdf.

National Center for Homeless Education (NCHE). 2021. "Federal Data Summary: School Years 2016–17 through 2018–19: Education for Homeless Children and Youth." University of North Carolina at Greensboro, NCHE, April. https:// nche.ed.gov/wp-content/uploads/2021/04/Federal-Data-Summary-SY-16.17 -to-18.19-Final.pdf.

National Conference of State Legislatures. 2021. *Affordable Care Act Medicaid Expansion.* July 1. https://www.kff.org/health-reform/state-indicator /state-activity-around-expanding-medicaid-under-the-affordable-care-act /?currentTimeframe (accessed July 10, 2021).

Neuberger, Zoë, and Katie Bergh. 2022. "Permanent Summer Grocery Benefits Are a Big Win for Children in Low-Income Families, Despite Disappointing Tradeoffs." Center on Budget and Policy Priorities, December 20. https:// www.cbpp.org/blog/permanent-summer-grocery-benefits-are-a-big-win-for -children-in-low-income-families-despite.

New York State Department of Labor. 2021. "Guidance on Use of Paid Sick Leave for COVID-19 Vaccine Recovery Time." May 28. https://dol.ny .gov/system/files/documents/2021/09/psl-and-vaccine-recovery-guidance -9-22-21.pdf.

Newville, David, and Gabriel Zucker. 2021. "GetCTC Helped Thousands of Families This Tax Season. How Do We Help Even More Next Year?" Code for America, November 17. https://codeforamerica.org/news/getctc-2021-update/.

Nolan, Laura, Irwin Garfinkel, Neeraj Kaushal, JaeHyun Nam, Jane Waldfogel, and Christopher Wimer. 2016. "Trends in Child Poverty by Race/Ethnicity: New Evidence Using an Anchored Historical Supplemental Poverty Measure." *Journal of Applied Research on Children: Informing Policy for Children at Risk* 7(1): article 3. https://files.eric.ed.gov/fulltext/EJ1188423.pdf.

Nord, Mark, Margaret Andrews, and Steven Carlson. 2008. "Household Food Security in the United States, 2007." Economic Research Report 66. U.S. Department of Agriculture Economic Research Service, November. https:// www.ers.usda.gov/webdocs/publications/46084/11227_err66.pdf?v=41056.

O'Connor, Alice. 2001. *Poverty Knowledge: Social Science, Social Policy, and the Poor in Twentieth-Century U.S. History.* Princeton, N.J.: Princeton University Press.

Office of Governor Gavin Newsom. 2021. "Governor Newsom Signs Legislation to Ensure Access to Supplemental Paid Sick Leave for Workers Impacted by the Pandemic." March 19. https://www.gov.ca.gov/2021/03/19/governor -newsom-signs-legislation-to-ensure-access-to-supplemental-paid-sick -leave-for-workers-impacted-by-the-pandemic/.

Organization for Economic Cooperation and Development (OECD). 2019. *Negotiating Our Way Up: Collective Bargaining in a Changing World of Work.* OECD, November. DOI: https://doi.org/10.1787/1fd2da34-en.

Pac, Jessica, Jaehyun Nam, Jane Waldfogel, and Chris Wimer. 2017. "Young Child Poverty in the United States: Analyzing Trends in Poverty and the Role of Anti-Poverty Programs Using the Supplemental Poverty Measure." *Children and Youth Services Review* 74(March): 35–49. DOI: https://doi.org/10.1016/j.childyouth.2017.01.022.

Parolin, Zachary. 2019a. "The Effect of Benefit Underreporting on Estimates of Poverty in the United States." *Social Indicators Research* 144(2, July): 869–98. DOI: https://doi.org/10.1007/s11205-018-02053-0.

———. 2019b. "Temporary Assistance for Needy Families and the Black–White Child Poverty Gap in the United States." *Socio-Economic Review* 19(3, July): 1005–35. DOI: https://doi.org/10.1093/ser/mwz025.

———. 2021a. "Decomposing the Decline of Cash Assistance in the United States, 1993 to 2016." *Demography* 58(3, June 1): 1119–41. DOI: https://doi.org/10.1215/00703370-9157471.

———. 2021b. "Income Support Policies and the Rise of Student and Family Homelessness." *Annals of the American Academy of Political and Social Science* 693 (1, January): 46–63. https://journals.sagepub.com/doi/full/10.1177/0002716220981847.

Parolin, Zachary, Elizabeth Ananat, Sophie M. Collyer, Megan Curran, and Christopher Wimer. 2021. "The Initial Effects of the Expanded Child Tax Credit on Material Hardship." Working Paper 29285. National Bureau of Economic Research, September. https://www.nber.org/papers/w29285.

Parolin, Zachary, Elizabeth Ananat, Sophie Collyer, Megan Curran, and Christopher Wimer. Forthcoming. "The Effects of the Monthly and Lump-Sum Child Tax Credit Payments on Food and Housing Hardship." *American Economic Association: Papers and Proceedings.*

Parolin, Zachary, and David Brady. 2018. "Extreme Child Poverty and the Role of Social Policy in the United States." *Journal of Poverty and Social Justice* 27 (1, February): 3–22. https://ideas.repec.org/p/osf/socarx/u5ecn.html.

Parolin, Zachary, Sophie Collyer, Megan Curran, Jordan Matsudaira, Jane Waldfogel, and Christopher Wimer. 2022. "Comparing the Performance of Monthly Poverty Measures." Working paper. Center on Poverty and Social Policy, August 22. https://www.povertycenter.columbia.edu/s/Comparing-Monthly-Poverty-Measures-CPSP-2022.pdf.

Parolin, Zachary, Sophie Collyer, Megan Curran, and Christopher Wimer. 2021a. "Monthly Poverty Rates among Children after the Expansion of the Child Tax Credit." *Poverty & Social Policy Brief* 5(4, August 20). Columbia University, Center on Poverty and Social Policy. https://www.povertycenter.columbia.edu/news-internal/monthly-poverty-july-2021.

———. 2021b. "The Potential Poverty Reduction Effect of the American Rescue Plan." *Poverty & Social Policy Fact Sheet* 20411. Columbia University, Center on Poverty and Social Policy, March 11. www.povertycenter.columbia.edu/news-internal/2021/presidential-policy/bideneconomic-relief-proposal-poverty-impact.

Parolin, Zachary, Christina J. Cross, and Rourke O'Brien. 2023. "Administrative Burdens and Economic Insecurity among Black, Latino, and White Families." *RSF: The Russell Sage Foundation Journal of the Social Sciences* 9(5): 56–75. DOI: 10.7758/RSF.2023.9.5.03.

Parolin, Zachary, Megan Curran, Jordan Matsudaira, Jane Waldfogel, and Christopher Wimer. 2022. "Estimating Monthly Poverty Rates in the United States." *Journal of Policy Analysis and Management* 41(4, Fall): 1177–1203. DOI: https://doi.org/10.1002/pam.22403.

Parolin, Zachary, Megan Curran, and Christopher Wimer. 2020. "The CARES ACT and Poverty in the COVID-19 Crisis: Promises and Pitfalls of the Recovery Rebates and Expanded Unemployment Benefits." *Poverty & Social Policy Brief* 4(8, June 21). Columbia University, Center on Poverty and Social Policy. https://www.povertycenter.columbia.edu/news-internal/coronavirus-cares-act-forecastingpoverty-estimates.

Parolin, Zachary, and Stefano Filauro. 2022. "The United States' Record-Low Child Poverty Rate in International and Historical Perspective." November. DOI: 10.31219/osf.io/su2fm.

Parolin, Zachary, Giulia Giupponi, Emma Lee, and Sophie Collyer. 2022. "Consumption Responses to an Unconditional Child Allowance in the United States." *OSF Preprints*, November 19. DOI: https://doi.org/10.31219/osf.io/k2mwy.

Parolin, Zachary, and Emma K. Lee. 2021a. "Large Socio-economic, Geographic, and Demographic Disparities Exist in Exposure to School Closures." *Nature Human Behaviour* 5(4, April): 522–28. DOI: https://doi.org/10.1038/s41562-021-01087-8.

———. 2021b. "The Care Burden during COVID-19: A National Database of Child Care Closures in the United States." *Socius* 7(July). DOI: https://doi.org/10.1177/23780231211032028.

———. 2022. "The Role of Poverty and Racial Discrimination in Exacerbating the Health Consequences of COVID-19." *Lancet Regional Health—Americas* 7(March): 100178. DOI: https://doi.org/10.1016/j.lana.2021.100178.

Parolin, Zachary, Jordan Matsudaira, Jane Waldfogel, and Christopher Wimer. 2022. "Exposure to Childhood Poverty and Racial Differences in Economic Opportunity in Young Adulthood." *Demography* 59(6, December 1): 2295–2319. DOI: https://doi.org/10.1215/00703370-10350740.

Parolin, Zachary, and Christopher Wimer. 2020. "Forecasting Estimates of Poverty during the COVID-19 Crisis." *Poverty & Social Policy Brief* 4(6, April 16). https://static1.squarespace.com/static/610831a16c95260dbd68934a/t/61153d43b7e14844e345854c/1628781891230/Forecasting-Poverty-Estimates-COVID19-CPSP-2020.pdf.

Patrick, Stephen W., Laura E. Henkhaus, Joseph S. Zickafoose, Kim Lovell, Alese Halvorson, Sarah Loch, Mia Letterie, and Matthew M. Davis. 2020. "Well-being of Parents and Children during the COVID-19 Pandemic: A National Survey." *Pediatrics* 146(4, October). DOI: https://doi.org/10.1542/peds.2020-016824.

Pew Research Center. 2013. "Table 40: Households, by Family Size, Race, and Ethnicity: 2013." In *Statistical Portrait of Hispanics in the United States, 2013.*

March 11. https://www.pewresearch.org/hispanic/ph_2015-03_statistical-portrait-of-hispanics-in-the-united-states-2013_current-40/.

Pilkauskas, Natasha, Katherine Michelmore, Nicole Kovski, and H. Luke Shaefer. 2022. "The Effects of Income on the Economic Wellbeing of Families with Low Incomes: Evidence from the 2021 Expanded Child Tax Credit." Working Paper 30533. National Bureau of Economic Research, October. DOI: https://doi.org/10.3386/w30533.

Press, Valerie G., Megan Huisingh-Scheetz, and Vineet M. Arora. 2021. "Inequities in Technology Contribute to Disparities in COVID-19 Vaccine Distribution." *JAMA Health Forum* 2(3, March 19): e210264. DOI: https://doi.org/10.1001/jamahealthforum.2021.0264.

Quan, Daniel, Lucía Luna Wong, Anita Shallal, Raghav Madan, Abel Hamdan, Heaveen Ahdi, Amir Daneshvar, Manasi Mahajan, Mohamed Nasereldin, Meredith Van Harn, Ijeoma Nnodim Opara, and Marcus Zervos. 2021. "Impact of Race and Socioeconomic Status on Outcomes in Patients Hospitalized with COVID-19." *Journal of General Internal Medicine* 36(5): 1302–9. DOI: https://doi.org/10.1007/s11606-020-06527-1.

Rainwater, Lee, and Timothy M. Smeeding. 2005. *Poor Kids in a Rich Country: America's Children in Comparative Perspective.* New York: Russell Sage Foundation.

Reardon, Sean F. 2011. "The Widening Academic Achievement Gap between the Rich and the Poor: New Evidence and Possible Explanations." In *Whither Opportunity? Rising Inequality, Schools, and Children's Life Chances,* edited by Greg J. Duncan and Richard J. Murnane. New York: Russell Sage Foundation.

RegionTrack. 2019. "Child Care in State Economies: 2019 Update." http://www.ced.org/assets/reports/childcareimpact/181104%20CCSE%20Report%20Jan30.pdf.

Rendall, Michael S., Bonnie Ghosh-Dastidar, Margaret M. Weden, Elizabeth H. Baker, and Zafar Nazarov. 2013. "Multiple Imputation for Combined-Survey Estimation with Incomplete Regressors in One but Not Both Surveys." *Sociological Methods & Research* 42(4). DOI: https://doi.org/10.1177/0049124113502947.

Rho, Hye Jin, Hayley Brown, and Shawn Fremstad. 2020. "A Basic Demographic Profile of Workers in Frontline Industries." Center for Economic and Policy Research, April. https://axelkra.us/wp-content/uploads/2020/12/2020-04-Frontline-Workers.pdf.

Rindfuss, Ronald R., David Guilkey, S. Philip Morgan, Øystein Kravdal, and Karen Benjamin Guzzo. 2007. "Child Care Availability and First-Birth Timing in Norway." *Demography* 44(2, May 1): 345–72. DOI: https://doi.org/10.1353/dem.2007.0017.

Roels, Natasja Ilonka, Amarylis Estrella, Melissa Maldonado-Salcedo, Rayna Rapp, Helena Hansen, and Anita Hardon. 2022. "Confident Futures: Community-Based Organizations as First Responders and Agents of Change in the Face of the Covid-19 Pandemic." *Social Science and Medicine* 294(February): 114639. DOI: https://doi.org/10.1016/j.socscimed.2021.114639.

Rosenbaum, Dottie. 2019. "SNAP's 'Broad-Based Categorical Eligibility' Supports Working Families and Those Saving for the Future." Center on Budget and Policy Priorities, July 30. https://www.cbpp.org/research /food-assistance/snaps-broad-based-categorical-eligibility-supports-working -families-and#_ftnref4.

Rothstein, Jesse. 2019. "The Lost Generation? Scarring after the Great Recession." University of California at Berkeley, May. https://eml.berkeley.edu/~jrothst /workingpapers/rothstein_scarring_052019.pdf.

Rothwell, Jonathan, and Ember Smith. 2021. "Socioeconomic Status as a Risk Factor in Economic and Physical Harm from COVID-19: Evidence from the United States." *Annals of the American Academy of Political and Social Science* 698(1, November): 12–38. DOI: https://doi.org/10.1177/00027162211062137.

Royston, Patrick. 2004. "Multiple Imputation of Missing Values." *Stata Journal* 4(3): 227–41. DOI: https://doi.org/10.1177/1536867x0400400301.

Roza, Marguerite, and Katherine Silberstein. 2022. "A Year Ago, School Districts Got a Windfall of Pandemic Aid. How's That Going?" Brookings Institution, March 31. https://www.brookings.edu/blog/brown-center-chalkboard /2022/03/31/a-year-ago-school-districts-got-a-windfall-of-pandemic-aid -hows-that-going/.

Sahm, Claudia. 2019. "Direct Stimulus Payments to Individuals." Hamilton Project, May 16. https://www.hamiltonproject.org/assets/files/Sahm_web _20190506.pdf.

Sandstrom, Heather, Gina Adams, and Archana Pyati. 2019. "Wellness Check: Material Hardship and Psychological Distress among Families with Infants and Toddlers." Urban Institute. https://www.urban.org/sites/default/files /publication/100387/wellness_check_material_hardship_and_psychological _distress_among_families_with_infants_and_toddlers_2.pdf.

Schanzenbach, Diane Whitmore. 2023. "The Impact of SNAP Emergency Allotments on SNAP Benefits and Food Insufficiency." Northwestern University Institute for Policy Research, January 27. https://www.ipr.northwestern .edu/documents/reports/ipr-rapid-research-report-snap-emergency-allotments -impact-27-january-2023.pdf.

Schanzenbach, Diane, and Abigail Pitts. 2020. "Food Insecurity Triples for Families with Children during COVID-19 Pandemic." Northwestern Institute for Policy Research, May 13. https://www.ipr.northwestern.edu/news/2020 /food-insecurity-triples-for-families-during-covid.html.

Schnake-Mahl, Alina S., and Usama Bilal. 2021. "Schnake-Mahl and Bilal Respond to 'Structural Racism and COVID-19 Mortality in the US.'" *American Journal of Epidemiology* 90(8, August): 1447–51. DOI: https://doi.org/10.1093 /aje/kwab058.

Schneider, Daniel, and Kristen Harknett. 2020. "Essential and Unprotected: COVID-19 Related Health and Safety Procedures for Service Sector Workers." SHIFT Project Research Brief, May. https://shift.hks.harvard.edu/files/2020/05 /Essential-and-Unprotected-COVID-19-Health-Safety.pdf.

Schott, Liz, Ladonna Pavetti, and Ife Floyd. 2018. "How States Use Federal and State Funds under the TANF Block Grant." Center on Budget and Policy Priorities, October 15. https://www.cbpp.org/sites/default/files/atoms/files /4-8-15tanf_0.pdf.

Schreiber, Melody. 2022. "What One Million COVID Dead Mean for the U.S.'s Future." *Scientific American*, March 29. https://www.scientificamerican.com /article/what-one-million-covid-dead-mean-for-the-u-s-s-future/.

Schwandt, Hannes, and Till von Wachter. 2019. "Unlucky Cohorts: Estimating the Long-Term Effects of Entering the Labor Market in a Recession in Large Cross-Sectional Data Sets." *Journal of Labor Economics* 37(S1, January): S161–98. DOI: https://doi.org/10.1086/701046.

Shaefer, H. Luke, Sophie Collyer, Greg Duncan, Kathryn Edin, Irwin Garfinkel, David Harris, Timothy M. Smeeding, Jane Waldfogel, Christopher Wimer, and Hirokazu Yoshikawa. 2018. "A Universal Child Allowance: A Plan to Reduce Poverty and Income Instability among Children in the United States." *RSF: The Russell Sage Foundation Journal of the Social Sciences* 4(2, February): 22–42. DOI: https://doi.org/10.7758/RSF.2018.4.2.02.

Shaefer, H. Luke, Patrick Cooney, Richard Rodems, and Marybeth J. Mattingly. 2020. "Hardship and Well-Being in the United States after the CARES Act." *Michigan Poverty Solutions* (University of Michigan), July. https://poverty .umich.edu/files/2020/07/PovertySolutions-Hardship-After-CARES-Act -PolicyBrief-r3.pdf.

Shaefer, H. Luke, and Kathryn Edin. 2013. "Rising Extreme Poverty in the United States and the Response of Federal Means-Tested Transfer Programs." *Social Service Review* 87(2, June): 250–68. DOI: https://doi.org/10.1086/671012.

Shaefer, H. Luke, Kathryn Edin, Vincent Fusaro, and Pinghui Wu. 2019. "The Decline of Cash Assistance and the Well-Being of Poor Households with Children." *Social Forces* 98(3, March): 1000–1025. DOI: https://doi.org/10.1093/sf/soz020.

Short, Kathleen. 2012. "The Research: Supplemental Poverty Measure: 2011." Report P60-244. U.S. Census Bureau, November 1. https://www.census.gov /library/publications/2012/demo/p60-244.html.

Shrivastava, Aditi, and Gina Azito Thompson. 2022. "TANF Cash Assistance Should Reach Millions More Families to Lessen Hardship." Center on Budget and Policy Priorities, February 18. https://www.cbpp.org/research/income -security/tanf-cash-assistance-should-reach-millions-more-families-to-lessen.

Smeeding, Timothy, Katherine Ross Phillips, and Michael O'Connor. 1999. "The EITC: Expectation, Knowledge, Use, and Economic and Social Mobility." Working Paper 13. Syracuse University, Center for Policy Research, April. https://surface.syr.edu/cgi/viewcontent.cgi?article=1146&context=cpr.

Sykes, Jennifer, Katrin Križ, Kathryn Edin, and Sarah Halpern-Meekin. 2014. "Dignity and Dreams: What the Earned Income Tax Credit (EITC) Means to Low-Income Families." *American Sociological Review* 80(2, April): 243–67. DOI: https://doi.org/10.1177/0003122414551552.

Thomson, Dana, Renee Ryberg, Kristin Harper, James Fuller, Katherine Paschall, Jody Franklin, and Lina Guzman. 2022. "Lessons from a Historic Decline in Child Poverty." *ChildTrends*. https://www.childtrends.org/publications/lessons -from-a-historic-decline-in-child-poverty.

Tobolowsky, Farrell A., et al. 2020. "COVID-19 Outbreak among Three Affiliated Homeless Service Sites—King County, Washington, 2020." *Morbidity and Mortality Weekly Report* 69(17, May 1): 523–26. DOI: https://doi.org/10.15585 /mmwr.mm6917e2.

Tolbert, Jennifer, Patrick Drake, and Anthony Damico, 2022. "Key Facts about the Uninsured Population." Kaiser Family Foundation, December 19. https://www.kff.org/uninsured/issue-brief/key-facts-about-the-uninsured -population.

Tomopoulos, Suzy, Benard P. Dreyer, Samantha Berkule, Arthur H. Fierman, Carolyn Brockmeyer, and Alan L. Mendelsohn. 2010. "Infant Media Exposure and Toddler Development." *Archives of Pediatrics and Adolescent Medicine* 164(12, December 6): 1105–11. DOI: https://doi.org/10.1001/archpediatrics .2010.235.

Torche, Florencia. 2014. "Analyses of Intergenerational Mobility: An Inter-disciplinary Review." *Annals of the American Academy of Political and Social Science* 657(1, January): 37–62. DOI: https://doi.org/10.1177/ 0002716214547476.

Townsend, Peter. 1979. *Poverty in the United Kingdom.* London: Allen Lane/Penguin Books.

U.S. Bureau of Labor Statistics. 2020. "Job Market Remains Tight in 2019, as the Unemployment Rate Falls to Its Lowest Level since 1969." *Monthly Labor Review* (April). https://www.bls.gov/opub/mlr/2020/article/job-market -remains-tight-in-2019-as-the-unemployment-rate-falls-to-its-lowest-level -since-1969.htm#top.

———. 2021. "Impact of the Coronavirus (COVID-19) Pandemic on the Employment Situation for January 2021." https://www.bls.gov/covid19 /employment-situation-covid19-faq-january-2021.htm#ques4.

U.S. Department of Agriculture. 2017. "Supplemental Nutrition Assistance Program (SNAP): National Level Annual Summary." USDA Food and Nutrition Service. https://www.fns.usda.gov/pd/supplemental-nutrition -assistance-program-snap

U.S. Department of Health, Education, and Welfare. 1976. *The Measure of Poverty: A Report to Congress as Mandated by the Education Amendments of 1974.* April. https://www.census.gov/content/dam/Census/library/publications /1976/demo/measureofpoverty.pdf.

U.S. Department of Labor. 2022. "Families First Coronavirus Response Act and Coronavirus Aid, Relief, and Economic Security (CARES) Act Funding to States through October 8, 2022." https://oui.doleta.gov/unemploy/docs /cares_act_funding_state.html.

U.S. Department of the Treasury. 2020. "Treasury, IRS Deliver 89.5 Million Economic Impact Payments in First Three Weeks, Release State-by-State Economic Impact Payment Figures." https://www.irs.gov/newsroom/treasury -irs-deliver-89-point-5-million-economic-impact-payments-in-first-three -weeks-release-state-by-state-economic-impact-payment-figures.

———. 2021. "Treasury and IRS Announce Families of Nearly 60 Million Children Receive $15 Billion in First Payments of Expanded and Newly Advanceable Child Tax Credit." July 15. https://home.treasury.gov/news/press-releases /Treasury-and-IRS-Announce-Families-of-Nearly-60-Million-Children -Receive-%2415-Billion-Dollars-in-First-Payments-of-Expanded-and-Newly -Advanceable-Child-Tax-Credit.

U.S. Government Accountability Office. 2007. *Advance Earned Income Tax Credit: Low Use and Small Dollars Paid Impede IRS's Efforts to Reduce High Noncompliance.* GAO-07-1110, August. https://www.gao.gov/assets/gao-07-1110.pdf.

———. 2022. "Current and Future Federal Preparedness Requires Fixes to Improve Health Data and Address Improper Payments." GAO-22-105397, April 27. https://files.gao.gov/reports/GAO-22-105397/index.html.

U.S. Secret Service. 2022. "Labor Watchdog's Pandemic Work Results in More than 1,000 Individuals Charged with UI Fraud and $45.6 Billion Identified in Potentially Fraudulent Pandemic UI Benefits." September 22. https://www .secretservice.gov/newsroom/releases/2022/09/labor-watchdogs-pandemic -work-results-more-1000-individuals-charged-ui.

Van Hook, Jennifer, James D. Bachmeier, Donna L. Coffman, and Ofer Harel. 2015. "Can We Spin Straw into Gold? An Evaluation of Immigrant Legal Status Imputation Approaches." *Demography* 52(1): 329–54. DOI: https://doi.org /10.1007/s13524-014-0358-x.

Wachter, Till von. 2019. "Unemployment Insurance Reform." *Annals of the American Academy of Political and Social Science* 686(1, November): 121–46. DOI: https://doi.org/10.1177/0002716219885339.

Waldfogel, Jane. 2013. *Britain's War on Poverty.* New York: Russell Sage Foundation.

Waldman, Annie, and Bianca Fortis. 2021. "The Federal Government Gave Billions to America's Schools for COVID-19 Relief. Where Did the Money Go?" *ProPublica*, October 20. https://www.propublica.org/article/the-federal -government-gave-billions-to-americas-schools-for-covid-19-relief-where -did-the-money-go.

Waller, Rebecca, Tralucia Powell, Yuheiry Rodriguez, Natalie Corbett, Samantha Perlstein, Lauren K. White, Ran Barzilay, and Nicholas J. Wagner. 2021. "The Impact of the COVID-19 Pandemic on Children's Conduct Problems and Callous-Unemotional Traits." *Child Psychiatry and Human Development* 52(6, December): 1012–23. DOI: https://doi.org/10.1007/s10578-020-01109-y.

Wancheck, John, and Robert Greenstein. 2011. "Earned Income Tax Credit Overpayment and Error Issues." Center on Budget and Policy Priorities. https://www.cbpp.org/sites/default/files/atoms/files/4-5-11tax.pdf.

Waxman, Elaine, and Poonam Gupta. 2021. "Stories of Hardship from Families with Young Children as the COVID-19 Pandemic Persists." Urban Institute, April. https://www.urban.org/sites/default/files/publication/104147/stories -of-hardship-from-families-with-young-children-as-the-covid-19-pandemic -persists_1.pdf.

Western, Bruce, and Jake Rosenfeld. 2011. "Unions, Norms, and the Rise in U.S. Wage Inequality." (review). *American Sociological Review* 76(4, August): 513–37. DOI: https://doi.org/10.1177/0003122411414817.

The White House. 2008. "President Bush Signs H.R. 5140, the Economic Stimulus Act of 2008." Office of the Secretary, February 13. https://georgewbush-white house.archives.gov/news/releases/2008/02/20080213-3.html.

Wimer, Christopher, Liana Fox, Irwin Garfinkel, Neeraj Kaushal, and Jane Waldfogel. 2016. "Progress on Poverty? New Estimates of Historical Trends Using an Anchored Supplemental Poverty Measure." *Demography* 53(4, August): 1207–18. DOI: https://doi.org/10.1007/s13524-016-0485-7.

Winship, Scott, and Angela Rachidi. 2020. "Has Hunger Swelled?" *American Enterprise Institute*, October 22. https://www.aei.org/research-products/report/has-hunger-swelled/.

Wolfe, Anna. 2022. "Gov. Phil Bryant Directed $1.1 Million Welfare Payment to Brett Favre, Defendant Says." *Mississippi Today*, July 12. https://mississippitoday.org/2022/07/12/phil-bryant-welfare-scandal-nancy-new-filing/.

Wright, Gwendolyn L., Lucas Hubbard, and William A. Darity. 2022. *The Pandemic Divide: How COVID Increased Inequality in America.* Durham, N.C.: Duke University Press.

Yeung, W. Jean, and Sandra L. Hofferth. 1998. "Family Adaptations to Income and Job Loss in the U.S." *Journal of Family and Economic Issues* 19(3, September): 255–83. DOI: https://doi.org/10.1023/A:1022962824012.

York, Erica, and Garrett Watson. 2021. "Sen. Romney's Child Tax Reform Proposal Aims to Expand the Social Safety Net and Simplify Tax Credits." Tax Foundation, February 5. https://taxfoundation.org/child-allowance-romney-tax-proposal/.

Zamarro, Gema, and María J. Prados. 2021. "Gender Differences in Couples' Division of Childcare, Work, and Mental Health during COVID-19." *Review of Economics of the Household* 19(1, January 16): 11–40. DOI: https://doi.org/10.1007/s11150-020-09534-7.

Ziliak, James P. 2021. "Food Hardship during the COVID-19 Pandemic and Great Recession." *Applied Economic Perspectives and Policy* 43(1, March): 132–52. DOI: https://doi.org/10.1002/aepp.13099.

Ziol-Guest, Kathleen M., Greg J. Duncan, Ariel Kalil, and W. Thomas Boyce. 2012. "Early Childhood Poverty, Immune-Mediated Disease Processes, and Adult Productivity." *Proceedings of the National Academy of Sciences* 109(suppl. 2, October 8): 17289–93. DOI: https://doi.org/10.1073/pnas.1203167109.

Index

Tables and figures are listed in **boldface**.